Shojo Beat

ANONYMOUS NOISE

Ryoko Fukuyama

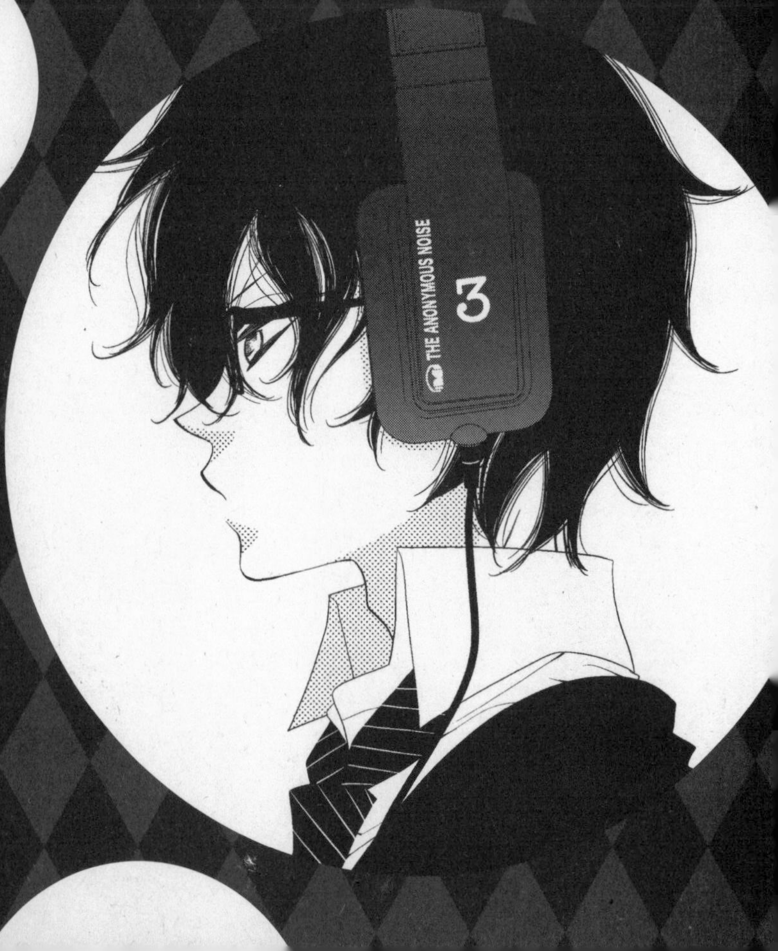
THE ANONYMOUS NOISE
3

Anonymous Noise

Volume 3

CONTENTS

Characters

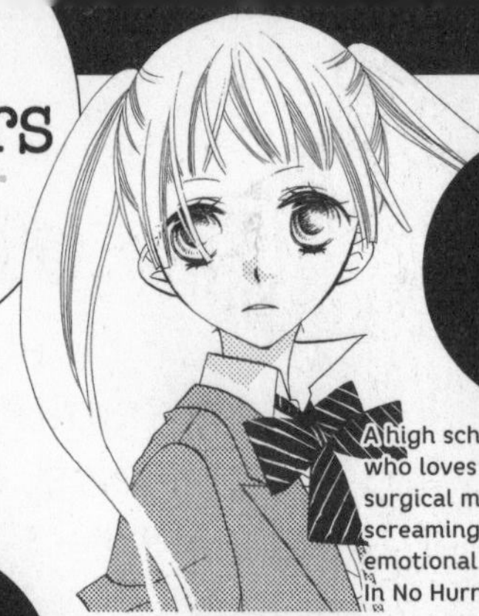

Nino Arisugawa [Nino]

A high school first-year student who loves to sing. She wears a surgical mask to stop herself fro screaming when she becomes emotional. How will her debut as In No Hurry's new singer go?!

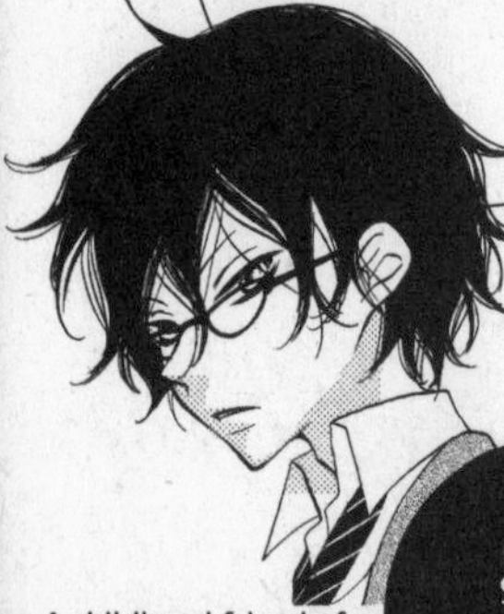

Momo Sakaki [Momo]

A childhood friend of Nino's who loves bad puns and works as a composer. He and Yuzu have become friends, but neither is aware of the other's connection to Nino.

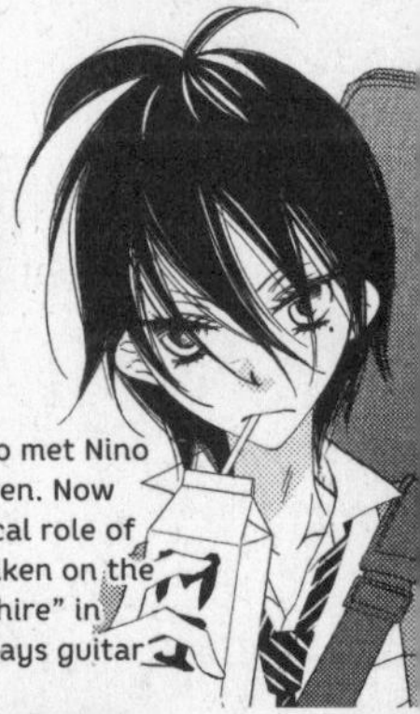

Kanade Yuzuriha [Yuzu]

A young composer who met Nino when they were children. Now that he's given the vocal role of "Alice" to Nino, he's taken on the guitarist role as "Cheshire" in In No Hurry. He also plays guitar in the Pop Music Club.

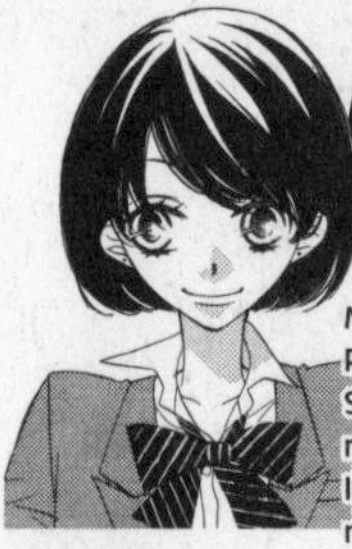

Miou Suguri

Miou sings in the Pop Music Club. She used to be the recording vocalist of In No Hurry, but she recently quit.

in NO hurry to shout; In No Hurry to Shout

A popular rock band whose members hide their identities with masks and eye patches.
Vocals: Alice
Guitar: Cheshire
Bass: Queen
Drums: Hatter

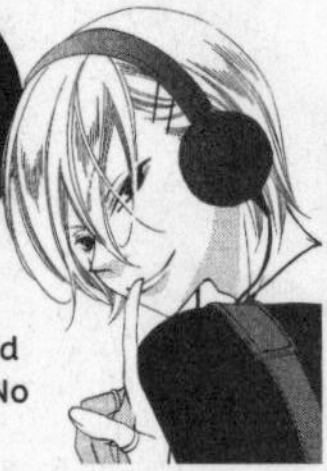

Yoshito Haruno [Haruyoshi]

President of the Pop Music Club and the bassist for In No Hurry as "Queen."

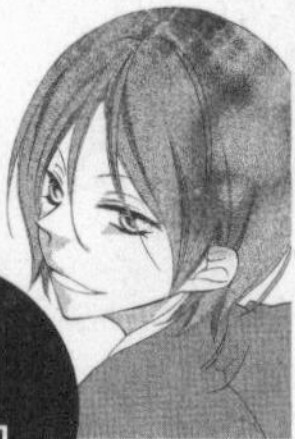

Ayumi Kurose [Kuro]

Kuro plays the drums in the Pop Music Club and is "Hatter" in In No Hurry.

Story

★ Music-loving Nino was abandoned twice in her youth—first by her girlhood crush Momo and then by the young composer Yuzu. Believing both their promises that they would find her again through her voice, Nino keeps singing. Later, in high school, she reunites with Yuzu, who invites her to become In No Hurry's new singer.
★ Nino auditions for a mysterious "Momo Kiryu" in the hope that he is actually her old friend. She's right, but Momo pushes her away. Unbeknownst to her, he feels shame for selling the songs he wrote for her. Immediately after that audition, Nino races to the studio to perform with In No Hurry on the TV show *Music King*...

*I CAN
BARELY
REMEMBER
ANYTHING
ABOUT HOW
I SANG IN
THOSE FIVE
MINUTES.*

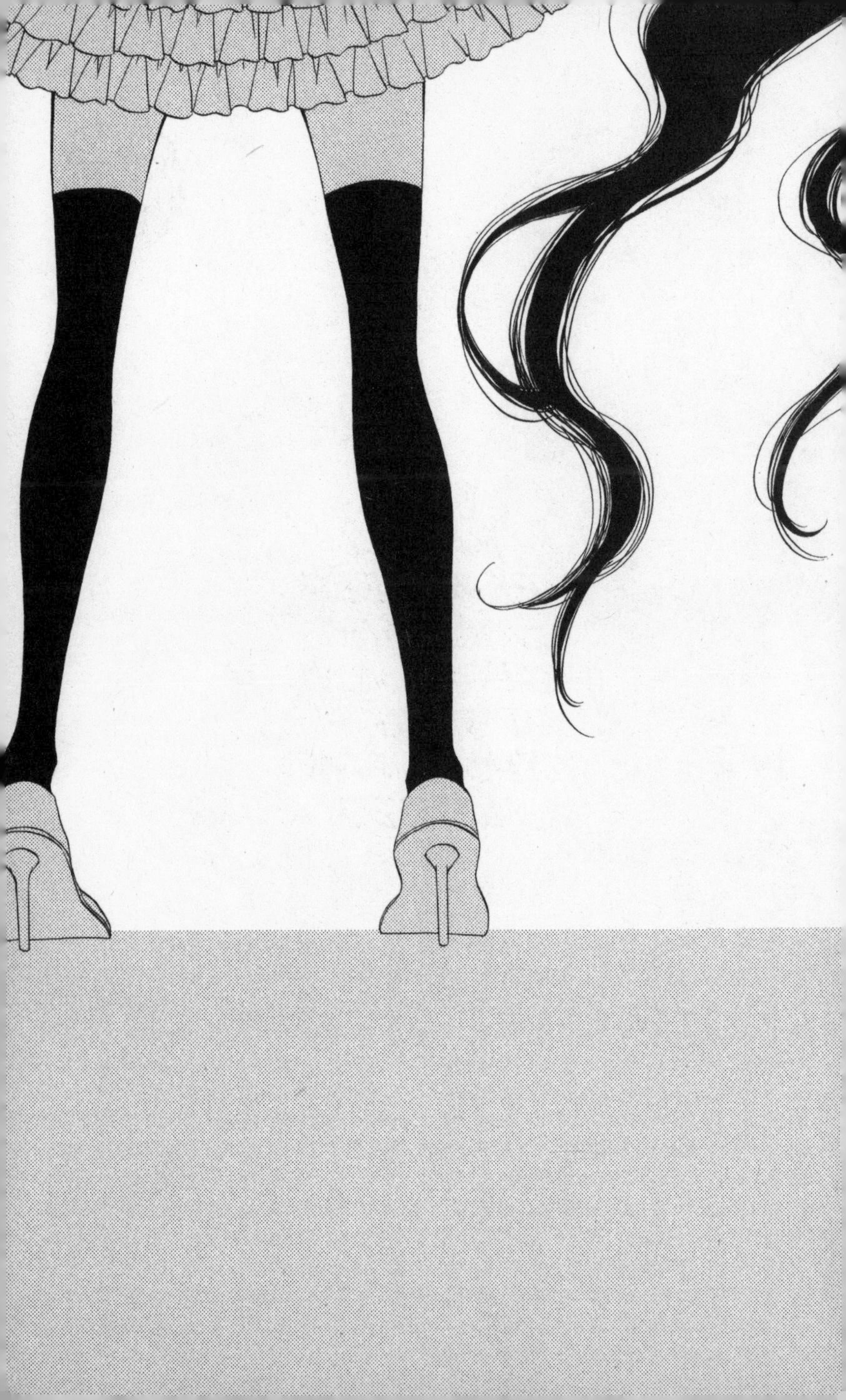

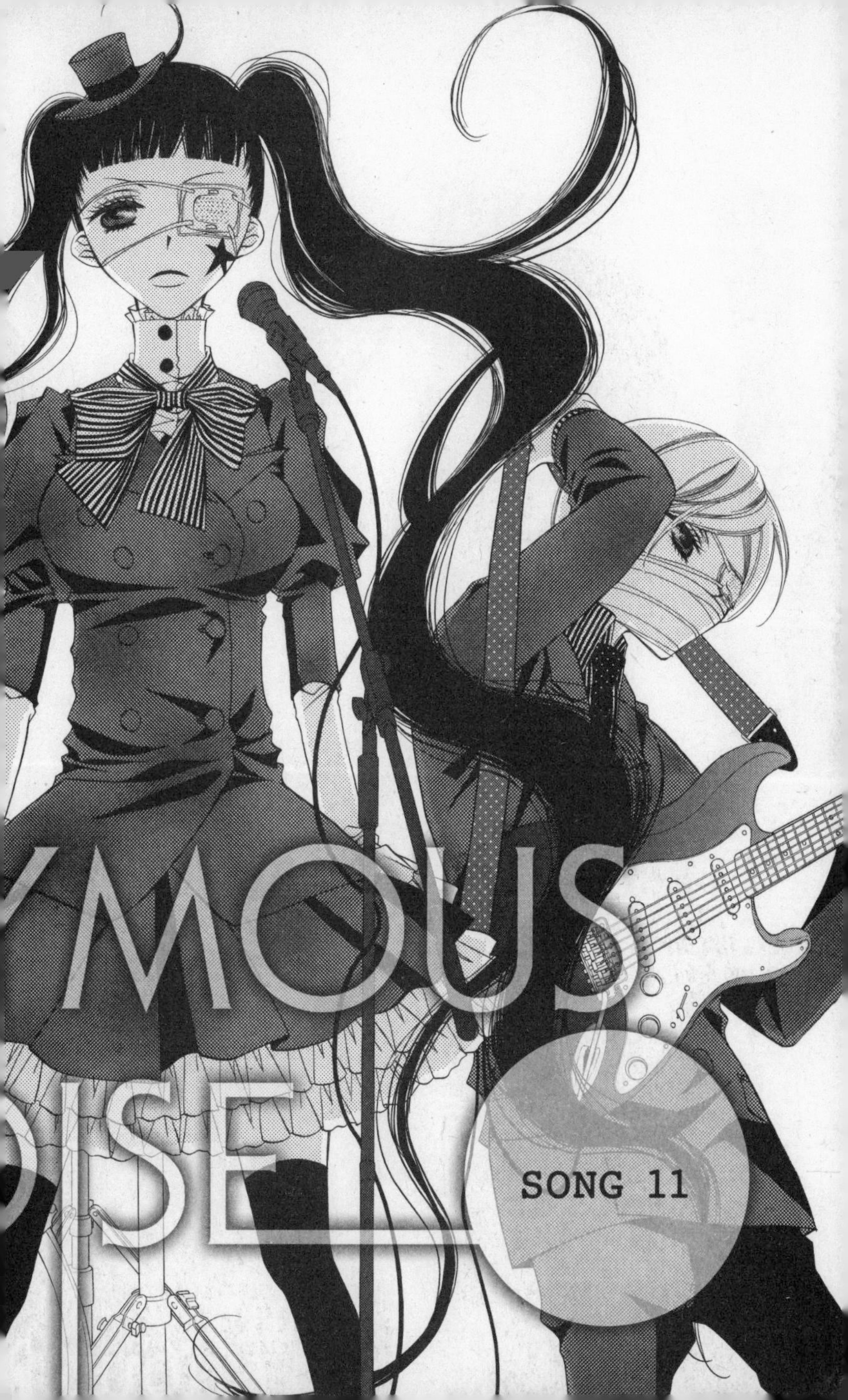
YMOUS
ISE
SONG 11

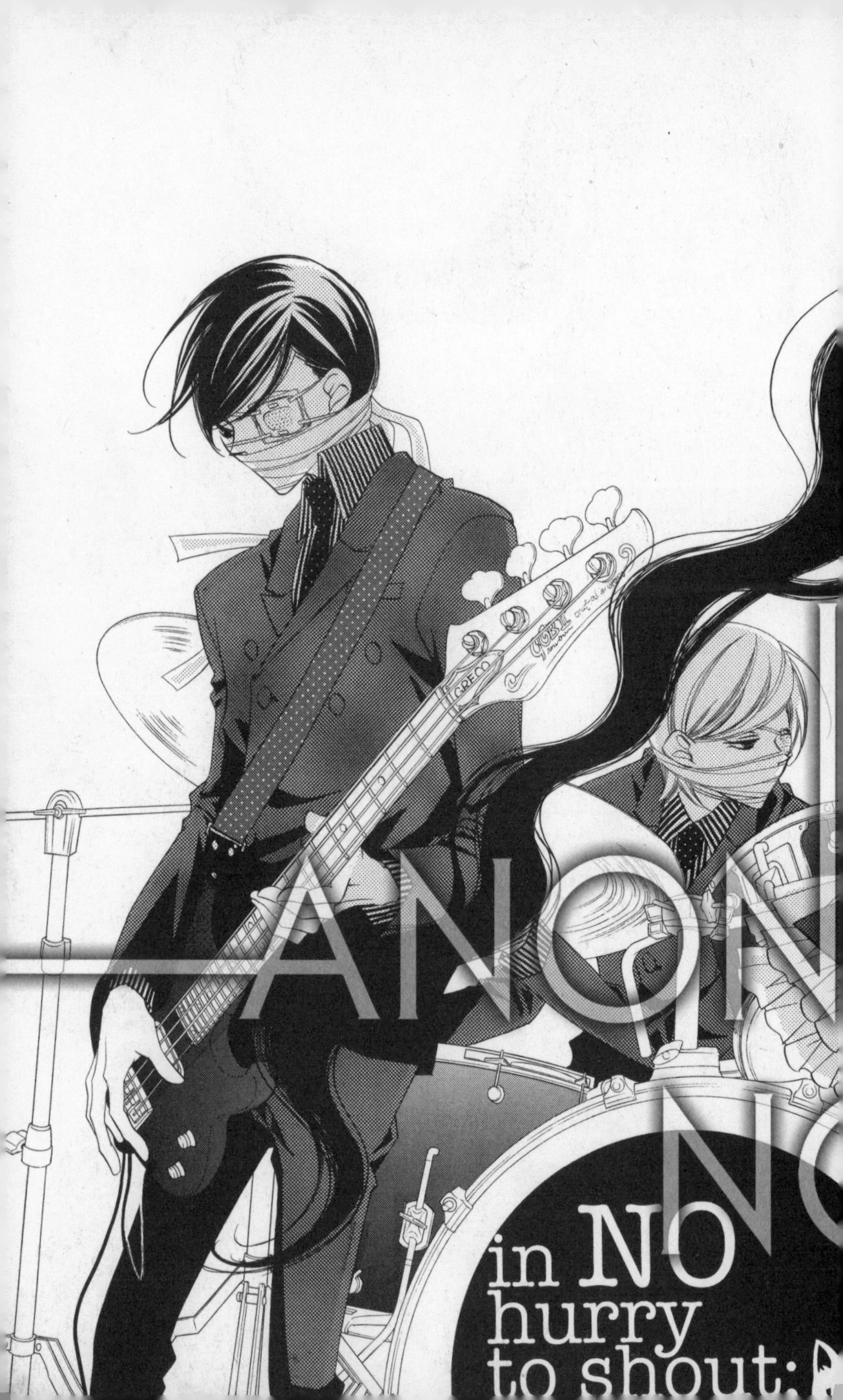
ANON
in NO
hurry
to shout:

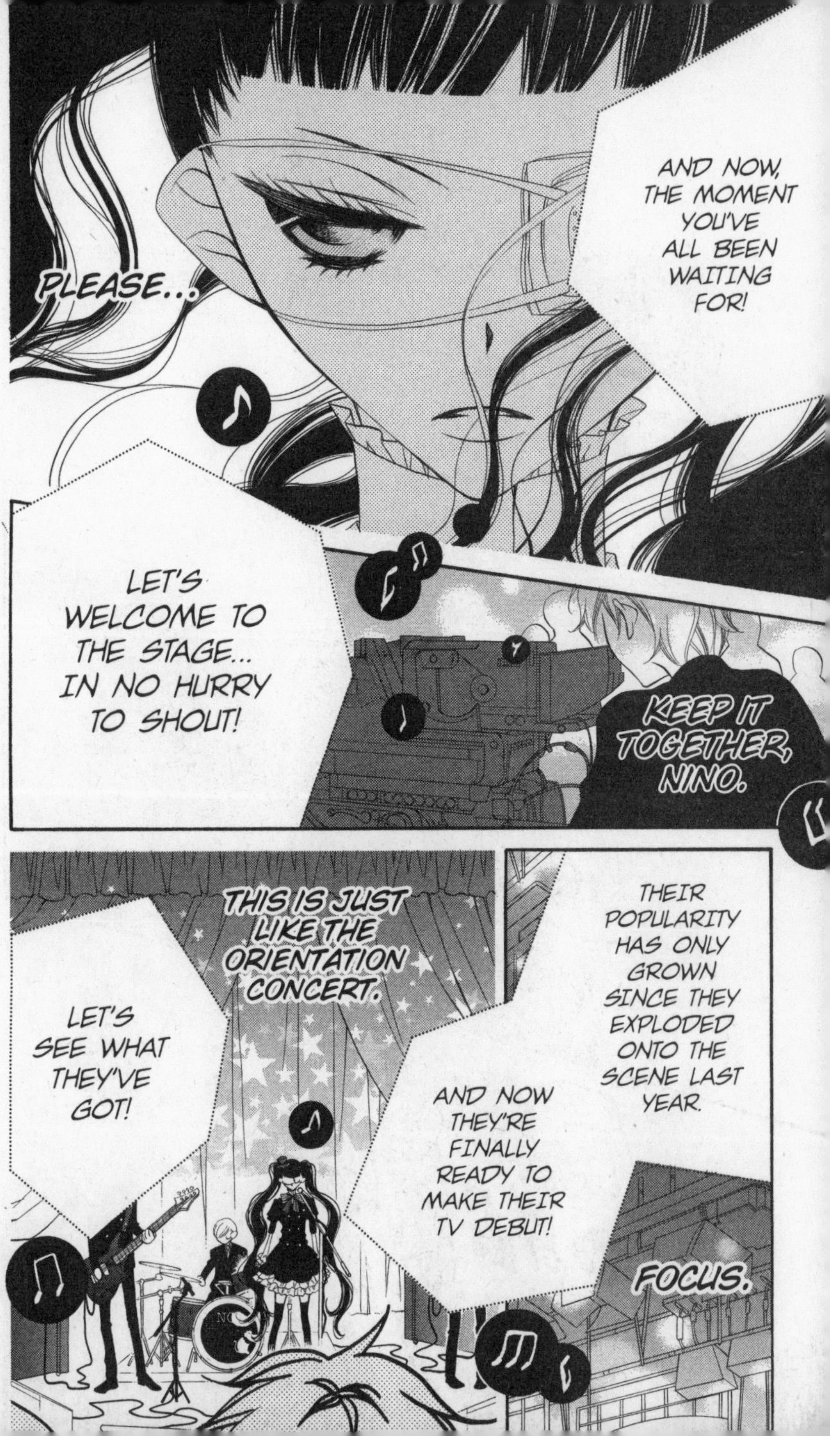
AND NOW, THE MOMENT YOU'VE ALL BEEN WAITING FOR!
PLEASE...
LET'S WELCOME TO THE STAGE... IN NO HURRY TO SHOUT!
KEEP IT TOGETHER, NINO.
THEIR POPULARITY HAS ONLY GROWN SINCE THEY EXPLODED ONTO THE SCENE LAST YEAR.
AND NOW THEY'RE FINALLY READY TO MAKE THEIR TV DEBUT!
FOCUS.
THIS IS JUST LIKE THE ORIENTATION CONCERT.
LET'S SEE WHAT THEY'VE GOT!

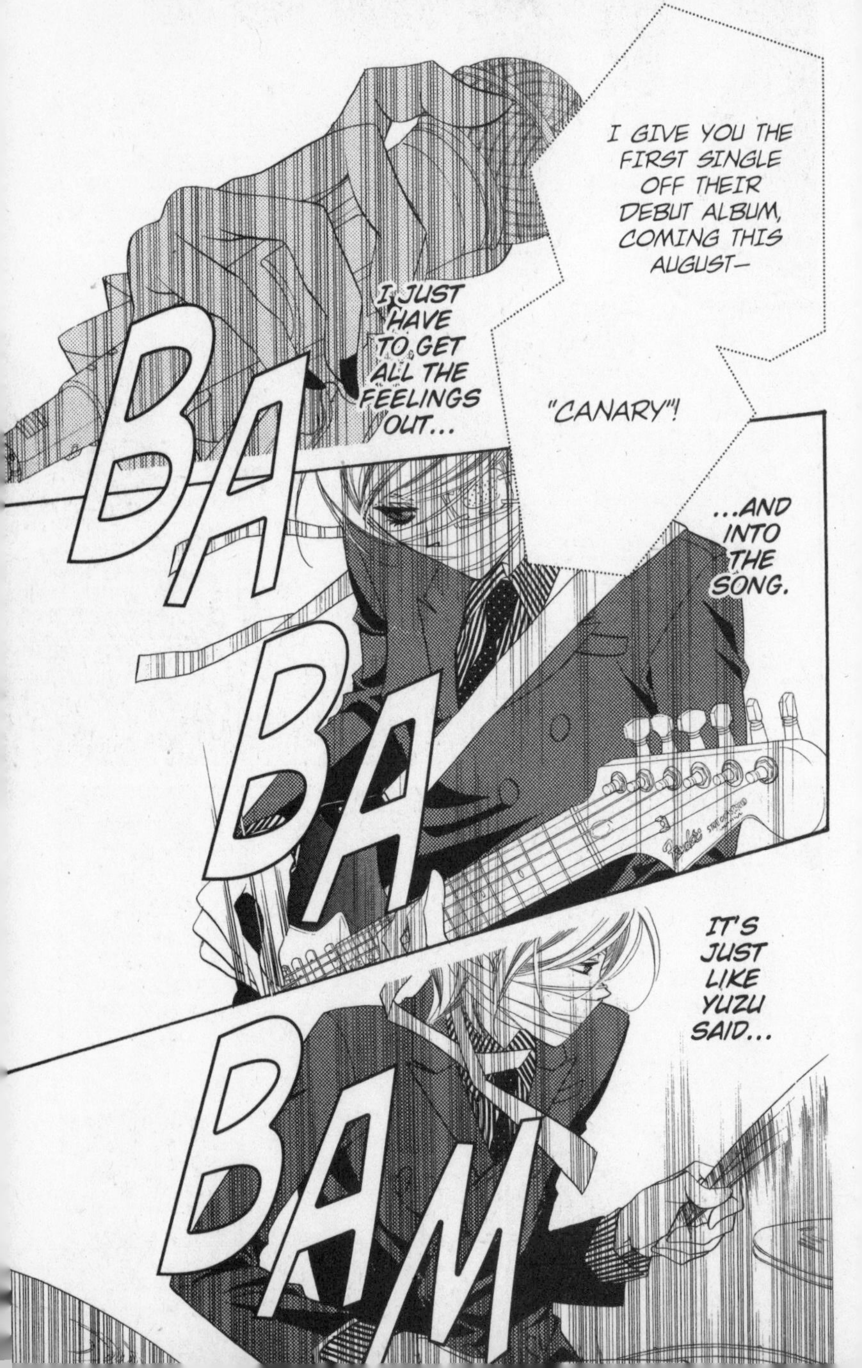
I GIVE YOU THE FIRST SINGLE OFF THEIR DEBUT ALBUM, COMING THIS AUGUST—
"CANARY"!
I JUST HAVE TO GET ALL THE FEELINGS OUT...
...AND INTO THE SONG.
BA
BA
BAM
IT'S JUST LIKE YUZU SAID...

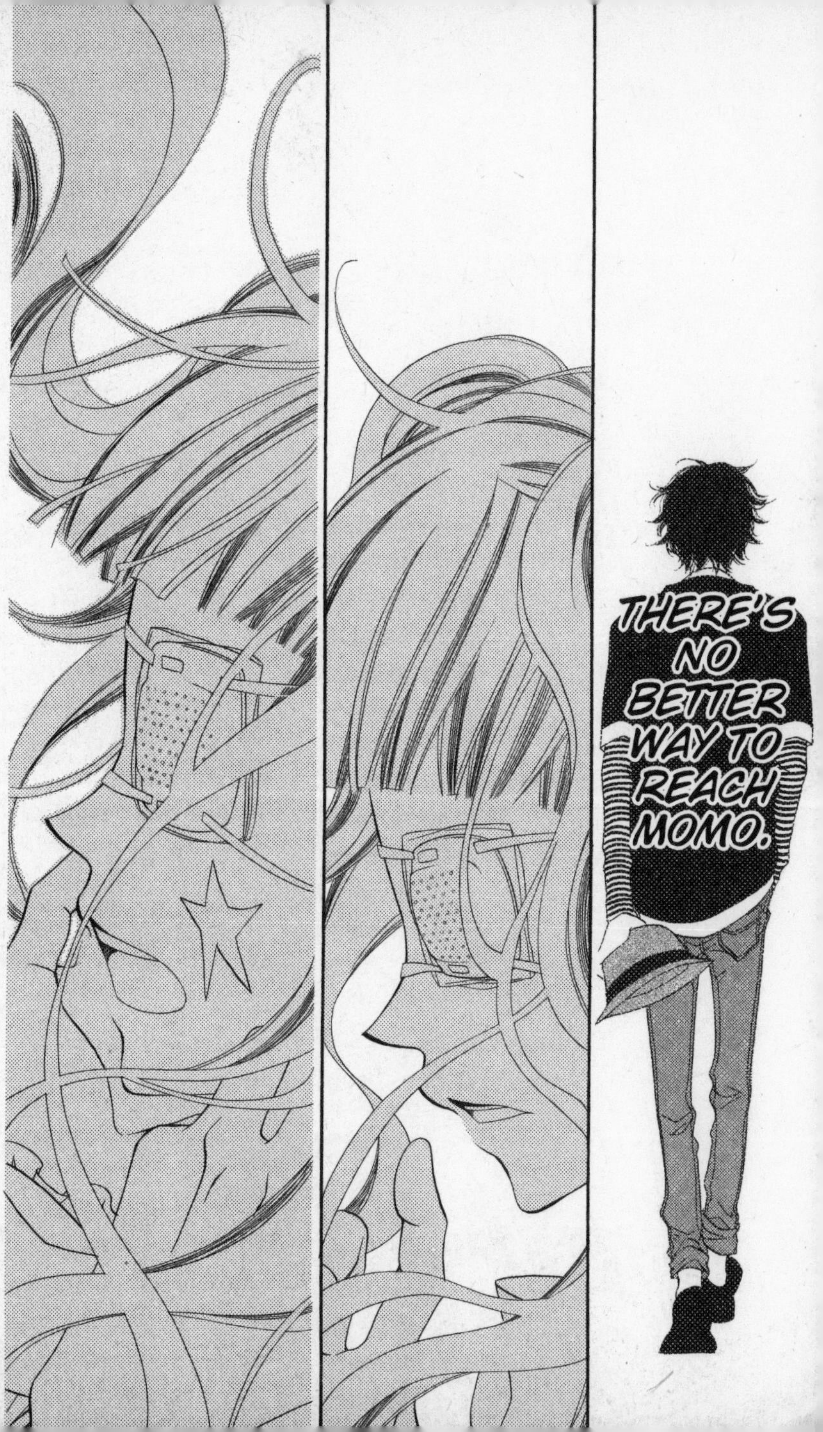
THERE'S NO BETTER WAY TO REACH MOMO.

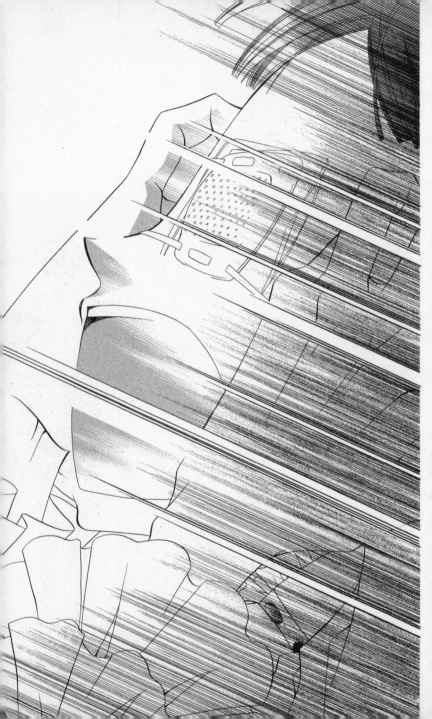

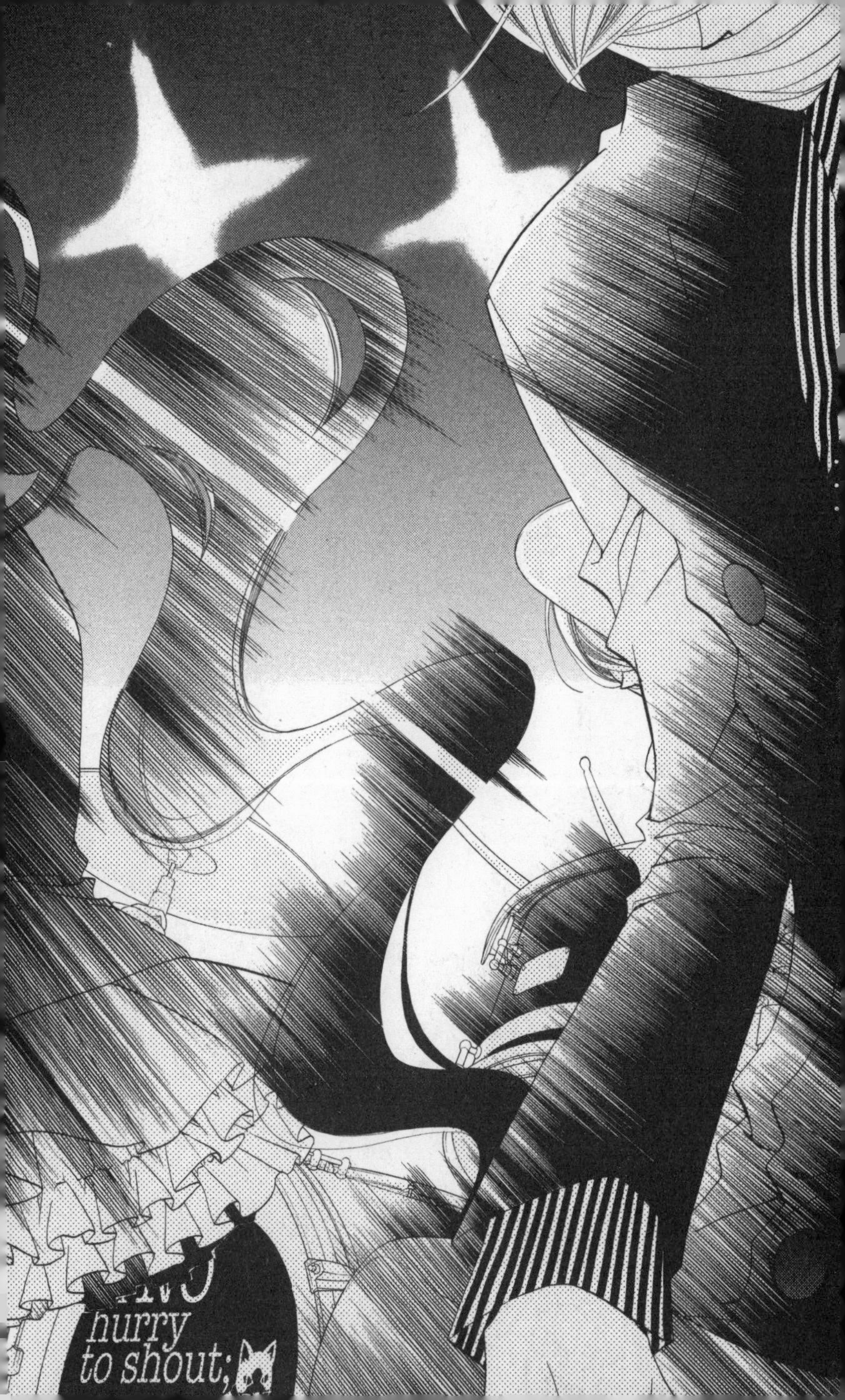
hurry
to shout;

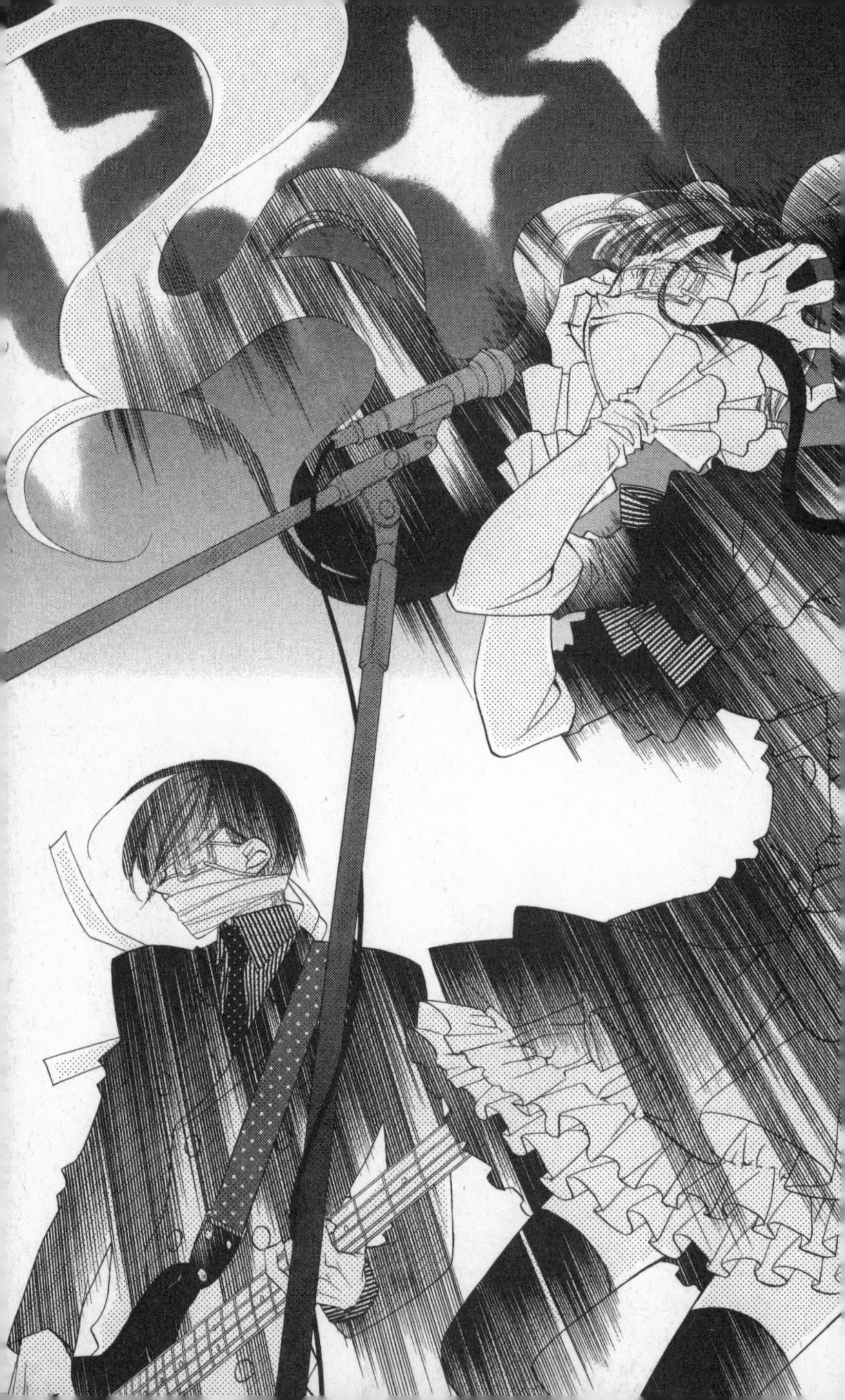

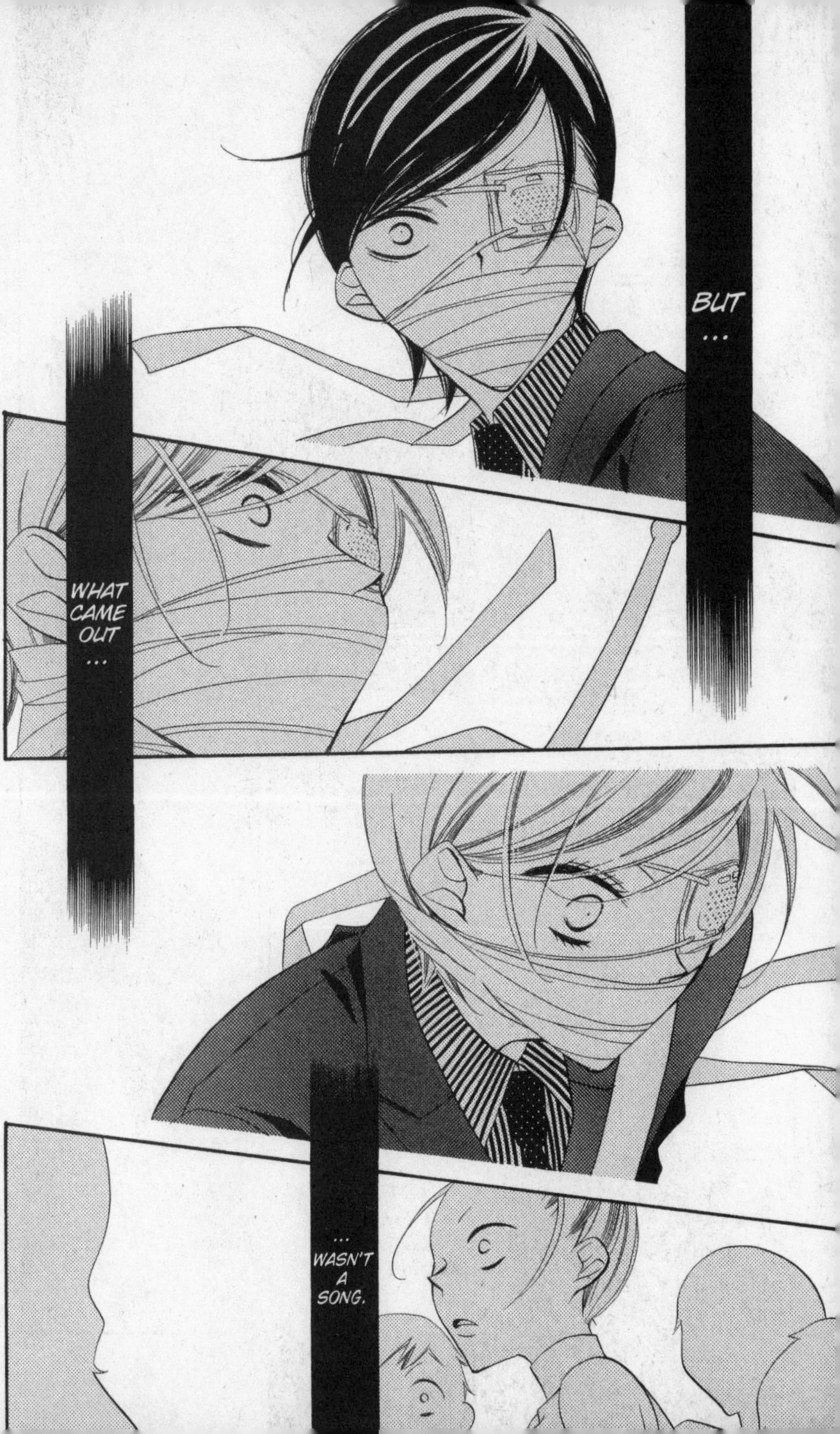
BUT ...
WHAT CAME OUT ...
... WASN'T A SONG.

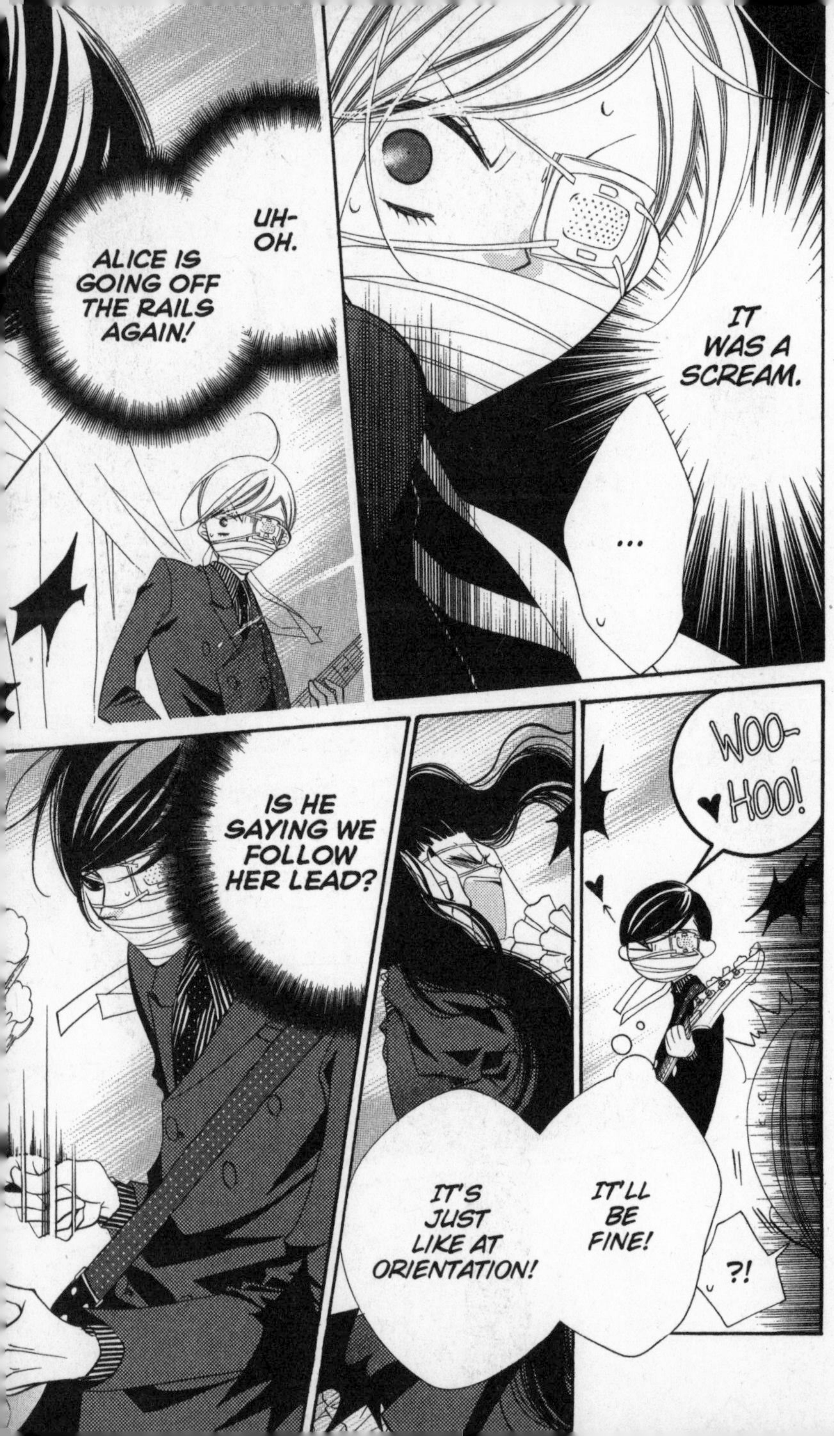
IT WAS A SCREAM.
...
UH-OH.
ALICE IS GOING OFF THE RAILS AGAIN!
WOO-HOO!
IT'LL BE FINE!
IT'S JUST LIKE AT ORIENTATION!
?!
IS HE SAYING WE FOLLOW HER LEAD?

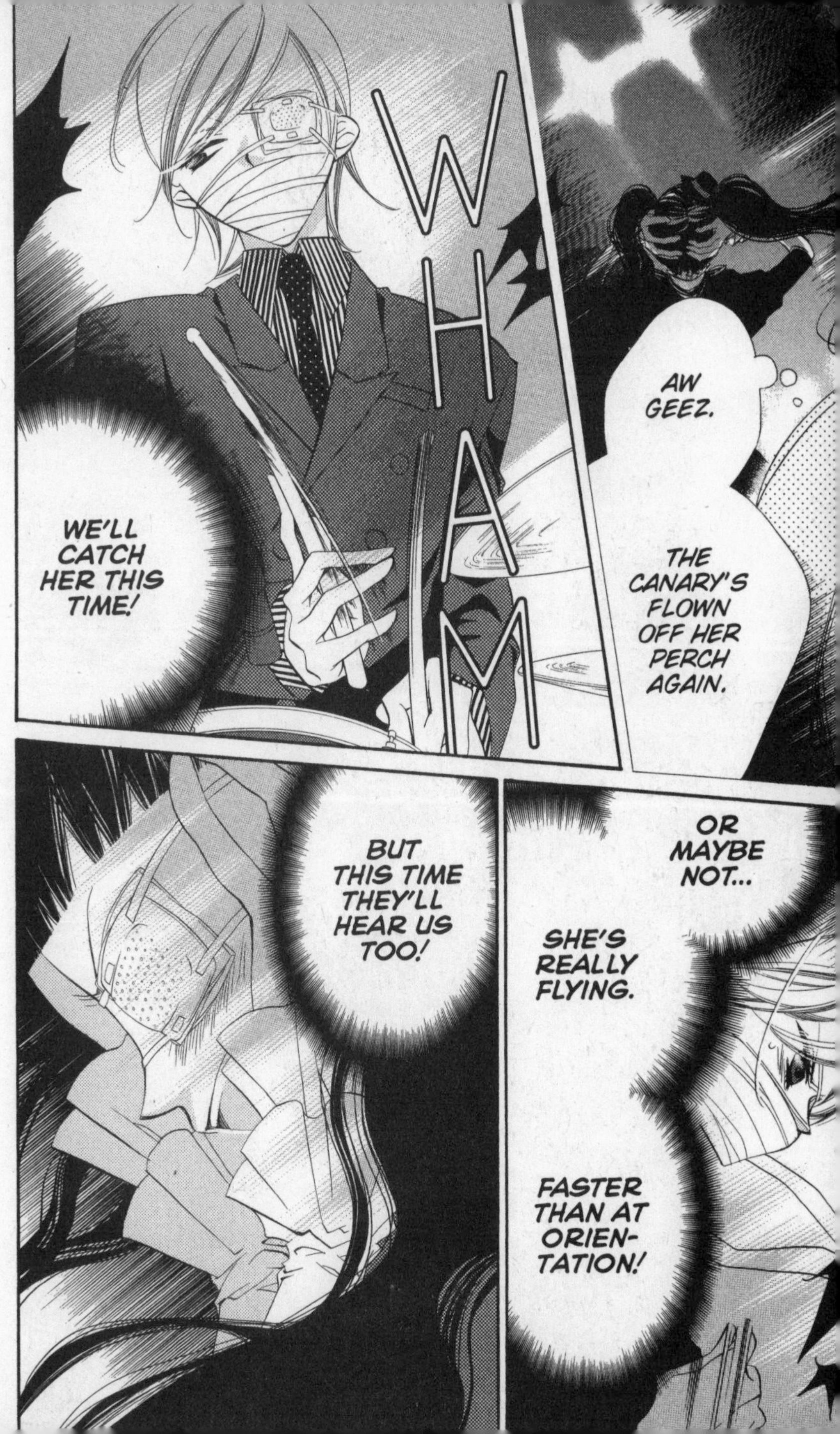
AW GEEZ.
THE CANARY'S FLOWN OFF HER PERCH AGAIN.
WHAM
WE'LL CATCH HER THIS TIME!
OR MAYBE NOT...
SHE'S REALLY FLYING.
FASTER THAN AT ORIENTATION!
BUT THIS TIME THEY'LL HEAR US TOO!

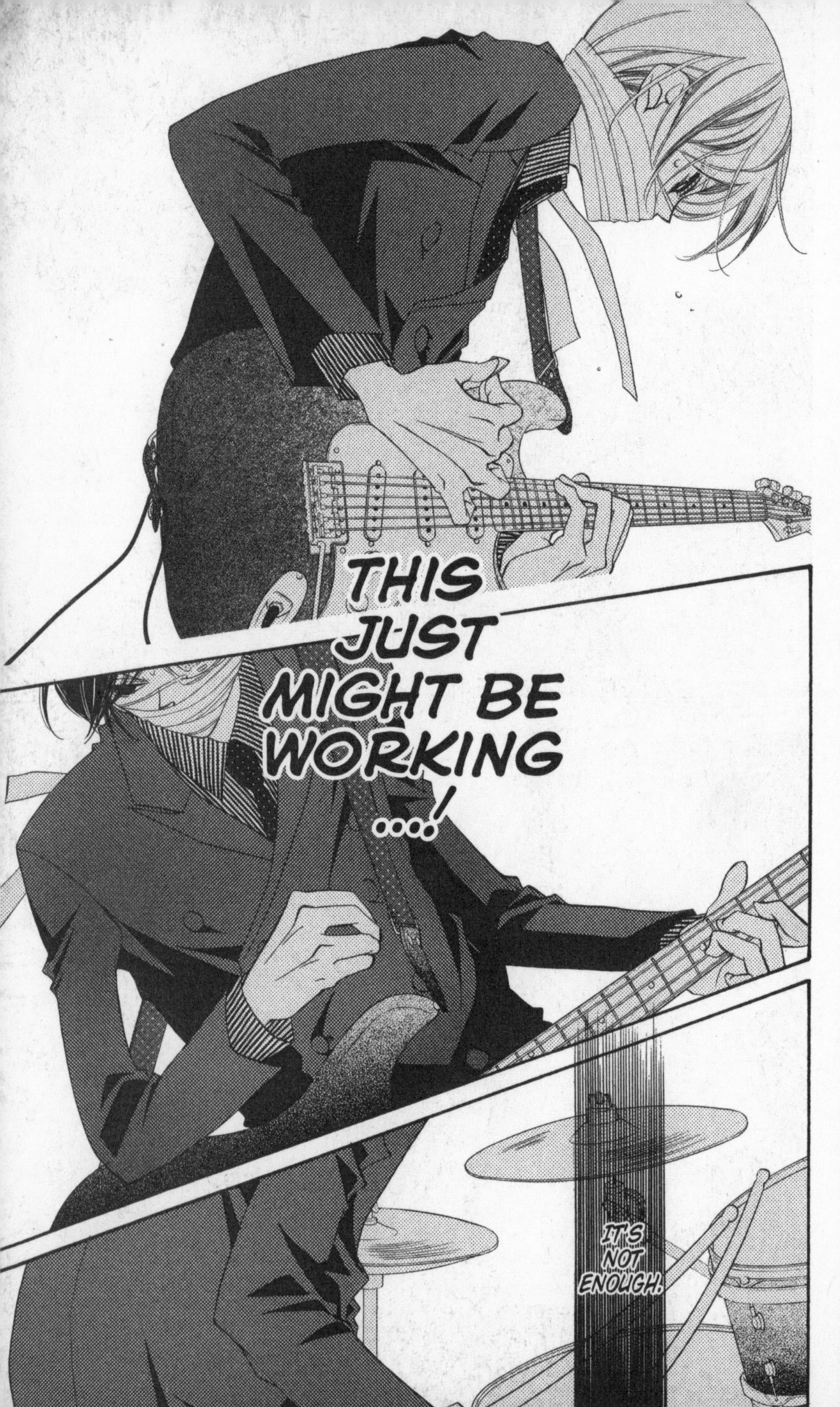
THIS JUST MIGHT BE WORKING ...!
IT'S NOT ENOUGH.

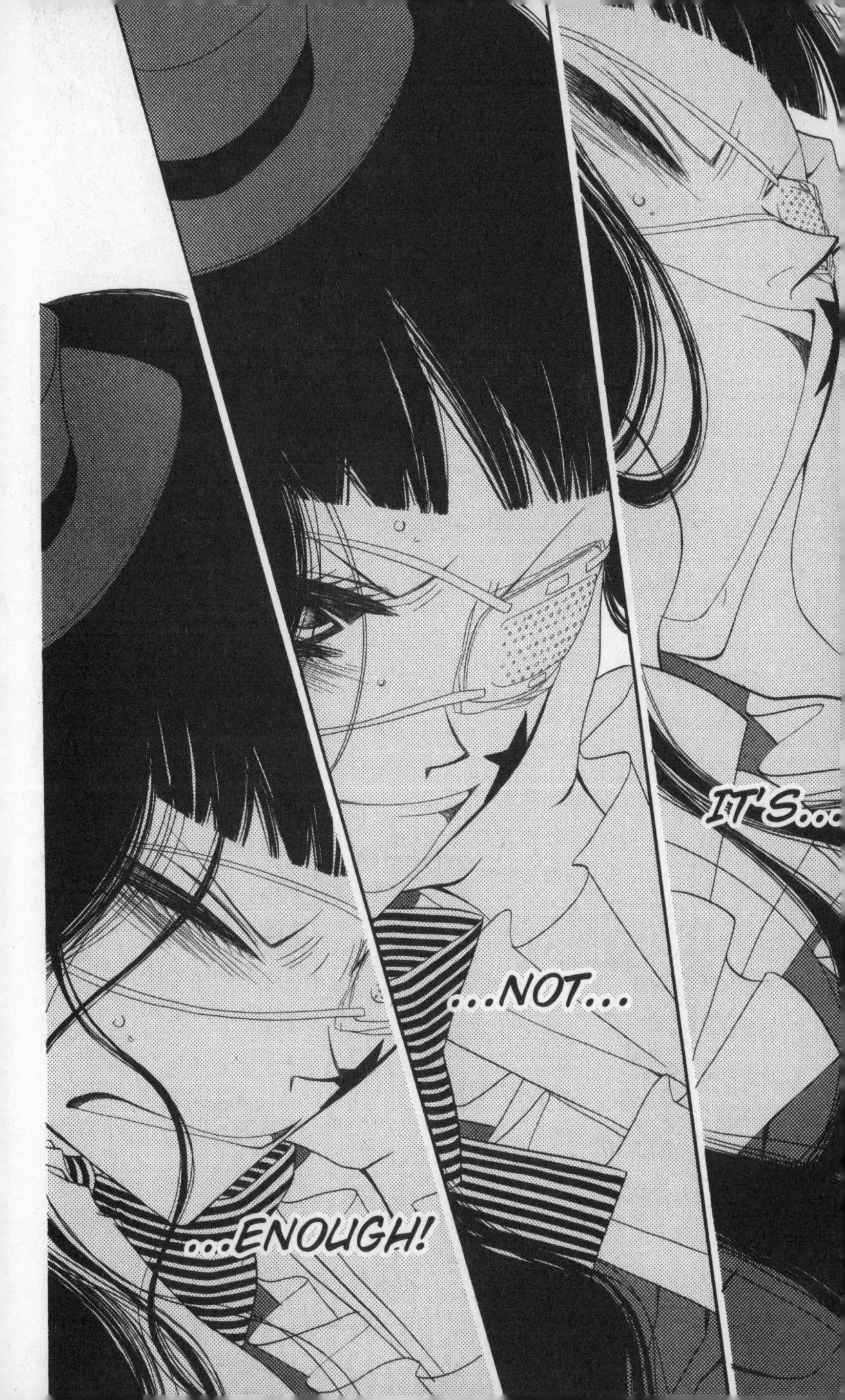
IT'S...
...NOT...
...ENOUGH!

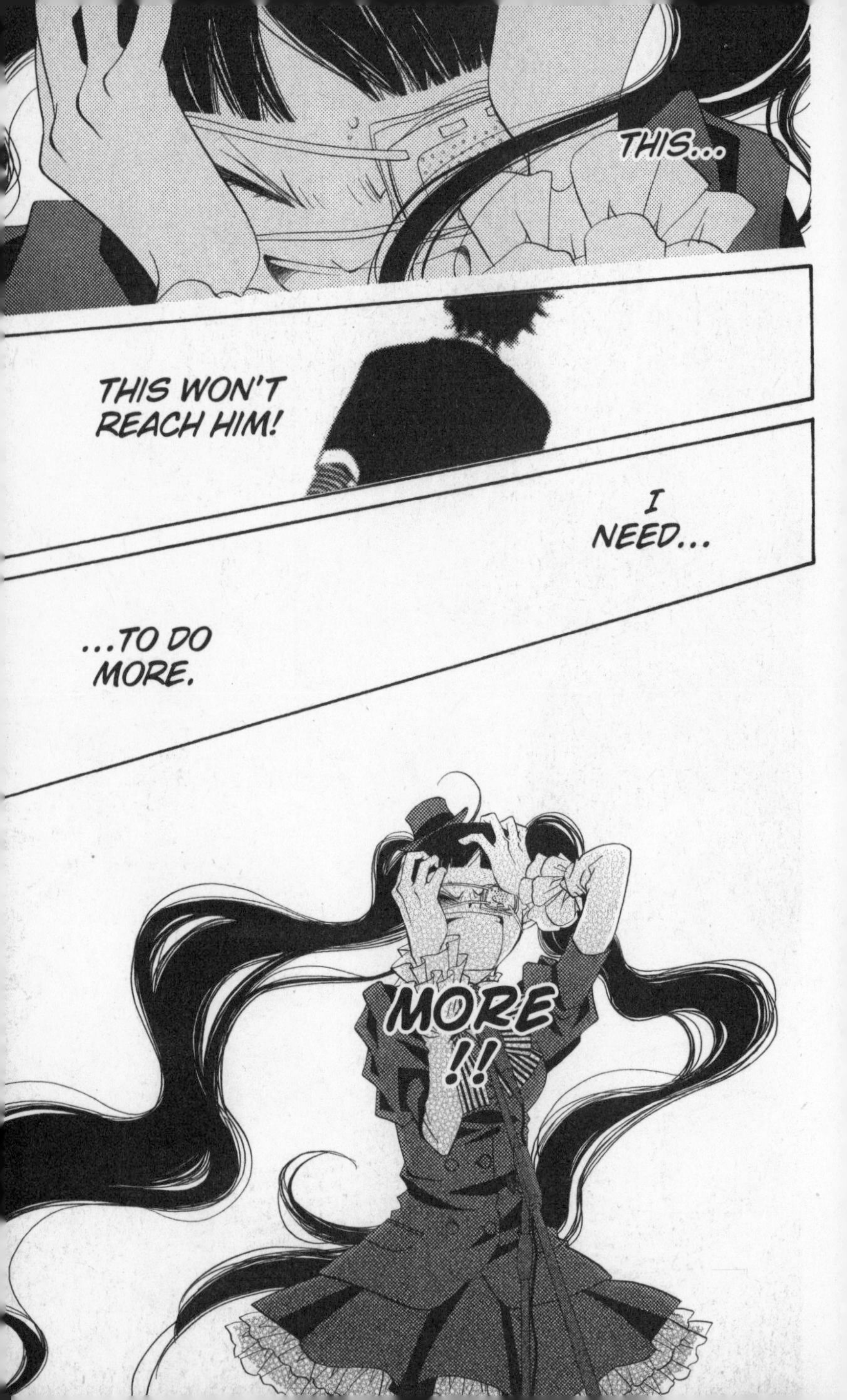
THIS...
THIS WON'T REACH HIM!
I NEED...
...TO DO MORE.
MORE !!

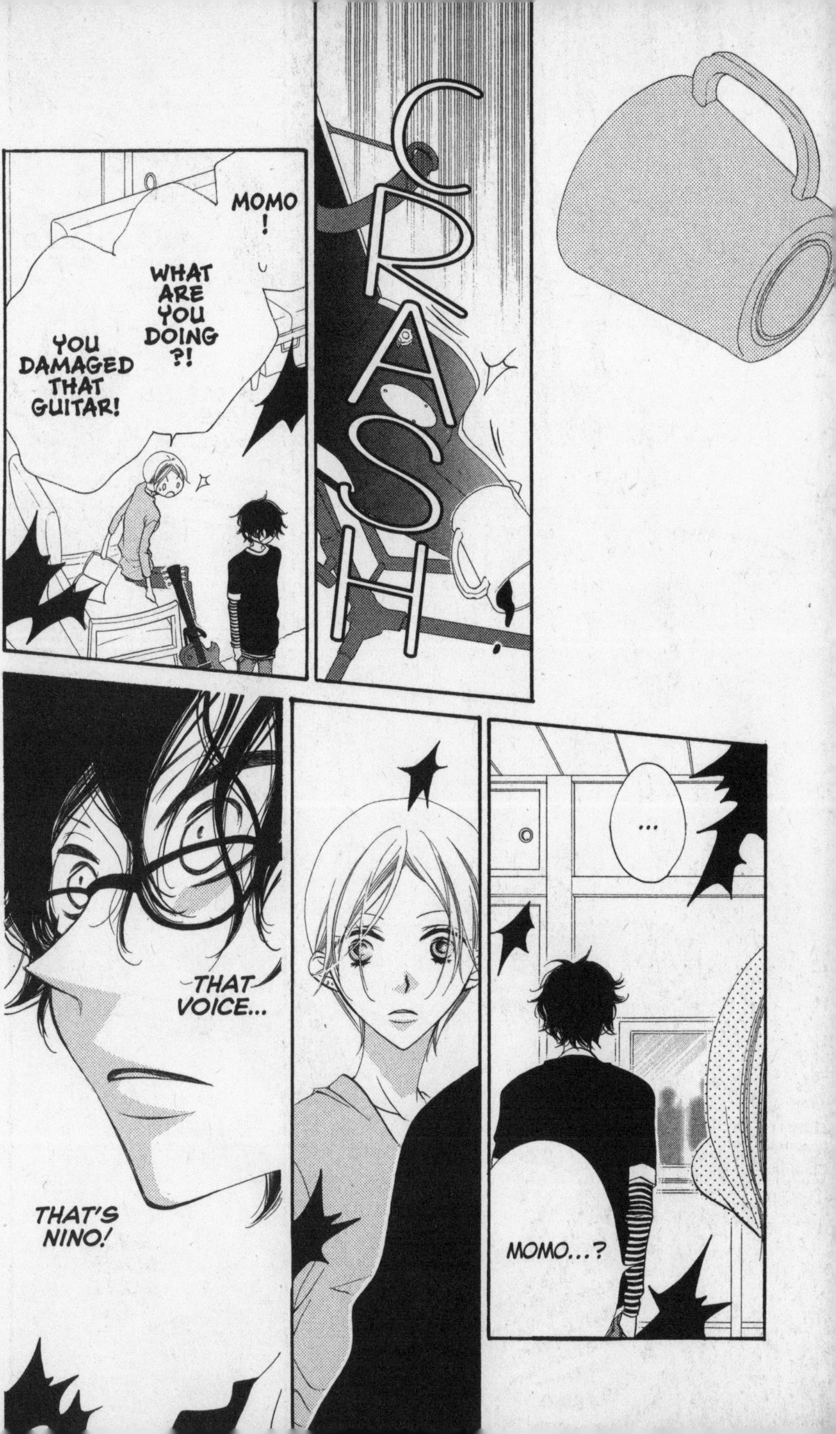
CRASH
MOMO!
WHAT ARE YOU DOING?!
YOU DAMAGED THAT GUITAR!
...
MOMO...?
THAT VOICE...
THAT'S NINO!

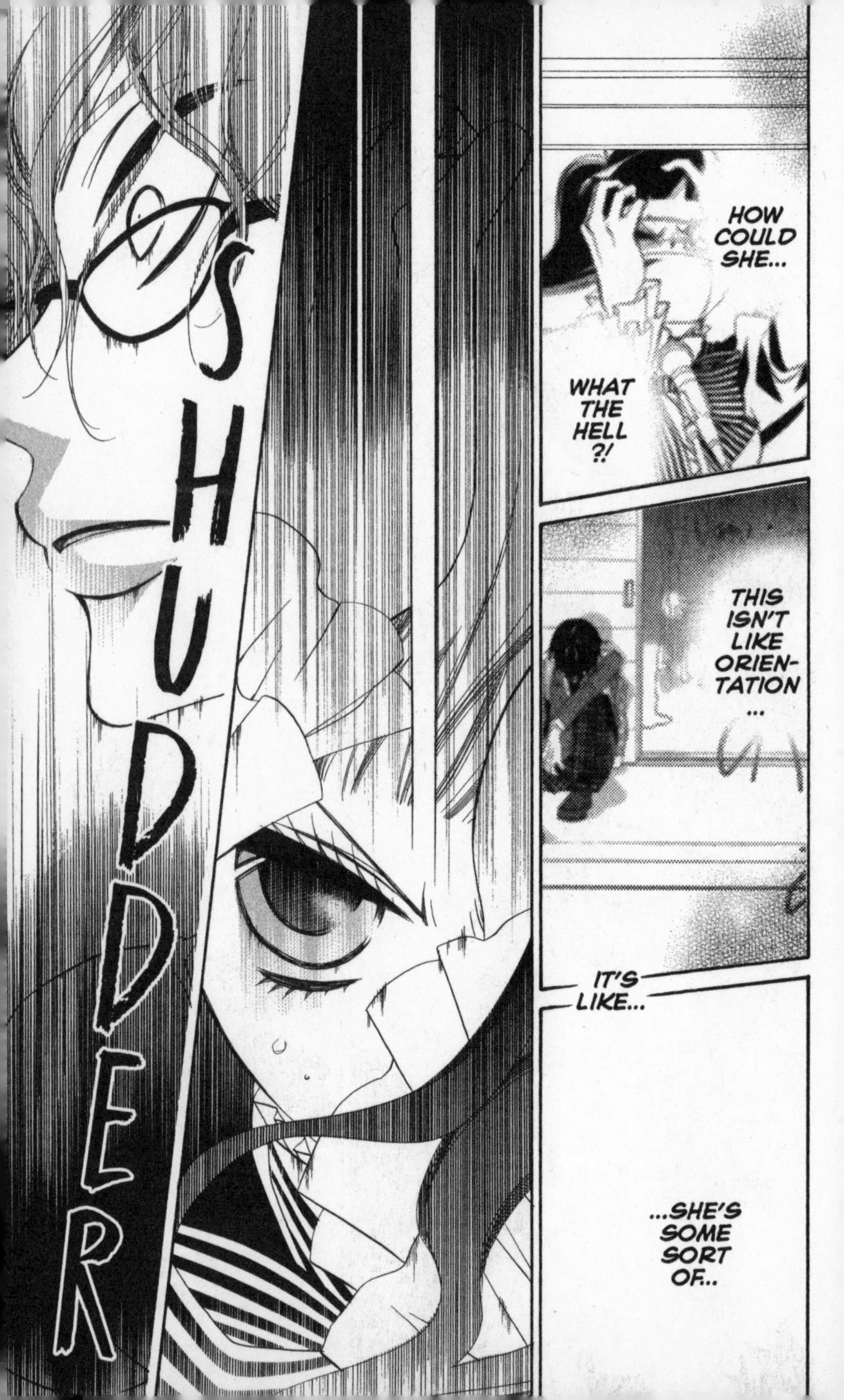
HOW COULD SHE...
WHAT THE HELL ?!
THIS ISN'T LIKE ORIEN-TATION ...
IT'S LIKE...
...SHE'S SOME SORT OF...
SHUDDER

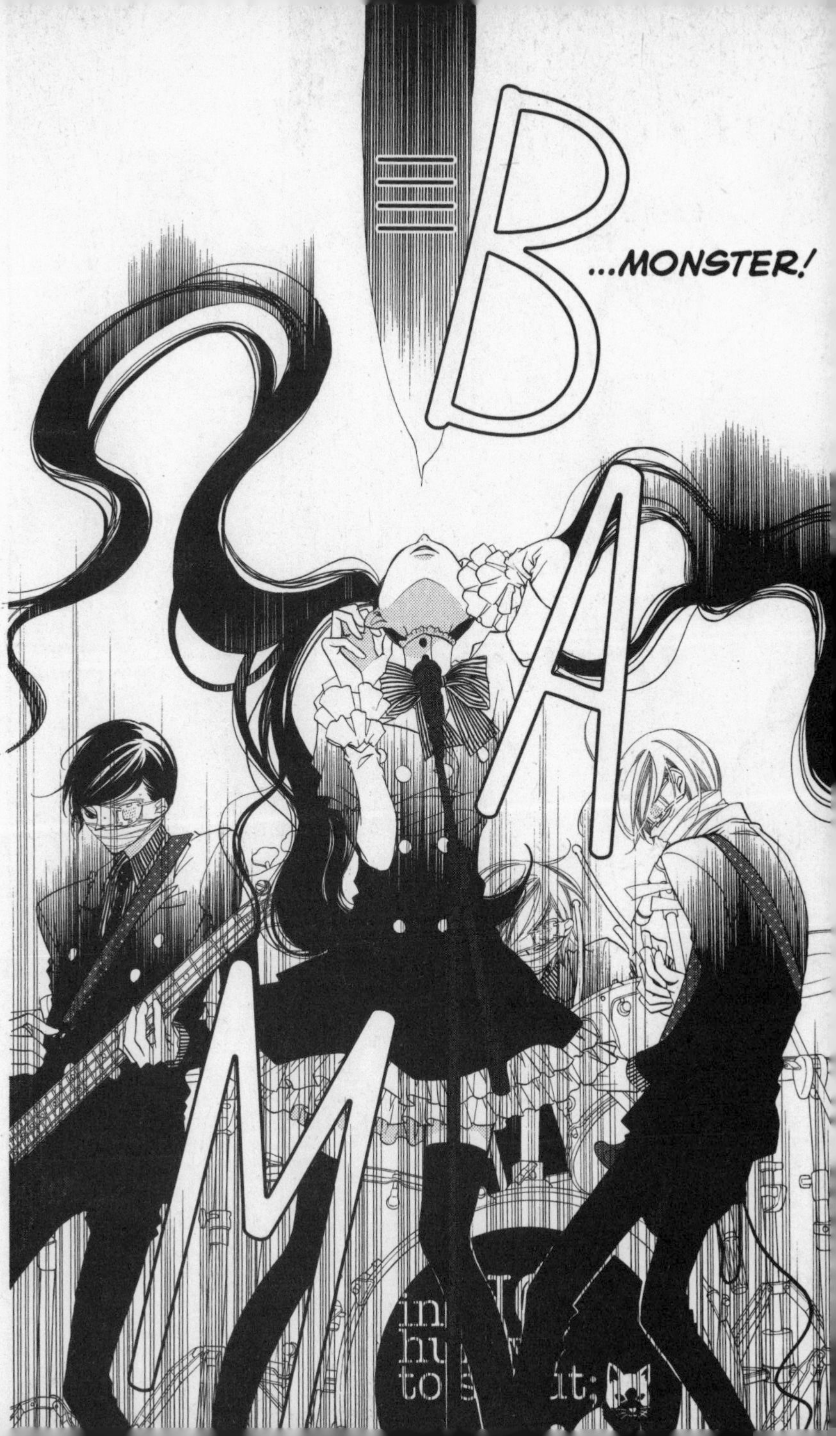
...MONSTER!
BAM

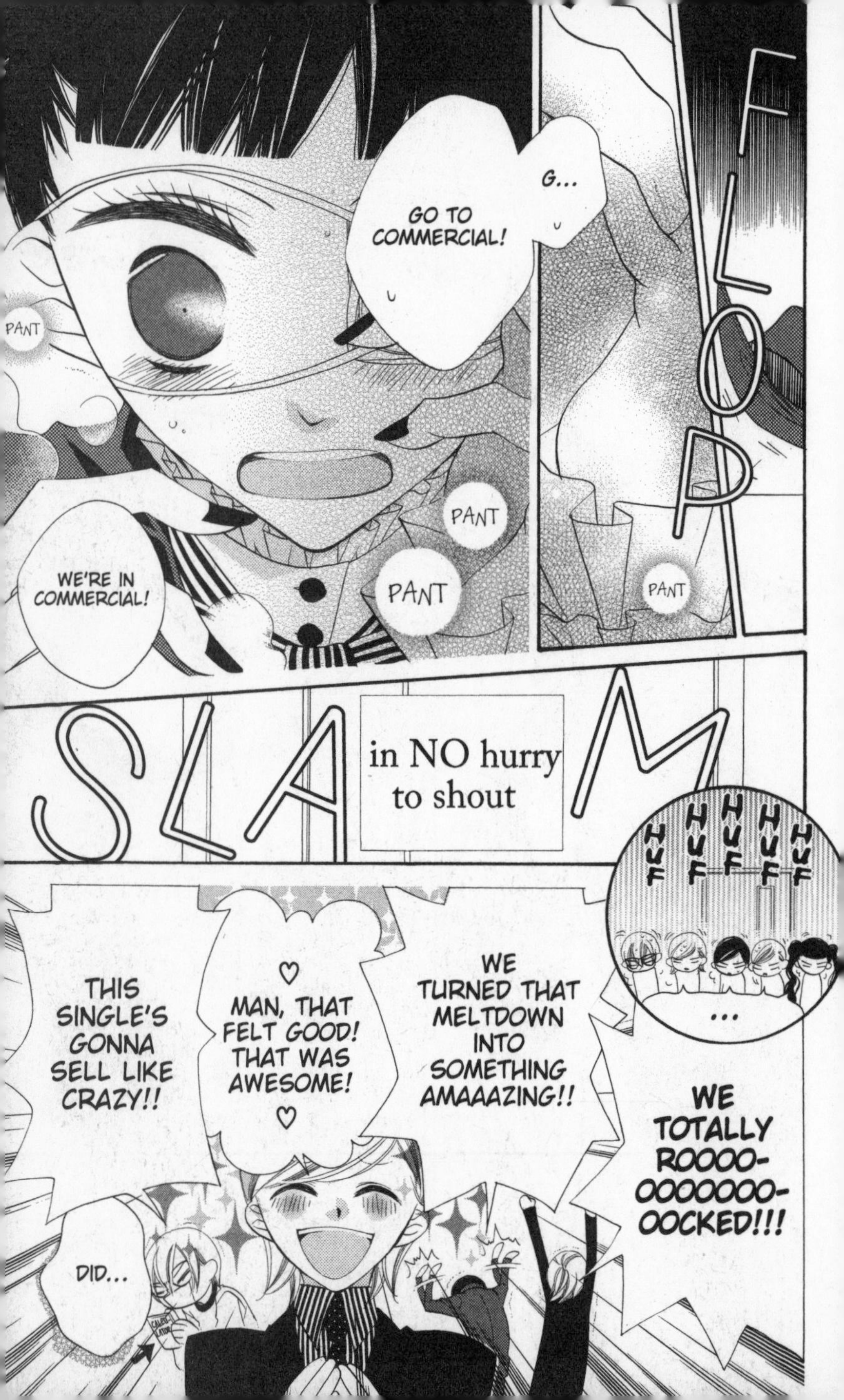
FLOP
PANT
G...
GO TO COMMERCIAL!
PANT
PANT
PANT
WE'RE IN COMMERCIAL!
SLAM
in NO hurry to shout
HUFF
HUFF
HUFF
HUFF
HUFF
...
WE TOTALLY ROOOO-OOOOOOO-OOCKED!!!
WE TURNED THAT MELTDOWN INTO SOMETHING AMAAAZING!!
MAN, THAT FELT GOOD! THAT WAS AWESOME!
THIS SINGLE'S GONNA SELL LIKE CRAZY!!
DID...

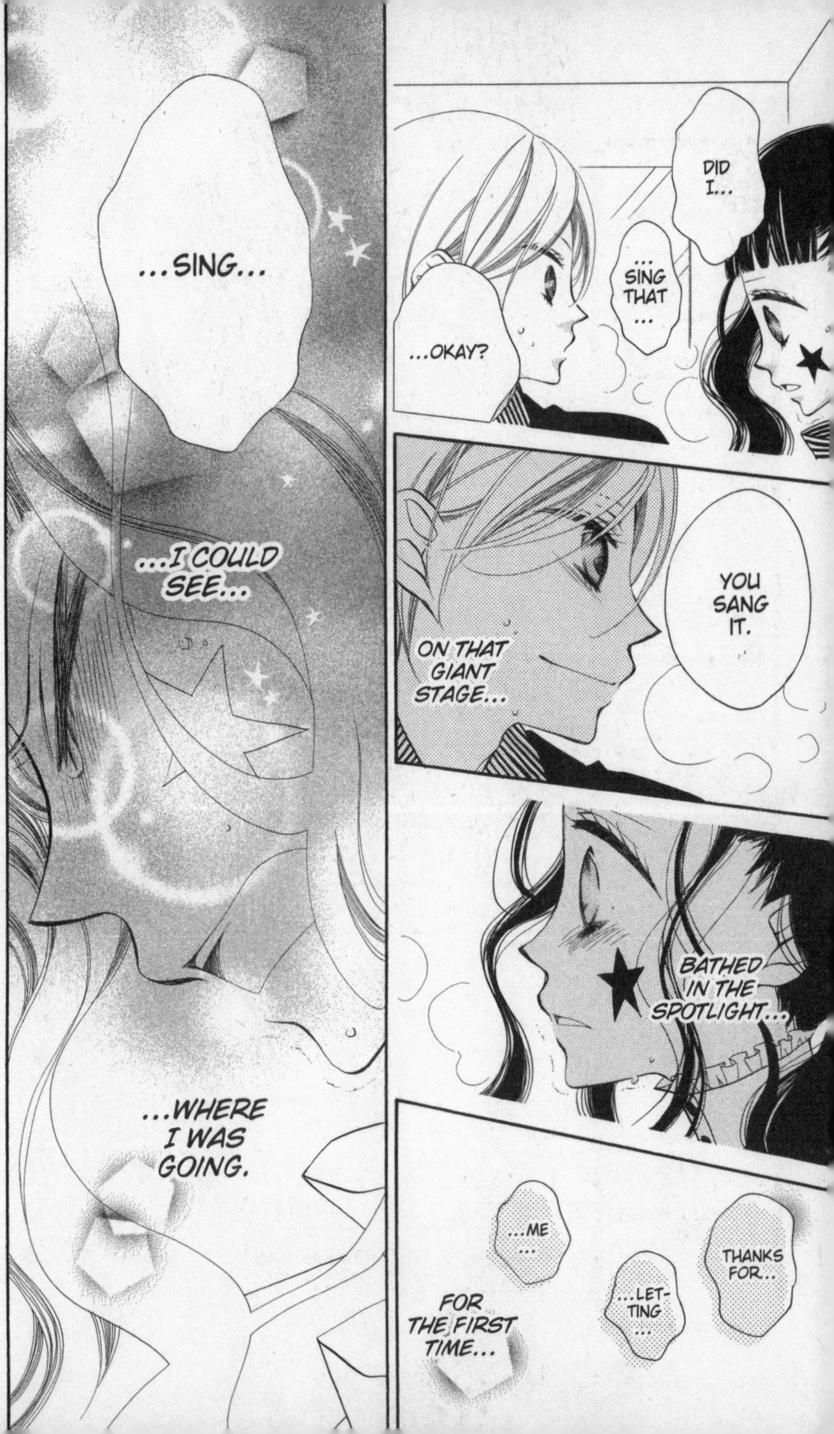
DID I...
...SING THAT...
...OKAY?
YOU SANG IT.
ON THAT GIANT STAGE...
BATHED IN THE SPOTLIGHT...
THANKS FOR...
...LET-TING...
...ME...
FOR THE FIRST TIME...
...SING...
...I COULD SEE...
...WHERE I WAS GOING.

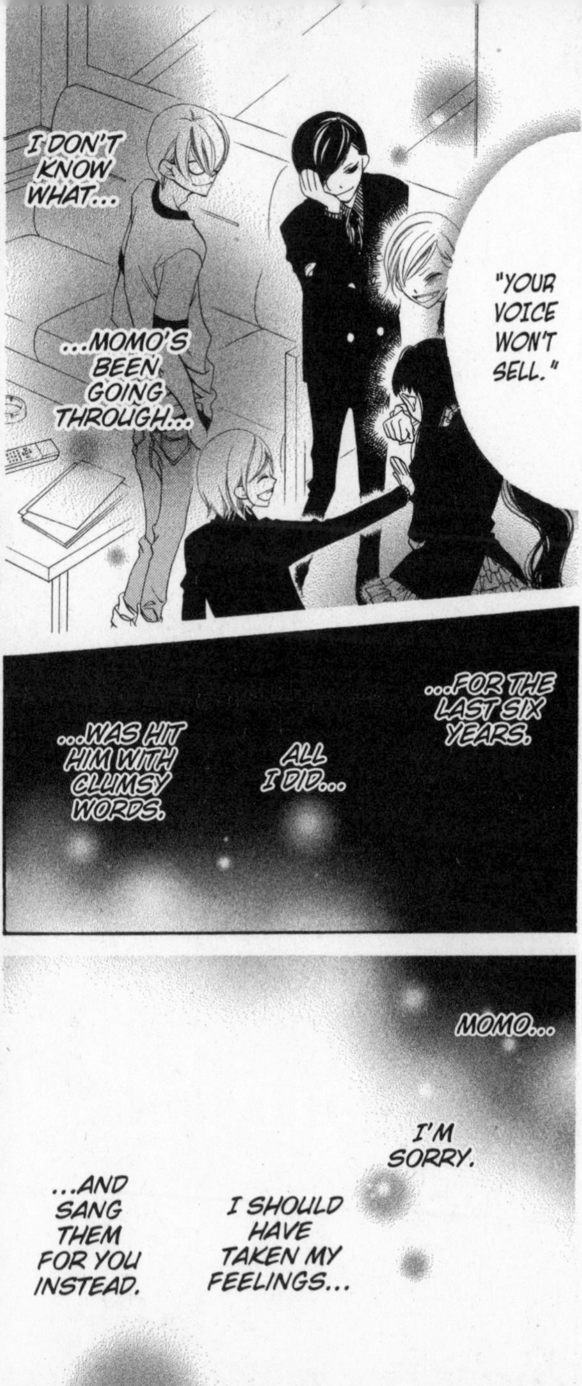
"YOUR VOICE WON'T SELL."
I DON'T KNOW WHAT...
...MOMO'S BEEN GOING THROUGH...
...FOR THE LAST SIX YEARS.
ALL I DID...
...WAS HIT HIM WITH CLUMSY WORDS.
MOMO...
I'M SORRY.
I SHOULD HAVE TAKEN MY FEELINGS...
...AND SANG THEM FOR YOU INSTEAD.

1

Greetings! This is Ryoko Fukuyama.

Thank you so much for reading volume 3 of Anonymous Noise! YAAAAY!

I can't believe we're already at volume 3! That was so fast! It's kinda scary! The cover of this volume has Momo on it. As with the volume 2 cover, I didn't like the original version and had to redo it. I really hope I can nail volume 4's cover on the first try! We'll see...

I always have the characters hold some sort of accessory, but this time I was torn between a black Les Paul and a Telecaster. I'll have to get that Telecaster on there one of these days! Anyway, I hope you enjoy volume 3!

FENDERS ARE HARD!

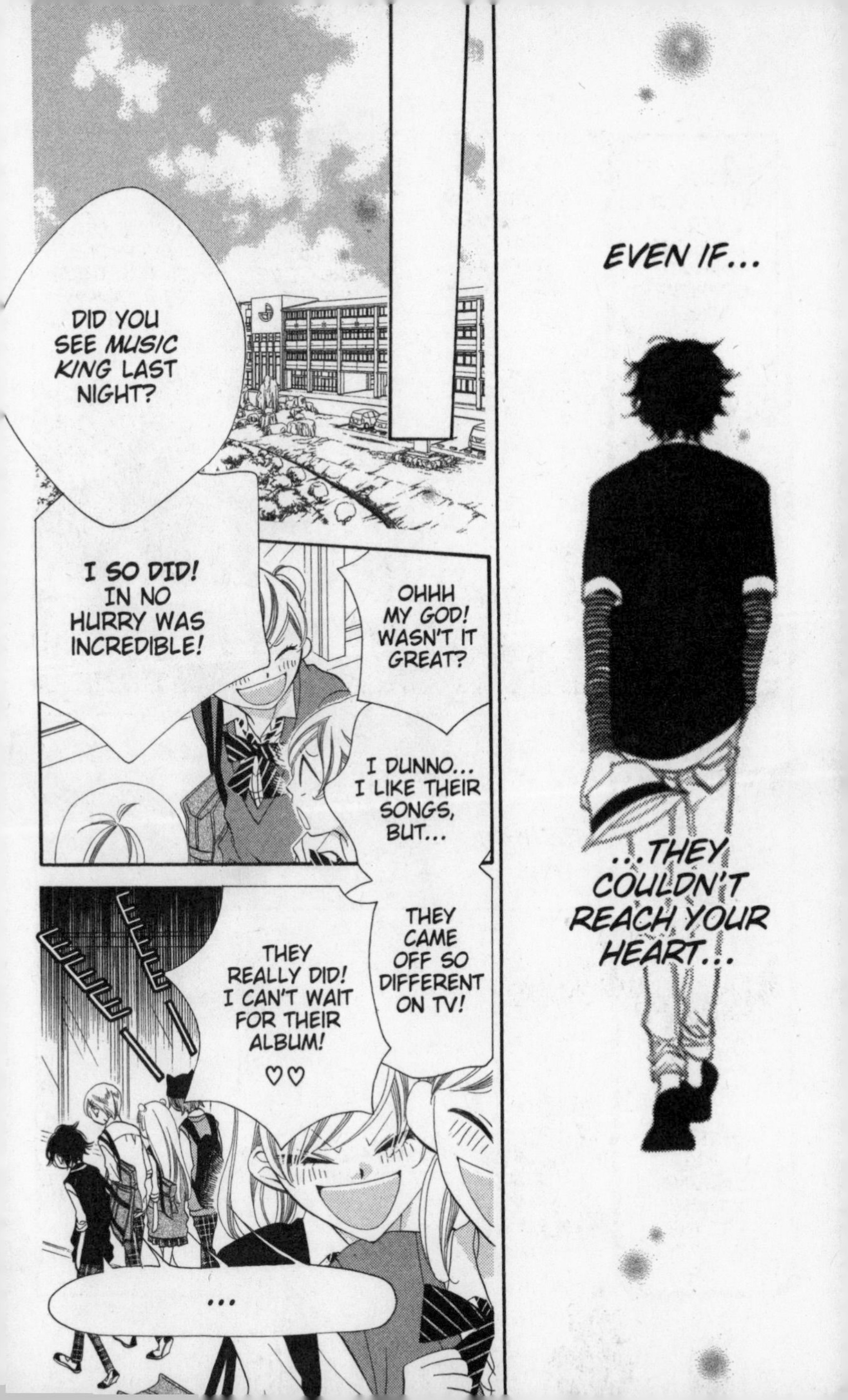
EVEN IF...
...THEY COULDN'T REACH YOUR HEART...
DID YOU SEE *MUSIC KING* LAST NIGHT?
I SO DID! IN NO HURRY WAS INCREDIBLE!
OHHH MY GOD! WASN'T IT GREAT?
I DUNNO... I LIKE THEIR SONGS, BUT...
THEY CAME OFF SO DIFFERENT ON TV!
THEY REALLY DID! I CAN'T WAIT FOR THEIR ALBUM! ♡♡
EEEE
EEEE
...

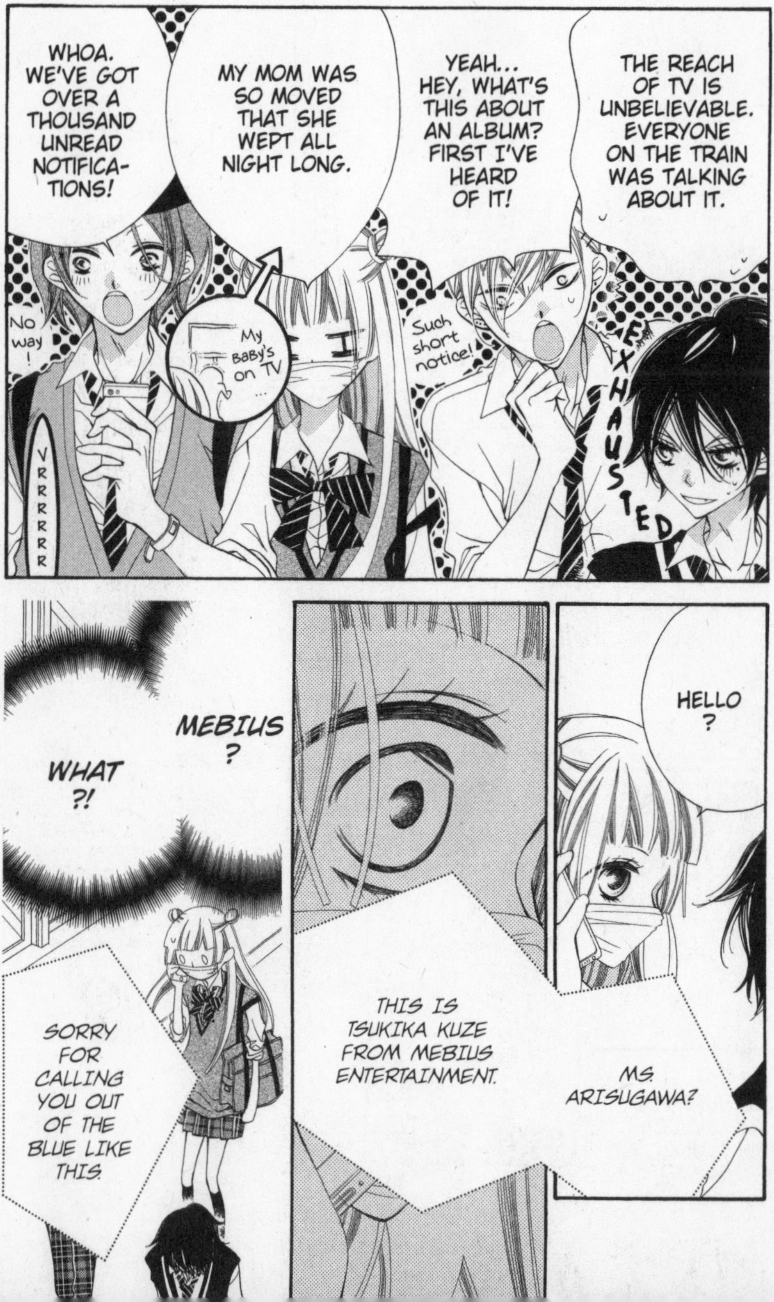

THE REACH OF TV IS UNBELIEVABLE. EVERYONE ON THE TRAIN WAS TALKING ABOUT IT.
EXHAUSTED
YEAH... HEY, WHAT'S THIS ABOUT AN ALBUM? FIRST I'VE HEARD OF IT!
Such short notice!
MY MOM WAS SO MOVED THAT SHE WEPT ALL NIGHT LONG.
My baby's on TV...
WHOA. WE'VE GOT OVER A THOUSAND UNREAD NOTIFICA-TIONS!
No way!
VRRRRRR
HELLO?
MS. ARISUGAWA?
THIS IS TSUKIKA KUZE FROM MEBIUS ENTERTAINMENT.
MEBIUS?
WHAT?!
SORRY FOR CALLING YOU OUT OF THE BLUE LIKE THIS.

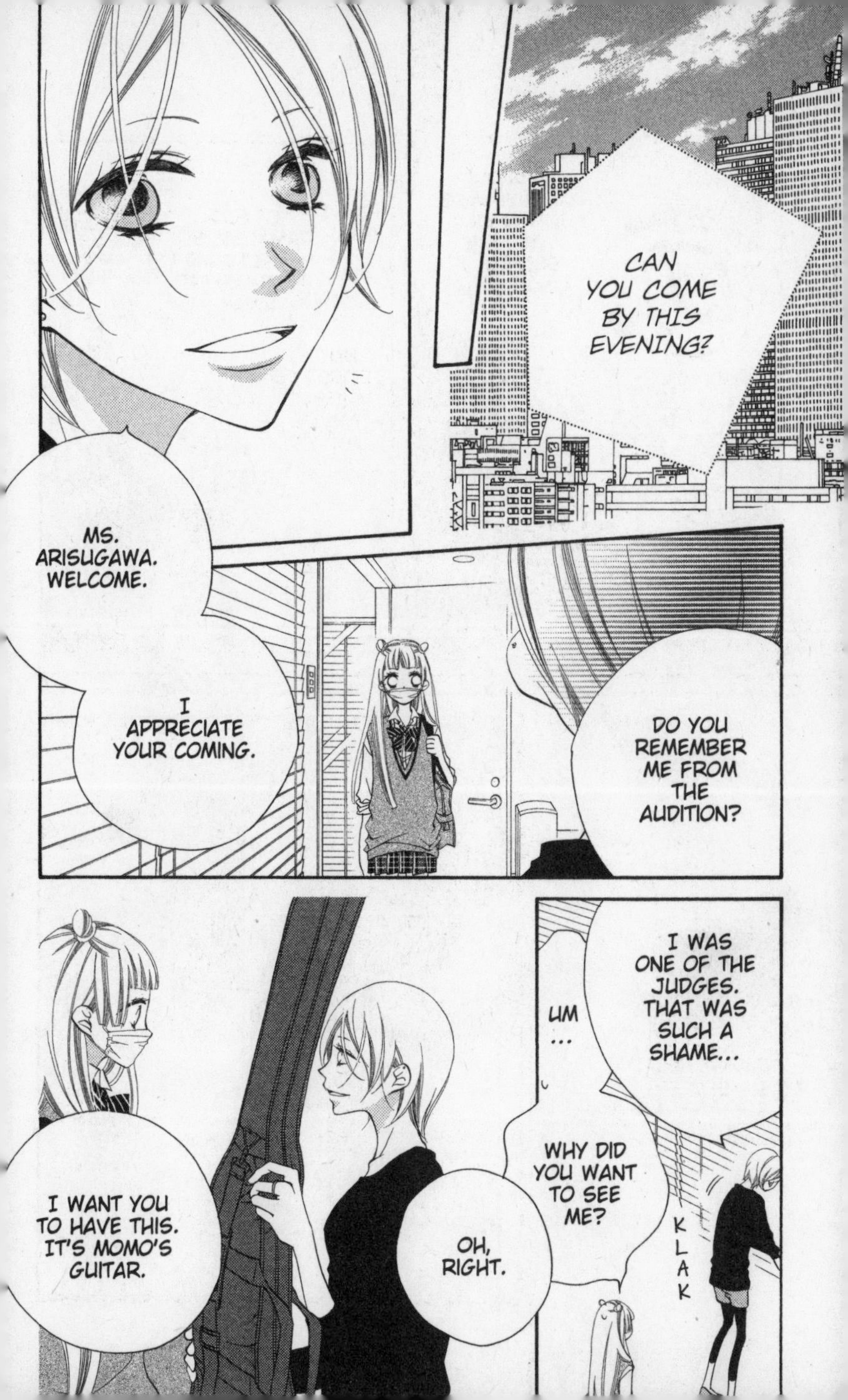
CAN YOU COME BY THIS EVENING?
MS. ARISUGAWA. WELCOME.
I APPRECIATE YOUR COMING.
DO YOU REMEMBER ME FROM THE AUDITION?
I WAS ONE OF THE JUDGES. THAT WAS SUCH A SHAME...
UM...
WHY DID YOU WANT TO SEE ME?
KLAK
OH, RIGHT.
I WANT YOU TO HAVE THIS. IT'S MOMO'S GUITAR.

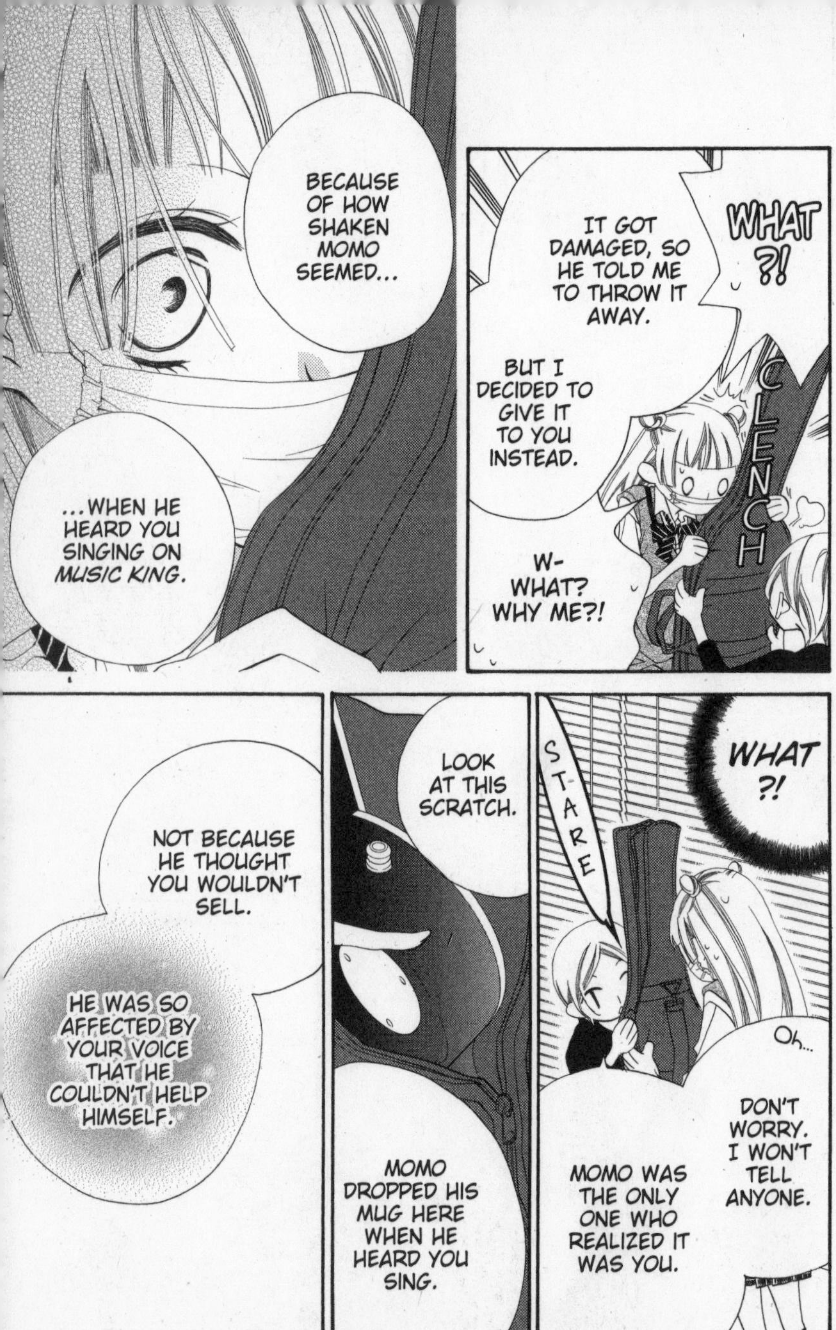
WHAT ?!
IT GOT DAMAGED, SO HE TOLD ME TO THROW IT AWAY.
BUT I DECIDED TO GIVE IT TO YOU INSTEAD.
CLENCH
W-WHAT? WHY ME?!
BECAUSE OF HOW SHAKEN MOMO SEEMED...
...WHEN HE HEARD YOU SINGING ON *MUSIC KING*.
WHAT ?!
STARE
Oh...
DON'T WORRY. I WON'T TELL ANYONE.
MOMO WAS THE ONLY ONE WHO REALIZED IT WAS YOU.
LOOK AT THIS SCRATCH.
MOMO DROPPED HIS MUG HERE WHEN HE HEARD YOU SING.
NOT BECAUSE HE THOUGHT YOU WOULDN'T SELL.
HE WAS SO AFFECTED BY YOUR VOICE THAT HE COULDN'T HELP HIMSELF.

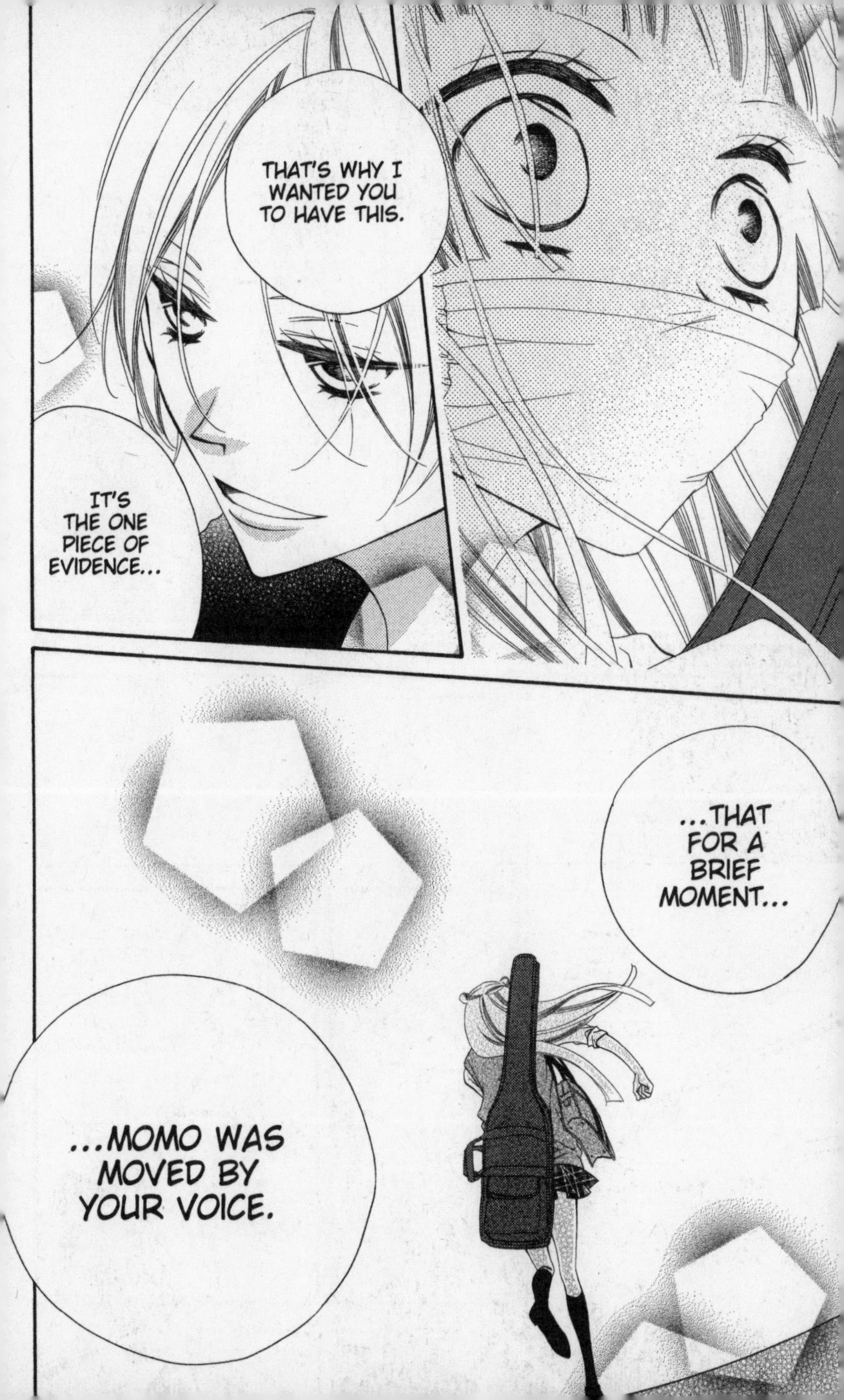
THAT'S WHY I WANTED YOU TO HAVE THIS.
IT'S THE ONE PIECE OF EVIDENCE...
...THAT FOR A BRIEF MOMENT...
...MOMO WAS MOVED BY YOUR VOICE.

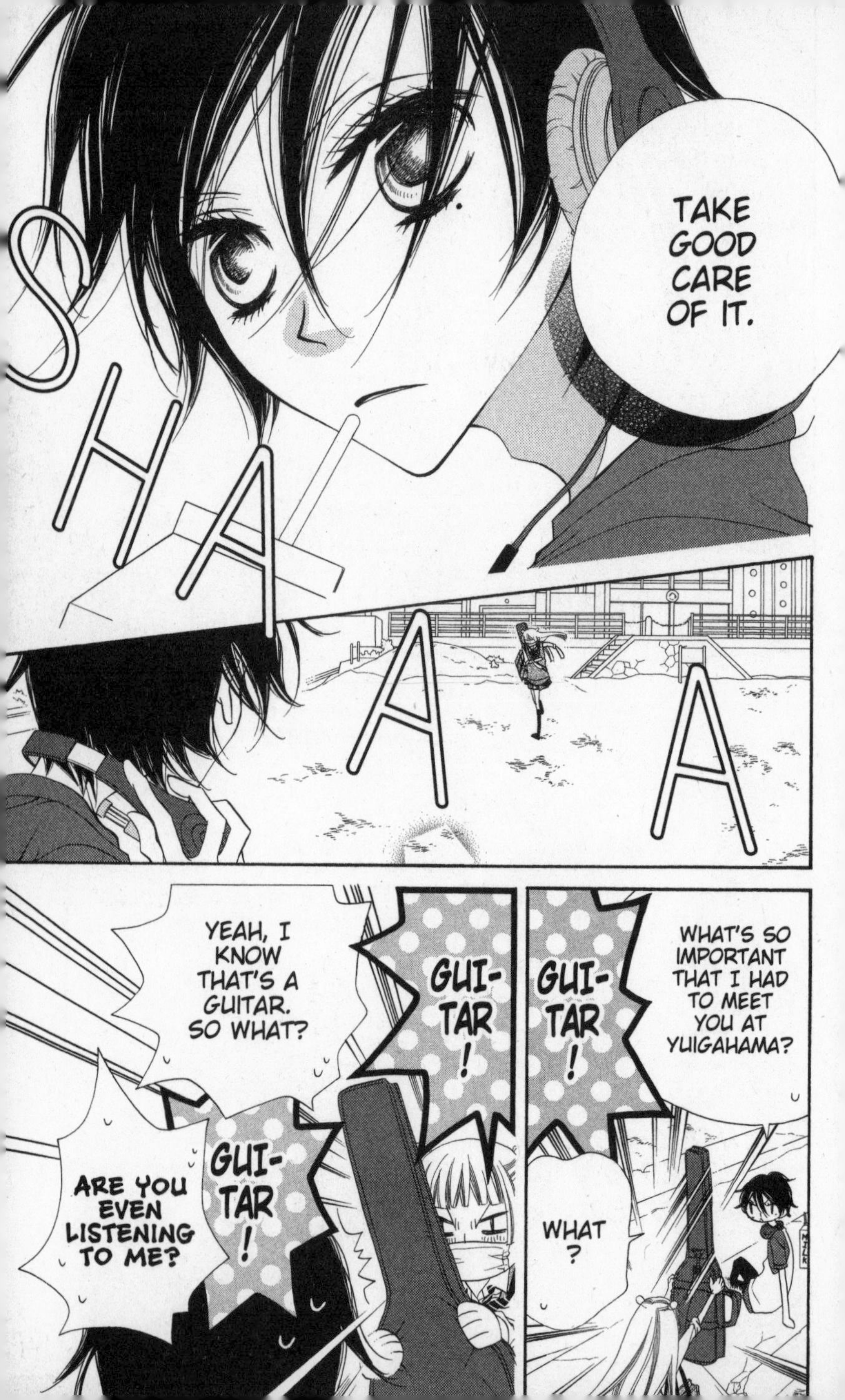
TAKE GOOD CARE OF IT.
SHAAA
WHAT'S SO IMPORTANT THAT I HAD TO MEET YOU AT YUIGAHAMA?
GUI-TAR!
WHAT?
GUI-TAR!
YEAH, I KNOW THAT'S A GUITAR. SO WHAT?
GUI-TAR!
ARE YOU EVEN LISTENING TO ME?

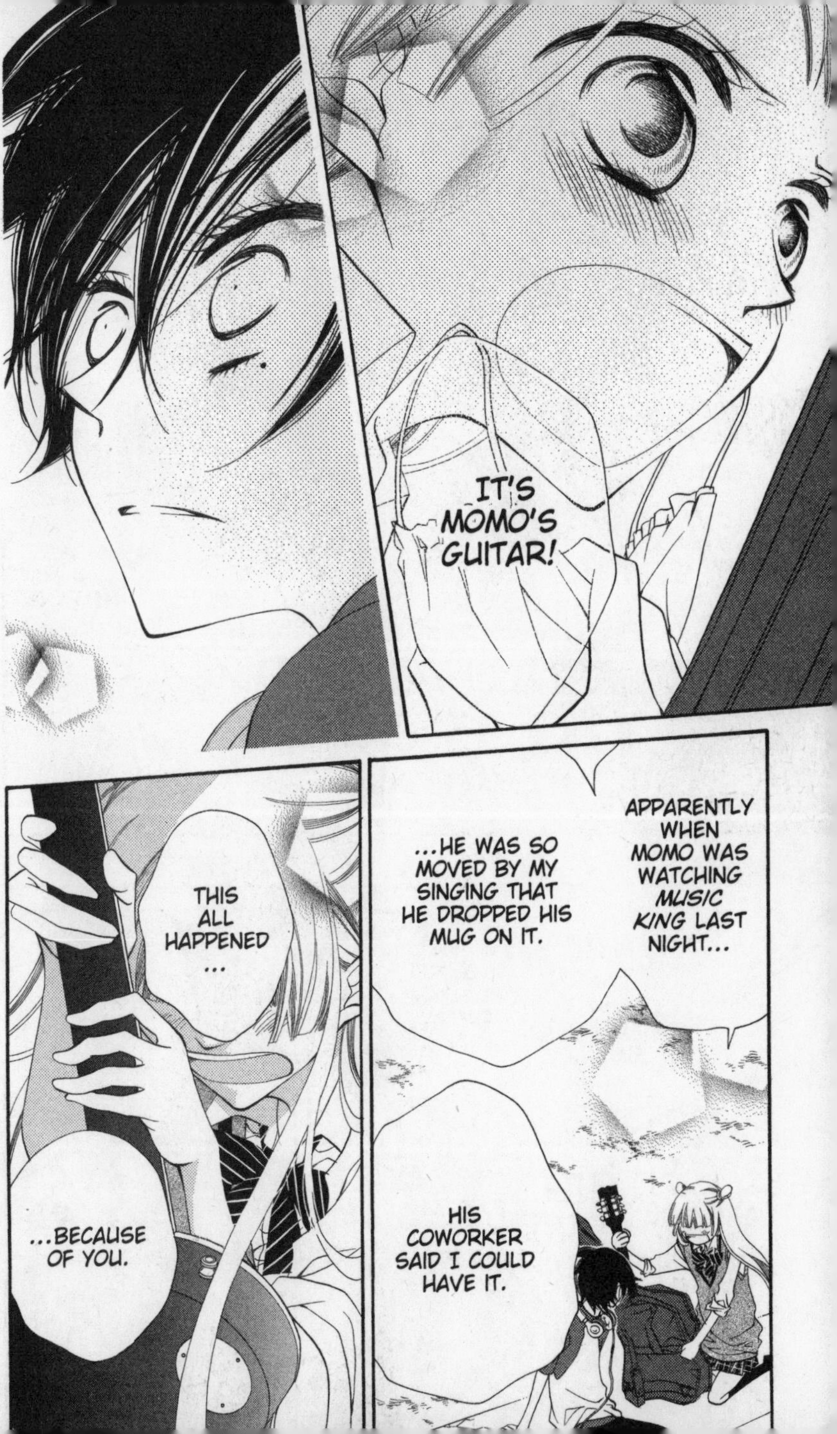
IT'S MOMO'S GUITAR!
APPARENTLY WHEN MOMO WAS WATCHING *MUSIC KING* LAST NIGHT...
...HE WAS SO MOVED BY MY SINGING THAT HE DROPPED HIS MUG ON IT.
HIS COWORKER SAID I COULD HAVE IT.
THIS ALL HAPPENED ...
...BECAUSE OF YOU.

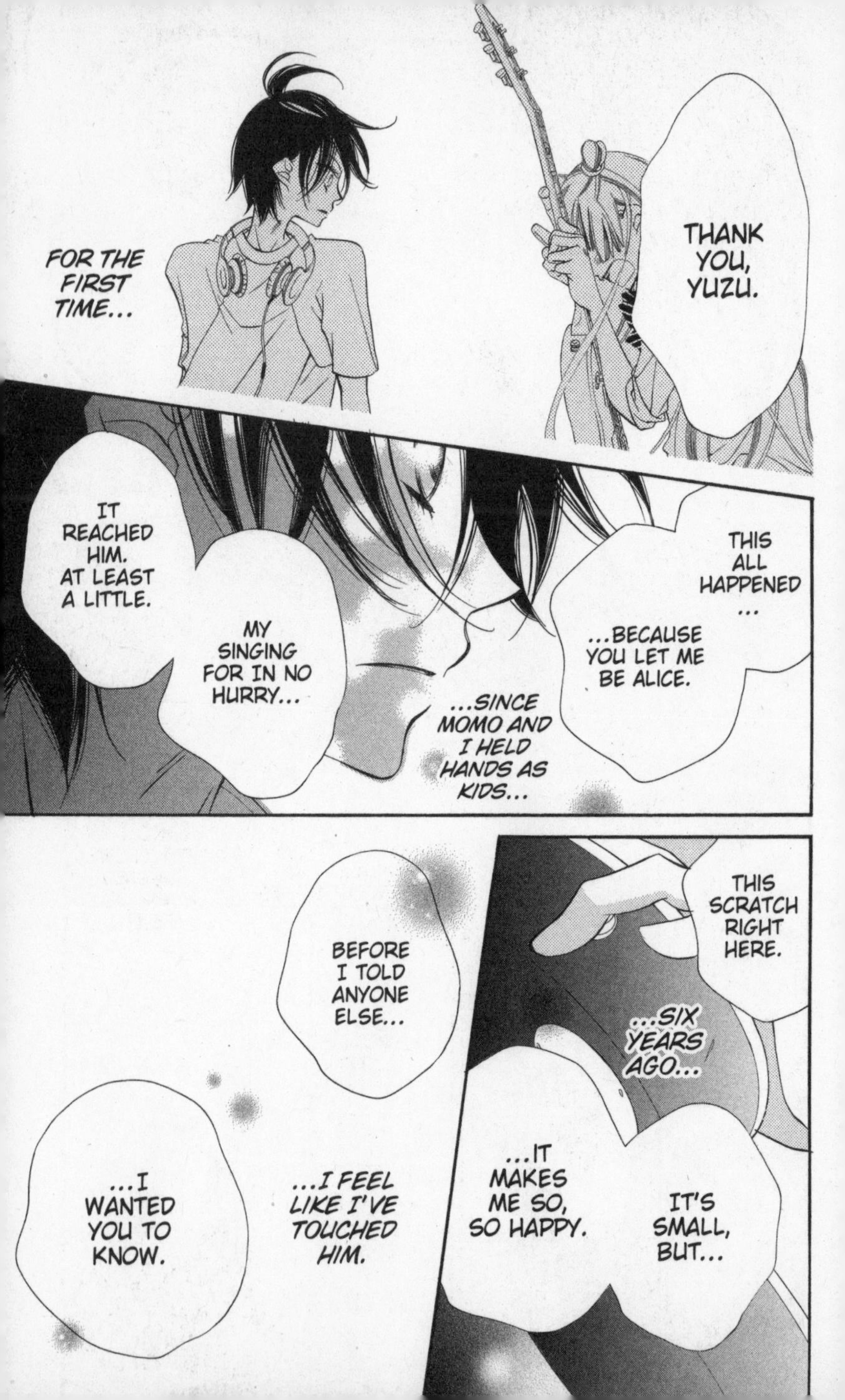
THANK YOU, YUZU.
FOR THE FIRST TIME...
THIS ALL HAPPENED...
...BECAUSE YOU LET ME BE ALICE.
...SINCE MOMO AND I HELD HANDS AS KIDS...
MY SINGING FOR IN NO HURRY...
IT REACHED HIM. AT LEAST A LITTLE.
THIS SCRATCH RIGHT HERE.
...SIX YEARS AGO...
IT'S SMALL, BUT...
...IT MAKES ME SO, SO HAPPY.
BEFORE I TOLD ANYONE ELSE...
...I FEEL LIKE I'VE TOUCHED HIM.
...I WANTED YOU TO KNOW.

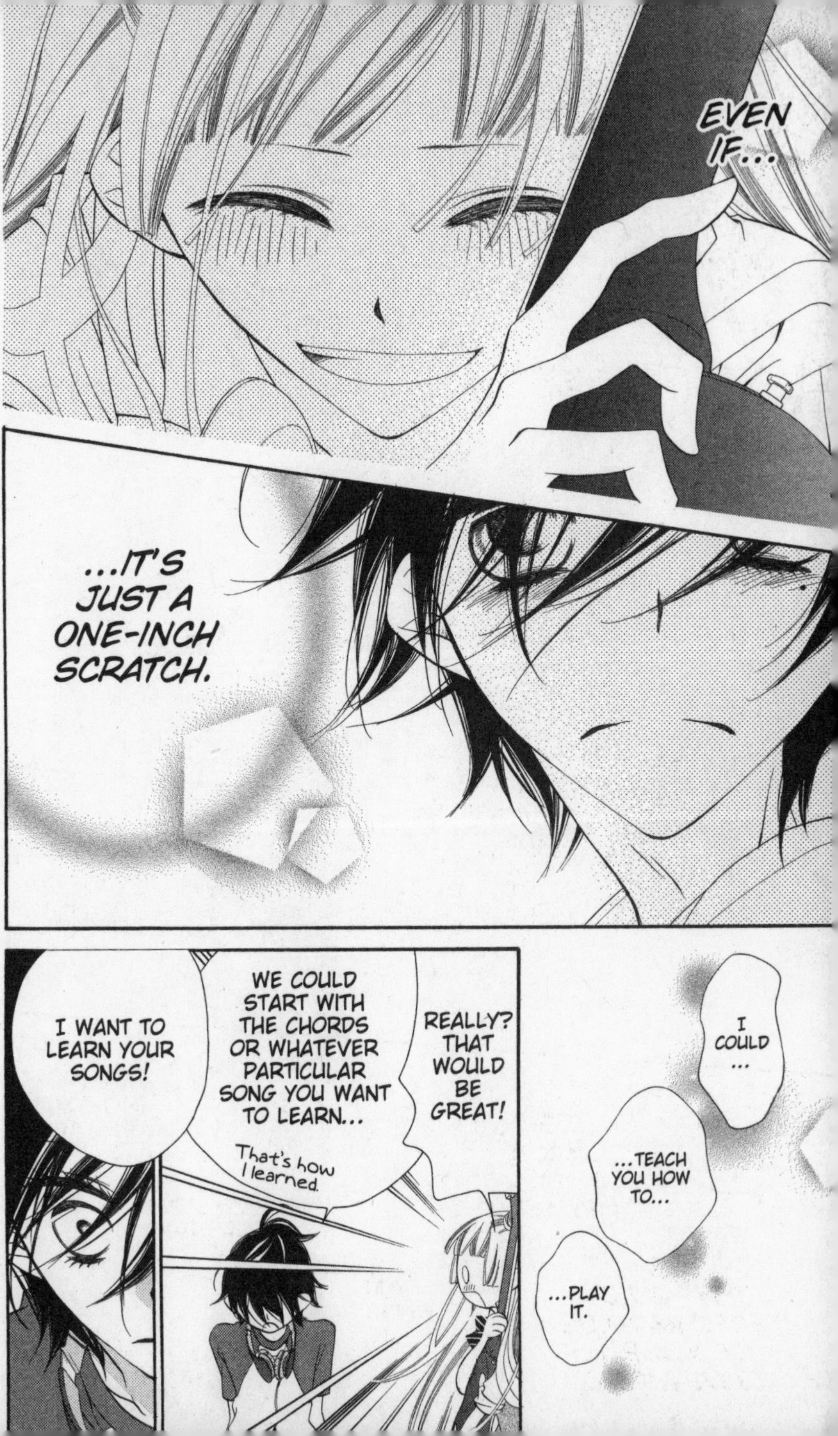
EVEN IF...
...IT'S JUST A ONE-INCH SCRATCH.
I COULD...
...TEACH YOU HOW TO...
...PLAY IT.
REALLY? THAT WOULD BE GREAT!
WE COULD START WITH THE CHORDS OR WHATEVER PARTICULAR SONG YOU WANT TO LEARN...
That's how I learned.
I WANT TO LEARN YOUR SONGS!

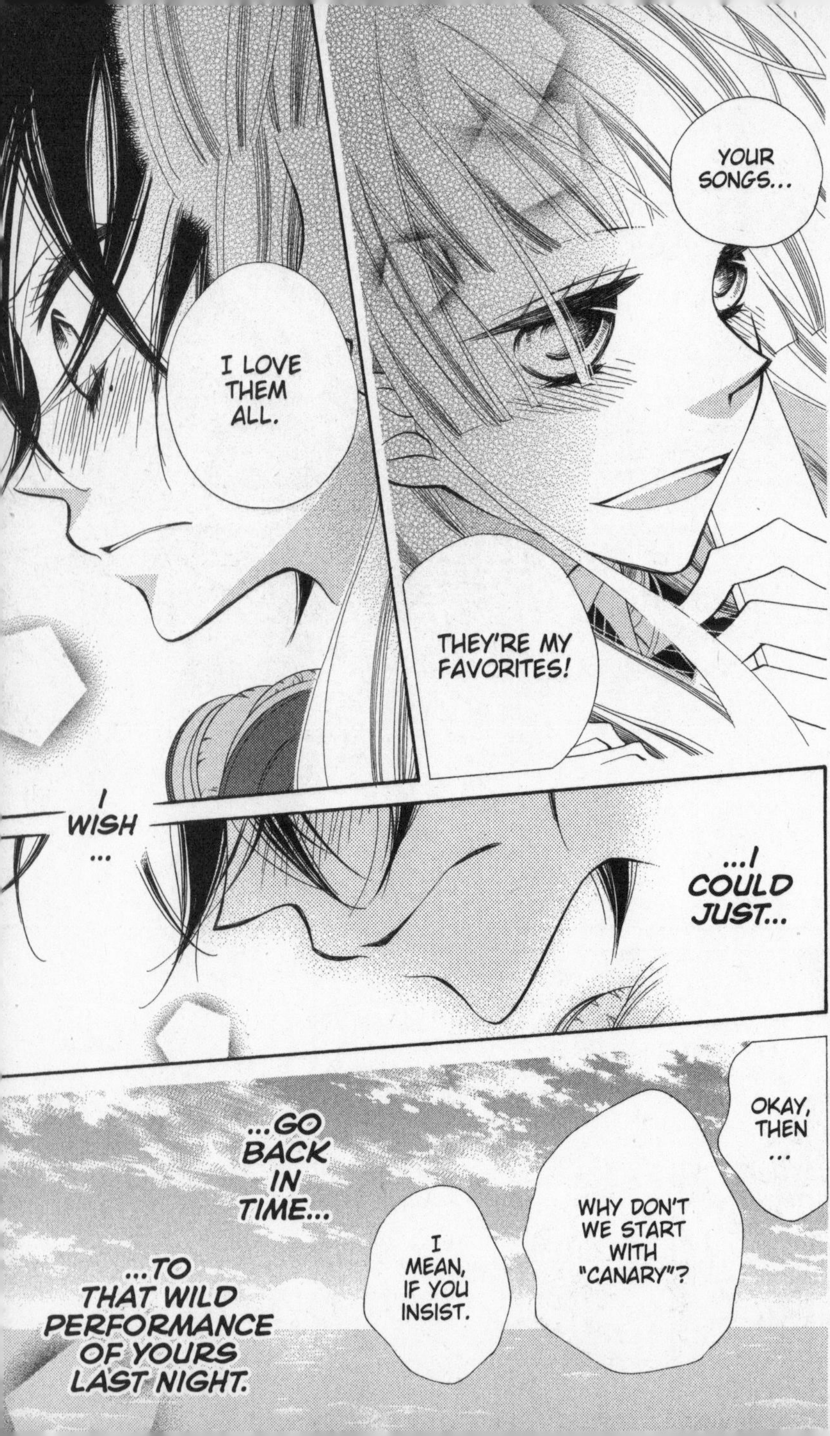
YOUR SONGS...
THEY'RE MY FAVORITES!
I LOVE THEM ALL.
I WISH...
...I COULD JUST...
OKAY, THEN...
WHY DON'T WE START WITH "CANARY"?
I MEAN, IF YOU INSIST.
...GO BACK IN TIME...
...TO THAT WILD PERFORMANCE OF YOURS LAST NIGHT.

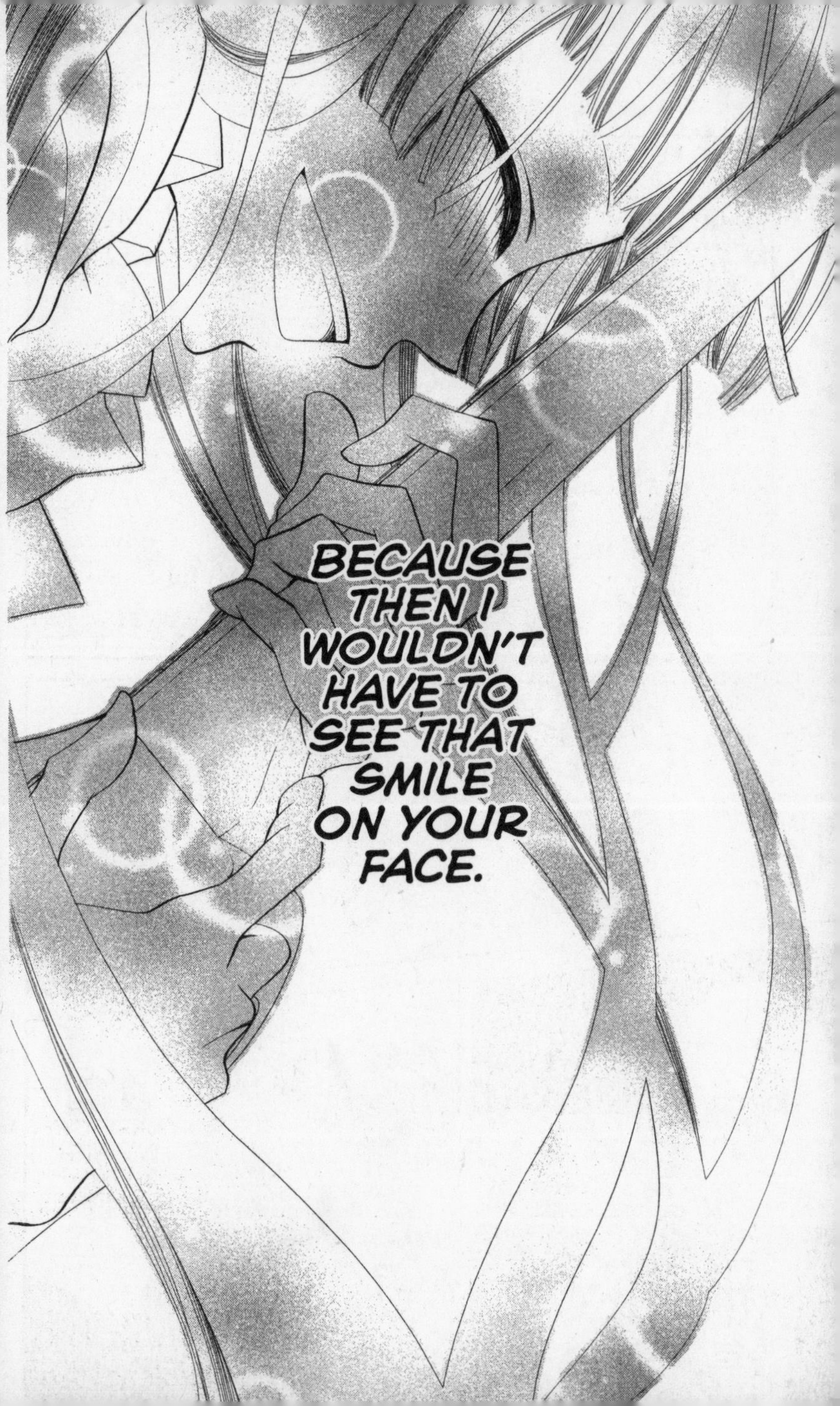
BECAUSE THEN I WOULDN'T HAVE TO SEE THAT SMILE ON YOUR FACE.

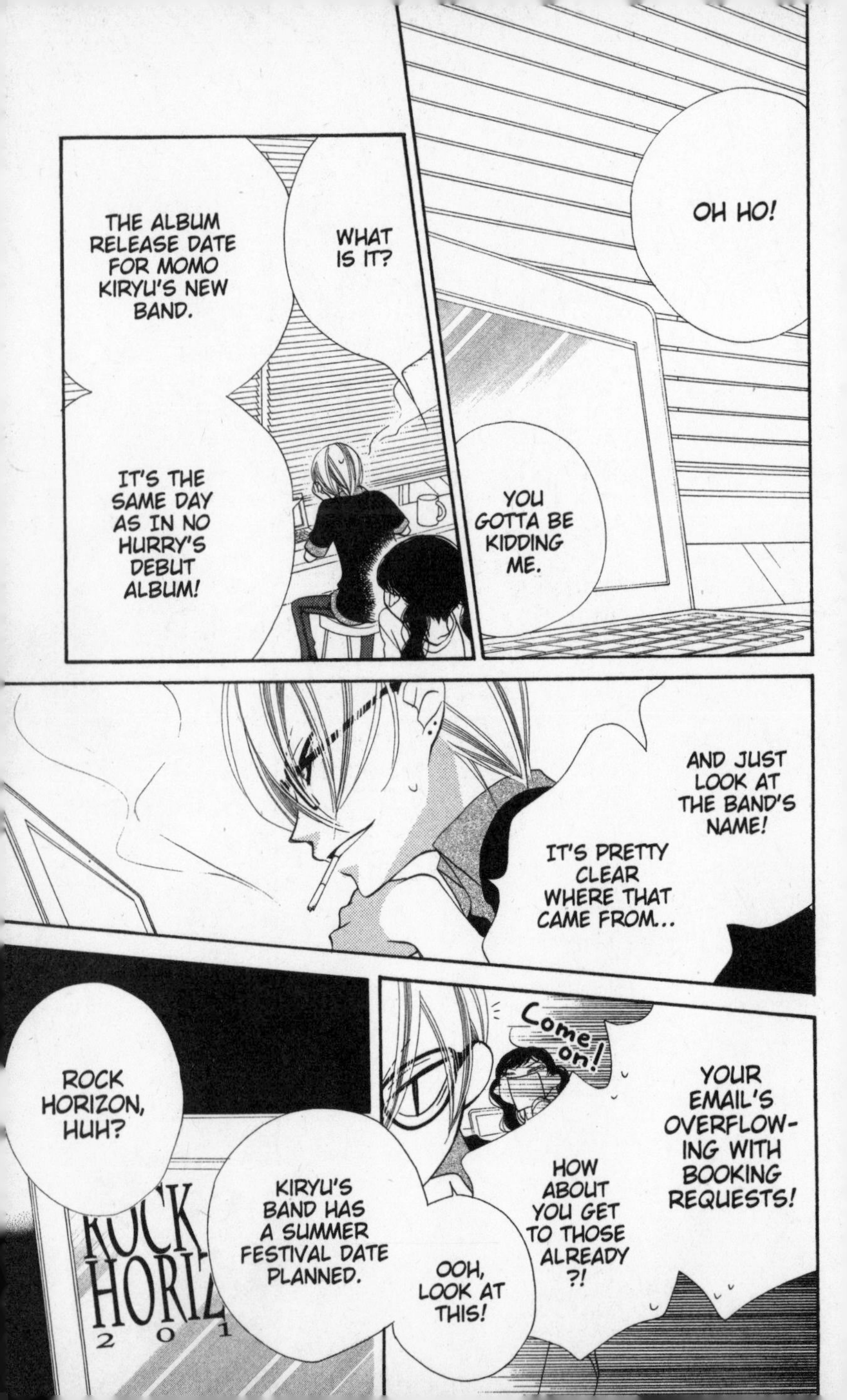
OH HO!
YOU GOTTA BE KIDDING ME.
WHAT IS IT?
THE ALBUM RELEASE DATE FOR MOMO KIRYU'S NEW BAND.
IT'S THE SAME DAY AS IN NO HURRY'S DEBUT ALBUM!
AND JUST LOOK AT THE BAND'S NAME!
IT'S PRETTY CLEAR WHERE THAT CAME FROM...
Come on!
YOUR EMAIL'S OVERFLOWING WITH BOOKING REQUESTS!
HOW ABOUT YOU GET TO THOSE ALREADY?!
OOH, LOOK AT THIS!
KIRYU'S BAND HAS A SUMMER FESTIVAL DATE PLANNED.
ROCK HORIZON, HUH?

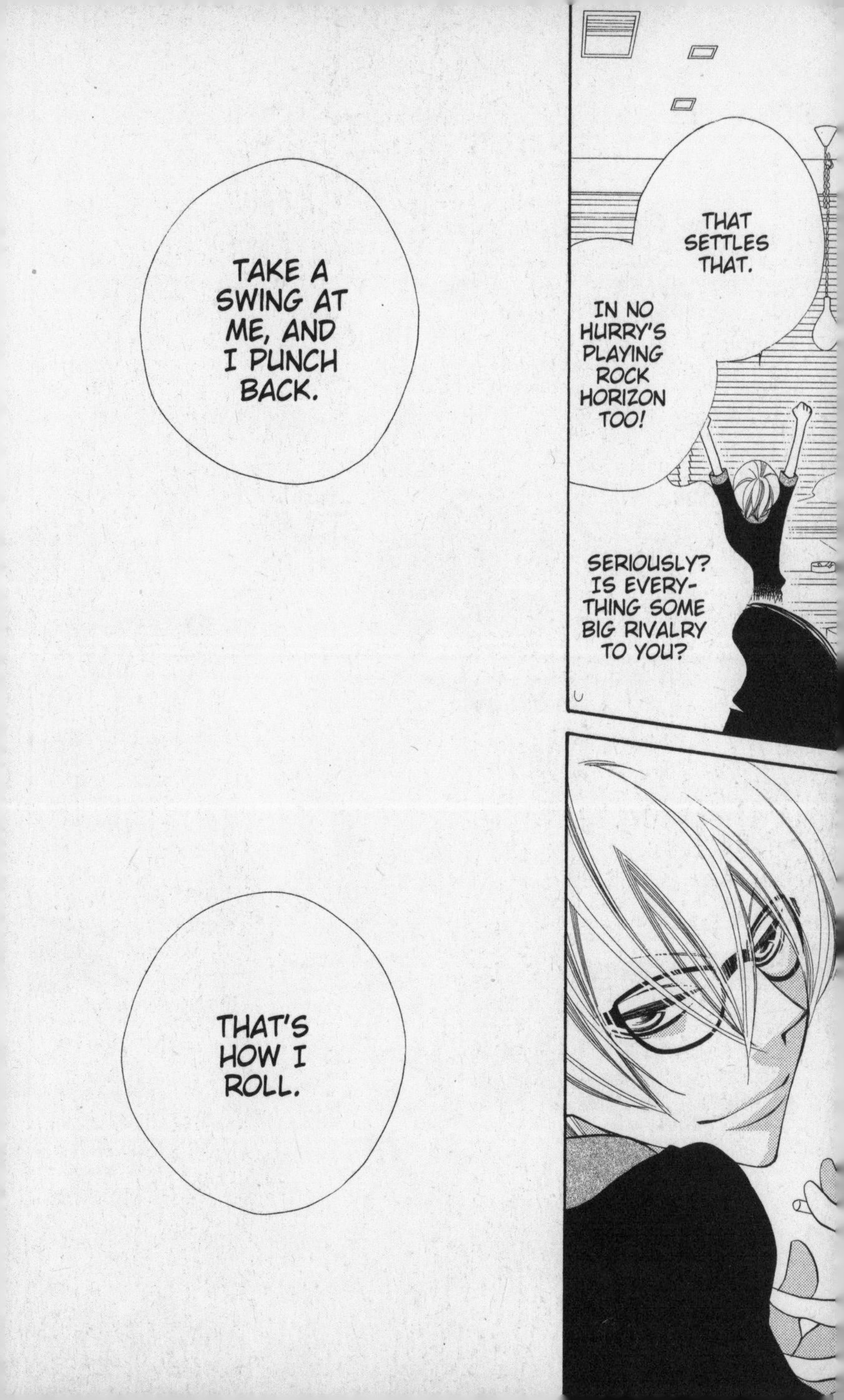
THAT SETTLES THAT.
IN NO HURRY'S PLAYING ROCK HORIZON TOO!
SERIOUSLY? IS EVERY-THING SOME BIG RIVALRY TO YOU?
TAKE A SWING AT ME, AND I PUNCH BACK.
THAT'S HOW I ROLL.

SONG 12

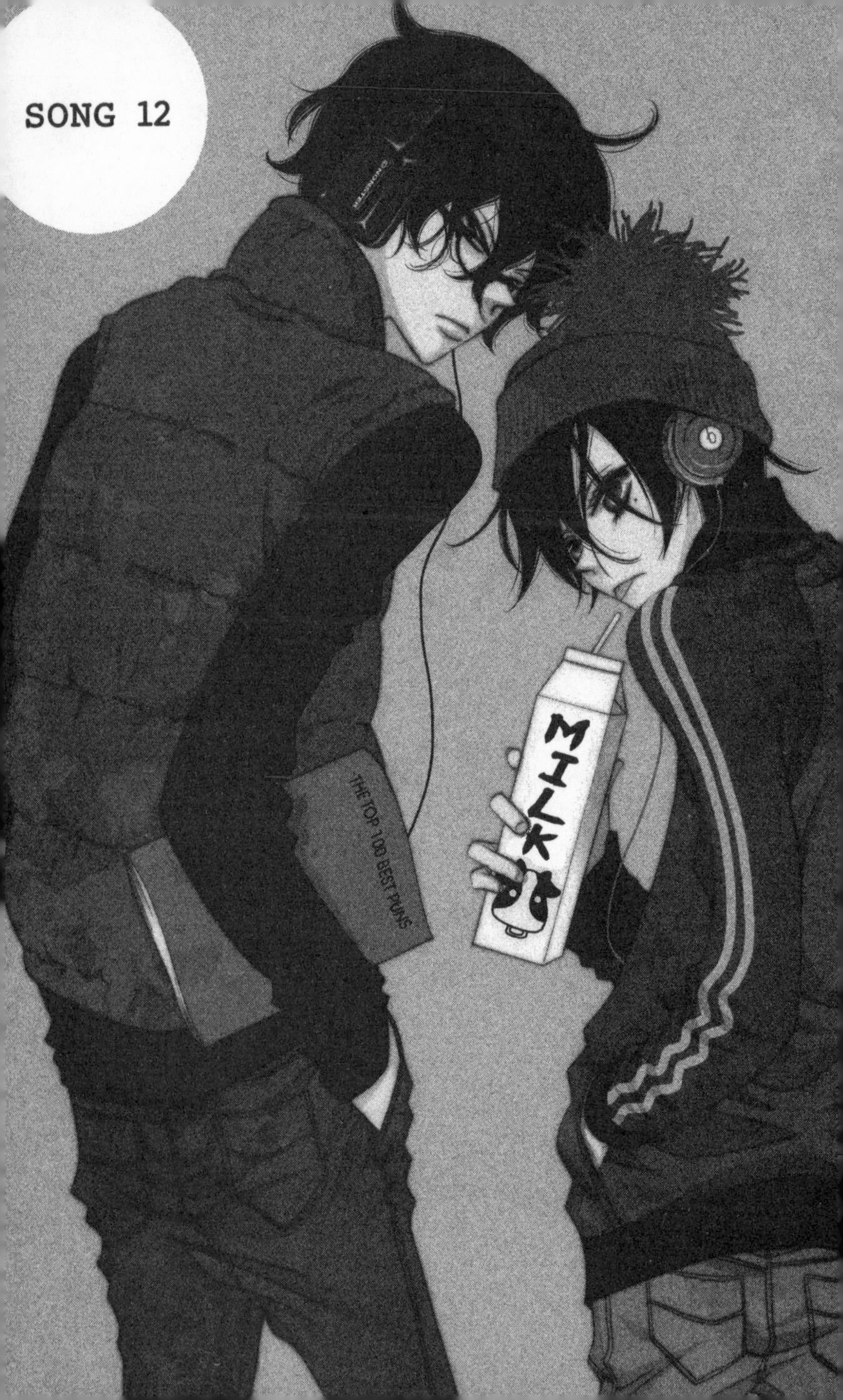
THE TOP 100 BEST PUNS
MILK

THE HEART-POUNDING EPIC SAGA OF YUZU AND HIS MILK EPISODE 4

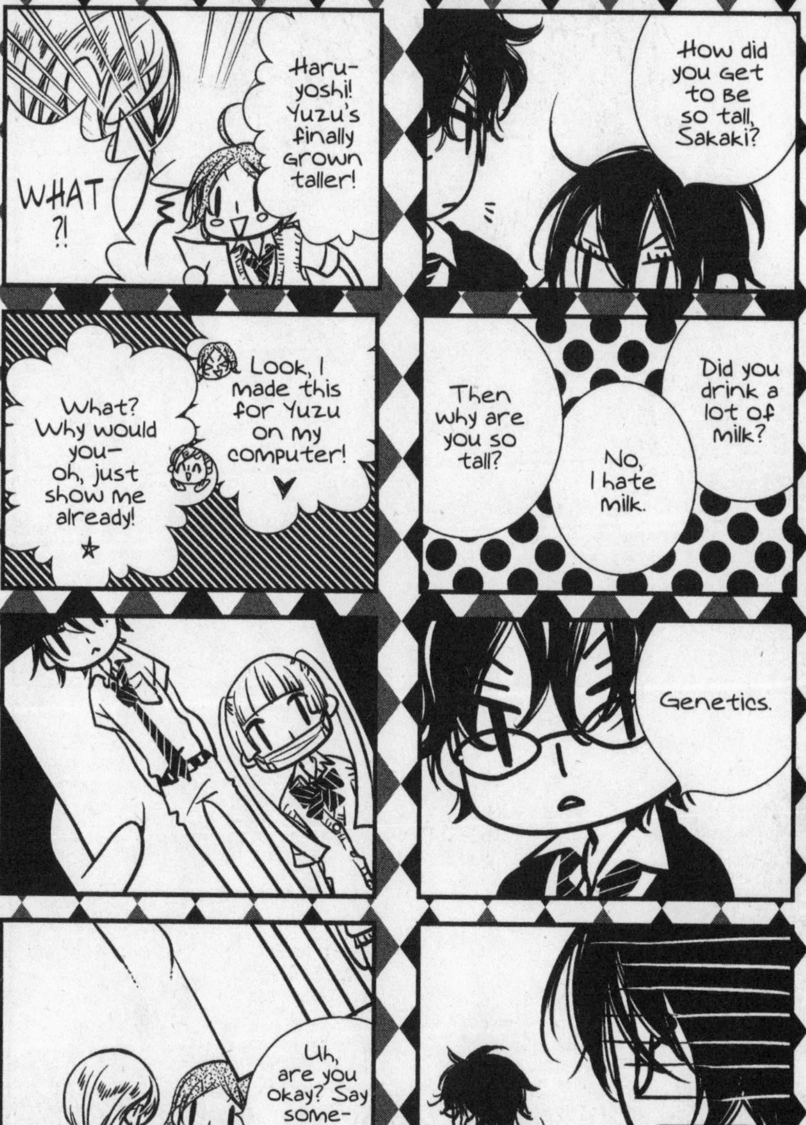
How did you get to be so tall, Sakaki?
Did you drink a lot of milk?
No, I hate milk.
Then why are you so tall?
Genetics.
Haru-yoshi! Yuzu's finally grown taller!
WHAT ?!
Look, I made this for Yuzu on my computer!
What? Why would you— oh, just show me already!
Uh, are you okay? Say some-thing, Haru-yoshi.

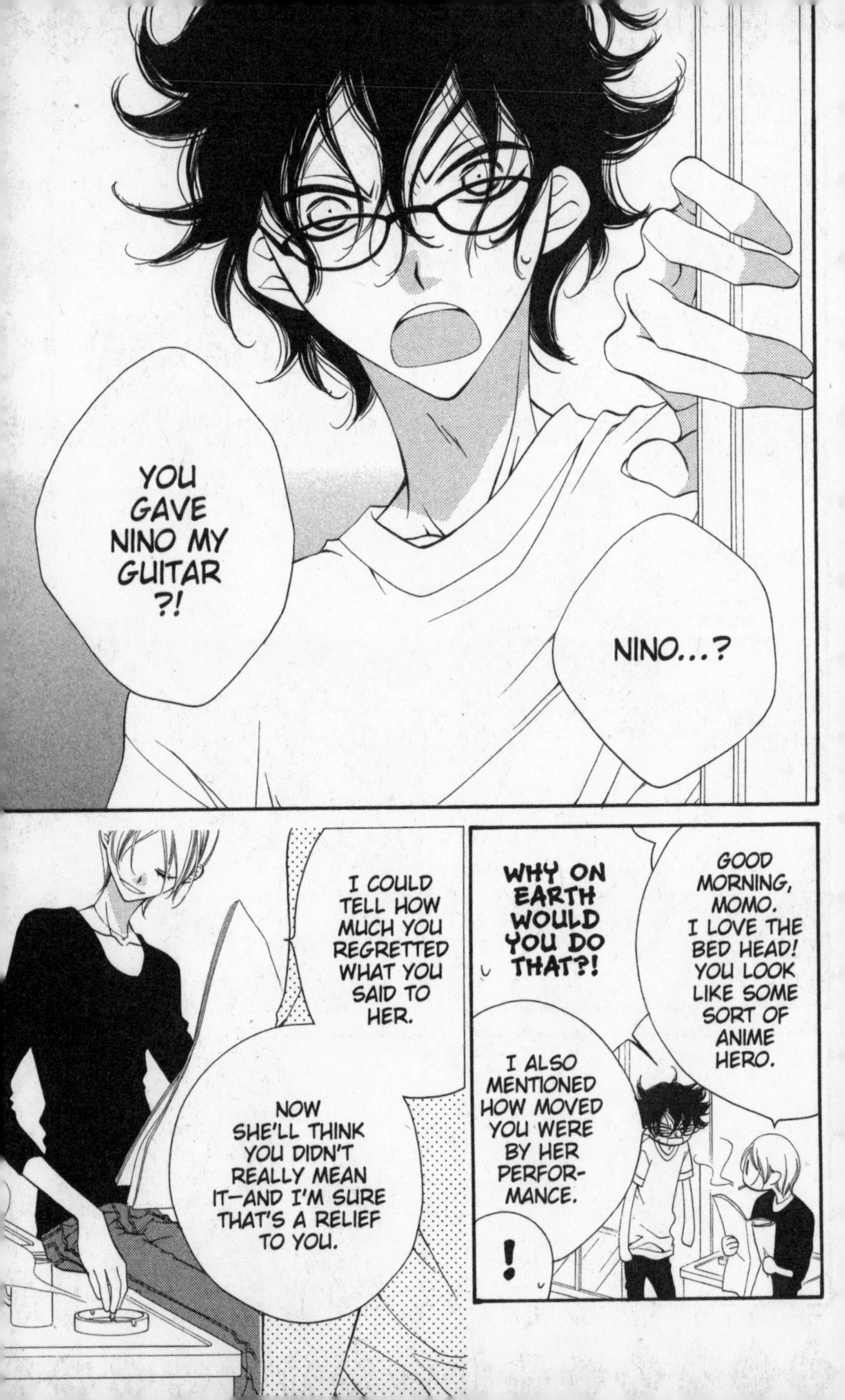
NINO...?
YOU GAVE NINO MY GUITAR ?!
GOOD MORNING, MOMO. I LOVE THE BED HEAD! YOU LOOK LIKE SOME SORT OF ANIME HERO.
WHY ON EARTH WOULD YOU DO THAT?!
I ALSO MENTIONED HOW MOVED YOU WERE BY HER PERFOR-MANCE.
!
I COULD TELL HOW MUCH YOU REGRETTED WHAT YOU SAID TO HER.
NOW SHE'LL THINK YOU DIDN'T REALLY MEAN IT—AND I'M SURE THAT'S A RELIEF TO YOU.

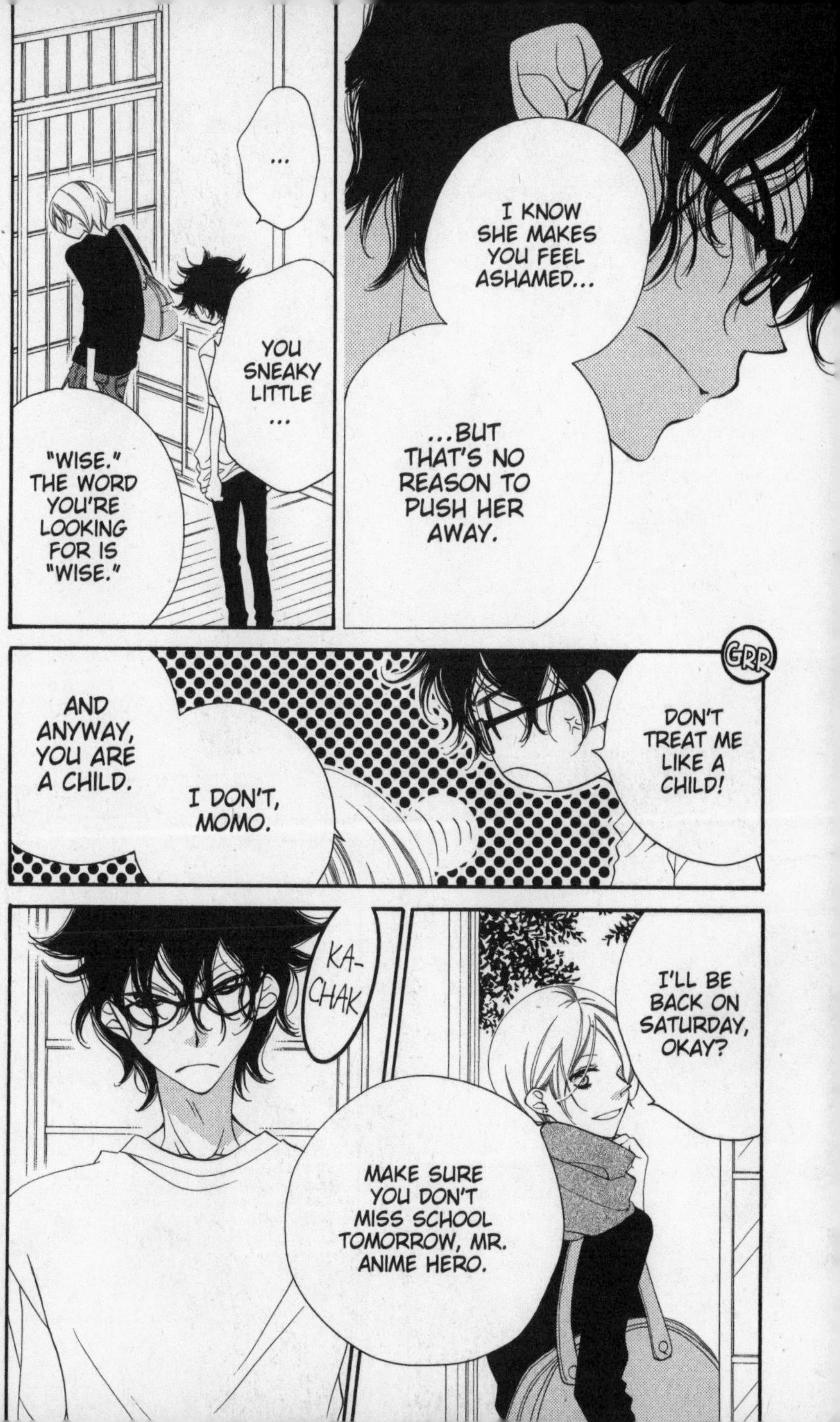
I KNOW SHE MAKES YOU FEEL ASHAMED...
...BUT THAT'S NO REASON TO PUSH HER AWAY.
...
YOU SNEAKY LITTLE ...
"WISE." THE WORD YOU'RE LOOKING FOR IS "WISE."
GRR
DON'T TREAT ME LIKE A CHILD!
I DON'T, MOMO.
AND ANYWAY, YOU ARE A CHILD.
I'LL BE BACK ON SATURDAY, OKAY?
MAKE SURE YOU DON'T MISS SCHOOL TOMORROW, MR. ANIME HERO.
KA-CHAK

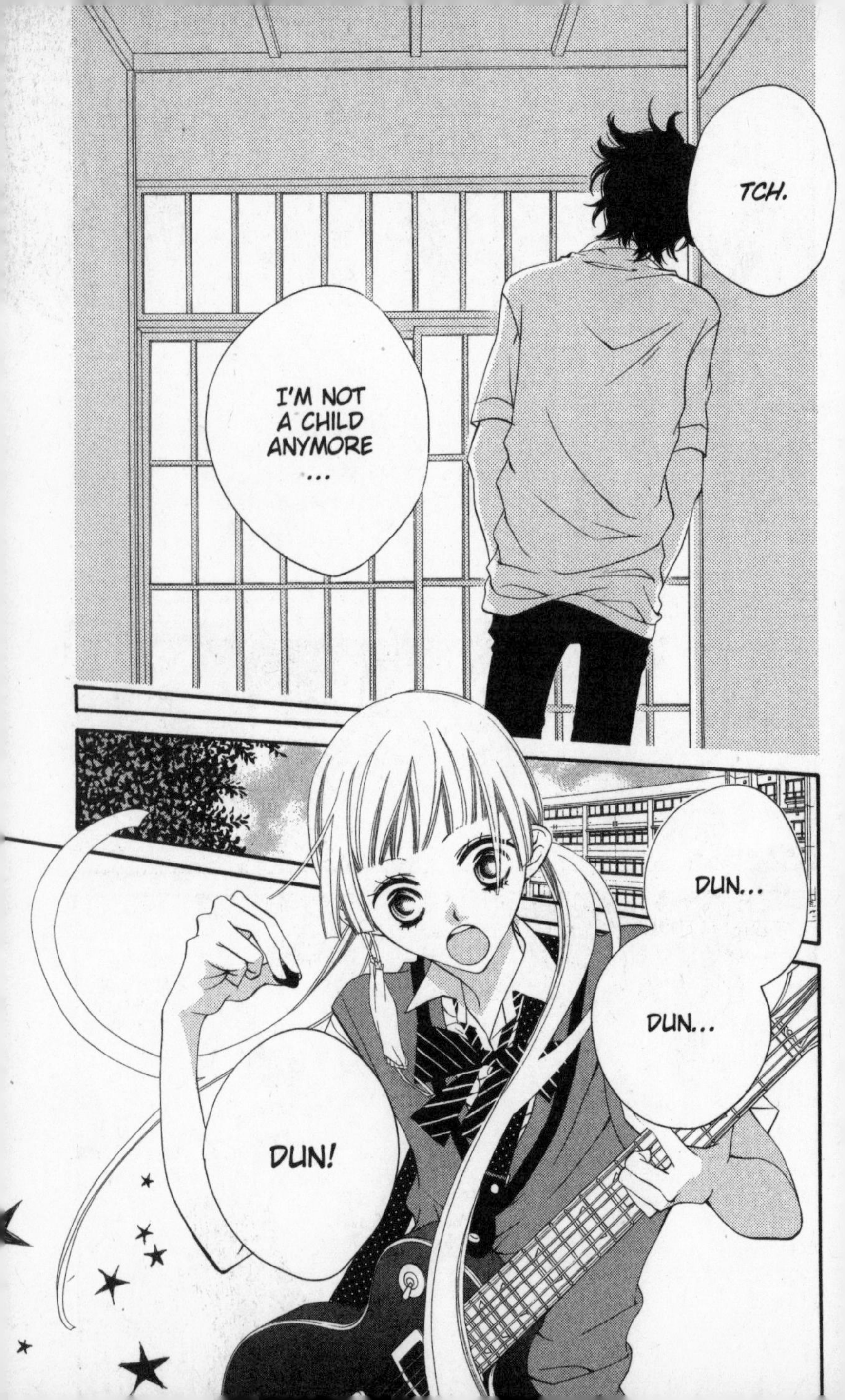
TCH.
I'M NOT A CHILD ANYMORE...
DUN...
DUN...
DUN!

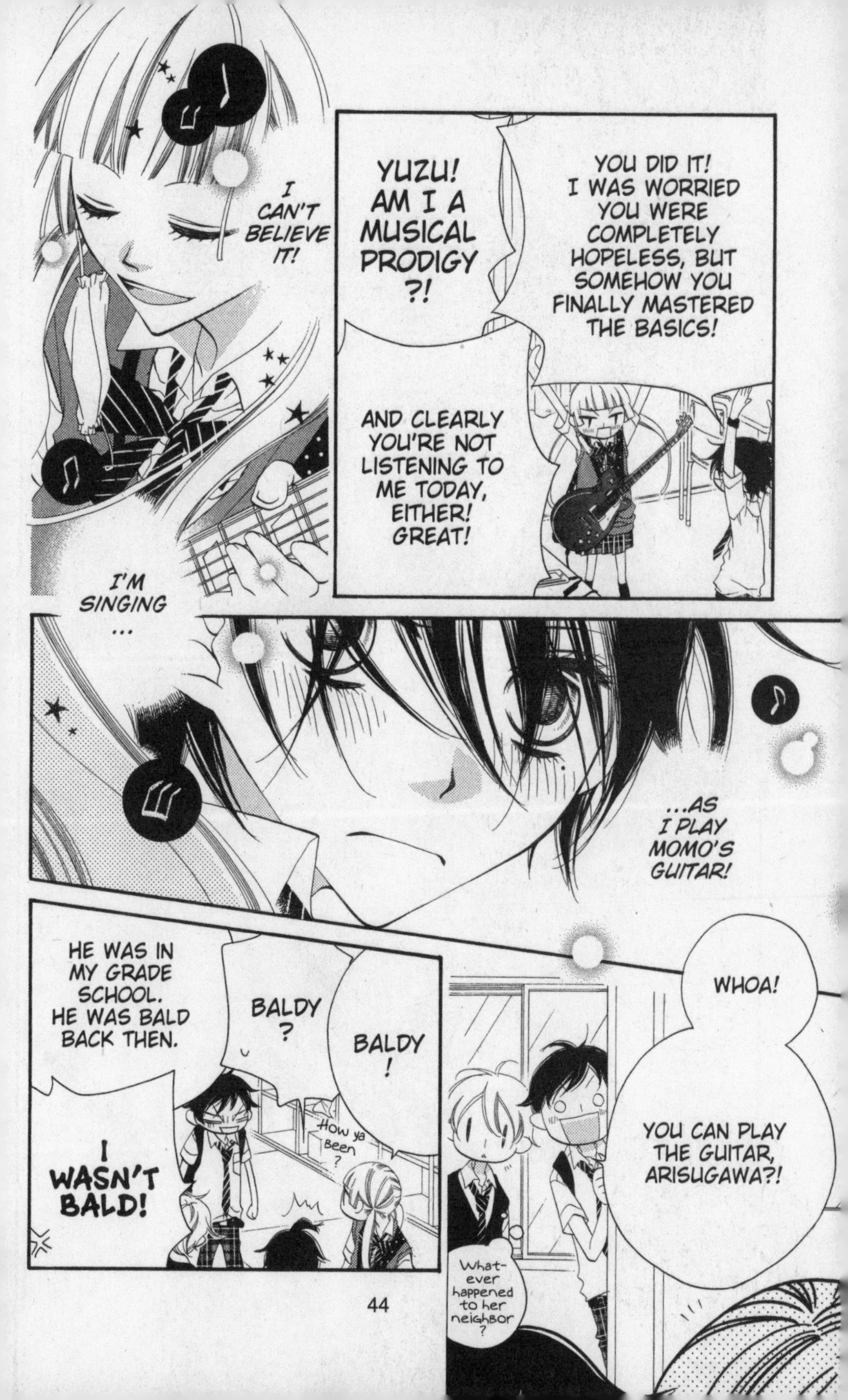
YOU DID IT! I WAS WORRIED YOU WERE COMPLETELY HOPELESS, BUT SOMEHOW YOU FINALLY MASTERED THE BASICS!
YUZU! AM I A MUSICAL PRODIGY?!
AND CLEARLY YOU'RE NOT LISTENING TO ME TODAY, EITHER! GREAT!
I CAN'T BELIEVE IT!
I'M SINGING...
...AS I PLAY MOMO'S GUITAR!
WHOA!
YOU CAN PLAY THE GUITAR, ARISUGAWA?!
What-ever happened to her neighbor?
BALDY!
BALDY?
HE WAS IN MY GRADE SCHOOL. HE WAS BALD BACK THEN.
How ya Been?
I WASN'T BALD!

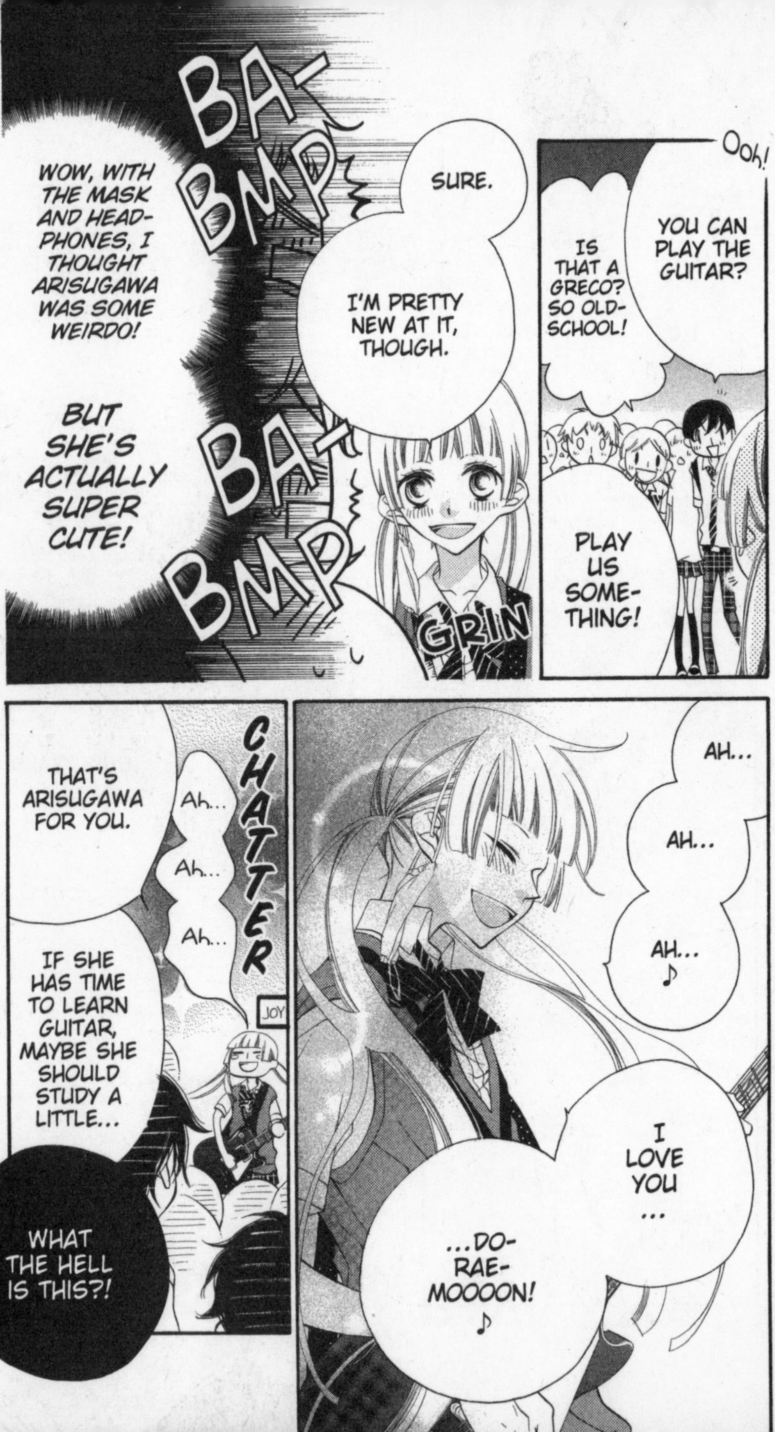
Ooh!
YOU CAN PLAY THE GUITAR?
IS THAT A GRECO? SO OLD-SCHOOL!
PLAY US SOME-THING!
SURE.
I'M PRETTY NEW AT IT, THOUGH.
BA-BMP
BA-BMP
WOW, WITH THE MASK AND HEAD-PHONES, I THOUGHT ARISUGAWA WAS SOME WEIRDO!
BUT SHE'S ACTUALLY SUPER CUTE!
GRIN
AH...
AH...
AH... ♪
I LOVE YOU ...
...DO-RAE-MOOOON! ♪
CHATTER
Ah...
Ah...
Ah...
JOY
THAT'S ARISUGAWA FOR YOU.
IF SHE HAS TIME TO LEARN GUITAR, MAYBE SHE SHOULD STUDY A LITTLE...
WHAT THE HELL IS THIS?!

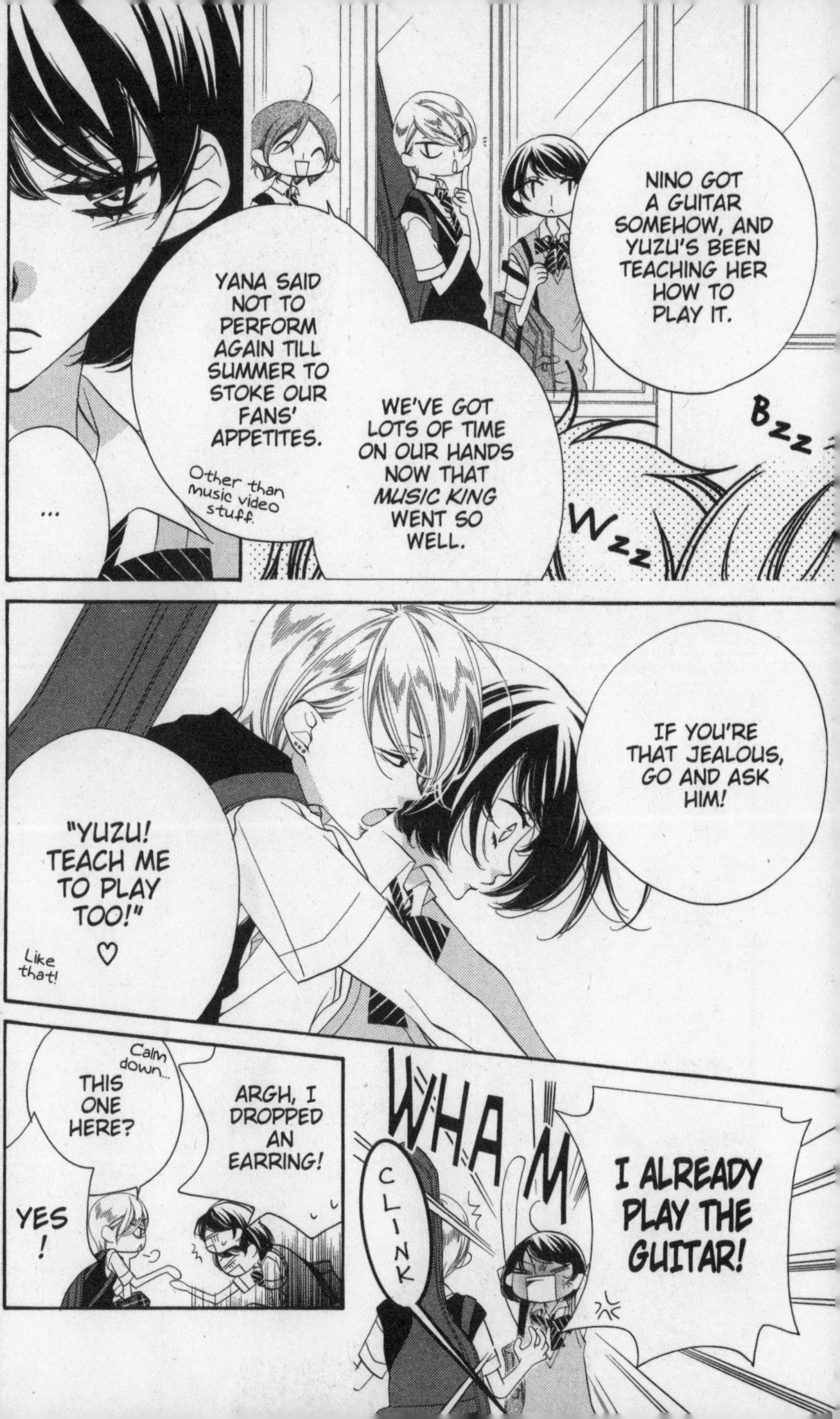
NINO GOT A GUITAR SOMEHOW, AND YUZU'S BEEN TEACHING HER HOW TO PLAY IT.
Bzzz
Wzzz
WE'VE GOT LOTS OF TIME ON OUR HANDS NOW THAT *MUSIC KING* WENT SO WELL.
YANA SAID NOT TO PERFORM AGAIN TILL SUMMER TO STOKE OUR FANS' APPETITES.
Other than music video stuff.
...
IF YOU'RE THAT JEALOUS, GO AND ASK HIM!
"YUZU! TEACH ME TO PLAY TOO!" ♡
Like that!
I ALREADY PLAY THE GUITAR!
WHAM
CLINK
ARGH, I DROPPED AN EARRING!
Calm down...
THIS ONE HERE?
YES!

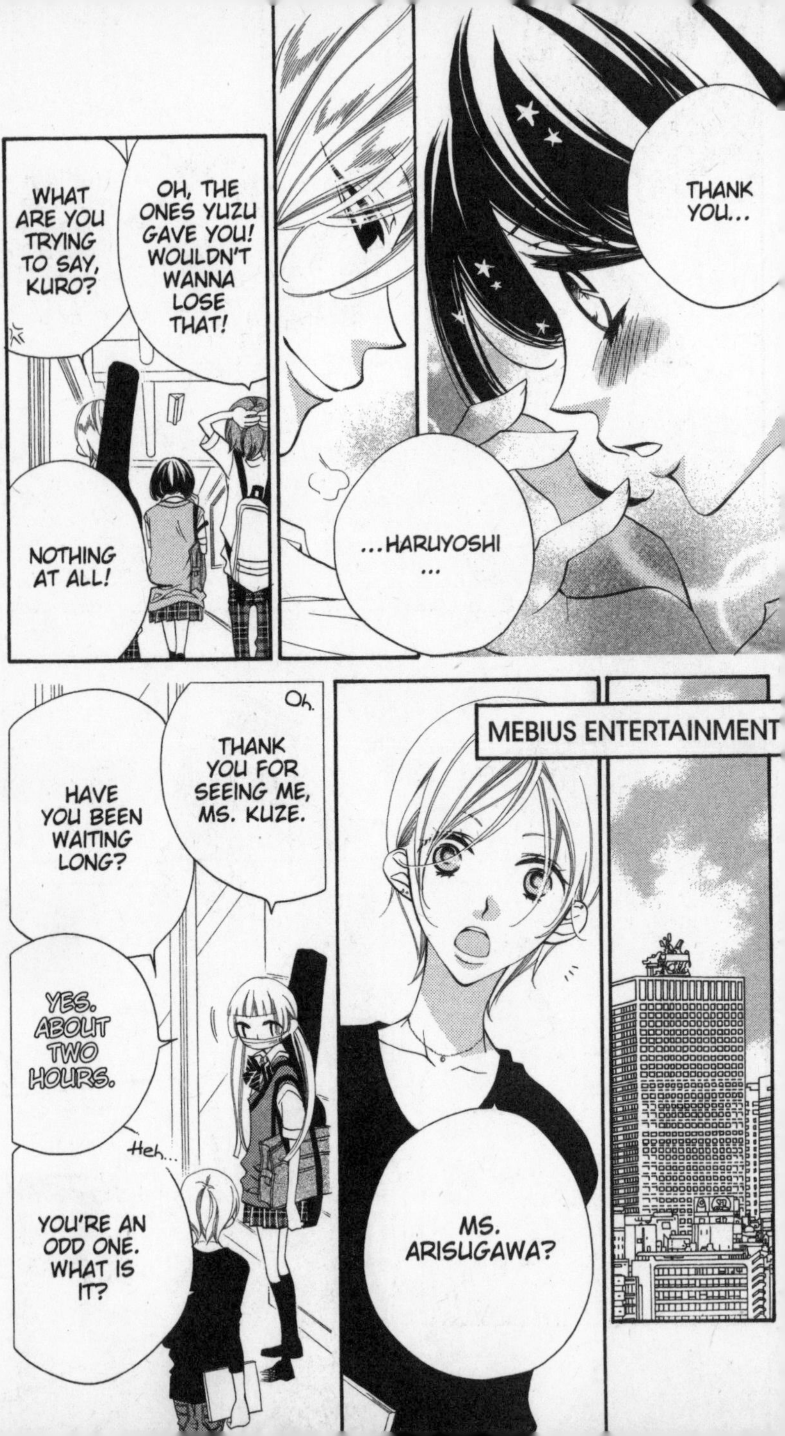
THANK YOU...
...HARUYOSHI ...
OH, THE ONES YUZU GAVE YOU! WOULDN'T WANNA LOSE THAT!
WHAT ARE YOU TRYING TO SAY, KURO?
NOTHING AT ALL!
MEBIUS ENTERTAINMENT
MS. ARISUGAWA?
Oh.
THANK YOU FOR SEEING ME, MS. KUZE.
HAVE YOU BEEN WAITING LONG?
YES. ABOUT TWO HOURS.
Heh...
YOU'RE AN ODD ONE. WHAT IS IT?

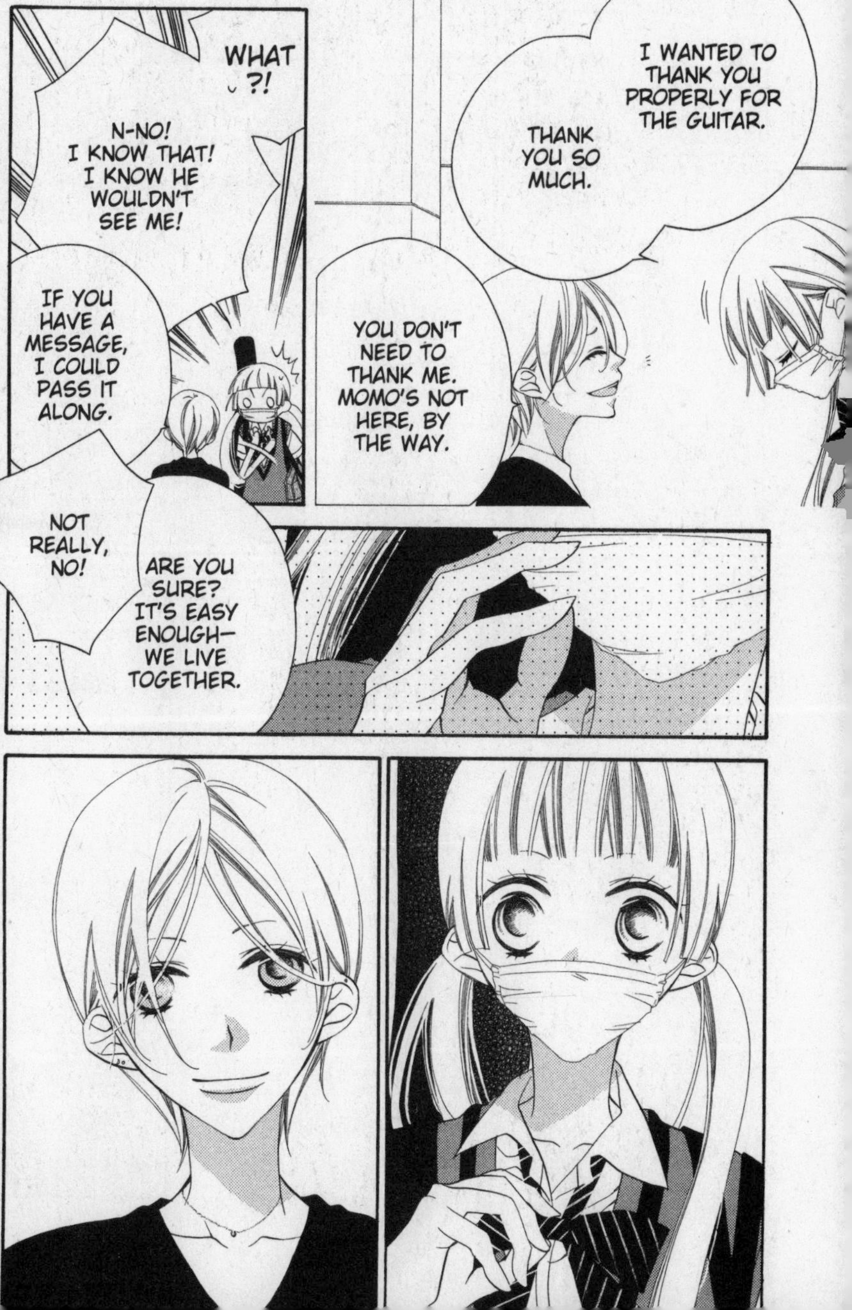
I WANTED TO THANK YOU PROPERLY FOR THE GUITAR.
THANK YOU SO MUCH.
YOU DON'T NEED TO THANK ME. MOMO'S NOT HERE, BY THE WAY.
WHAT ?!
N-NO! I KNOW THAT! I KNOW HE WOULDN'T SEE ME!
IF YOU HAVE A MESSAGE, I COULD PASS IT ALONG.
NOT REALLY, NO!
ARE YOU SURE? IT'S EASY ENOUGH— WE LIVE TOGETHER.

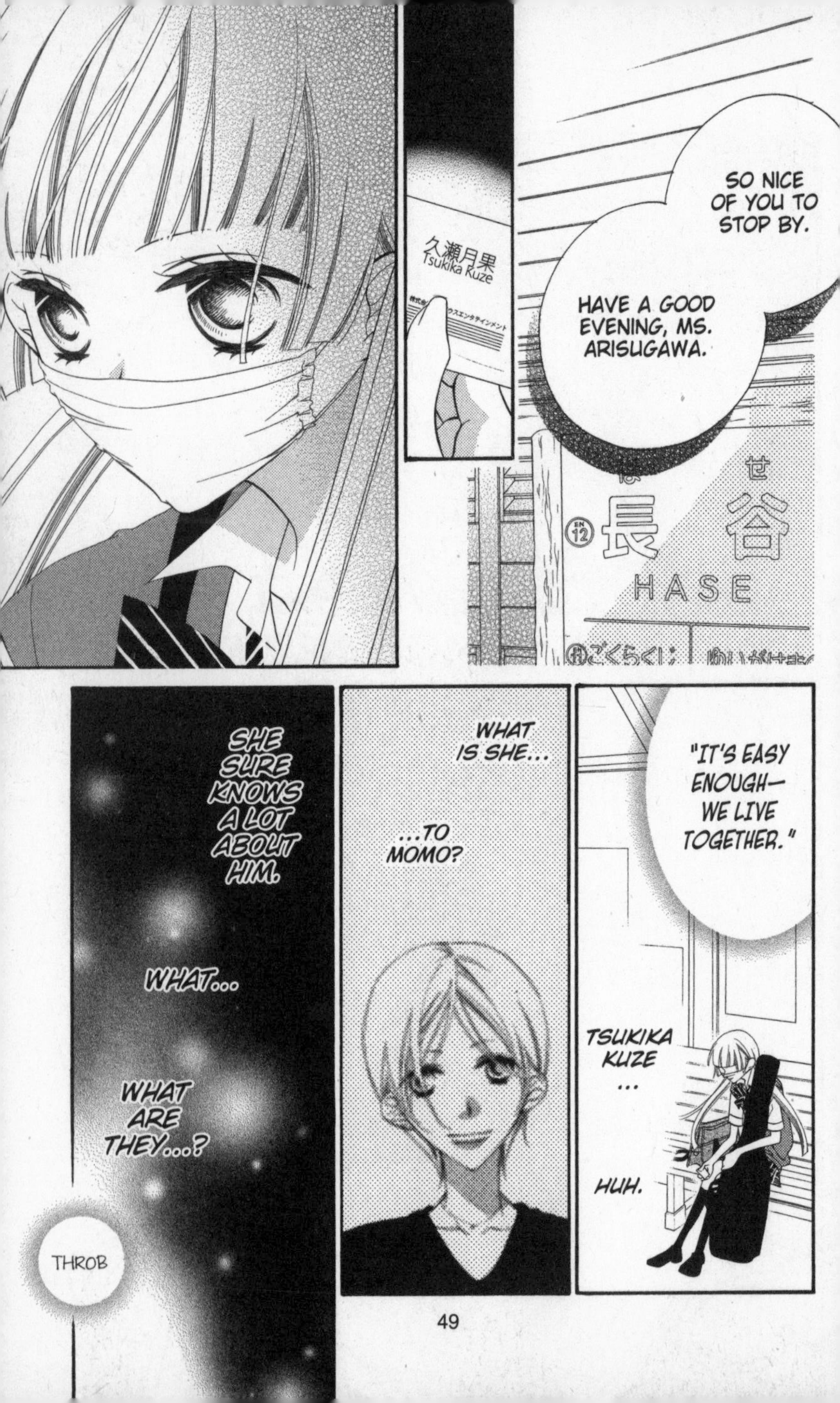
SO NICE OF YOU TO STOP BY.
HAVE A GOOD EVENING, MS. ARISUGAWA.
長谷
HASE
久瀬月果
Tsukika Kuze
"IT'S EASY ENOUGH—WE LIVE TOGETHER."
TSUKIKA KUZE...
HUH.
WHAT IS SHE...
...TO MOMO?
SHE SURE KNOWS A LOT ABOUT HIM.
WHAT...
WHAT ARE THEY...?
THROB

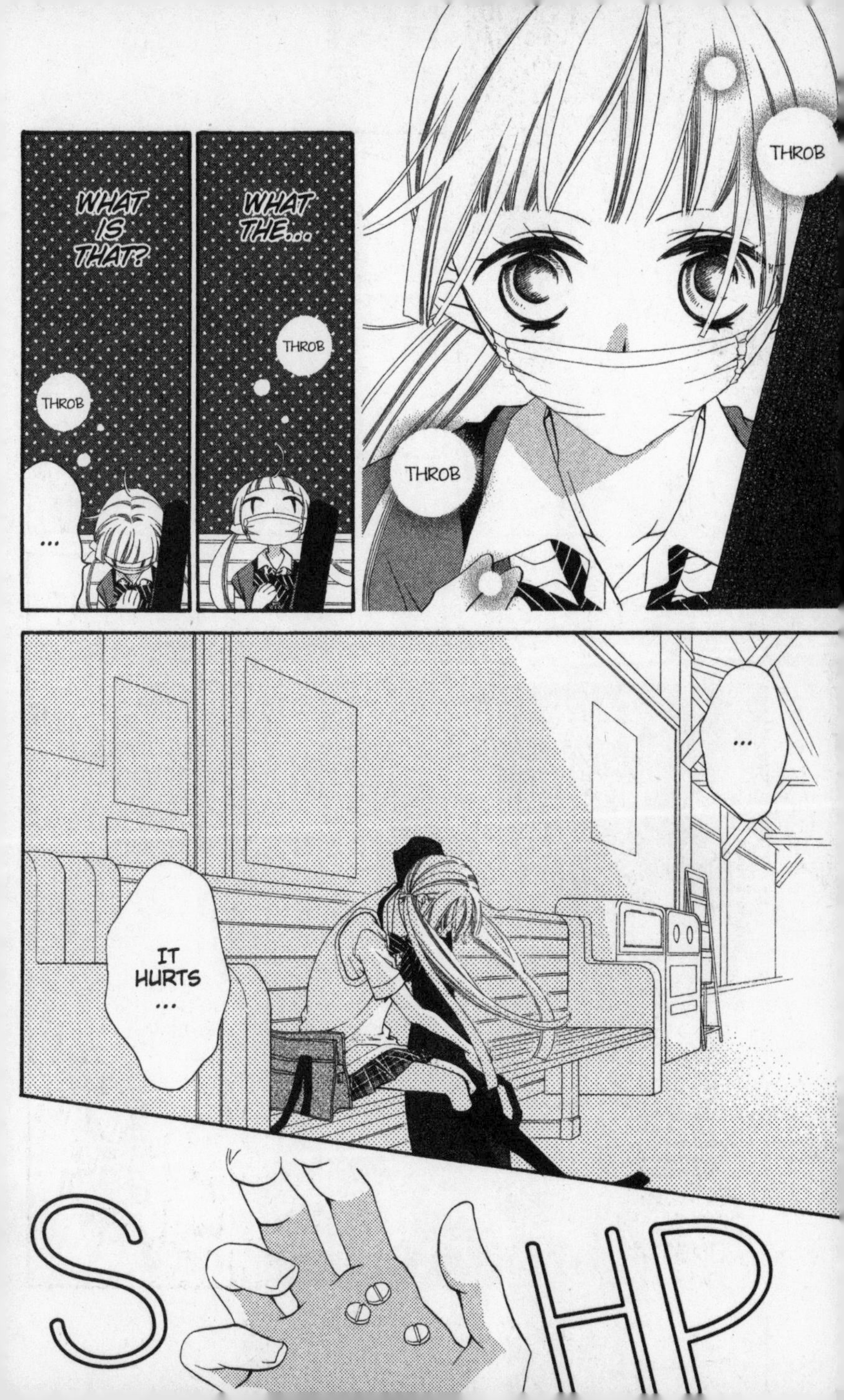
THROB
THROB
WHAT THE...
THROB
WHAT IS THAT?
THROB
...
...
IT HURTS ...
SHP

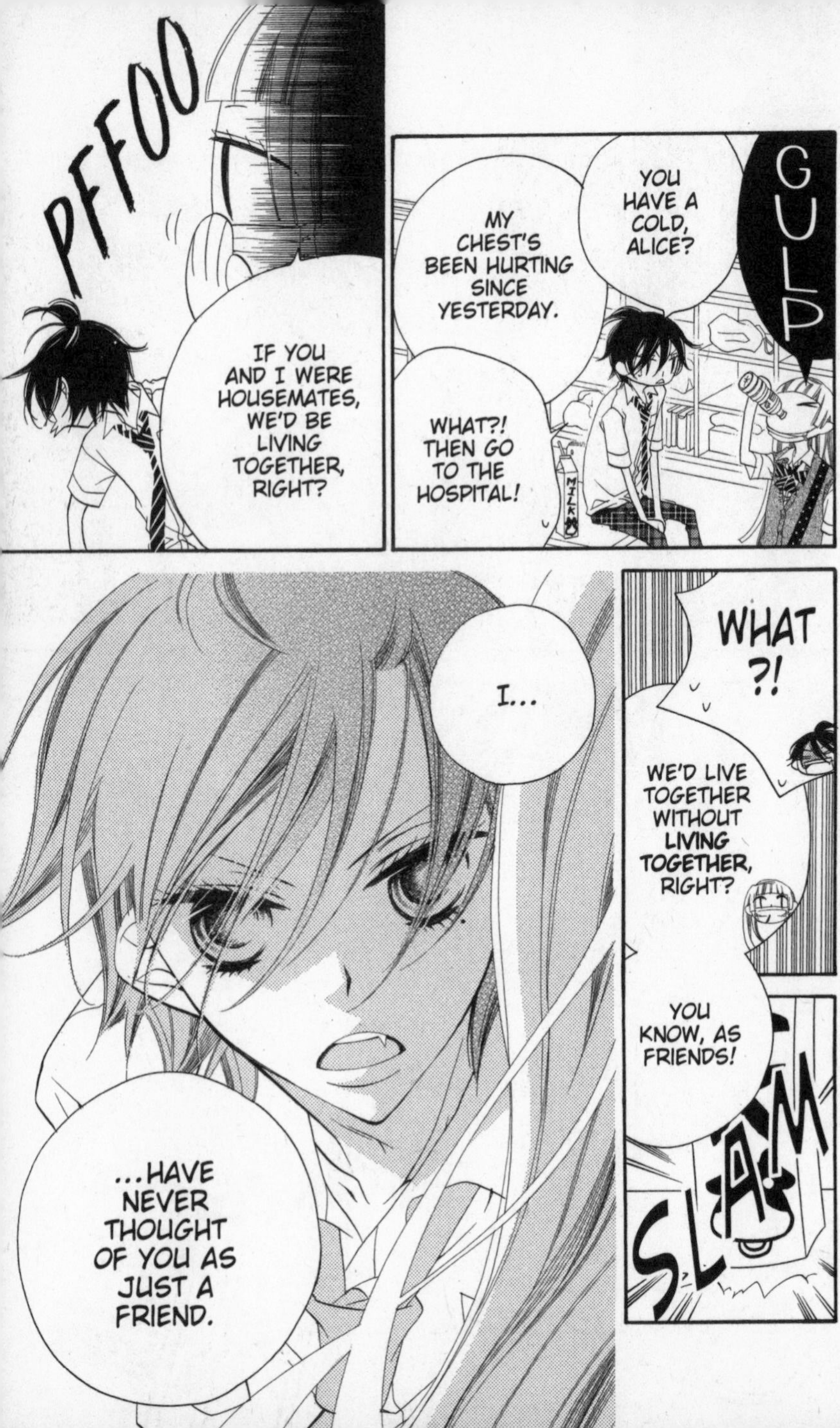
GULP
YOU HAVE A COLD, ALICE?
MY CHEST'S BEEN HURTING SINCE YESTERDAY.
WHAT?! THEN GO TO THE HOSPITAL!
MILK
PFFOO
IF YOU AND I WERE HOUSEMATES, WE'D BE LIVING TOGETHER, RIGHT?
WHAT ?!
WE'D LIVE TOGETHER WITHOUT LIVING TOGETHER, RIGHT?
YOU KNOW, AS FRIENDS!
SLAM
I...
...HAVE NEVER THOUGHT OF YOU AS JUST A FRIEND.

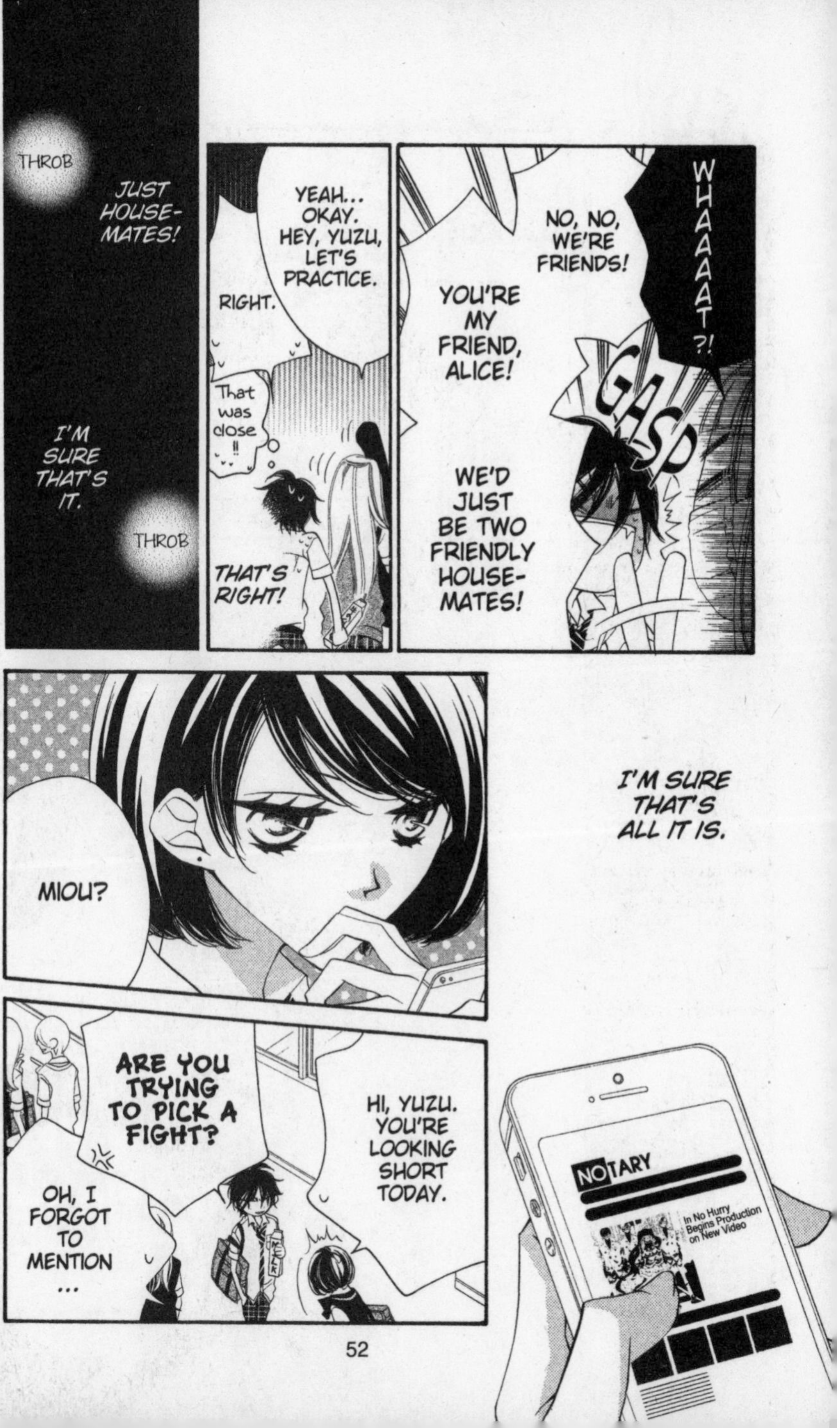
WHAAAAT?!
GASP
NO, NO, WE'RE FRIENDS!
YOU'RE MY FRIEND, ALICE!
WE'D JUST BE TWO FRIENDLY HOUSE-MATES!
YEAH... OKAY. HEY, YUZU, LET'S PRACTICE.
RIGHT.
That was close!!
THAT'S RIGHT!
THROB
JUST HOUSE-MATES!
I'M SURE THAT'S IT.
THROB
I'M SURE THAT'S ALL IT IS.
NOTARY
In No Hurry Begins Production on New Video
MIOU?
HI, YUZU. YOU'RE LOOKING SHORT TODAY.
ARE YOU TRYING TO PICK A FIGHT?
OH, I FORGOT TO MENTION ...

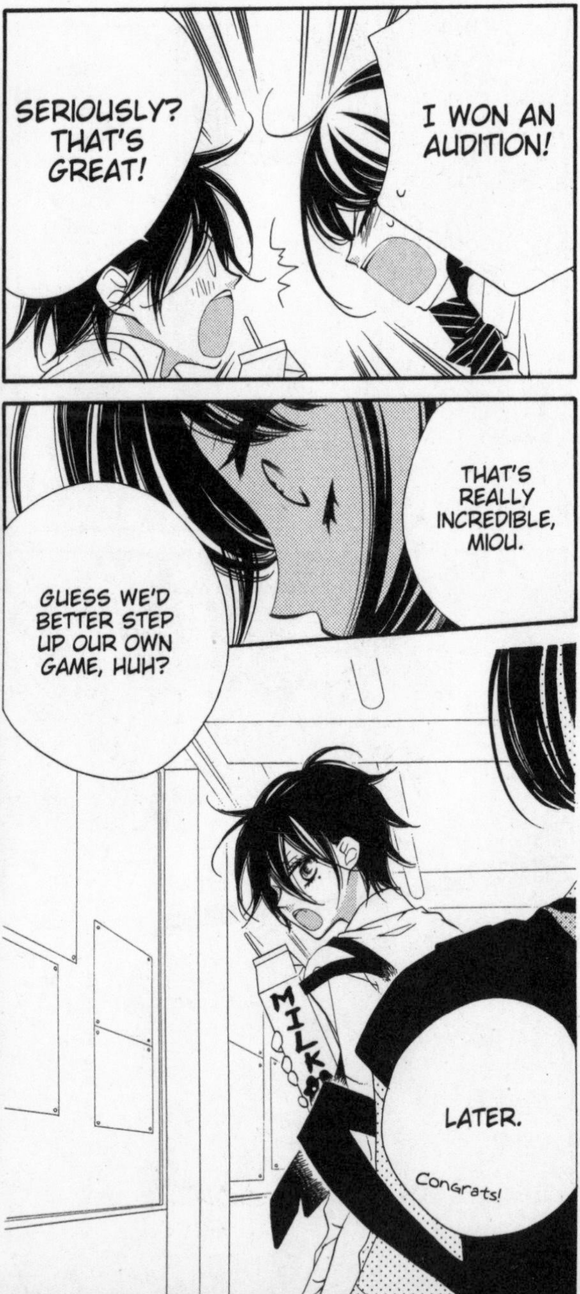
I WON AN AUDITION!
SERIOUSLY? THAT'S GREAT!
THAT'S REALLY INCREDIBLE, MIOU.
GUESS WE'D BETTER STEP UP OUR OWN GAME, HUH?
MILK
LATER.
Congrats!

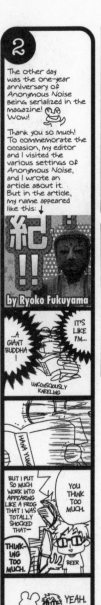

2

The other day was the one-year anniversary of Anonymous Noise being serialized in the magazine! Wow!

Thank you so much! To commemorate the occasion, my editor and I visited the various settings of Anonymous Noise, and I wrote an article about it. But in the article, my name appeared like this: ↓

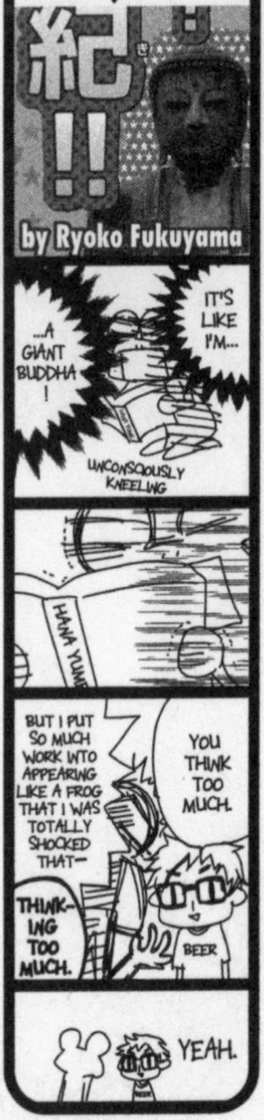
紀
!!
by Ryoko Fukuyama
IT'S LIKE I'M...
...A GIANT BUDDHA!
UNCONSCIOUSLY KNEELING
HANA YUME
YOU THINK TOO MUCH.
BUT I PUT SO MUCH WORK INTO APPEARING LIKE A FROG THAT I WAS TOTALLY SHOCKED THAT—
THINKING TOO MUCH.
BEER
YEAH.

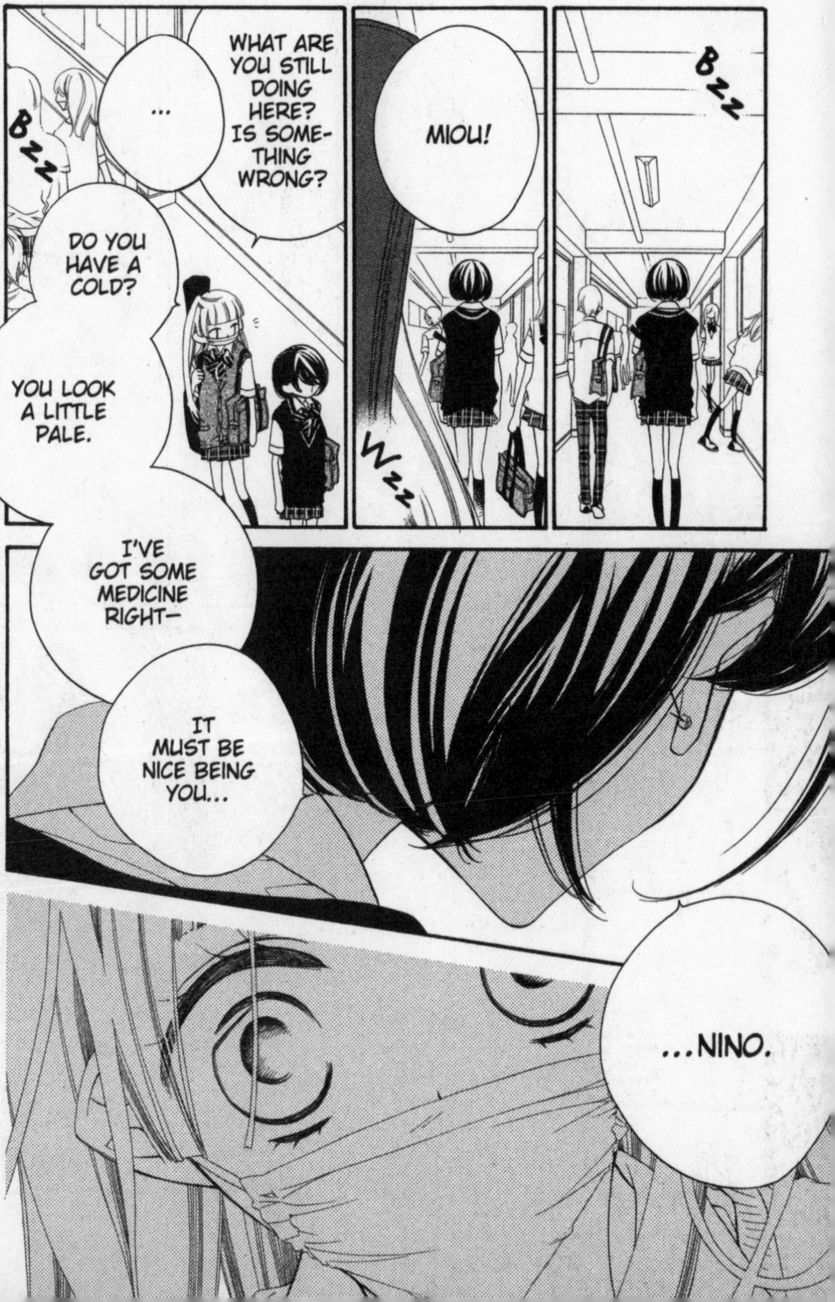
Bzz
Wzz
MIOU!
WHAT ARE YOU STILL DOING HERE? IS SOME-THING WRONG?
...
Bzz
DO YOU HAVE A COLD?
YOU LOOK A LITTLE PALE.
I'VE GOT SOME MEDICINE RIGHT—
IT MUST BE NICE BEING YOU...
...NINO.

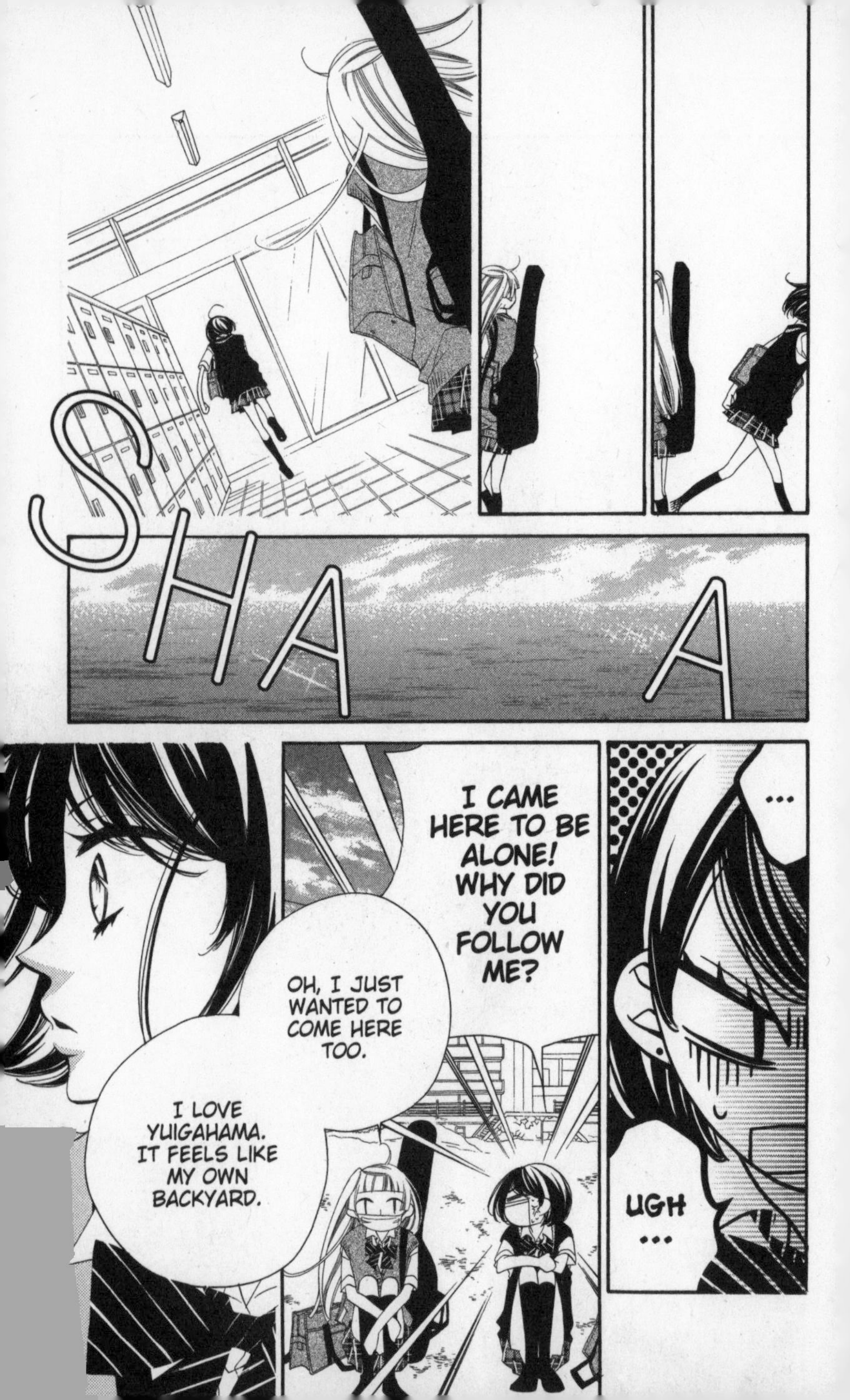
SHAA
...
UGH...
I CAME HERE TO BE ALONE! WHY DID YOU FOLLOW ME?
OH, I JUST WANTED TO COME HERE TOO.
I LOVE YUIGAHAMA. IT FEELS LIKE MY OWN BACKYARD.

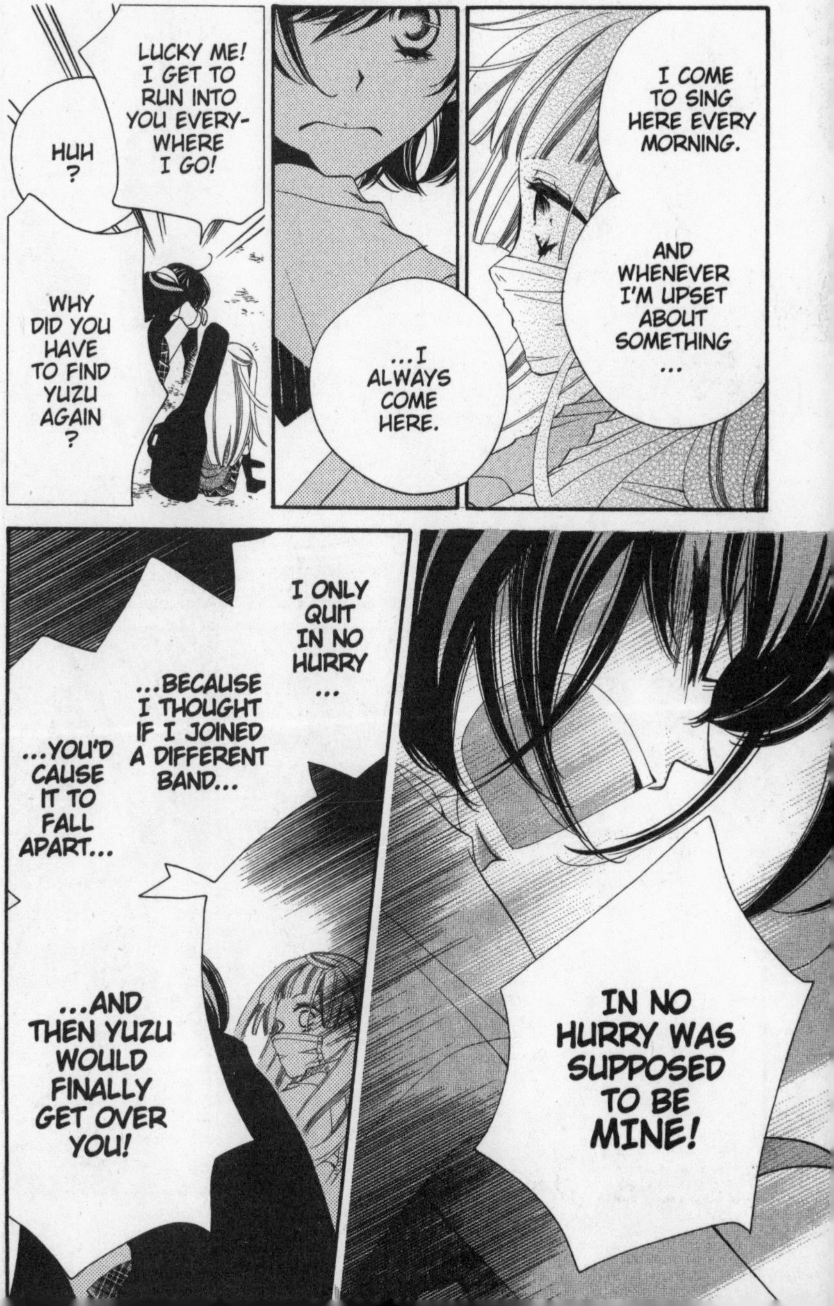
I COME TO SING HERE EVERY MORNING.
AND WHENEVER I'M UPSET ABOUT SOMETHING...
...I ALWAYS COME HERE.
LUCKY ME! I GET TO RUN INTO YOU EVERY-WHERE I GO!
HUH?
WHY DID YOU HAVE TO FIND YUZU AGAIN?
IN NO HURRY WAS SUPPOSED TO BE MINE!
I ONLY QUIT IN NO HURRY...
...BECAUSE I THOUGHT IF I JOINED A DIFFERENT BAND...
...YOU'D CAUSE IT TO FALL APART...
...AND THEN YUZU WOULD FINALLY GET OVER YOU!

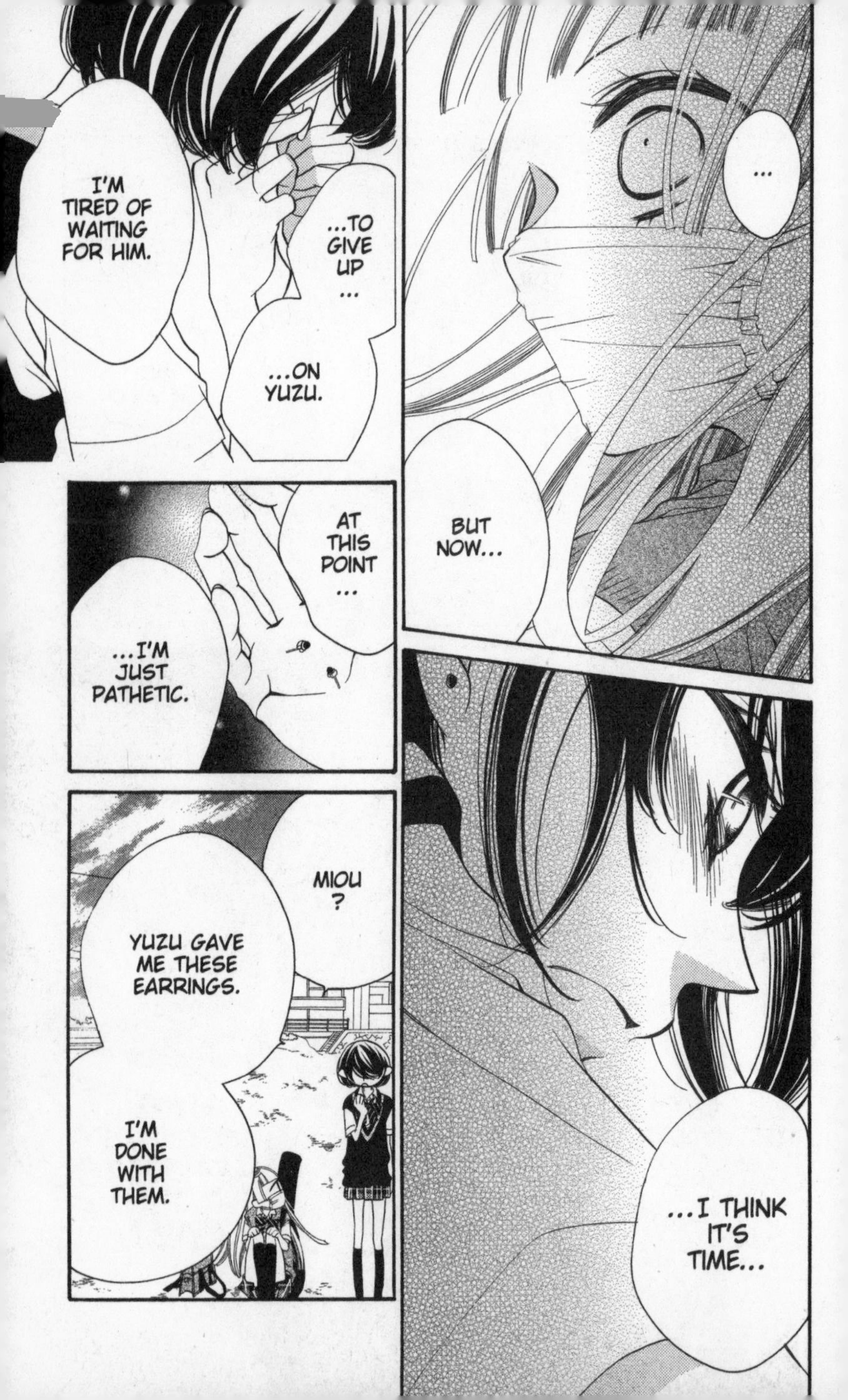
...
BUT NOW...
...I THINK IT'S TIME...
...TO GIVE UP ...
...ON YUZU.
I'M TIRED OF WAITING FOR HIM.
AT THIS POINT ...
...I'M JUST PATHETIC.
MIOU ?
YUZU GAVE ME THESE EARRINGS.
I'M DONE WITH THEM.

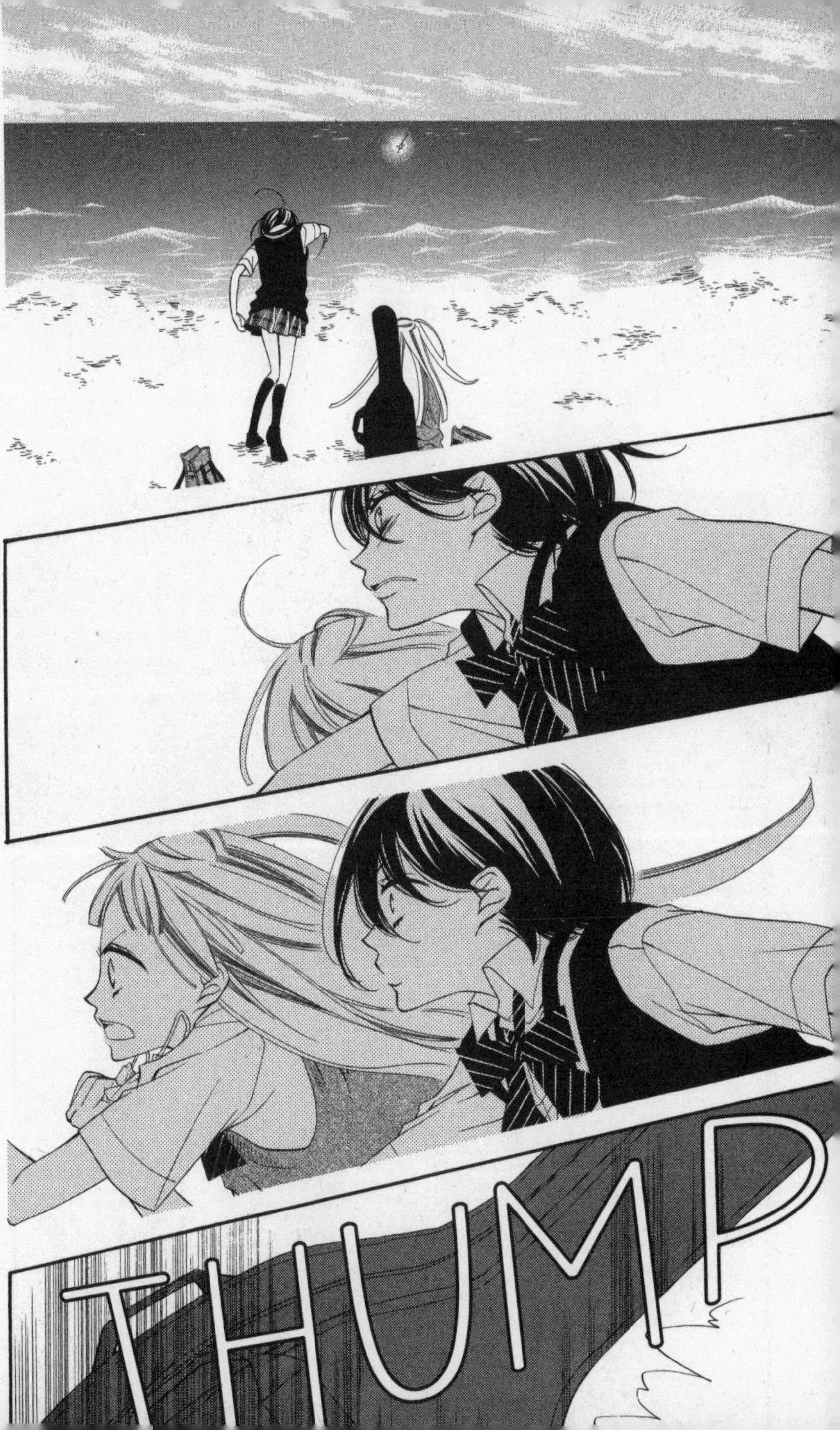
THUMP

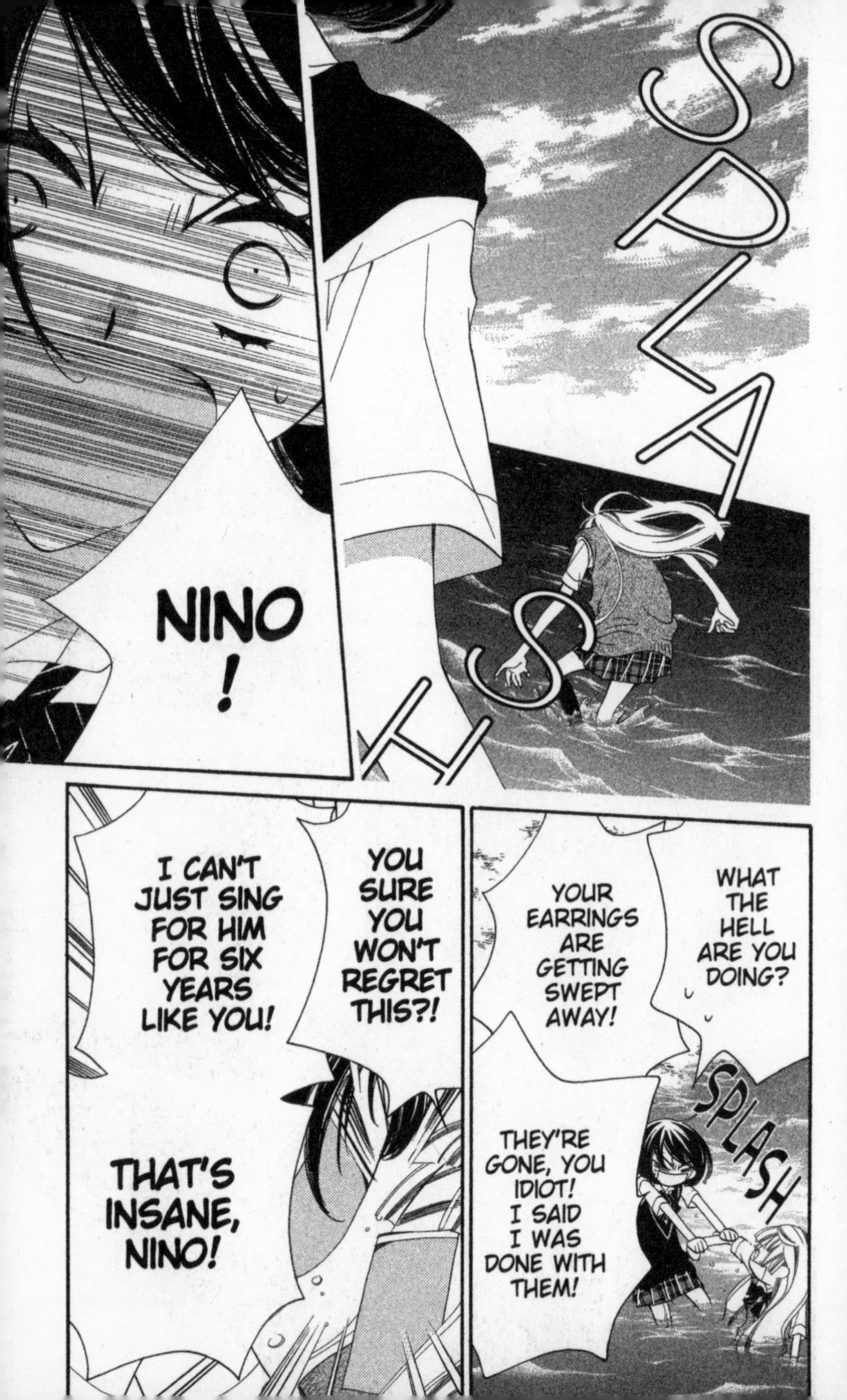
SPLASH
NINO!
WHAT THE HELL ARE YOU DOING?
YOUR EARRINGS ARE GETTING SWEPT AWAY!
SPLASH
THEY'RE GONE, YOU IDIOT! I SAID I WAS DONE WITH THEM!
YOU SURE YOU WON'T REGRET THIS?!
I CAN'T JUST SING FOR HIM FOR SIX YEARS LIKE YOU!
THAT'S INSANE, NINO!

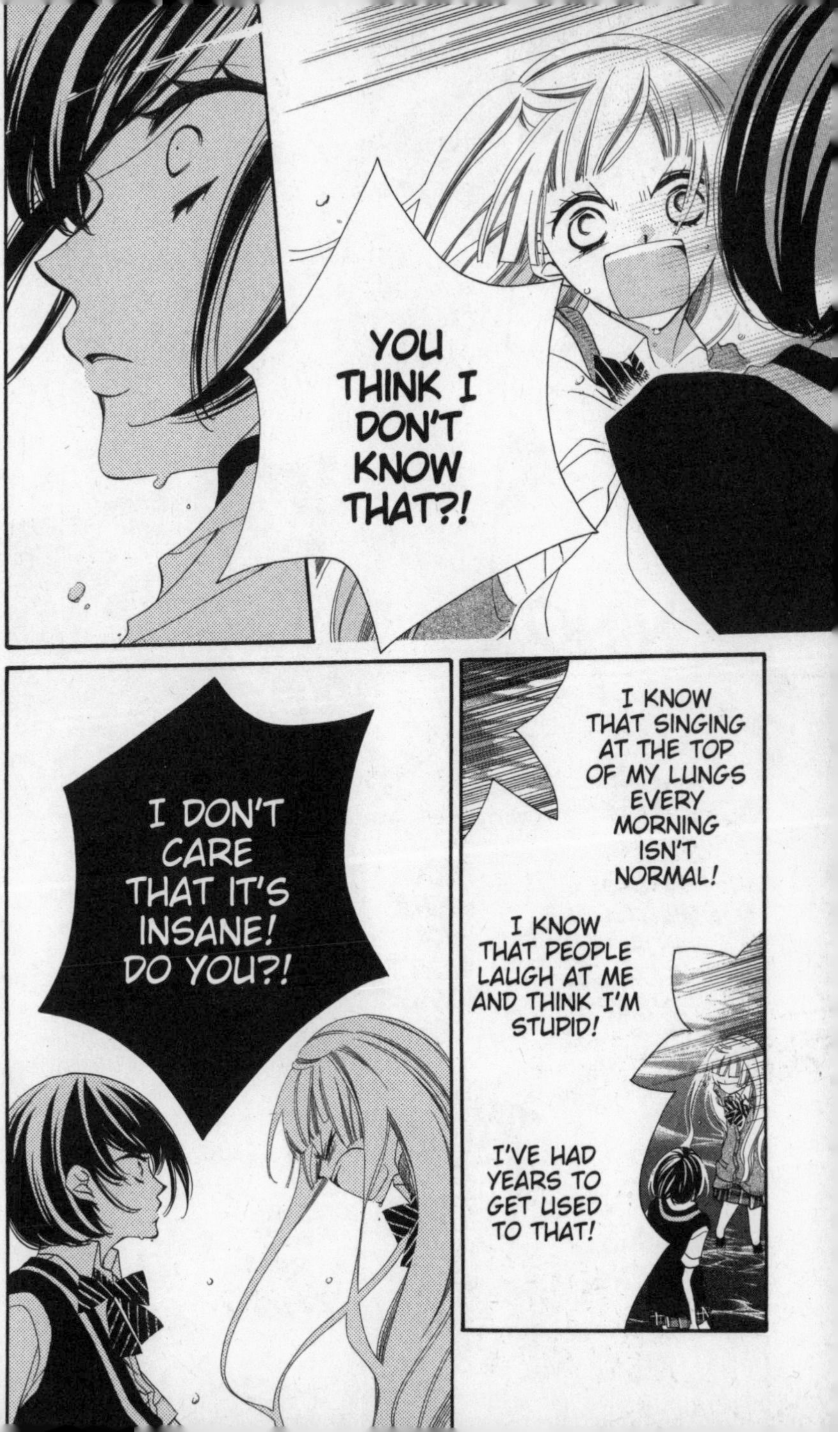
YOU THINK I DON'T KNOW THAT?!
I KNOW THAT SINGING AT THE TOP OF MY LUNGS EVERY MORNING ISN'T NORMAL!
I KNOW THAT PEOPLE LAUGH AT ME AND THINK I'M STUPID!
I'VE HAD YEARS TO GET USED TO THAT!
I DON'T CARE THAT IT'S INSANE! DO YOU?!

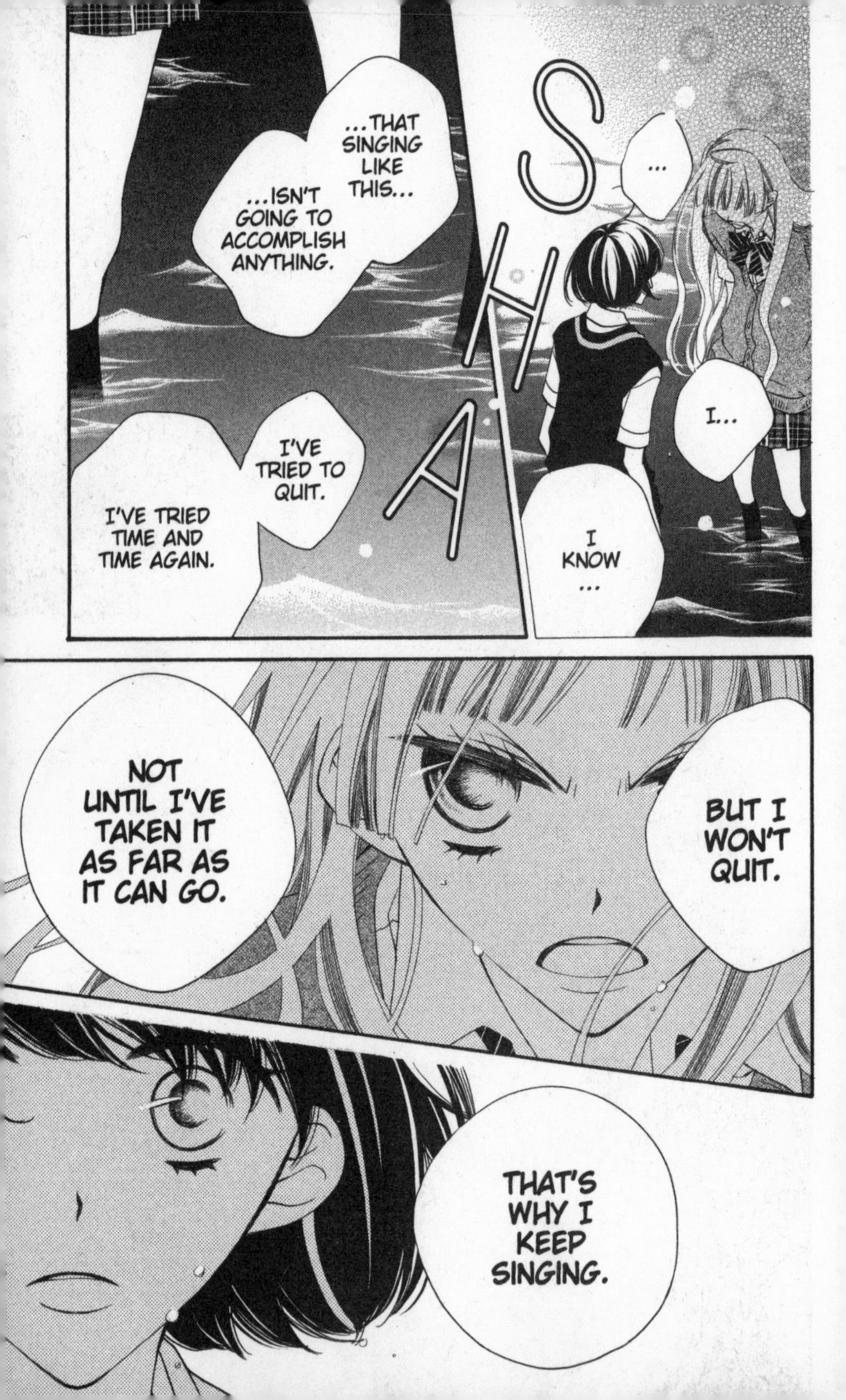
...
SHA
I...
I KNOW ...
...THAT SINGING LIKE THIS...
...ISN'T GOING TO ACCOMPLISH ANYTHING.
I'VE TRIED TO QUIT.
I'VE TRIED TIME AND TIME AGAIN.
BUT I WON'T QUIT.
NOT UNTIL I'VE TAKEN IT AS FAR AS IT CAN GO.
THAT'S WHY I KEEP SINGING.

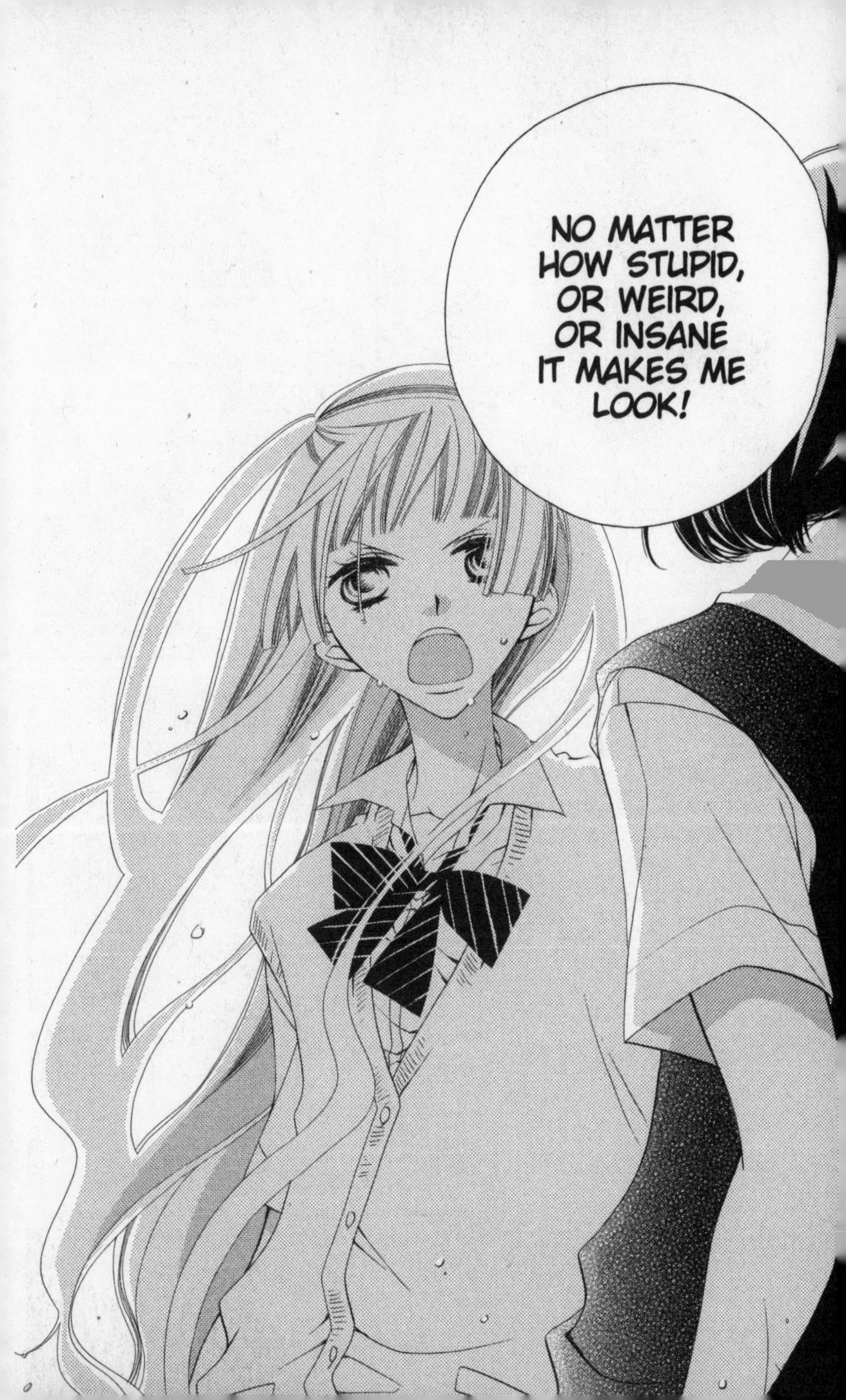
NO MATTER HOW STUPID, OR WEIRD, OR INSANE IT MAKES ME LOOK!

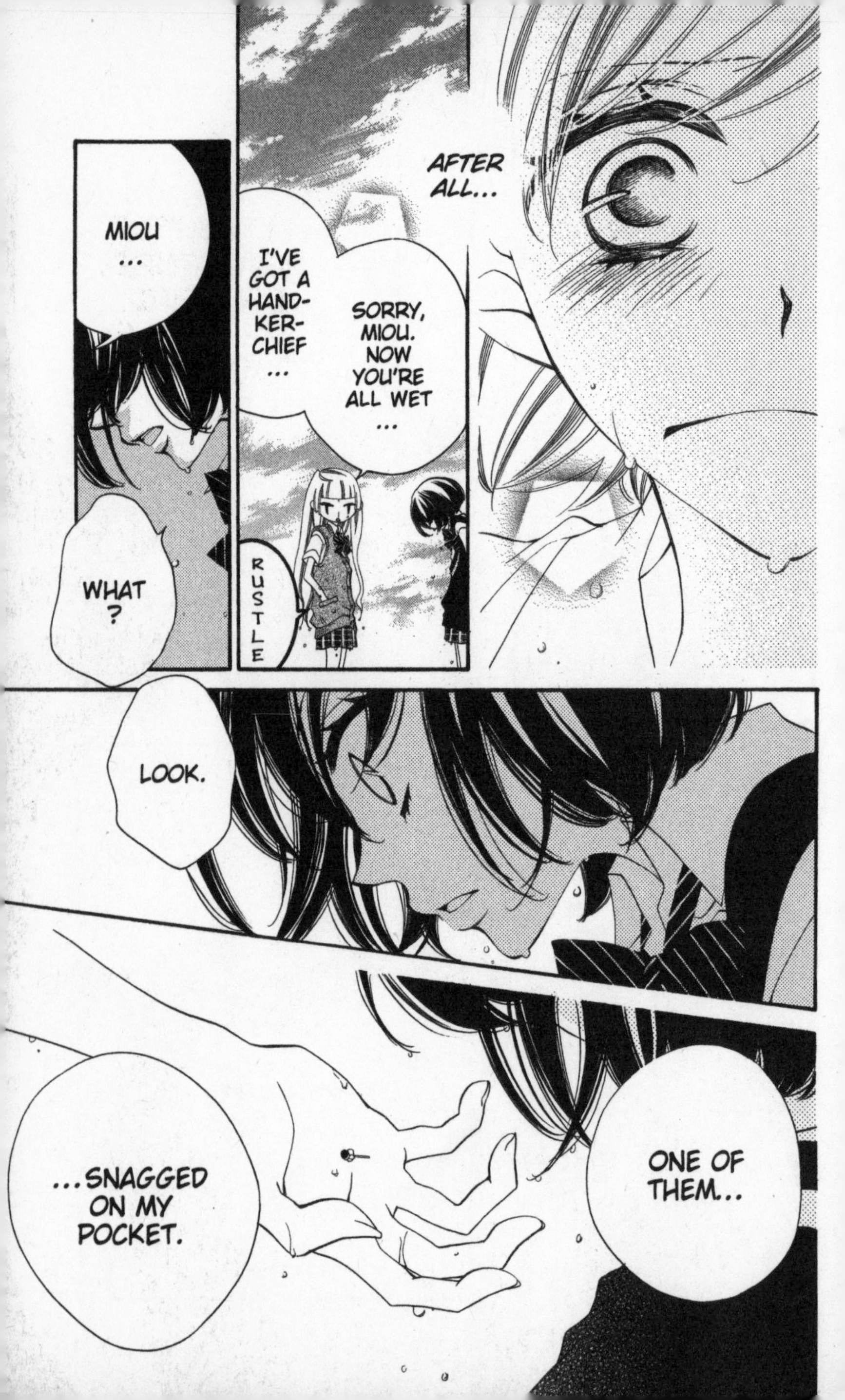
AFTER ALL...
SORRY, MIOU. NOW YOU'RE ALL WET...
I'VE GOT A HANDKERCHIEF...
RUSTLE
MIOU...
WHAT?
LOOK.
ONE OF THEM...
...SNAGGED ON MY POCKET.

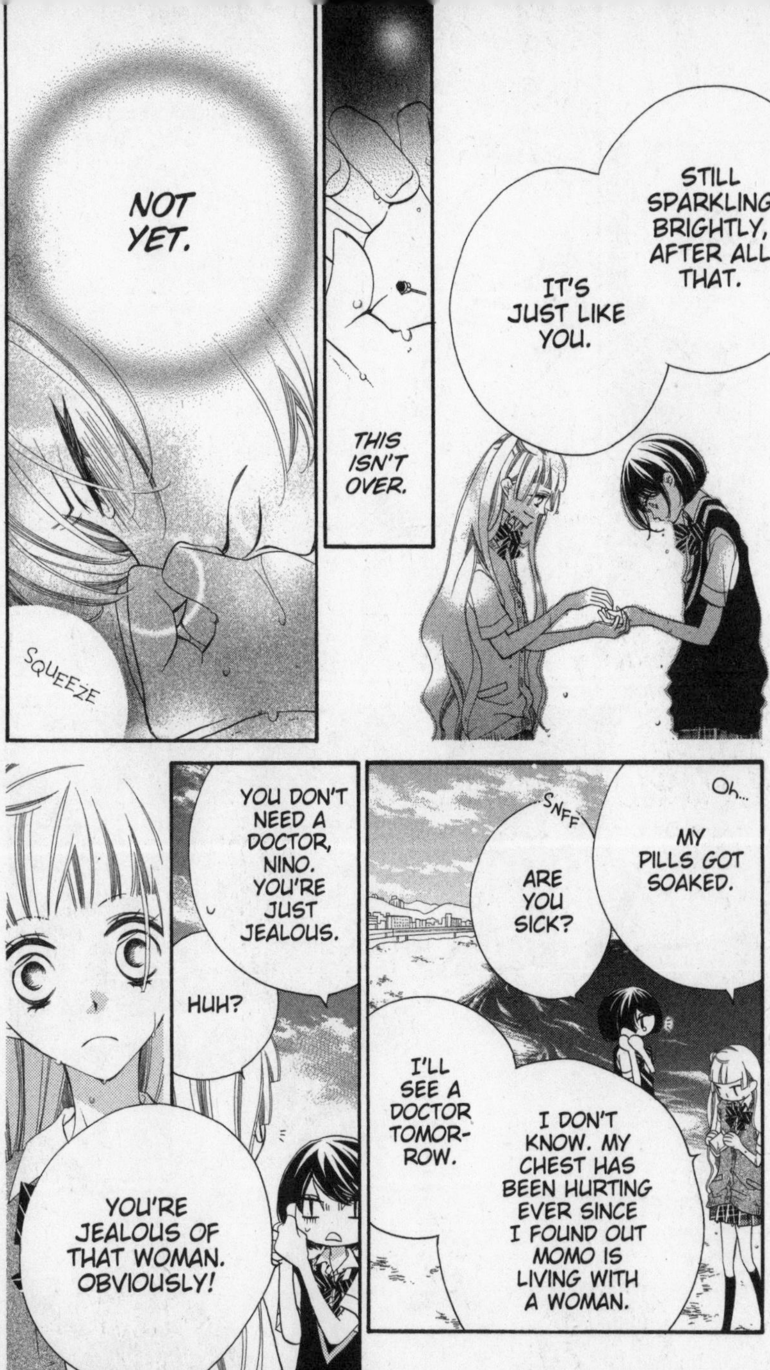
STILL SPARKLING BRIGHTLY, AFTER ALL THAT.
IT'S JUST LIKE YOU.
THIS ISN'T OVER.
NOT YET.
SQUEEZE
Oh...
MY PILLS GOT SOAKED.
SNFF
ARE YOU SICK?
I DON'T KNOW. MY CHEST HAS BEEN HURTING EVER SINCE I FOUND OUT MOMO IS LIVING WITH A WOMAN.
I'LL SEE A DOCTOR TOMOR-ROW.
YOU DON'T NEED A DOCTOR, NINO. YOU'RE JUST JEALOUS.
HUH?
YOU'RE JEALOUS OF THAT WOMAN. OBVIOUSLY!

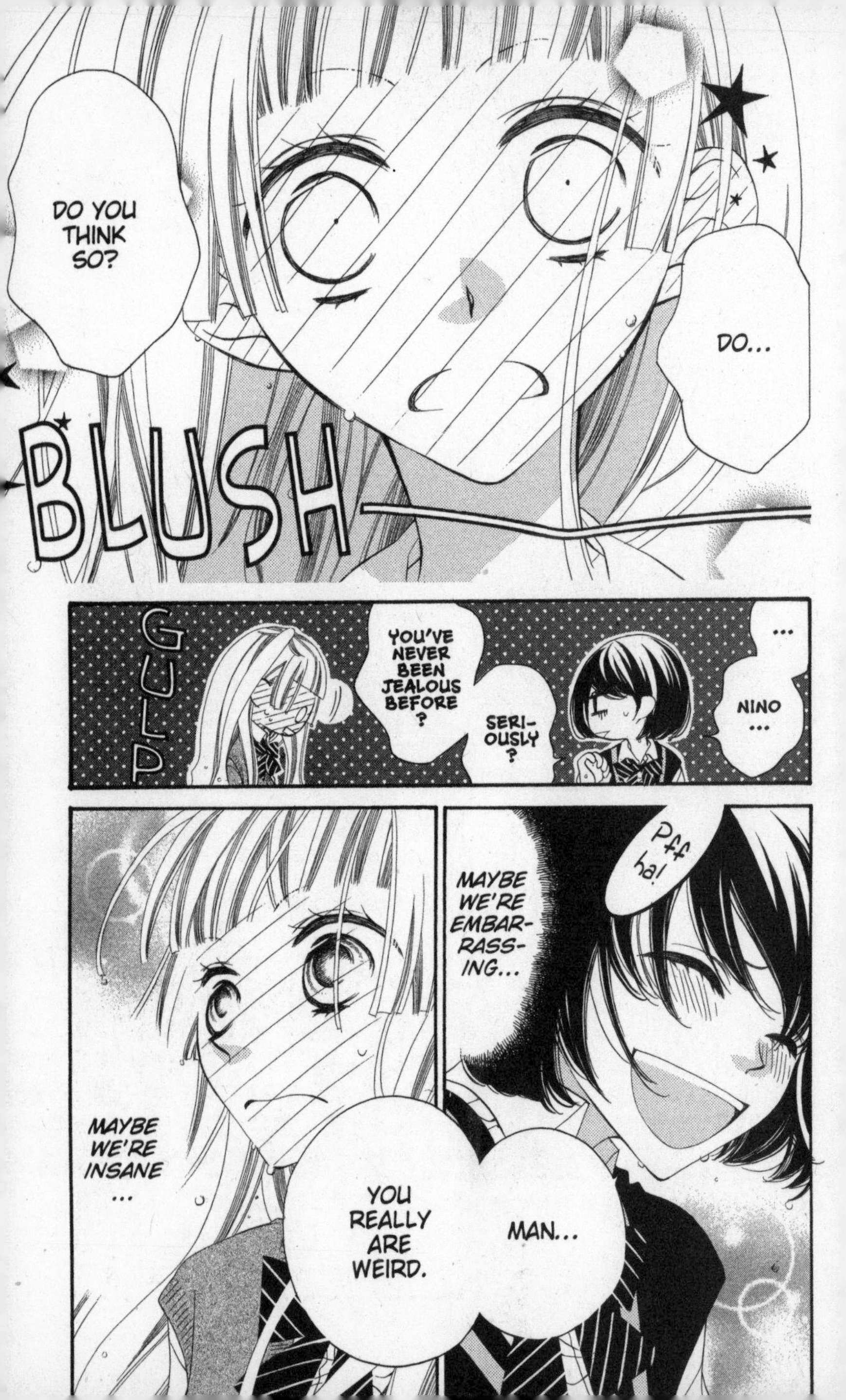
DO...
DO YOU THINK SO?
BLUSH
...
NINO...
SERIOUSLY?
YOU'VE NEVER BEEN JEALOUS BEFORE?
GULP
Pff ha!
MAYBE WE'RE EMBARRASSING...
MAN...
YOU REALLY ARE WEIRD.
MAYBE WE'RE INSANE...

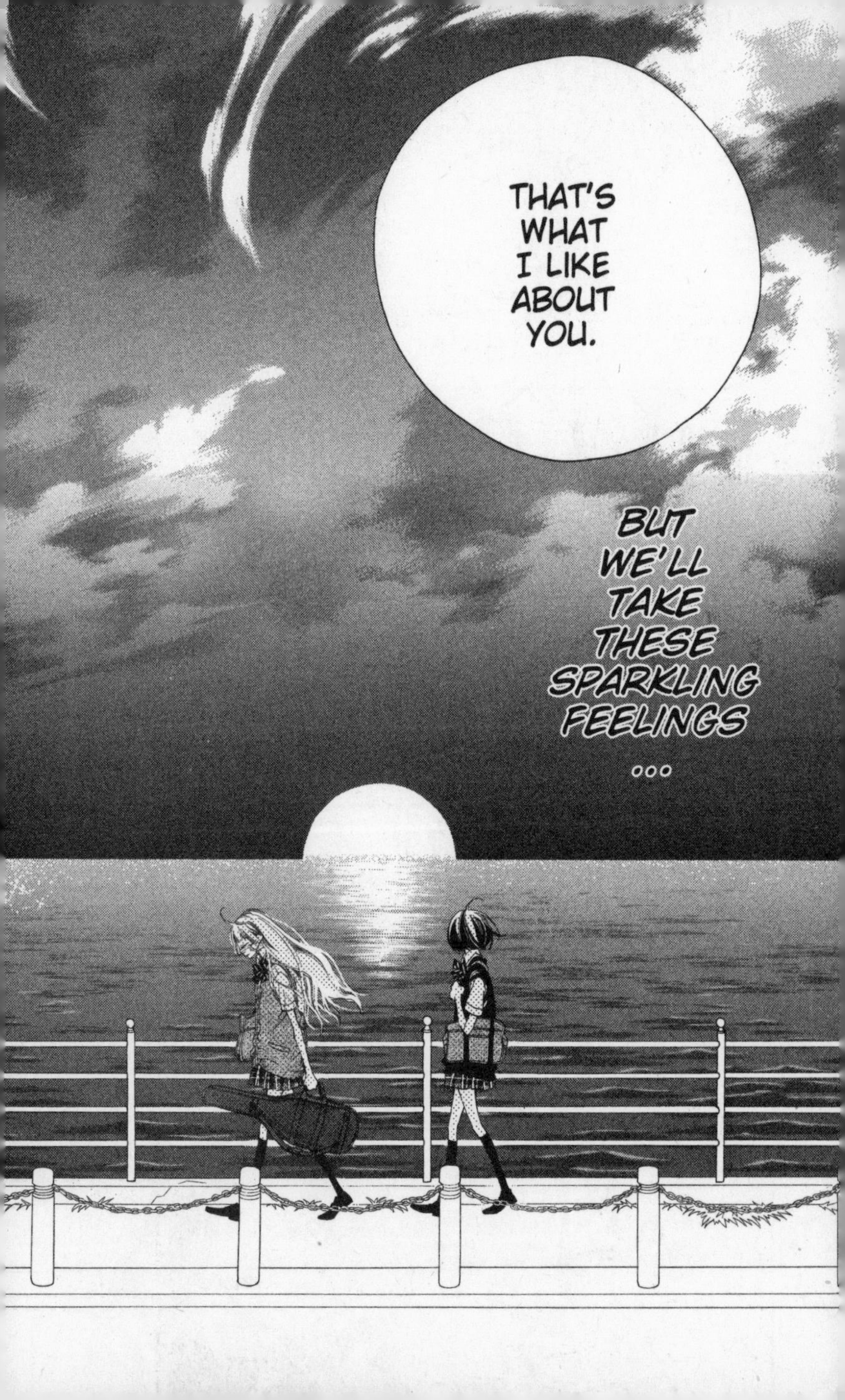
THAT'S WHAT I LIKE ABOUT YOU.
BUT WE'LL TAKE THESE SPARKLING FEELINGS ...

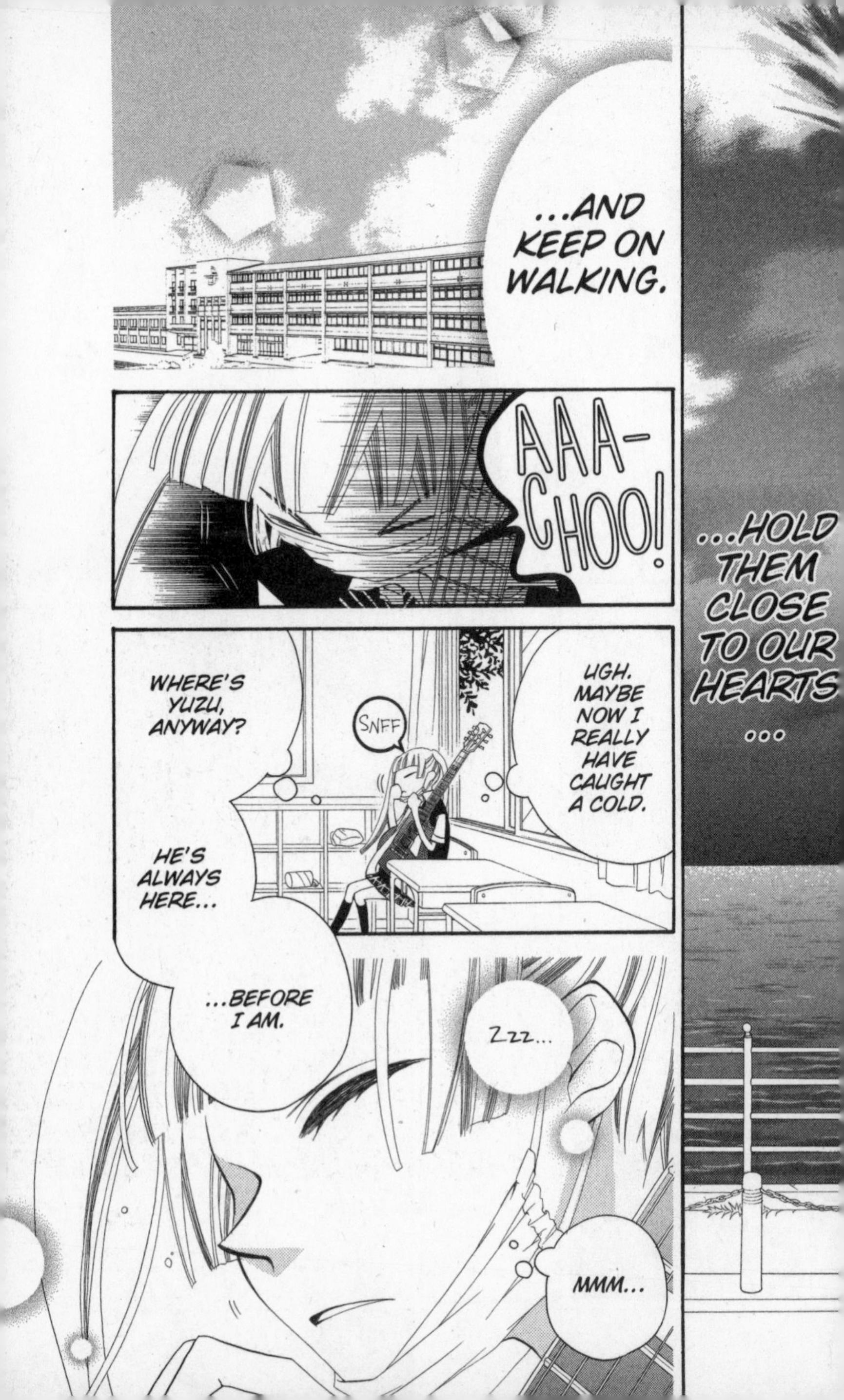
...HOLD THEM CLOSE TO OUR HEARTS...
...AND KEEP ON WALKING.
AAA-CHOO!
UGH. MAYBE NOW I REALLY HAVE CAUGHT A COLD.
SNFF
WHERE'S YUZU, ANYWAY?
HE'S ALWAYS HERE... ...BEFORE I AM.
Zzz...
MMM...

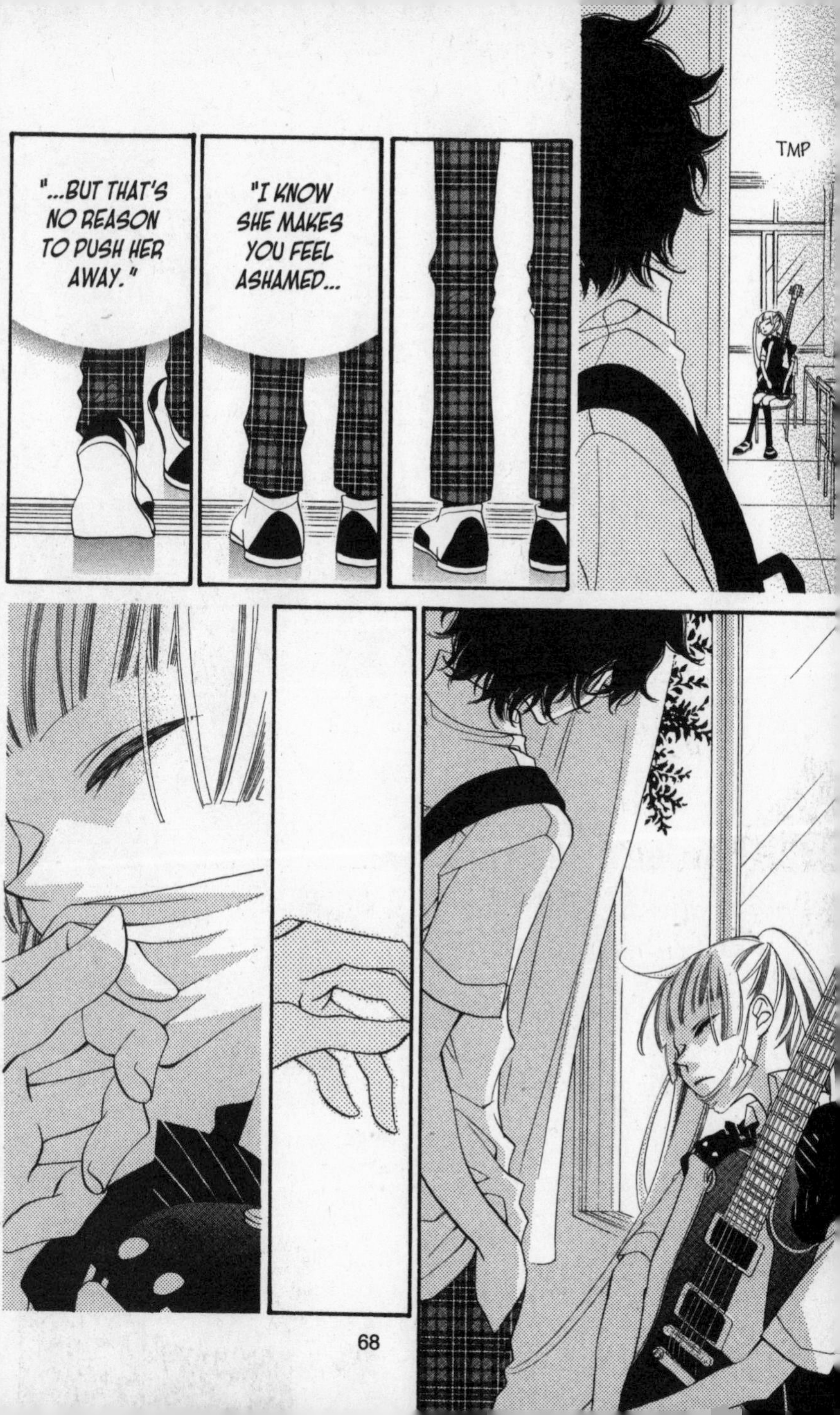
TMP
"I KNOW SHE MAKES YOU FEEL ASHAMED...
"...BUT THAT'S NO REASON TO PUSH HER AWAY."

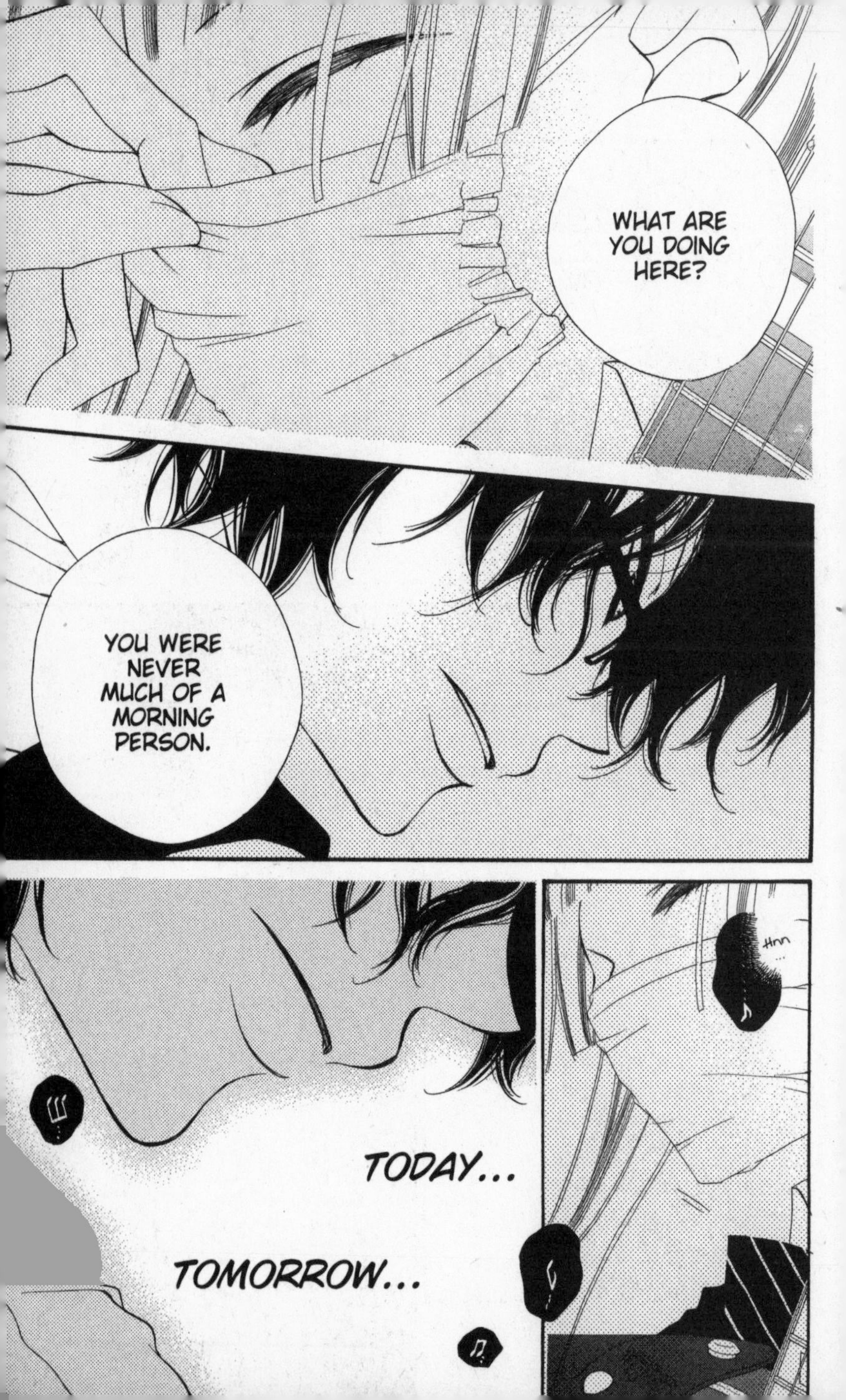
WHAT ARE YOU DOING HERE?
YOU WERE NEVER MUCH OF A MORNING PERSON.
Hnn...
TODAY...
TOMORROW...

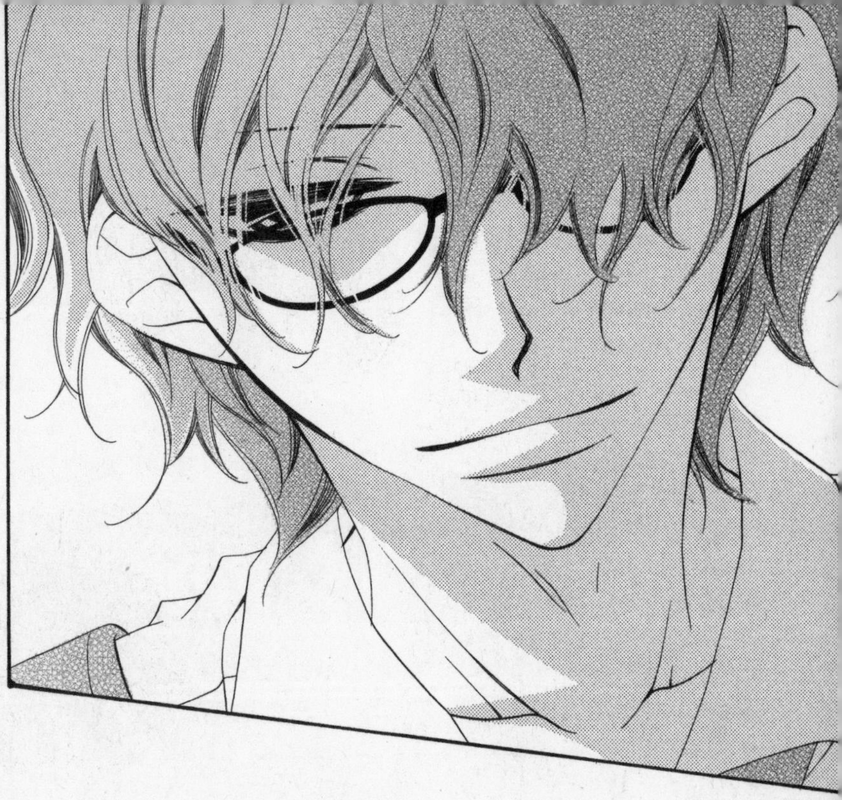

WE'LL
JUST KEEP
WALKING.

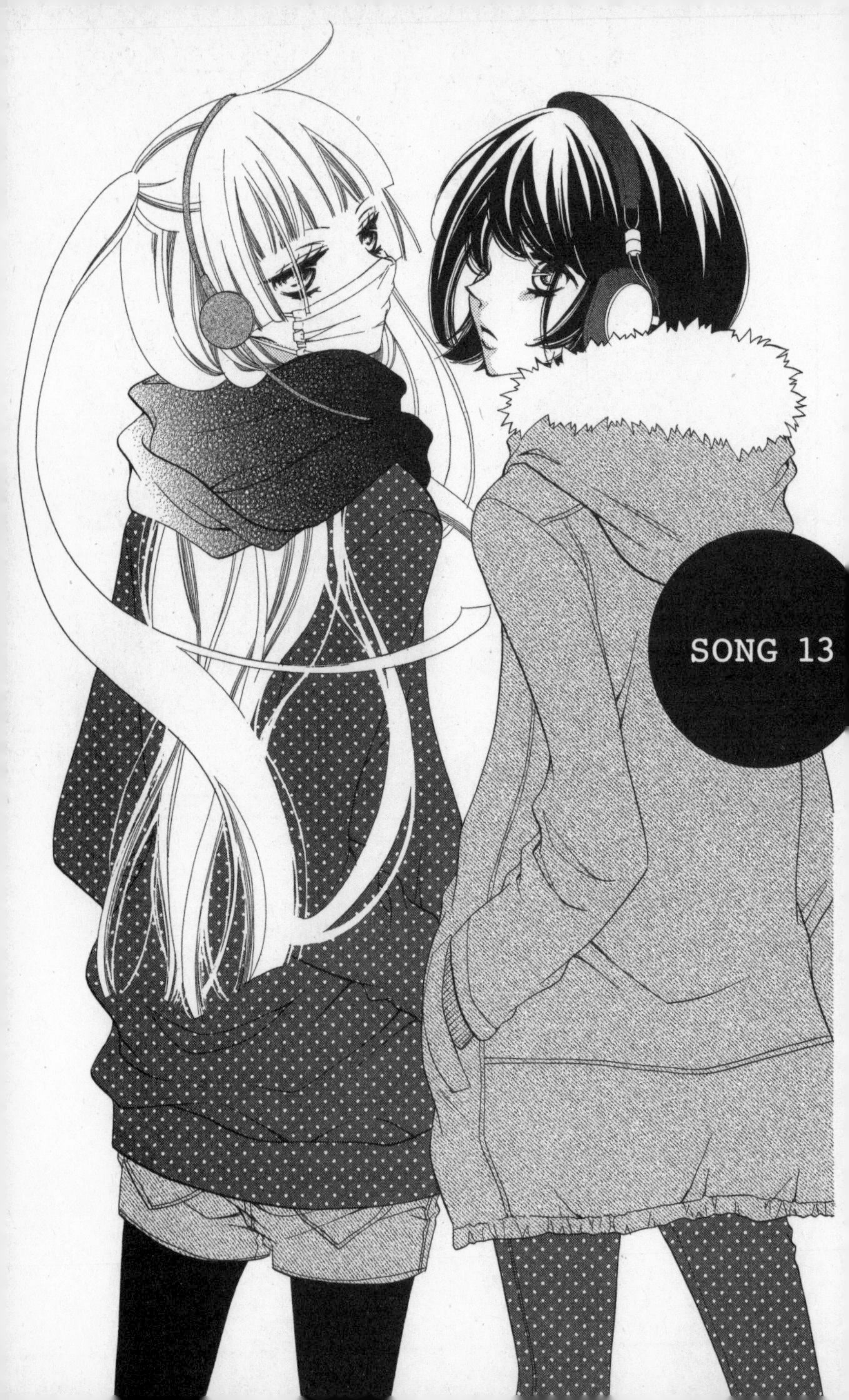
SONG 13

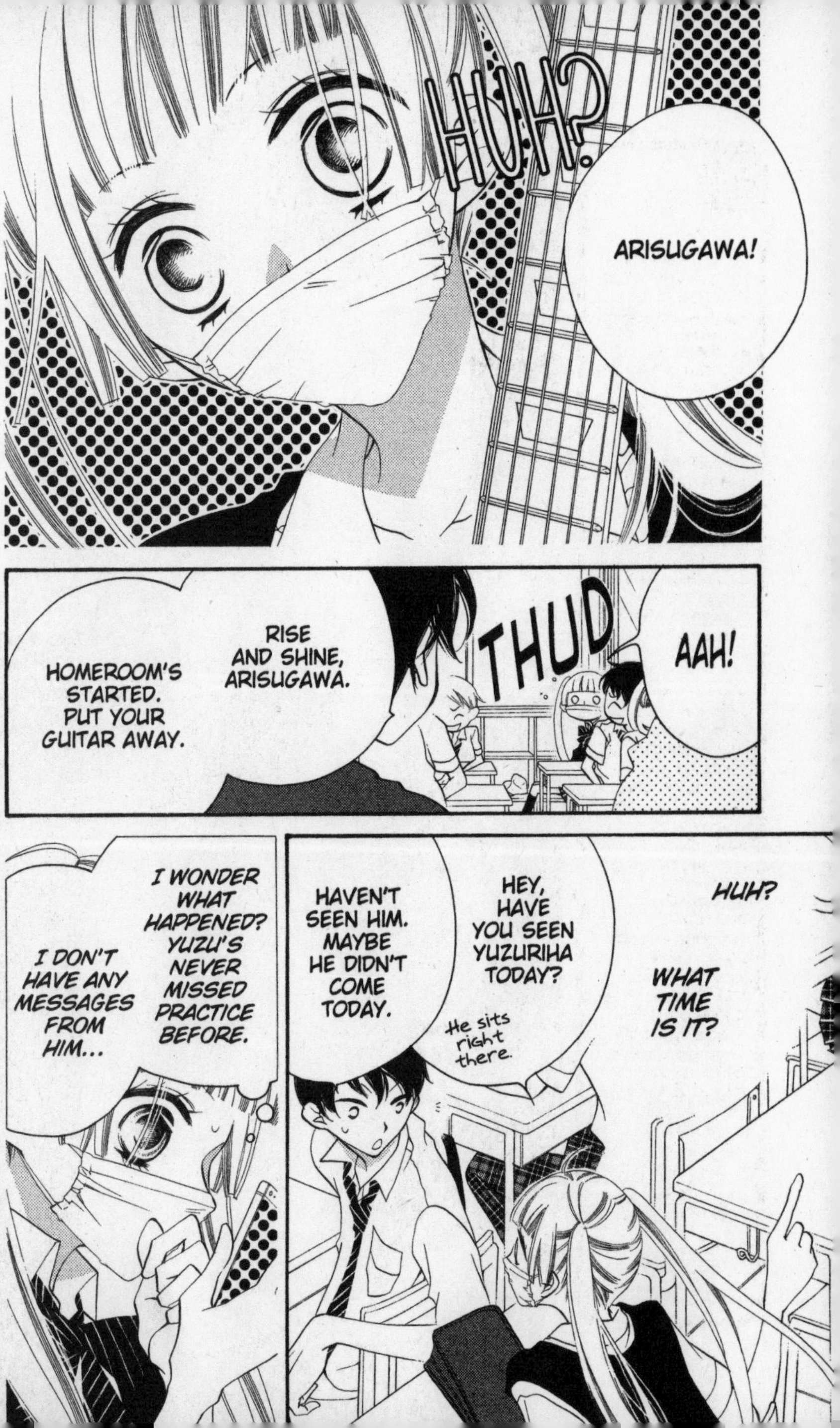
ARISUGAWA!
HUH?
AAH!
THUD
RISE AND SHINE, ARISUGAWA.
HOMEROOM'S STARTED. PUT YOUR GUITAR AWAY.
HUH?
WHAT TIME IS IT?
HEY, HAVE YOU SEEN YUZURIHA TODAY?
He sits right there.
HAVEN'T SEEN HIM. MAYBE HE DIDN'T COME TODAY.
I WONDER WHAT HAPPENED? YUZU'S NEVER MISSED PRACTICE BEFORE.
I DON'T HAVE ANY MESSAGES FROM HIM...

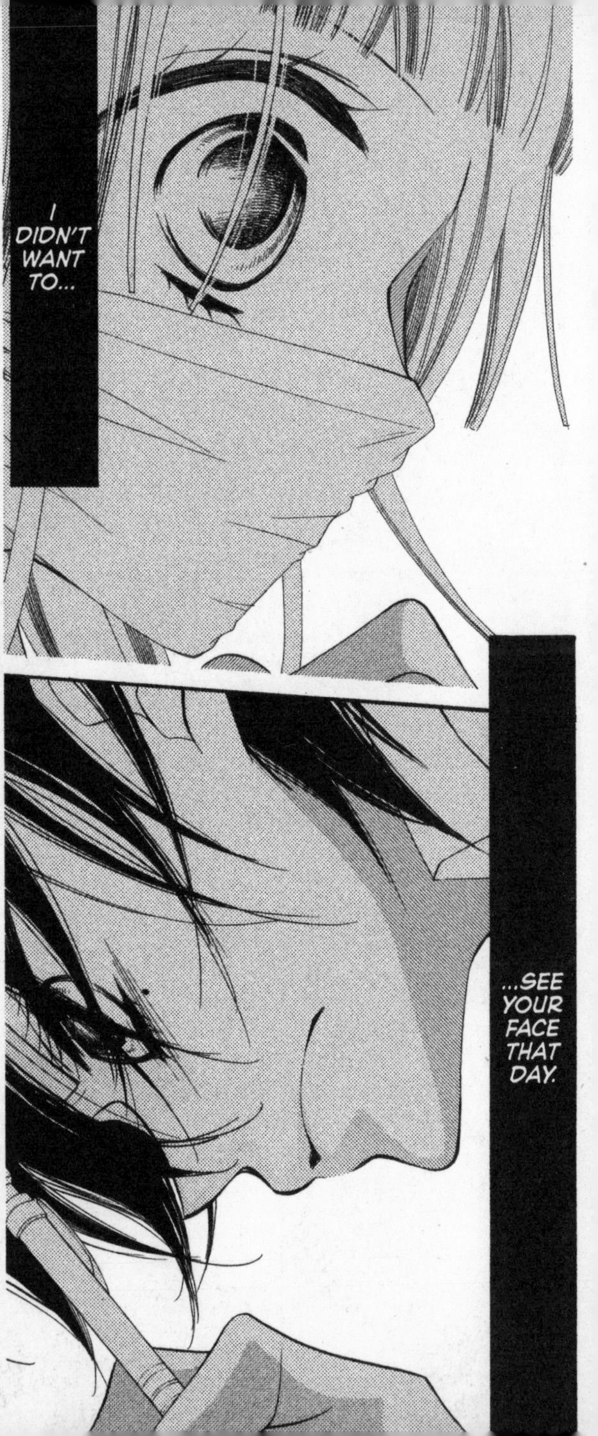
I DIDN'T WANT TO...
...SEE YOUR FACE THAT DAY.

3

When Yuzu runs away from home in Song 13, he runs into [redacted] BEEEP ← SPOILER at the steps of Engaku-ji temple near Kita-Kamakura Station.

The cherry trees and autumn foliage there are really beautiful, so you should pay a visit if you're ever nearby. It's the spot that made me fall in love with Kamakura.

Visit on a weekday just past tourist season and there's hardly anyone around.

Once I wandered down the road all the way to Tsurugaoka Hachimangu! And there was the cutest café down an alley nearby! This isn't really related to Kamakura, but I recommend the Tenugui Café Ichigeya near Goryo Shrine. Now I'm dying to go there!

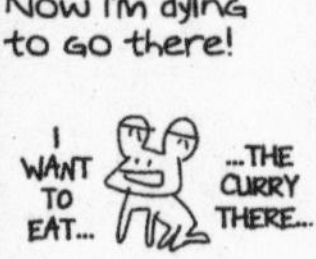
I WANT TO EAT...
...THE CURRY THERE...

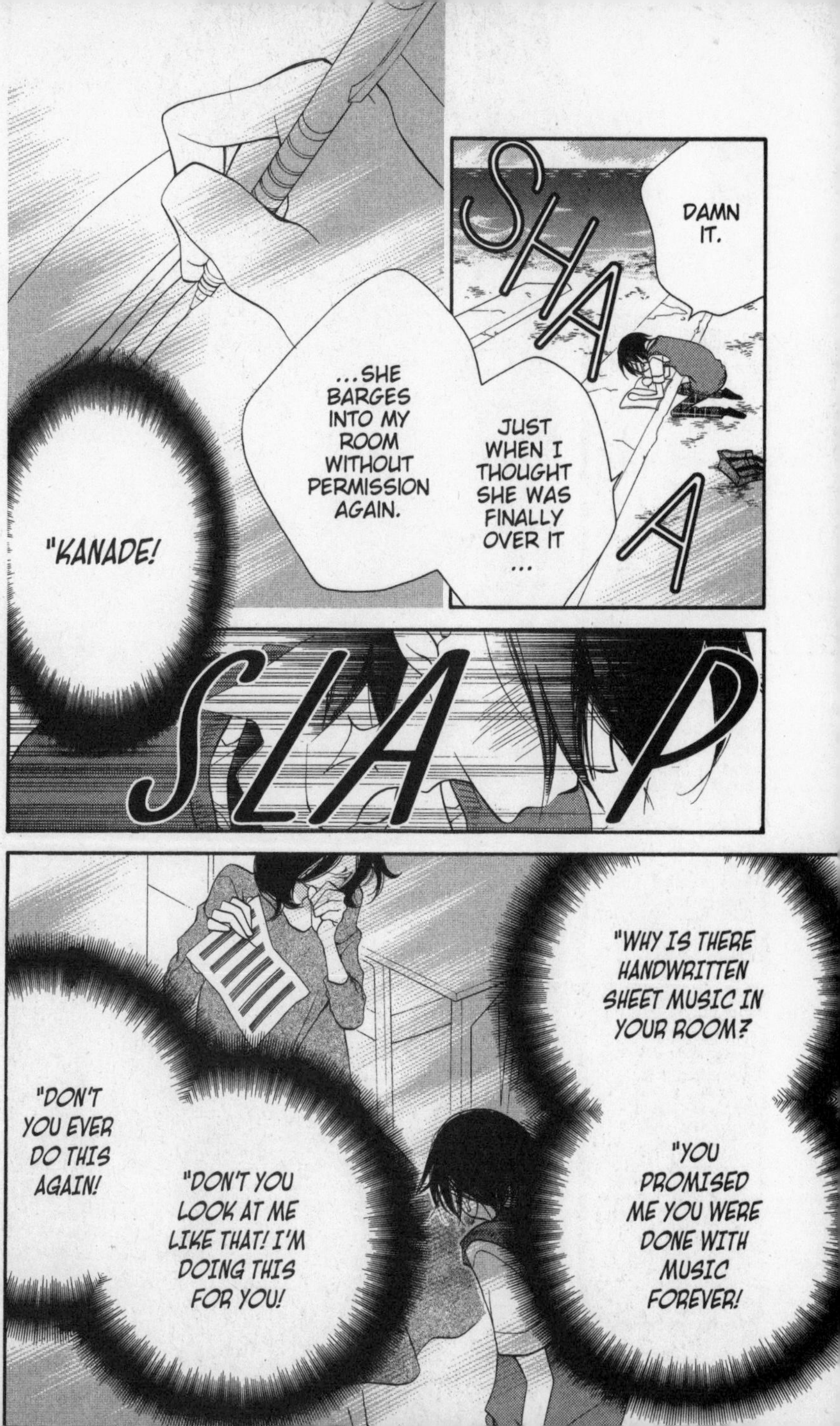
SHA A
DAMN IT.
JUST WHEN I THOUGHT SHE WAS FINALLY OVER IT ...
...SHE BARGES INTO MY ROOM WITHOUT PERMISSION AGAIN.
"KANADE!
SLAP
"WHY IS THERE HANDWRITTEN SHEET MUSIC IN YOUR ROOM?
"YOU PROMISED ME YOU WERE DONE WITH MUSIC FOREVER!
"DON'T YOU LOOK AT ME LIKE THAT! I'M DOING THIS FOR YOU!
"DON'T YOU EVER DO THIS AGAIN!

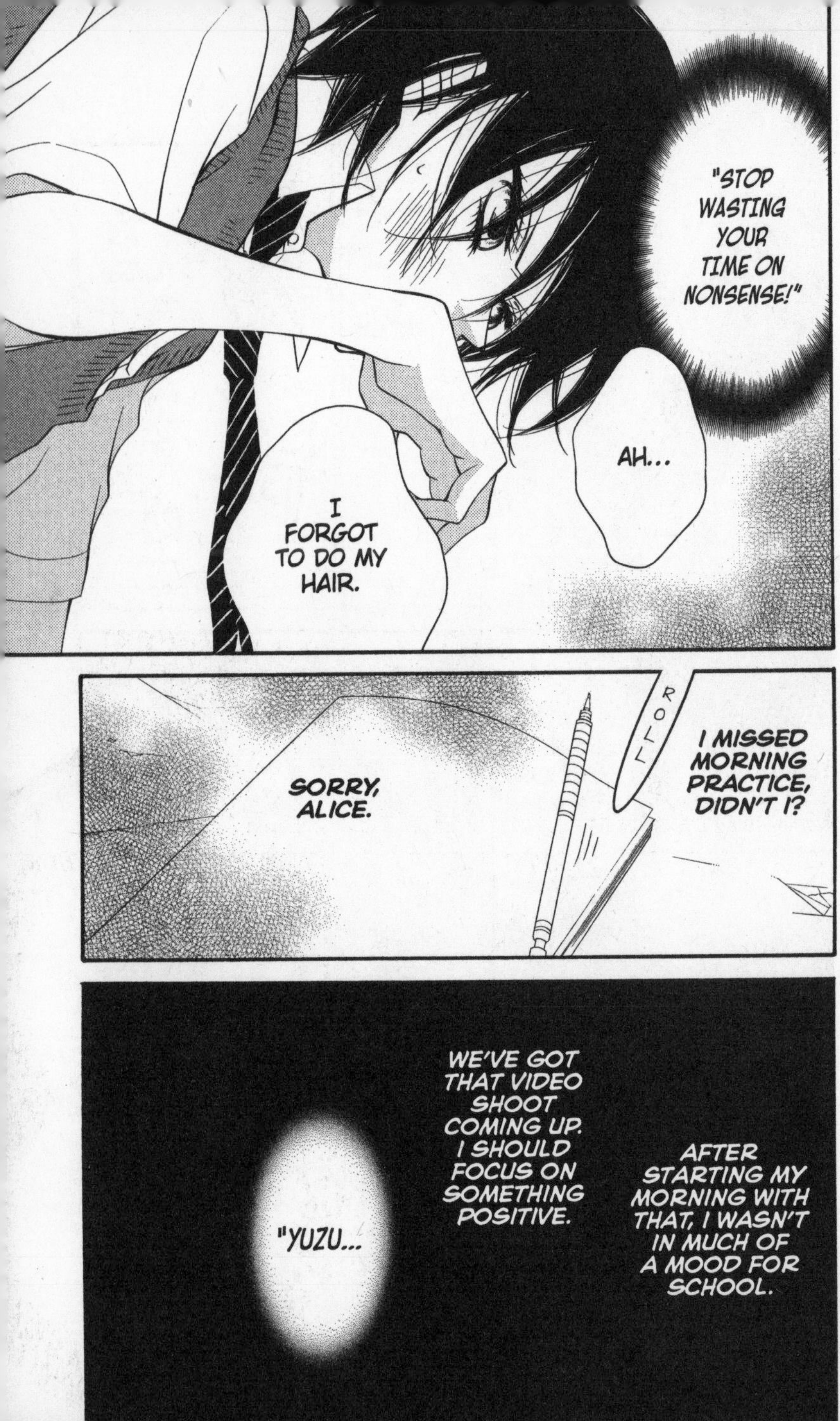
"STOP WASTING YOUR TIME ON NONSENSE!"
AH...
I FORGOT TO DO MY HAIR.
I MISSED MORNING PRACTICE, DIDN'T I?
ROLL
SORRY, ALICE.
AFTER STARTING MY MORNING WITH THAT, I WASN'T IN MUCH OF A MOOD FOR SCHOOL.
WE'VE GOT THAT VIDEO SHOOT COMING UP. I SHOULD FOCUS ON SOMETHING POSITIVE.
"YUZU...

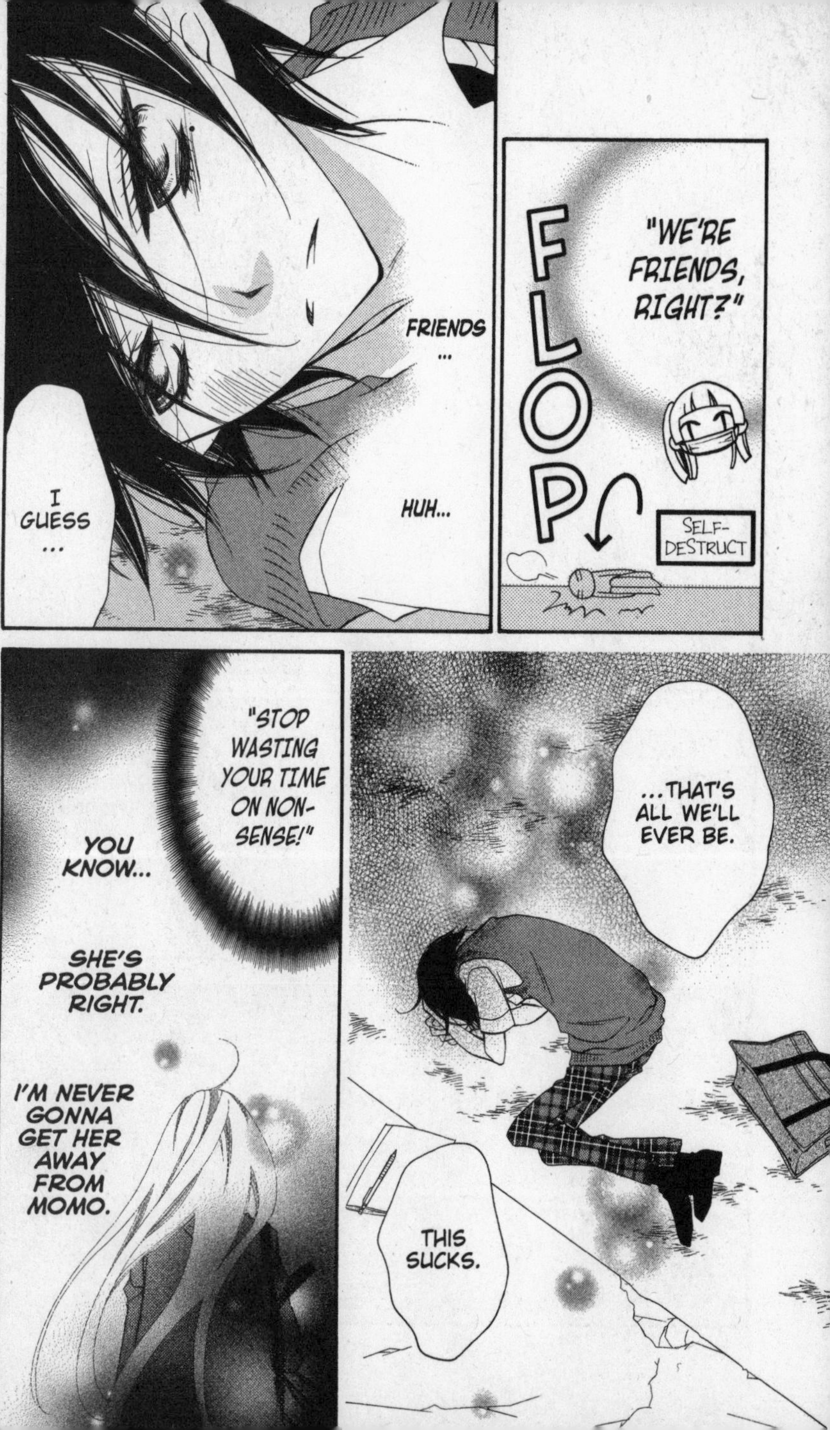
"WE'RE FRIENDS, RIGHT?"
FLOP
SELF-DESTRUCT
FRIENDS ...
HUH...
I GUESS ...
...THAT'S ALL WE'LL EVER BE.
THIS SUCKS.
"STOP WASTING YOUR TIME ON NON-SENSE!"
YOU KNOW...
SHE'S PROBABLY RIGHT.
I'M NEVER GONNA GET HER AWAY FROM MOMO.

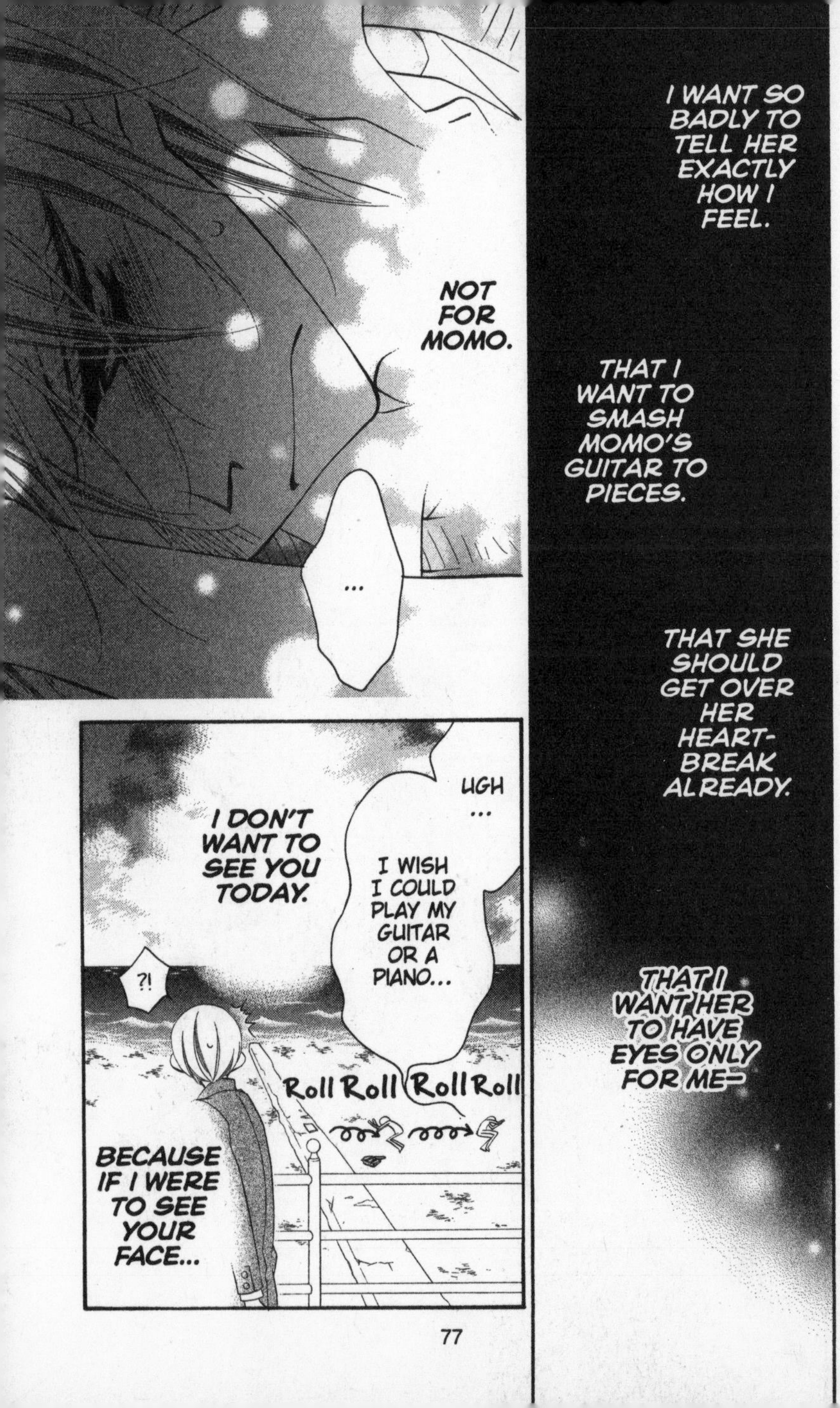
I WANT SO BADLY TO TELL HER EXACTLY HOW I FEEL.
THAT I WANT TO SMASH MOMO'S GUITAR TO PIECES.
THAT SHE SHOULD GET OVER HER HEART-BREAK ALREADY.
THAT I WANT HER TO HAVE EYES ONLY FOR ME—
NOT FOR MOMO.
...
UGH ...
I WISH I COULD PLAY MY GUITAR OR A PIANO...
I DON'T WANT TO SEE YOU TODAY.
?!
Roll Roll Roll Roll
BECAUSE IF I WERE TO SEE YOUR FACE...

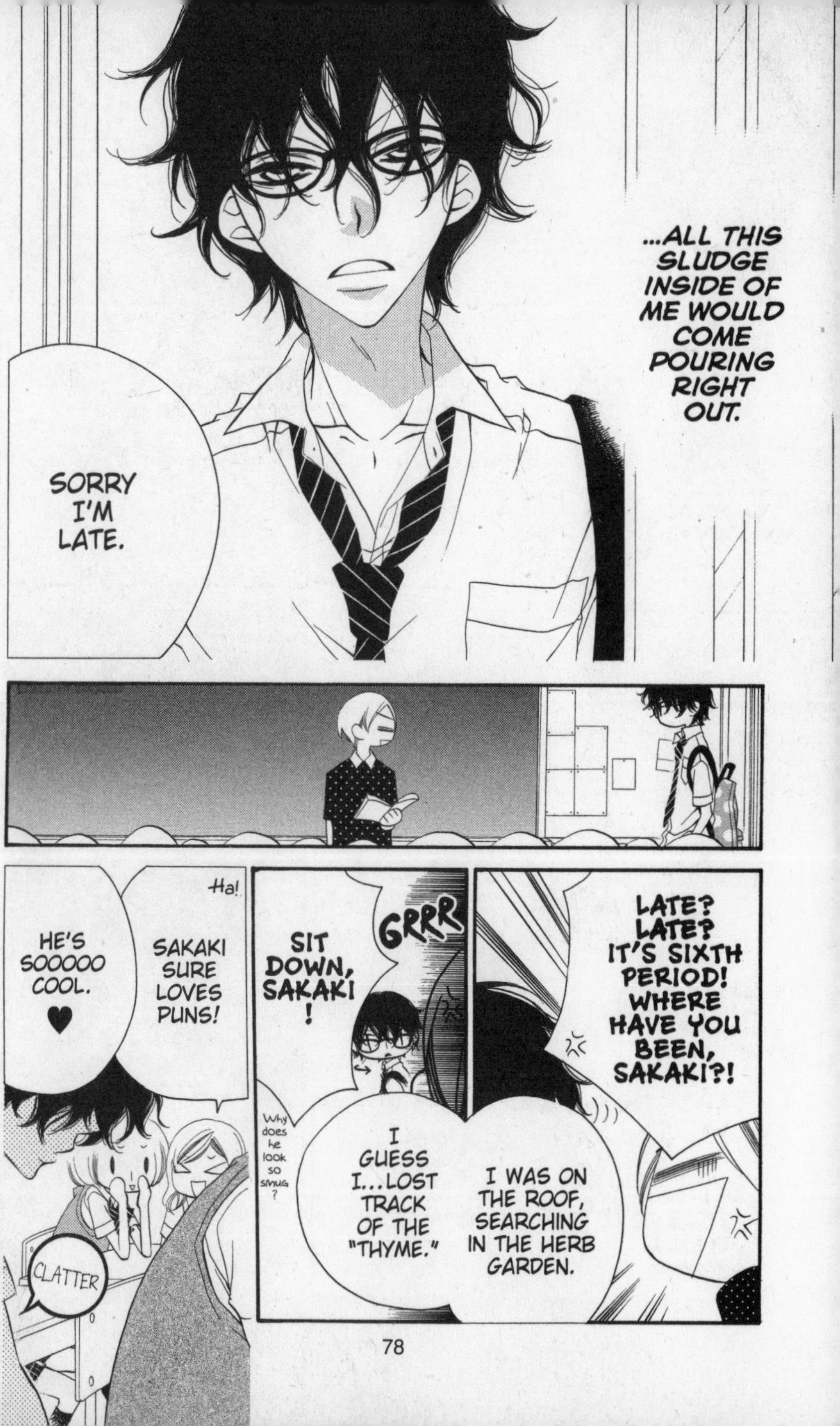
...ALL THIS SLUDGE INSIDE OF ME WOULD COME POURING RIGHT OUT.
SORRY I'M LATE.
LATE? LATE? IT'S SIXTH PERIOD! WHERE HAVE YOU BEEN, SAKAKI?!
I WAS ON THE ROOF, SEARCHING IN THE HERB GARDEN.
GRRR
SIT DOWN, SAKAKI!
I GUESS I...LOST TRACK OF THE "THYME."
Why does he look so smug?
Ha!
SAKAKI SURE LOVES PUNS!
HE'S SOOOOO COOL. ♥
CLATTER

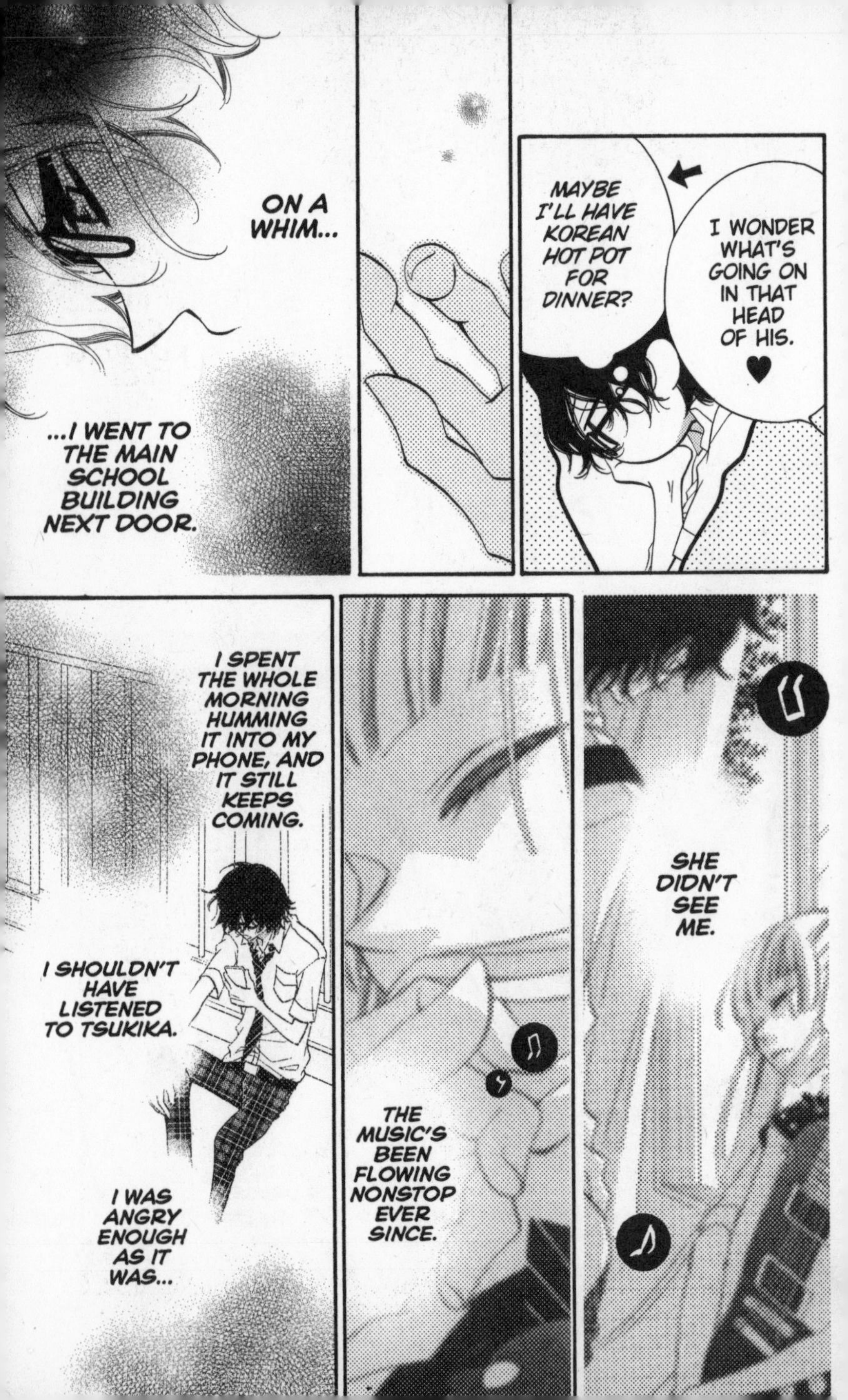
I WONDER WHAT'S GOING ON IN THAT HEAD OF HIS. ♥
MAYBE I'LL HAVE KOREAN HOT POT FOR DINNER?
ON A WHIM...
...I WENT TO THE MAIN SCHOOL BUILDING NEXT DOOR.
SHE DIDN'T SEE ME.
THE MUSIC'S BEEN FLOWING NONSTOP EVER SINCE.
I SPENT THE WHOLE MORNING HUMMING IT INTO MY PHONE, AND IT STILL KEEPS COMING.
I SHOULDN'T HAVE LISTENED TO TSUKIKA.
I WAS ANGRY ENOUGH AS IT WAS...

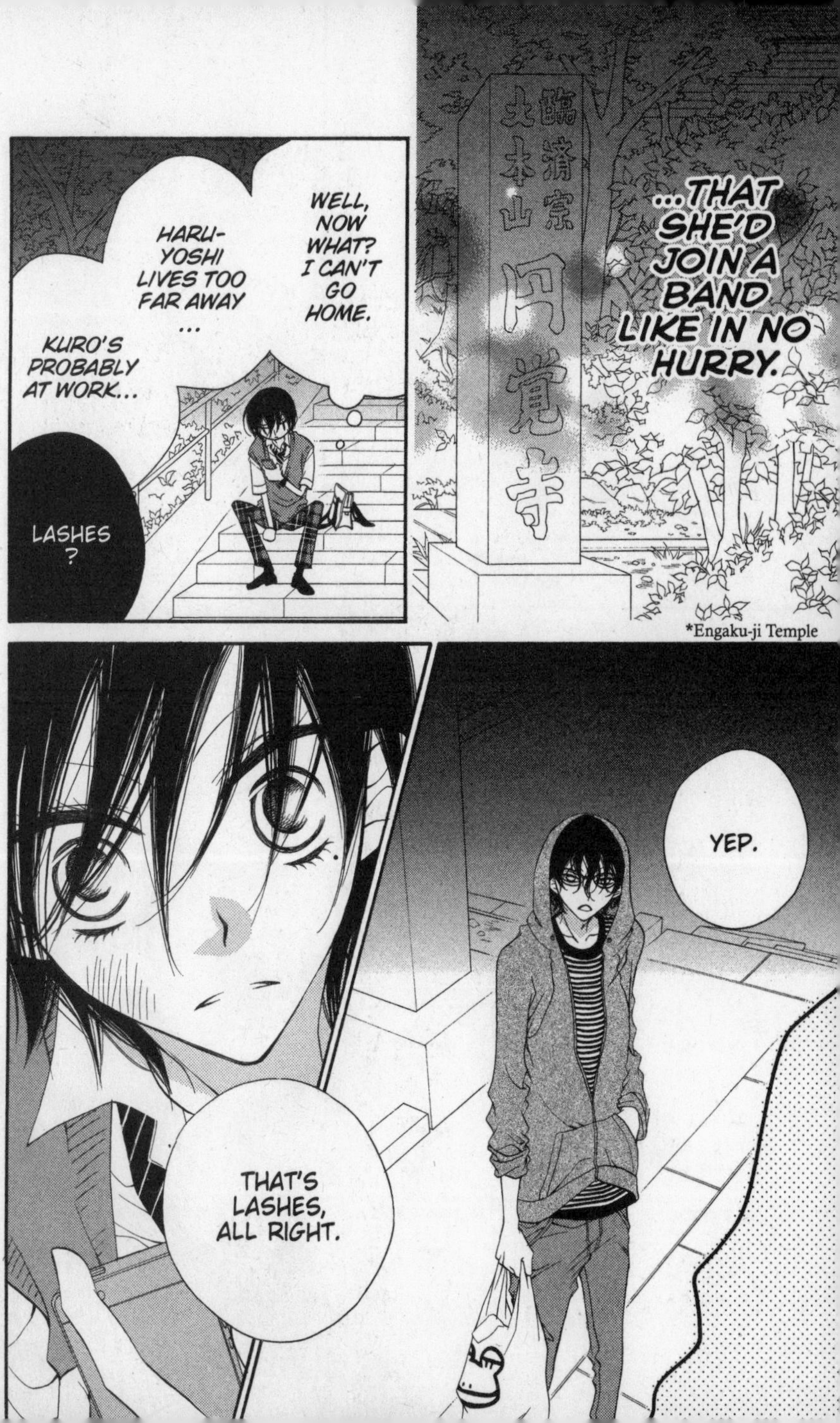
臨済宗
大本山
円覚寺
...THAT SHE'D JOIN A BAND LIKE IN NO HURRY.
WELL, NOW WHAT? I CAN'T GO HOME.
HARU-YOSHI LIVES TOO FAR AWAY ...
KURO'S PROBABLY AT WORK...
LASHES ?
YEP.
THAT'S LASHES, ALL RIGHT.
*Engaku-ji Temple

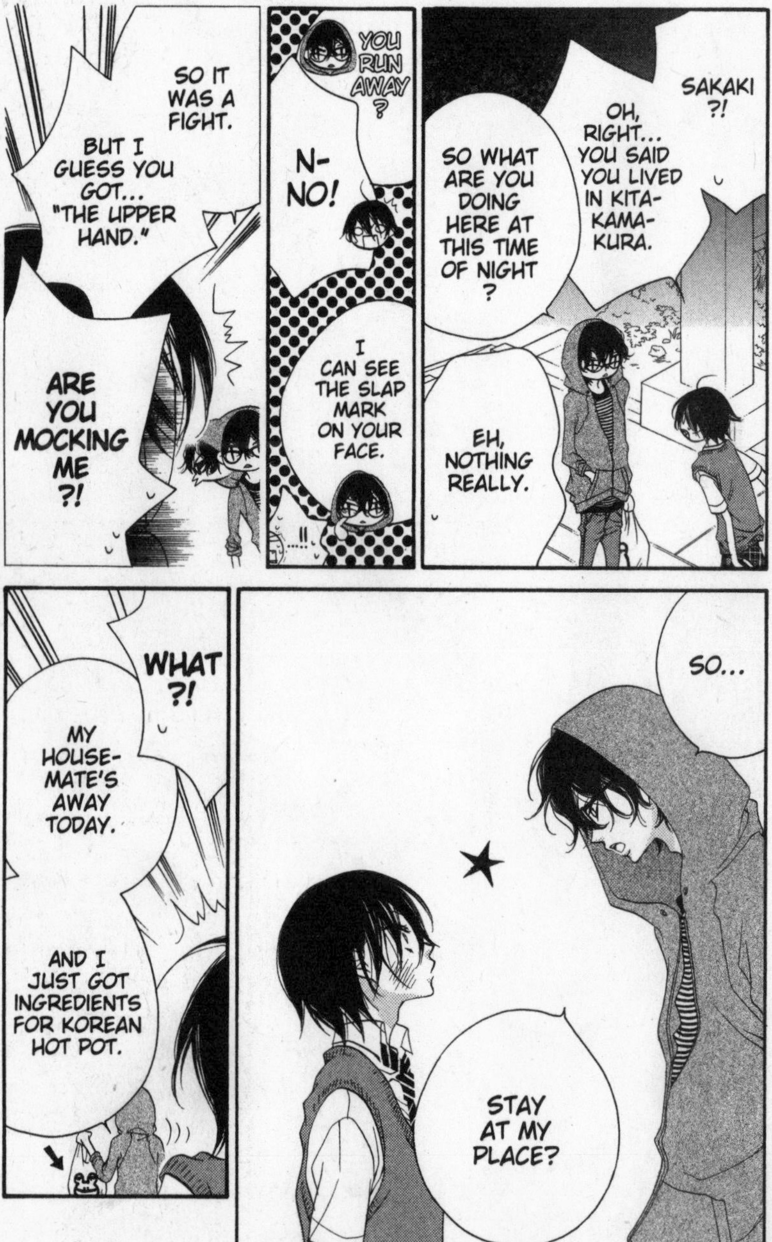
SAKAKI ?!
OH, RIGHT... YOU SAID YOU LIVED IN KITA-KAMA-KURA.
SO WHAT ARE YOU DOING HERE AT THIS TIME OF NIGHT ?
EH, NOTHING REALLY.
YOU RUN AWAY ?
N-NO!
I CAN SEE THE SLAP MARK ON YOUR FACE.
...!!
SO IT WAS A FIGHT.
BUT I GUESS YOU GOT... "THE UPPER HAND."
ARE YOU MOCKING ME ?!
SO...
STAY AT MY PLACE?
WHAT ?!
MY HOUSE-MATE'S AWAY TODAY.
AND I JUST GOT INGREDIENTS FOR KOREAN HOT POT.

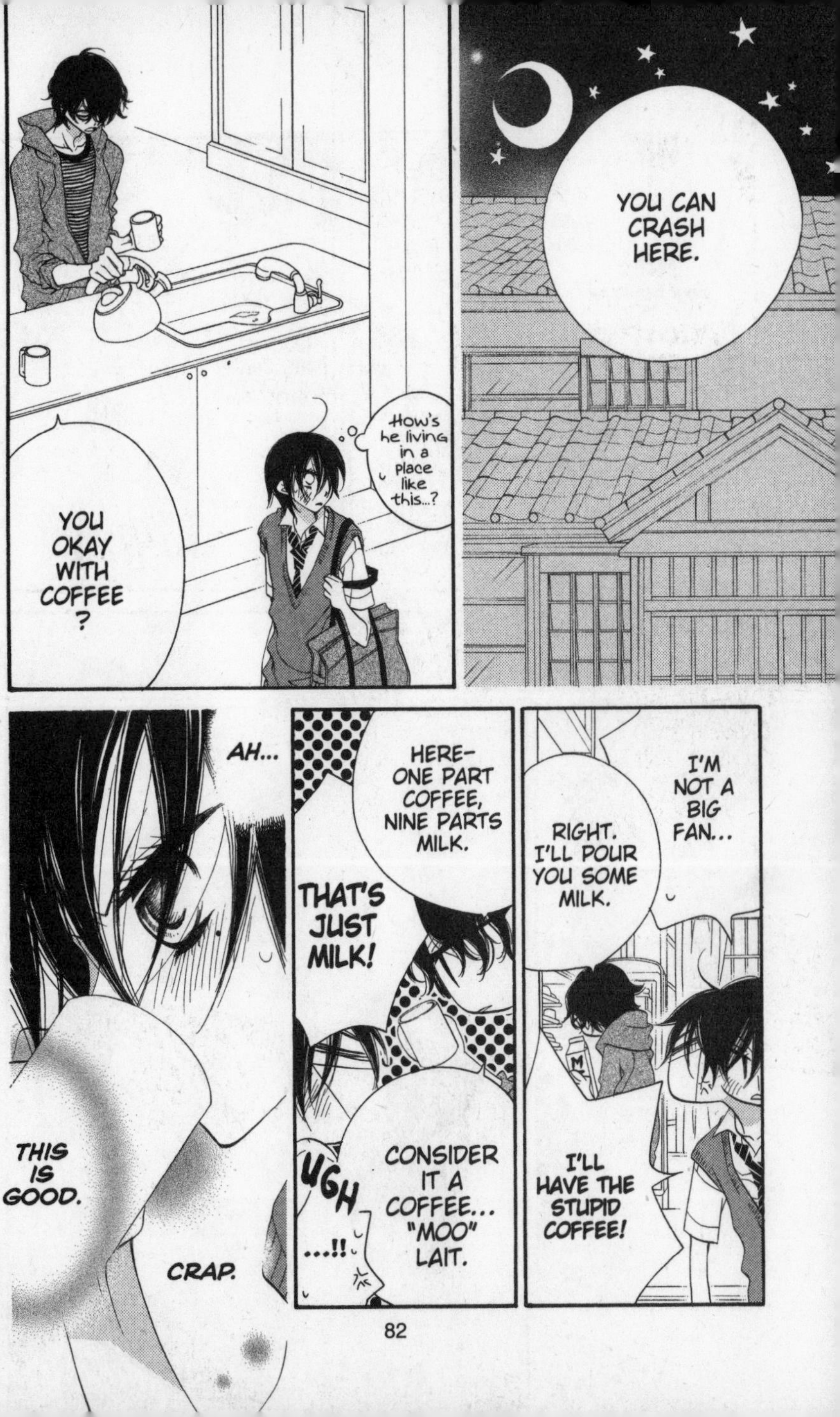
YOU CAN CRASH HERE.
How's he living in a place like this...?
YOU OKAY WITH COFFEE?
I'M NOT A BIG FAN...
RIGHT. I'LL POUR YOU SOME MILK.
I'LL HAVE THE STUPID COFFEE!
HERE- ONE PART COFFEE, NINE PARTS MILK.
THAT'S JUST MILK!
CONSIDER IT A COFFEE... "MOO" LAIT.
UGH
...!!
AH...
THIS IS GOOD.
CRAP.

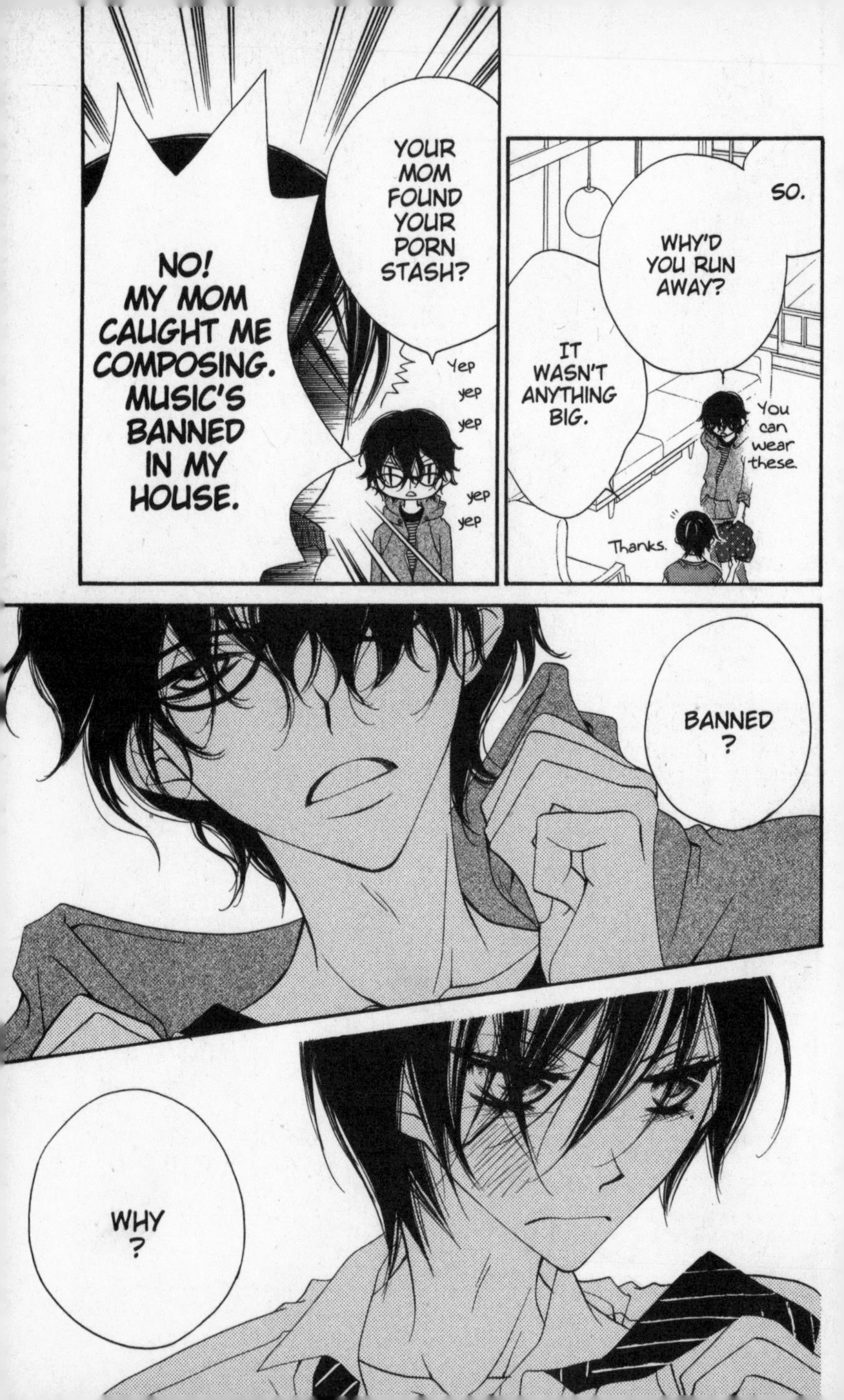
SO.
WHY'D YOU RUN AWAY?
IT WASN'T ANYTHING BIG.
You can wear these.
Thanks.
YOUR MOM FOUND YOUR PORN STASH?
NO! MY MOM CAUGHT ME COMPOSING. MUSIC'S BANNED IN MY HOUSE.
Yep yep yep yep yep
BANNED?
WHY?

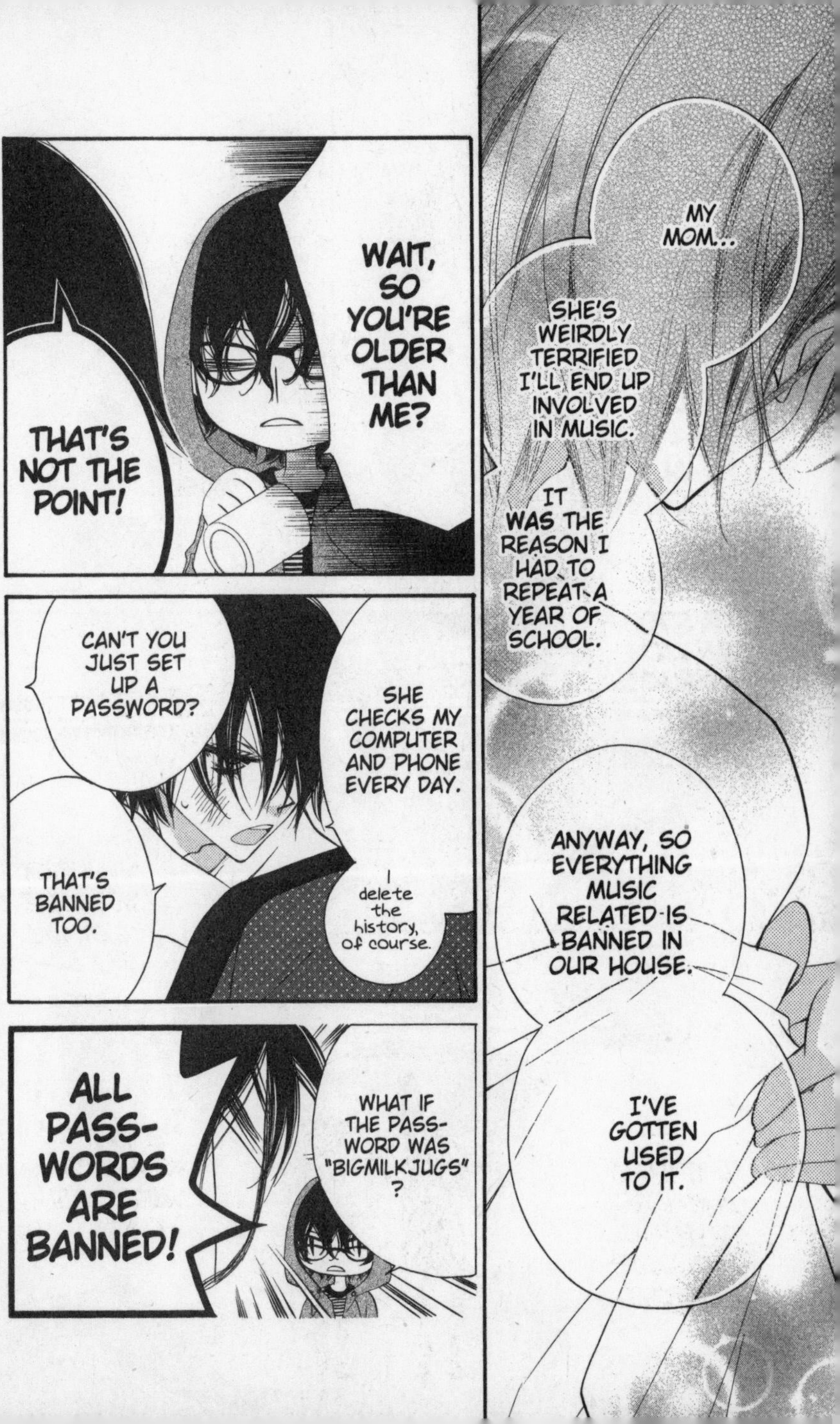
MY MOM...
SHE'S WEIRDLY TERRIFIED I'LL END UP INVOLVED IN MUSIC.
IT WAS THE REASON I HAD TO REPEAT A YEAR OF SCHOOL.
ANYWAY, SO EVERYTHING MUSIC RELATED IS BANNED IN OUR HOUSE.
I'VE GOTTEN USED TO IT.
WAIT, SO YOU'RE OLDER THAN ME?
THAT'S NOT THE POINT!
SHE CHECKS MY COMPUTER AND PHONE EVERY DAY.
I delete the history, of course.
CAN'T YOU JUST SET UP A PASSWORD?
THAT'S BANNED TOO.
WHAT IF THE PASS-WORD WAS "BIGMILKJUGS" ?
ALL PASS-WORDS ARE BANNED!

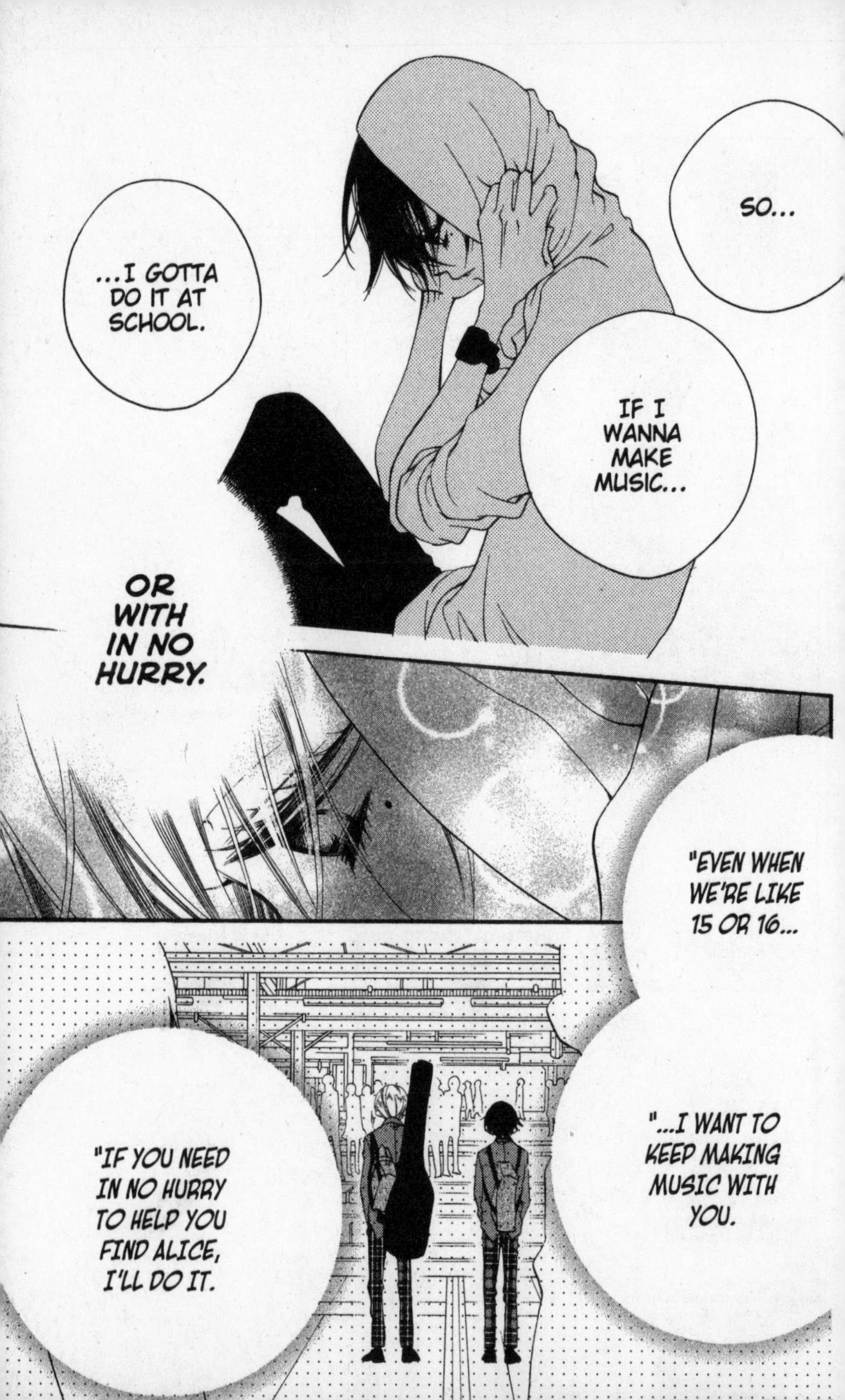
SO...
IF I WANNA MAKE MUSIC...
...I GOTTA DO IT AT SCHOOL.
OR WITH IN NO HURRY.
"EVEN WHEN WE'RE LIKE 15 OR 16...
"...I WANT TO KEEP MAKING MUSIC WITH YOU.
"IF YOU NEED IN NO HURRY TO HELP YOU FIND ALICE, I'LL DO IT.

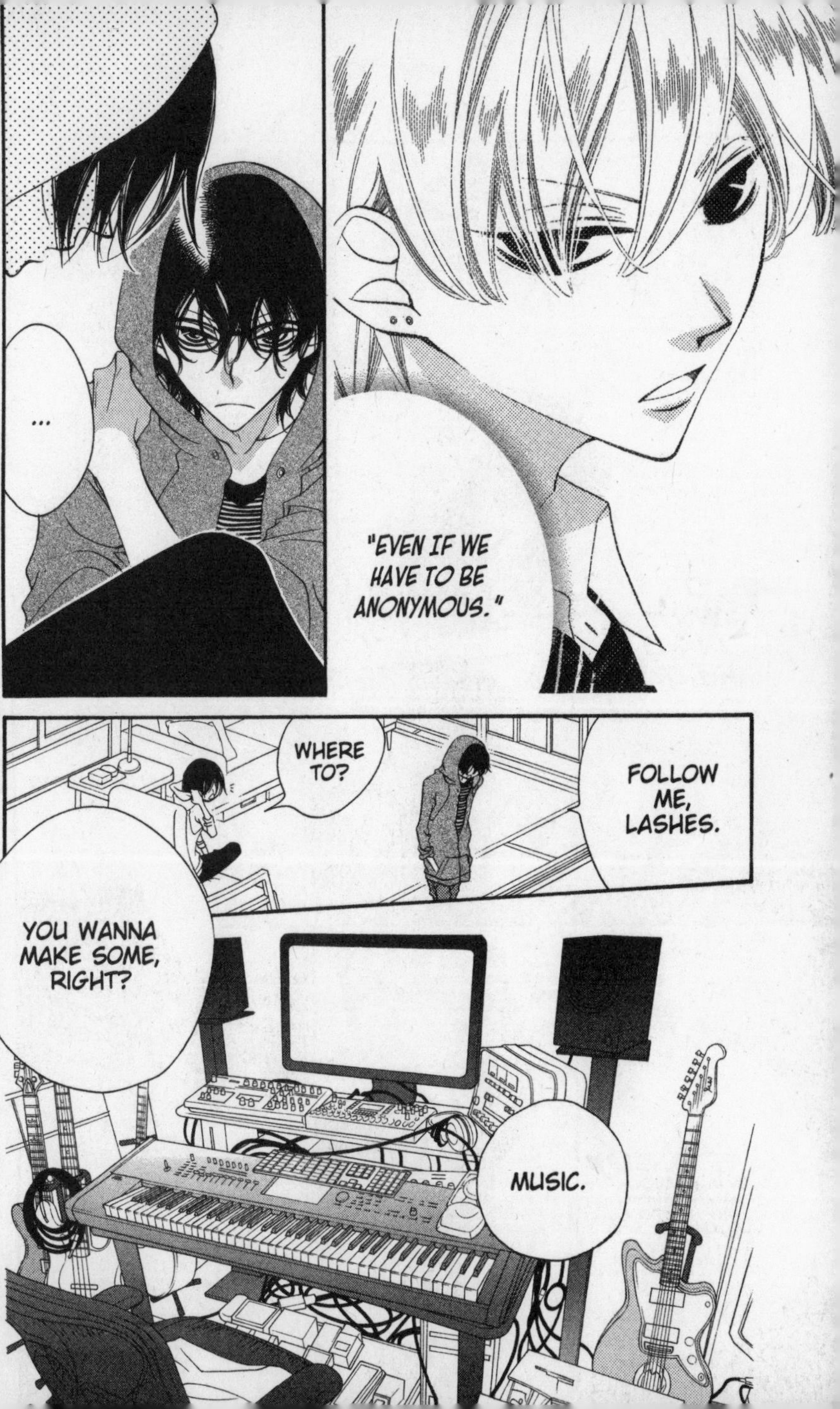
"EVEN IF WE HAVE TO BE ANONYMOUS."
...
FOLLOW ME, LASHES.
WHERE TO?
YOU WANNA MAKE SOME, RIGHT?
MUSIC.

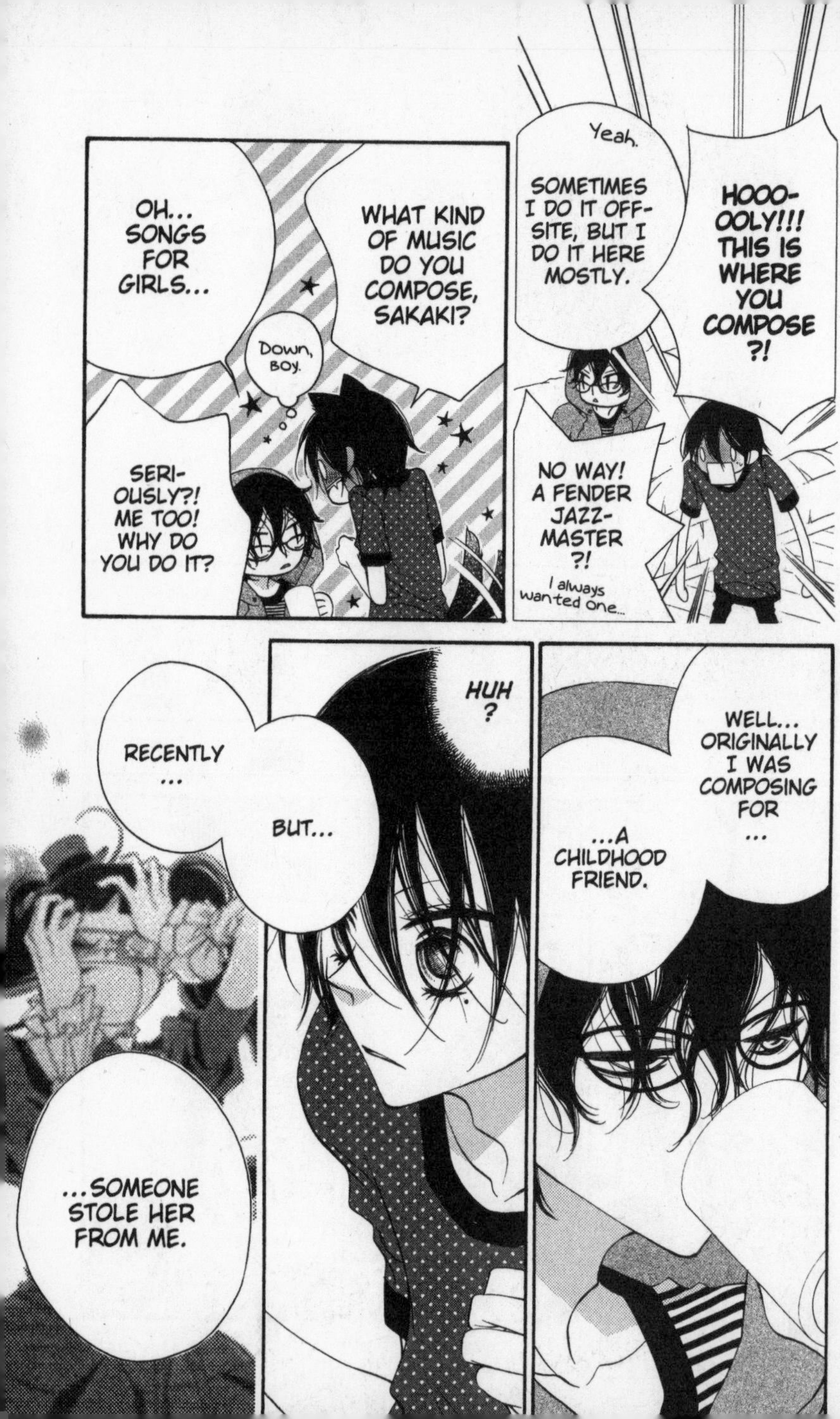
HOOOO-OOLY!!! THIS IS WHERE YOU COMPOSE?!
Yeah.
SOMETIMES I DO IT OFF-SITE, BUT I DO IT HERE MOSTLY.
NO WAY! A FENDER JAZZ-MASTER?!
I always wanted one...
WHAT KIND OF MUSIC DO YOU COMPOSE, SAKAKI?
Down, boy.
OH... SONGS FOR GIRLS...
SERI-OUSLY?! ME TOO! WHY DO YOU DO IT?
WELL... ORIGINALLY I WAS COMPOSING FOR ...
...A CHILDHOOD FRIEND.
HUH?
BUT...
RECENTLY ...
...SOMEONE STOLE HER FROM ME.

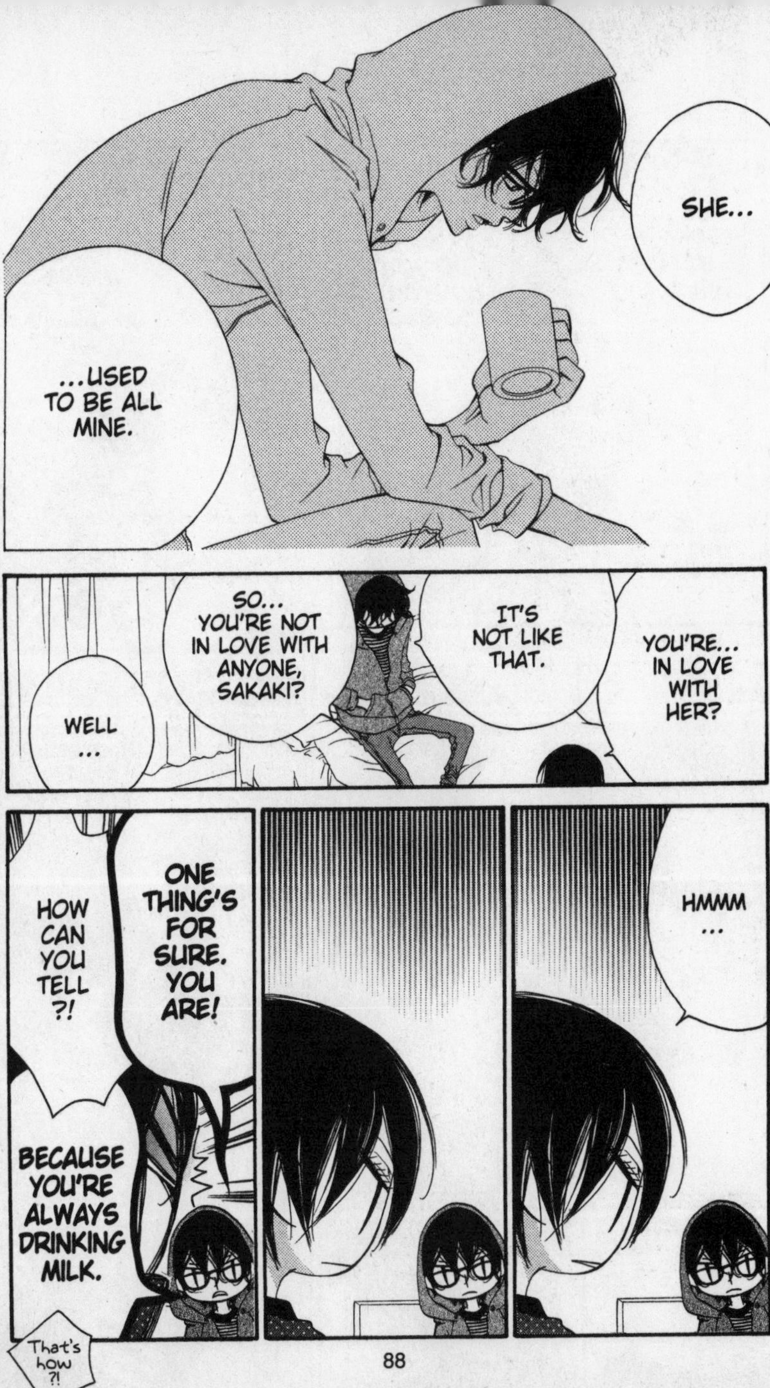
SHE...
...USED TO BE ALL MINE.
YOU'RE... IN LOVE WITH HER?
IT'S NOT LIKE THAT.
SO... YOU'RE NOT IN LOVE WITH ANYONE, SAKAKI?
WELL...
HMMM...
ONE THING'S FOR SURE. YOU ARE!
HOW CAN YOU TELL?!
BECAUSE YOU'RE ALWAYS DRINKING MILK.
That's how?!

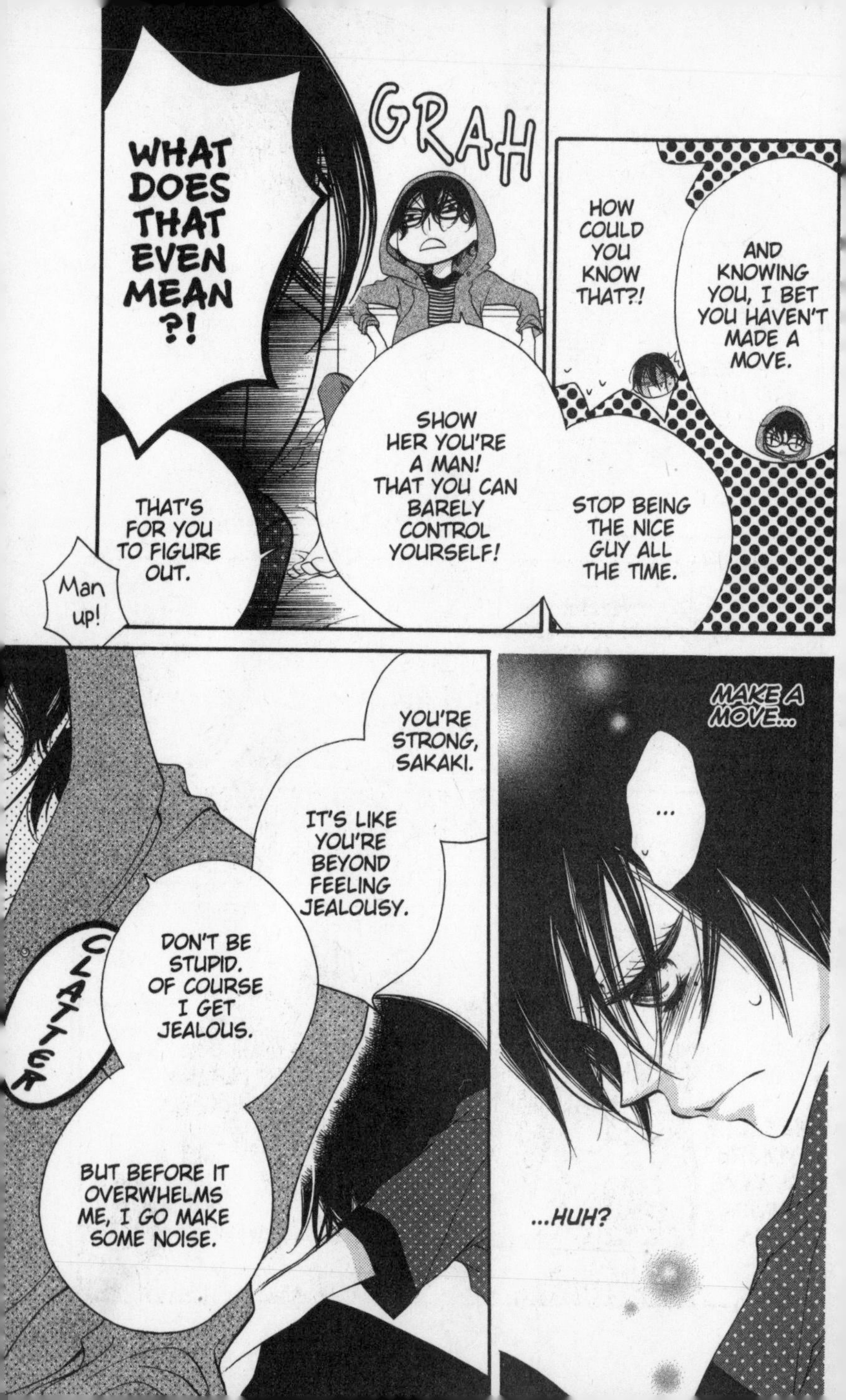
AND KNOWING YOU, I BET YOU HAVEN'T MADE A MOVE.
HOW COULD YOU KNOW THAT?!
STOP BEING THE NICE GUY ALL THE TIME.
GRAH
SHOW HER YOU'RE A MAN! THAT YOU CAN BARELY CONTROL YOURSELF!
WHAT DOES THAT EVEN MEAN?!
THAT'S FOR YOU TO FIGURE OUT.
Man up!
MAKE A MOVE...
...
...HUH?
YOU'RE STRONG, SAKAKI.
IT'S LIKE YOU'RE BEYOND FEELING JEALOUSY.
DON'T BE STUPID. OF COURSE I GET JEALOUS.
CLATTER
BUT BEFORE IT OVERWHELMS ME, I GO MAKE SOME NOISE.

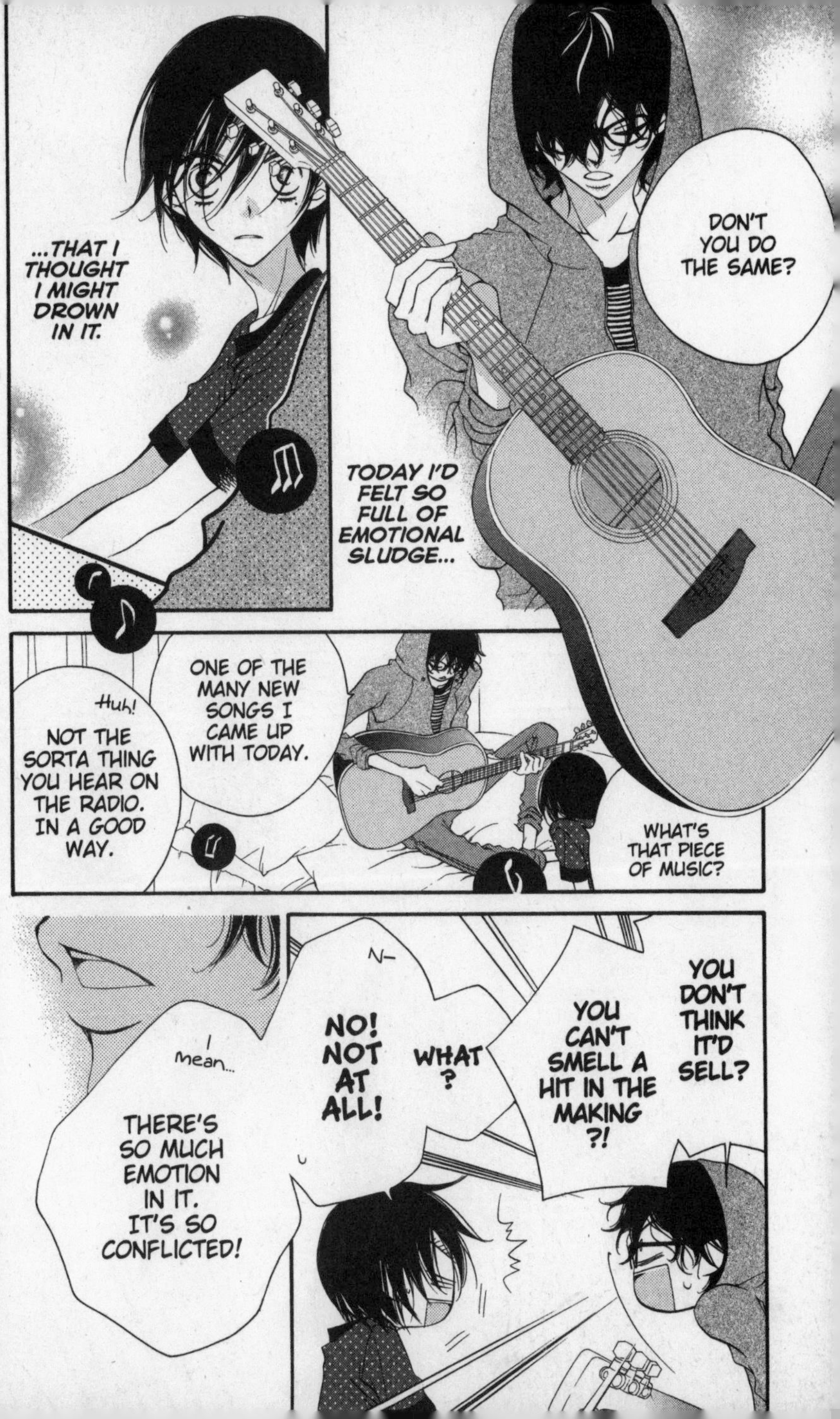
DON'T YOU DO THE SAME?
TODAY I'D FELT SO FULL OF EMOTIONAL SLUDGE...
...THAT I THOUGHT I MIGHT DROWN IN IT.
WHAT'S THAT PIECE OF MUSIC?
ONE OF THE MANY NEW SONGS I CAME UP WITH TODAY.
Huh!
NOT THE SORTA THING YOU HEAR ON THE RADIO. IN A GOOD WAY.
YOU DON'T THINK IT'D SELL?
YOU CAN'T SMELL A HIT IN THE MAKING ?!
WHAT ?
N–
NO! NOT AT ALL!
I mean...
THERE'S SO MUCH EMOTION IN IT. IT'S SO CONFLICTED!

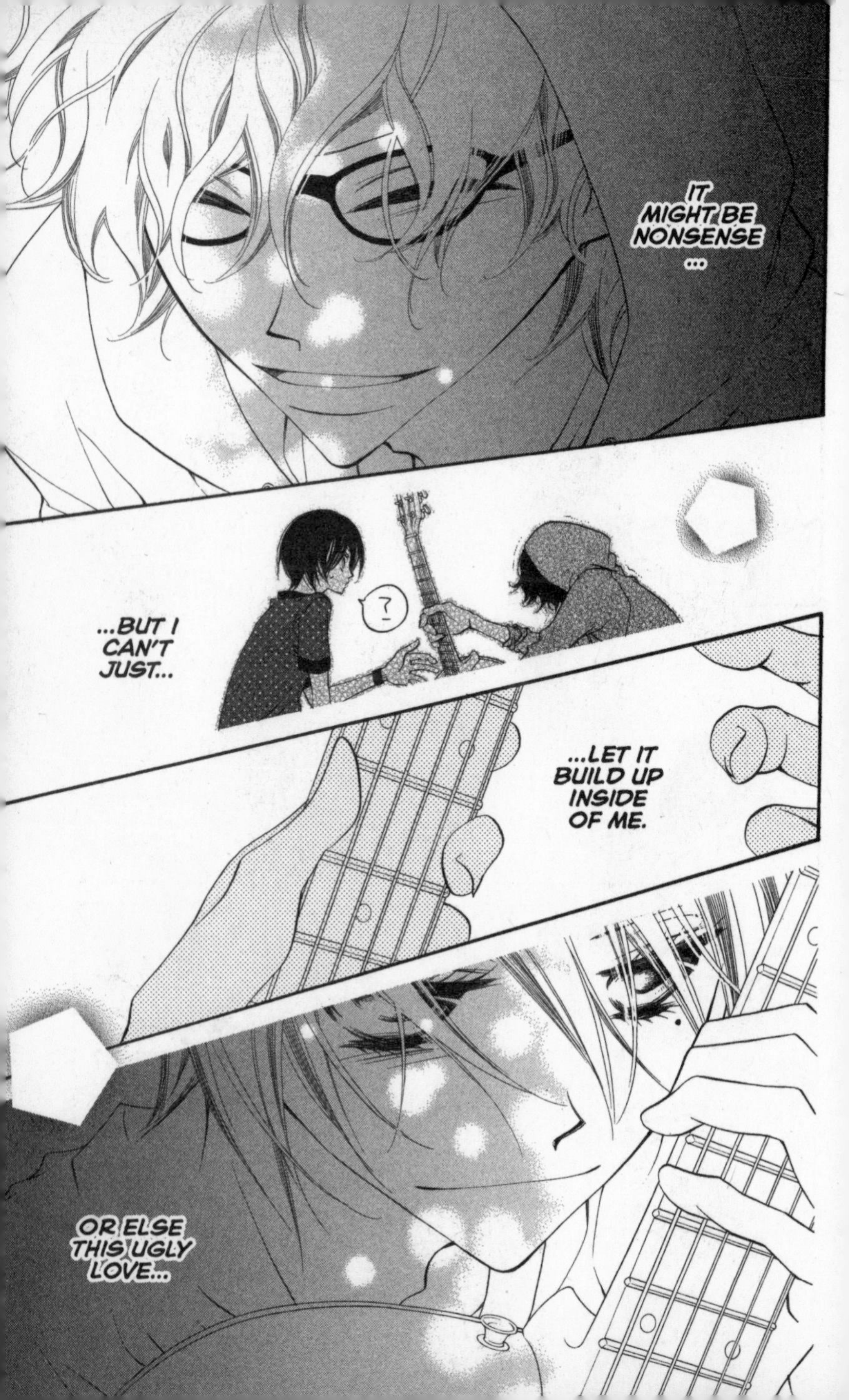
IT MIGHT BE NONSENSE...
?
...BUT I CAN'T JUST...
...LET IT BUILD UP INSIDE OF ME.
OR ELSE THIS UGLY LOVE...

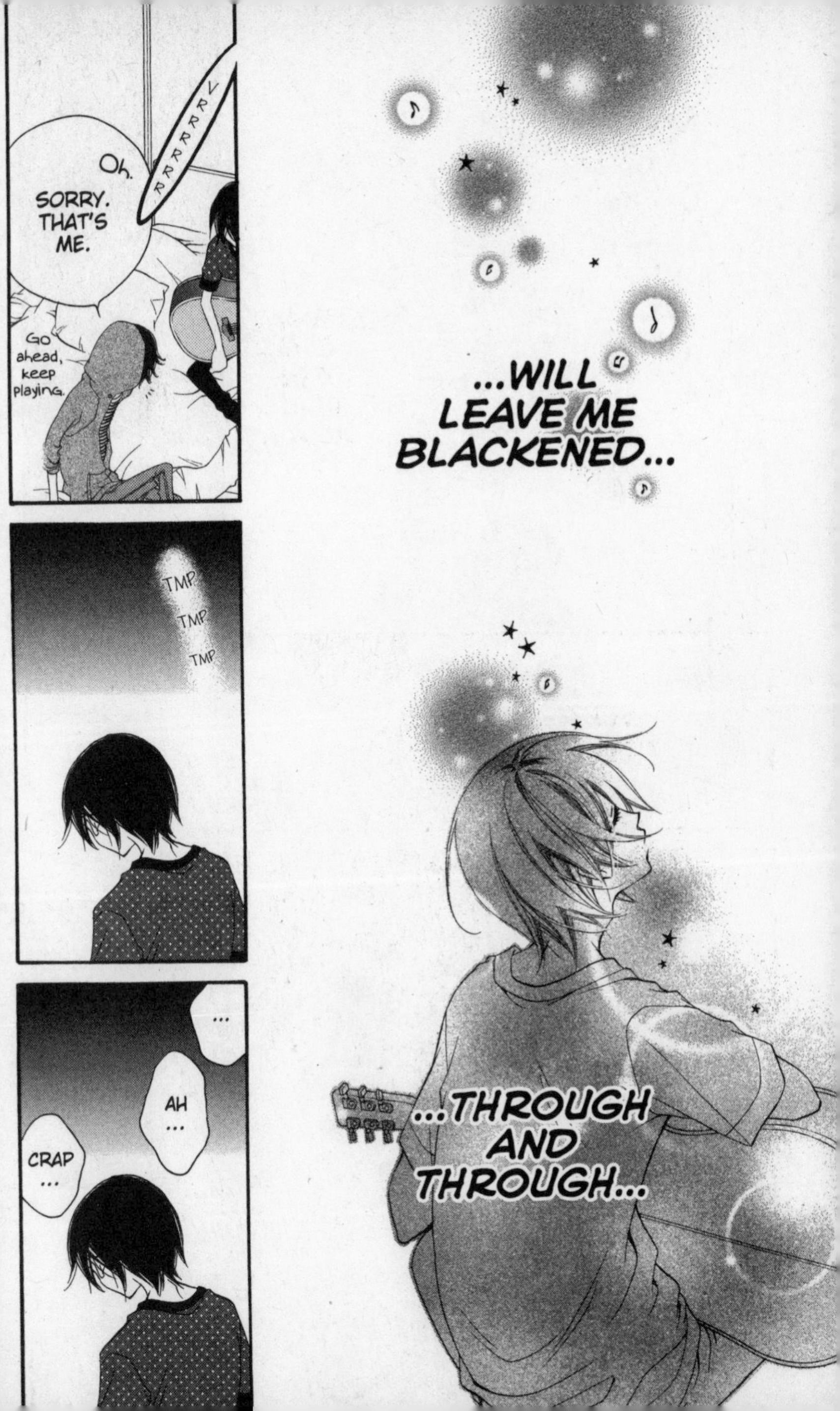
...WILL LEAVE ME BLACKENED...
...THROUGH AND THROUGH...
VRRRRRR
Oh.
SORRY. THAT'S ME.
Go ahead, keep playing.
TMP
TMP
TMP
...
AH...
CRAP...

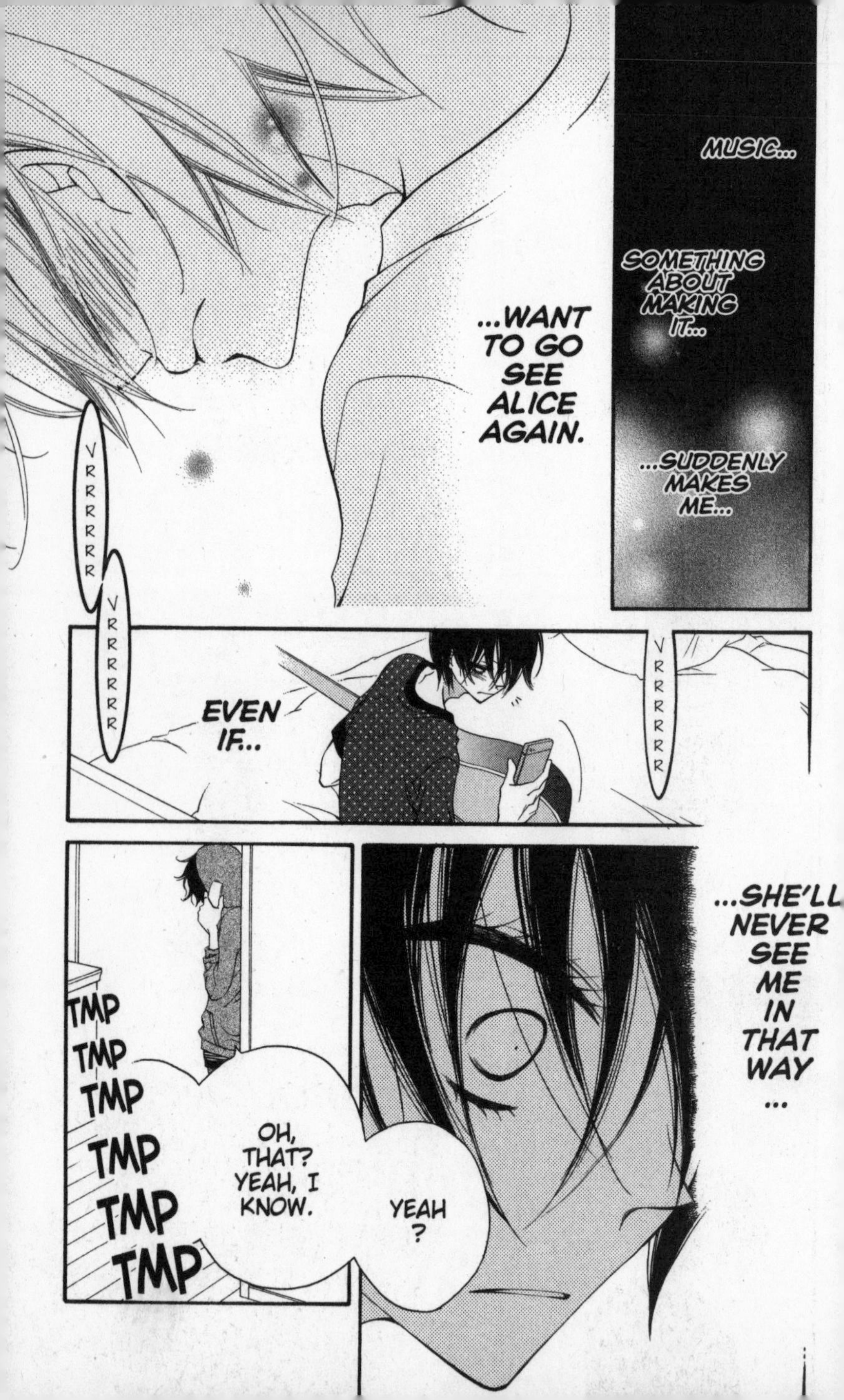
MUSIC...
SOMETHING ABOUT MAKING IT...
...SUDDENLY MAKES ME...
...WANT TO GO SEE ALICE AGAIN.
VRRRRRR
VRRRRRR
VRRRRRR
EVEN IF...
...SHE'LL NEVER SEE ME IN THAT WAY ...
YEAH?
OH, THAT? YEAH, I KNOW.
TMP TMP TMP TMP TMP TMP

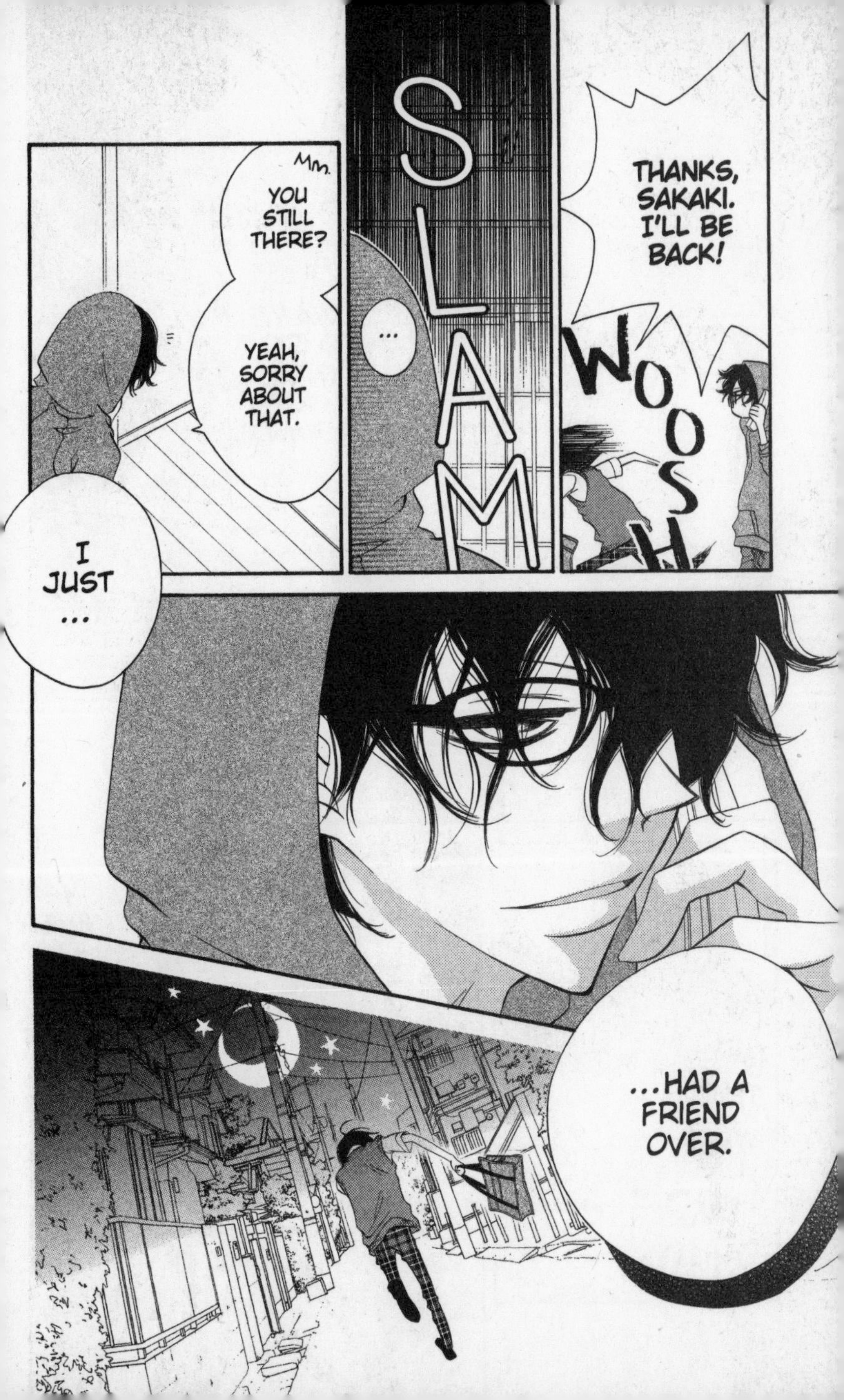
THANKS, SAKAKI. I'LL BE BACK!
WOOSH
SLAM
...
Mm.
YOU STILL THERE?
YEAH, SORRY ABOUT THAT.
I JUST...
...HAD A FRIEND OVER.

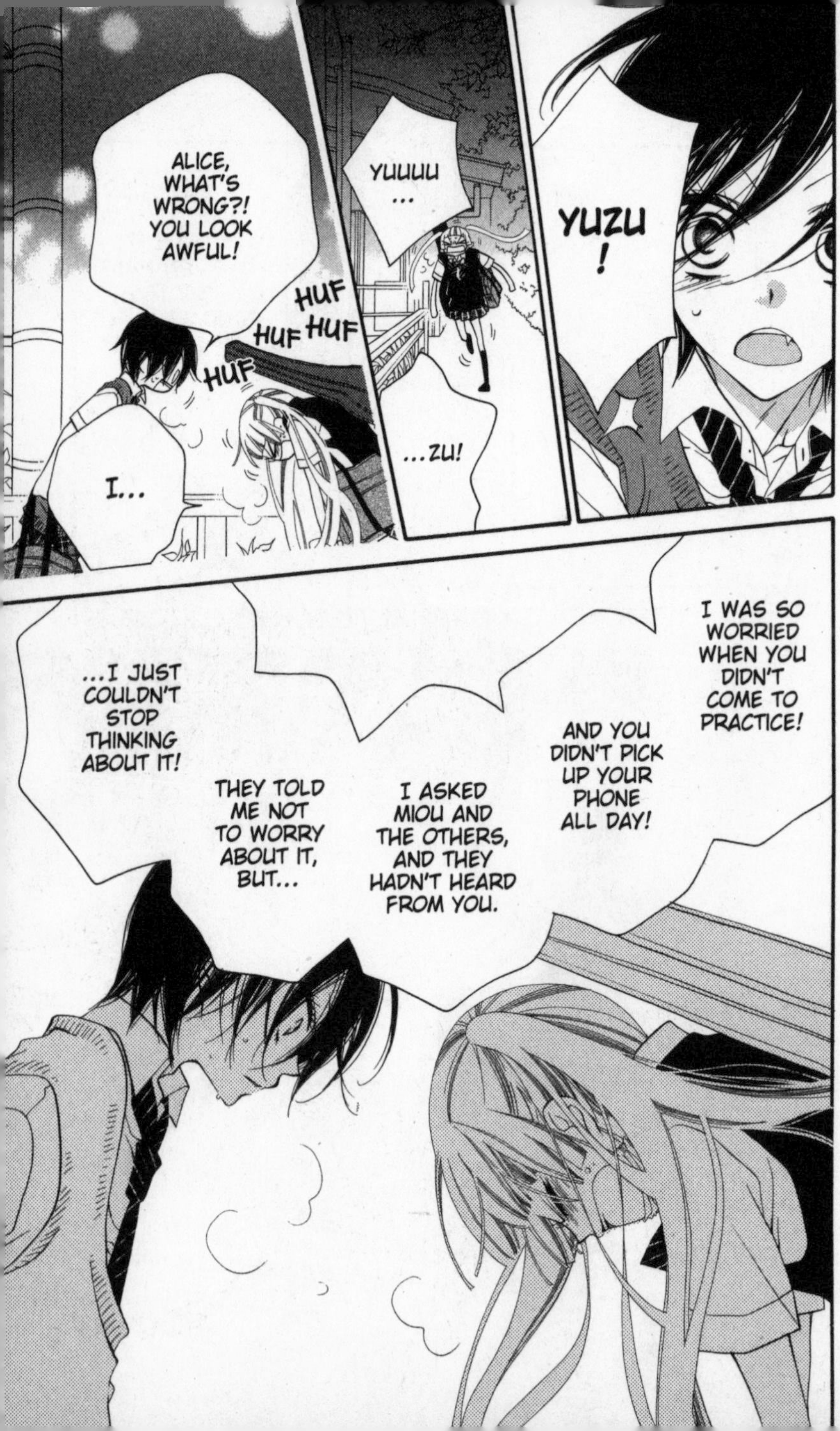
YUZU !
YUUUU ...
...ZU!
ALICE, WHAT'S WRONG?! YOU LOOK AWFUL!
HUF
HUF
HUF
HUF
I...
I WAS SO WORRIED WHEN YOU DIDN'T COME TO PRACTICE!
AND YOU DIDN'T PICK UP YOUR PHONE ALL DAY!
I ASKED MIOU AND THE OTHERS, AND THEY HADN'T HEARD FROM YOU.
THEY TOLD ME NOT TO WORRY ABOUT IT, BUT...
...I JUST COULDN'T STOP THINKING ABOUT IT!

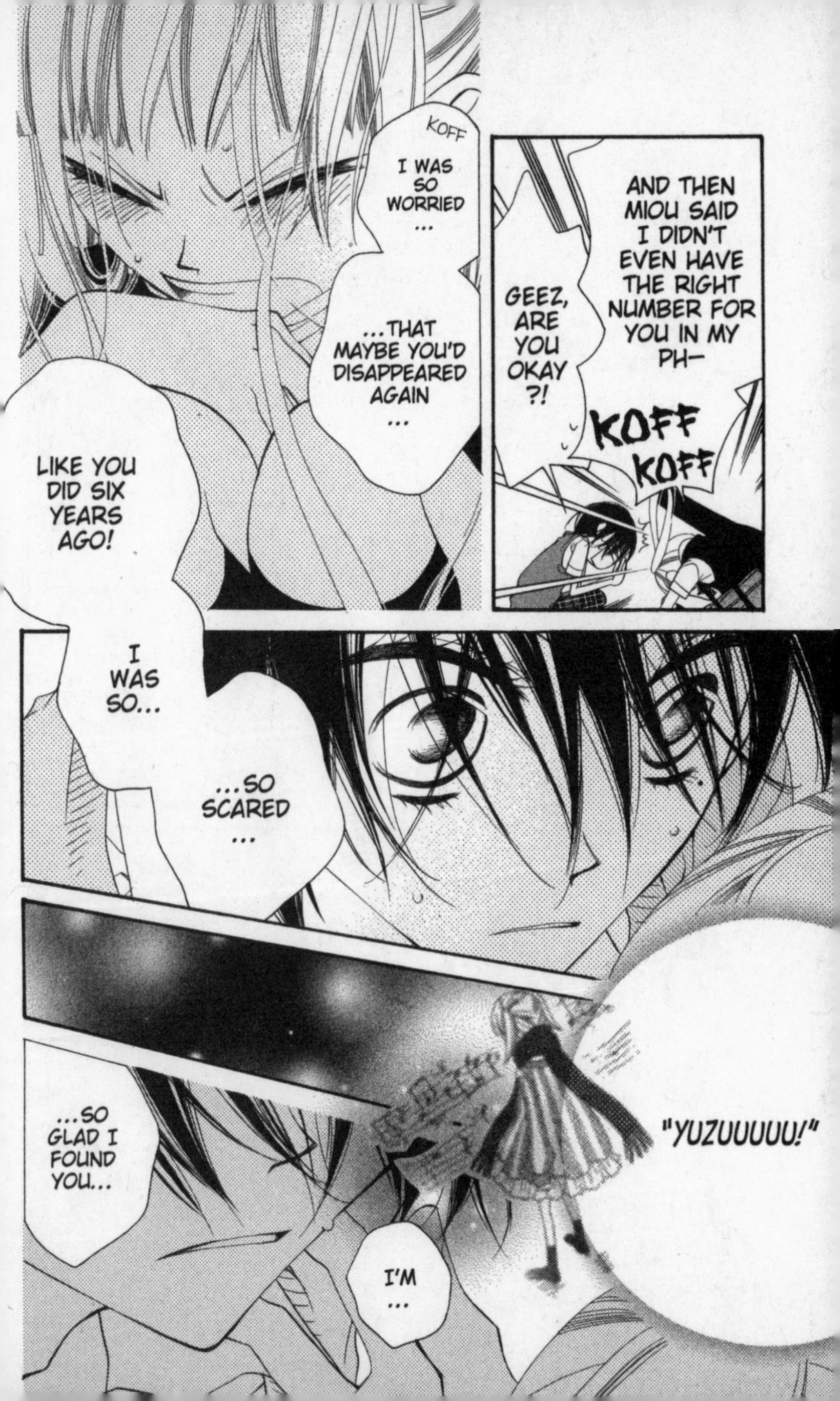

AND THEN MIOU SAID I DIDN'T EVEN HAVE THE RIGHT NUMBER FOR YOU IN MY PH—
GEEZ, ARE YOU OKAY ?!
KOFF KOFF
KOFF
I WAS SO WORRIED ...
...THAT MAYBE YOU'D DISAPPEARED AGAIN ...
LIKE YOU DID SIX YEARS AGO!
I WAS SO...
...SO SCARED ...
"YUZUUUUU!"
...SO GLAD I FOUND YOU...
I'M ...

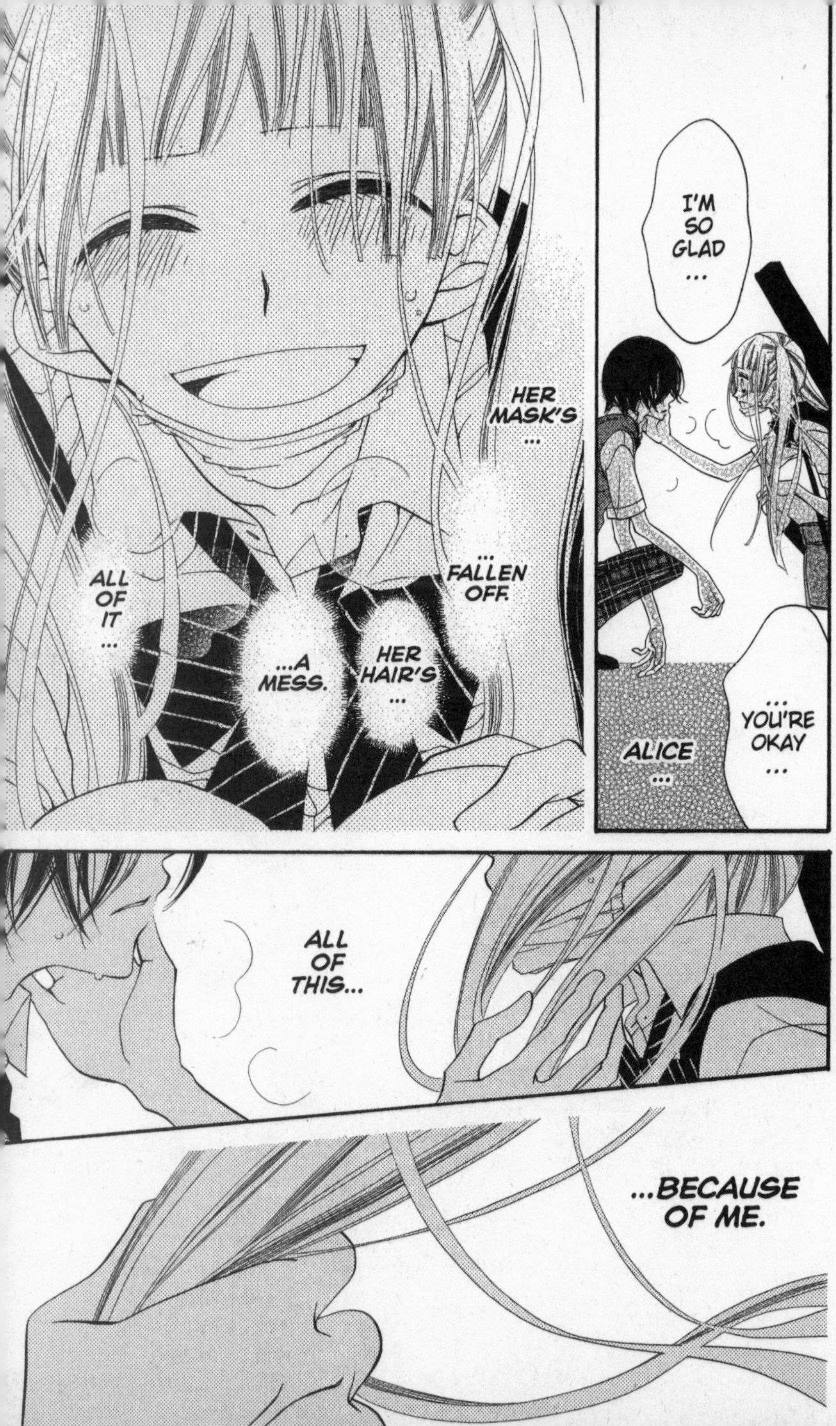
I'M SO GLAD...
...YOU'RE OKAY...
ALICE...
HER MASK'S...
...FALLEN OFF.
HER HAIR'S...
...A MESS.
ALL OF IT...
ALL OF THIS...
...BECAUSE OF ME.

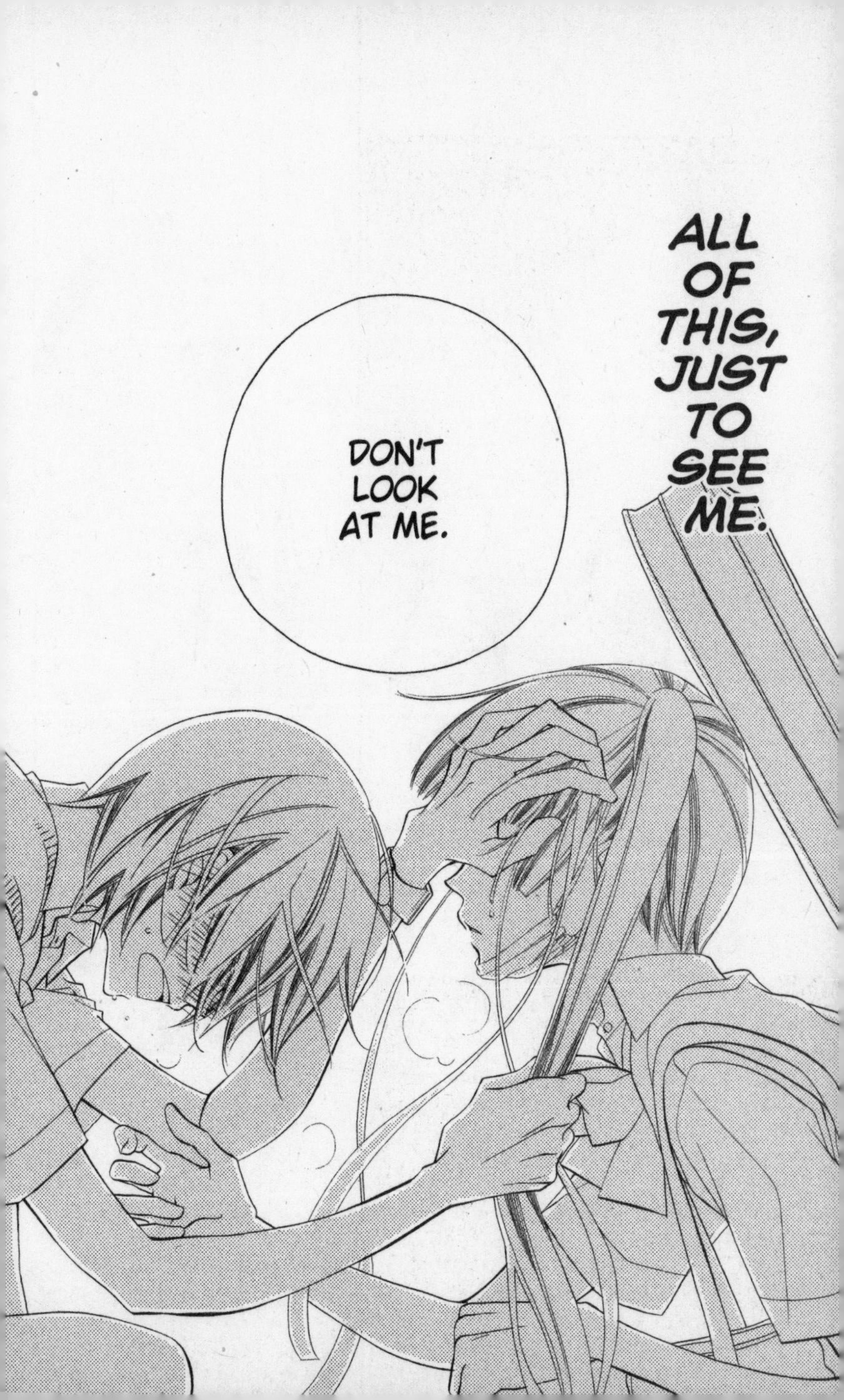
ALL OF THIS, JUST TO SEE ME.
DON'T LOOK AT ME.

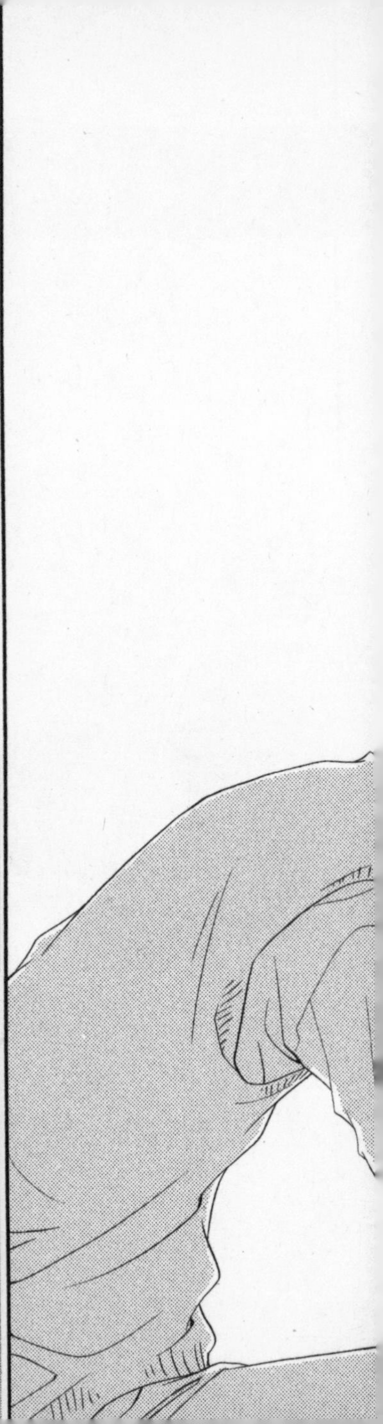

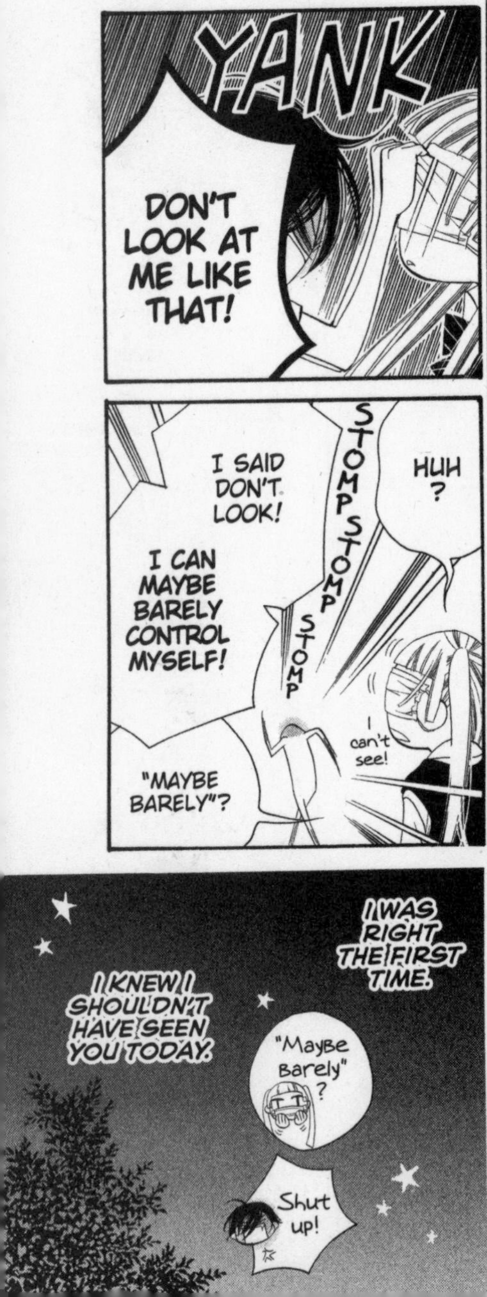
YANK
DON'T LOOK AT ME LIKE THAT!
HUH?
STOMP STOMP
STOMP
I SAID DON'T LOOK!
I CAN MAYBE BARELY CONTROL MYSELF!
STOMP
I can't see!
"MAYBE BARELY"?
I WAS RIGHT THE FIRST TIME.
I KNEW I SHOULDN'T HAVE SEEN YOU TODAY.
"Maybe Barely"?
Shut up!

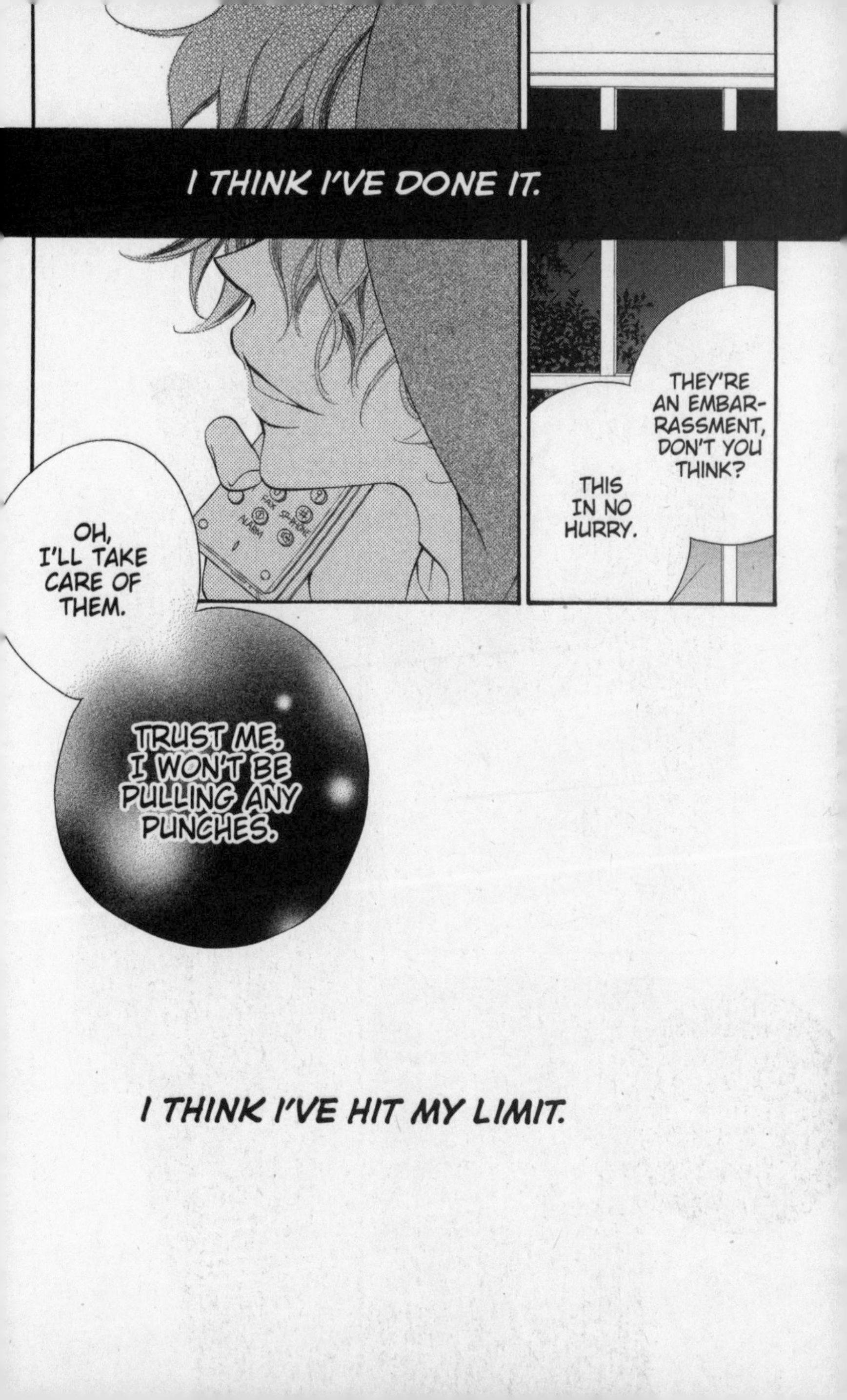
I THINK I'VE DONE IT.
THEY'RE AN EMBARRASSMENT, DON'T YOU THINK?
THIS IN NO HURRY.
OH, I'LL TAKE CARE OF THEM.
TRUST ME. I WON'T BE PULLING ANY PUNCHES.
I THINK I'VE HIT MY LIMIT.

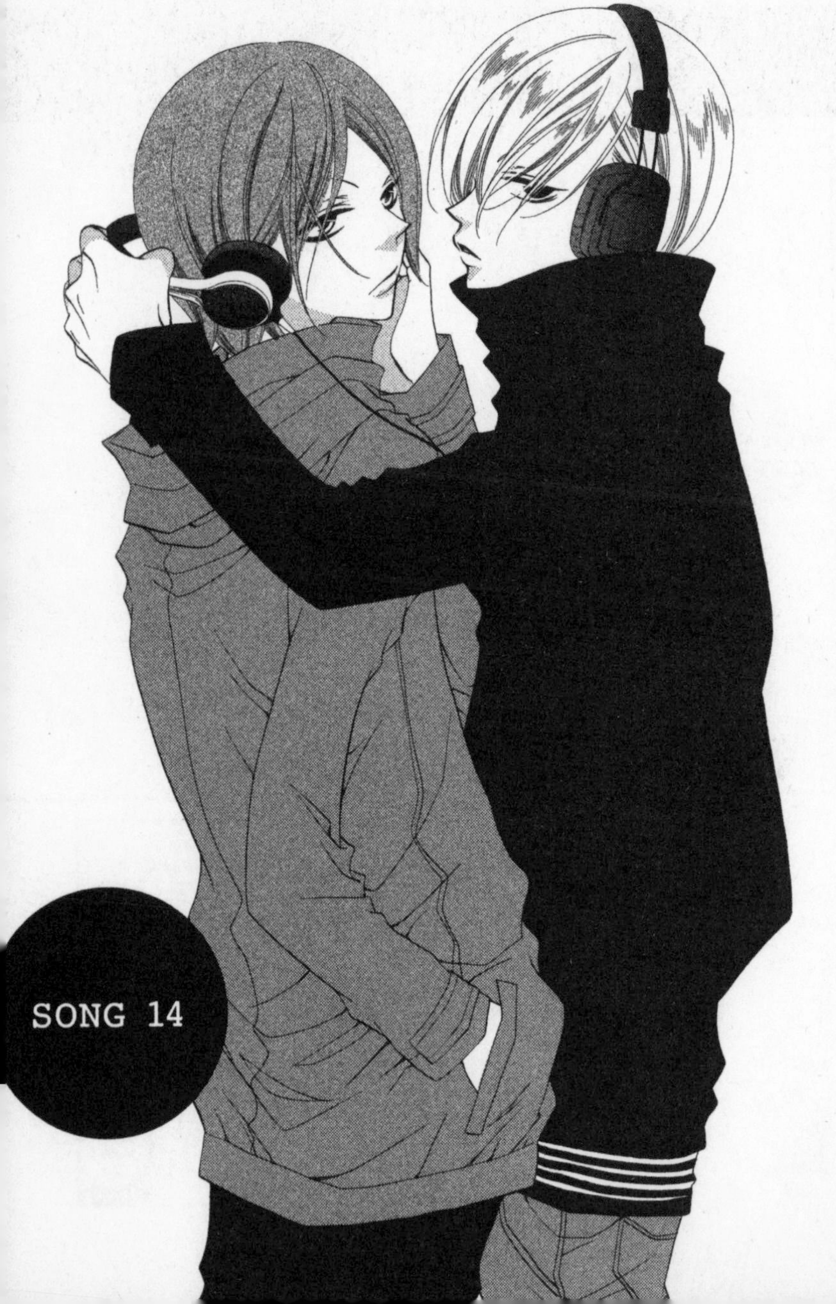
SONG 14

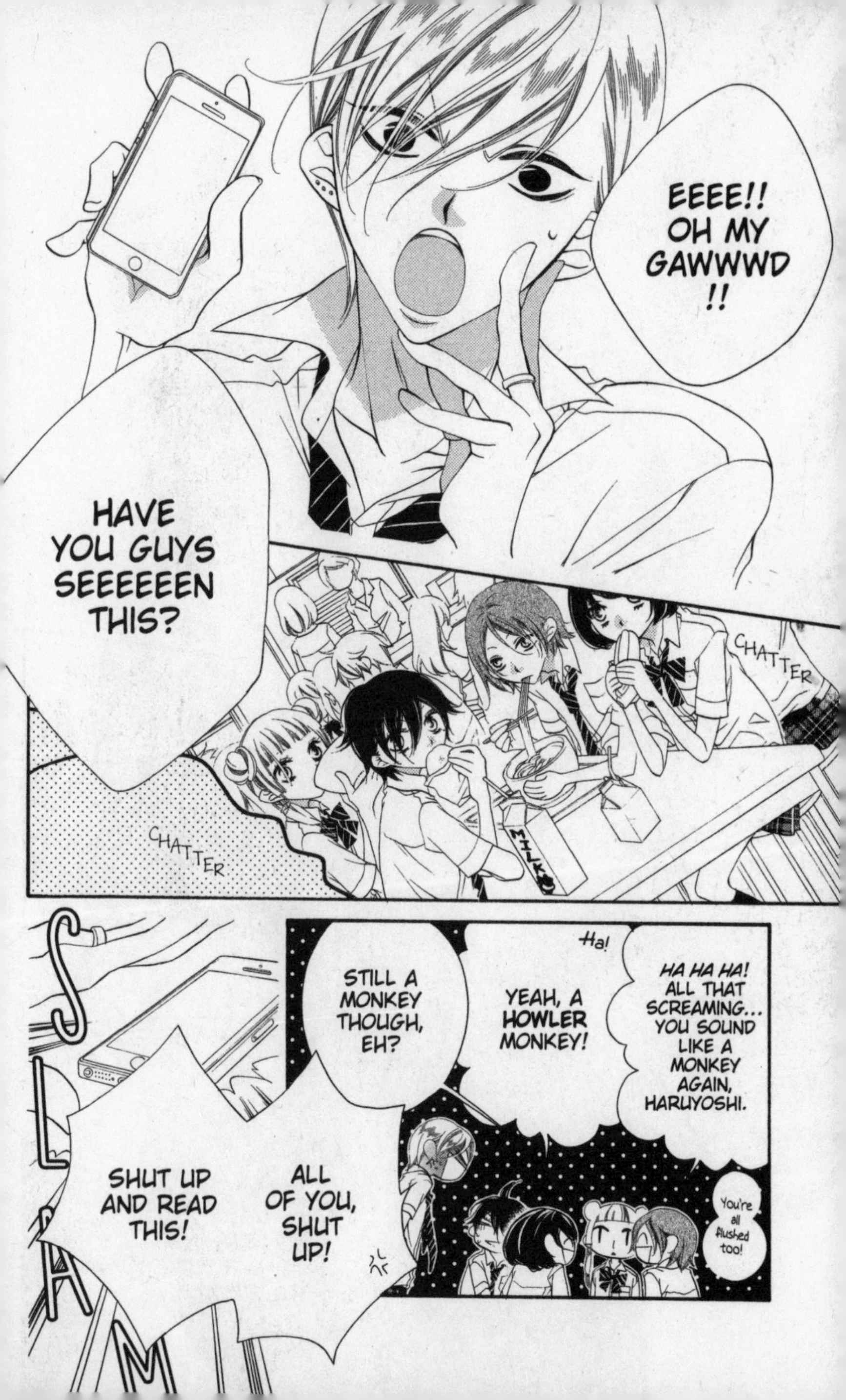
EEEE!! OH MY GAWWWD !!
HAVE YOU GUYS SEEEEEEN THIS?
CHATTER
CHATTER
MILK
HA HA HA! ALL THAT SCREAMING... YOU SOUND LIKE A MONKEY AGAIN, HARUYOSHI.
Ha!
YEAH, A HOWLER MONKEY!
STILL A MONKEY THOUGH, EH?
You're all flushed too!
ALL OF YOU, SHUT UP!
SHUT UP AND READ THIS!
SLAM

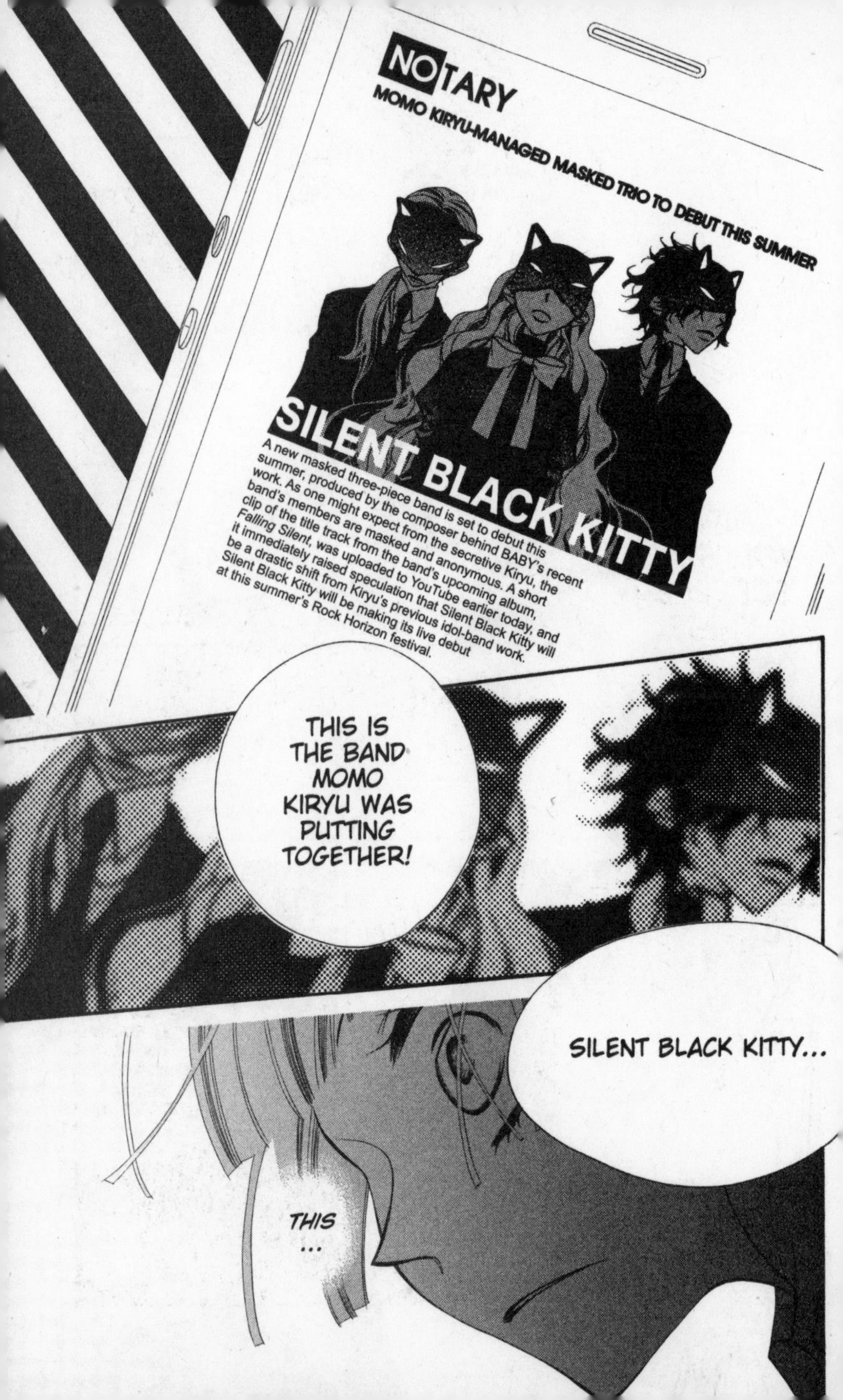
NOTARY
MOMO KIRYU-MANAGED MASKED TRIO TO DEBUT THIS SUMMER
SILENT BLACK KITTY
A new masked three-piece band is set to debut this summer, produced by the composer behind BABY's recent work. As one might expect from the secretive Kiryu, the band's members are masked and anonymous. A short clip of the title track from the band's upcoming album, Falling Silent, was uploaded to YouTube earlier today, and it immediately raised speculation that Silent Black Kitty will be a drastic shift from Kiryu's previous idol-band work. Silent Black Kitty will be making its live debut at this summer's Rock Horizon festival.
THIS IS THE BAND MOMO KIRYU WAS PUTTING TOGETHER!
SILENT BLACK KITTY...
THIS ...

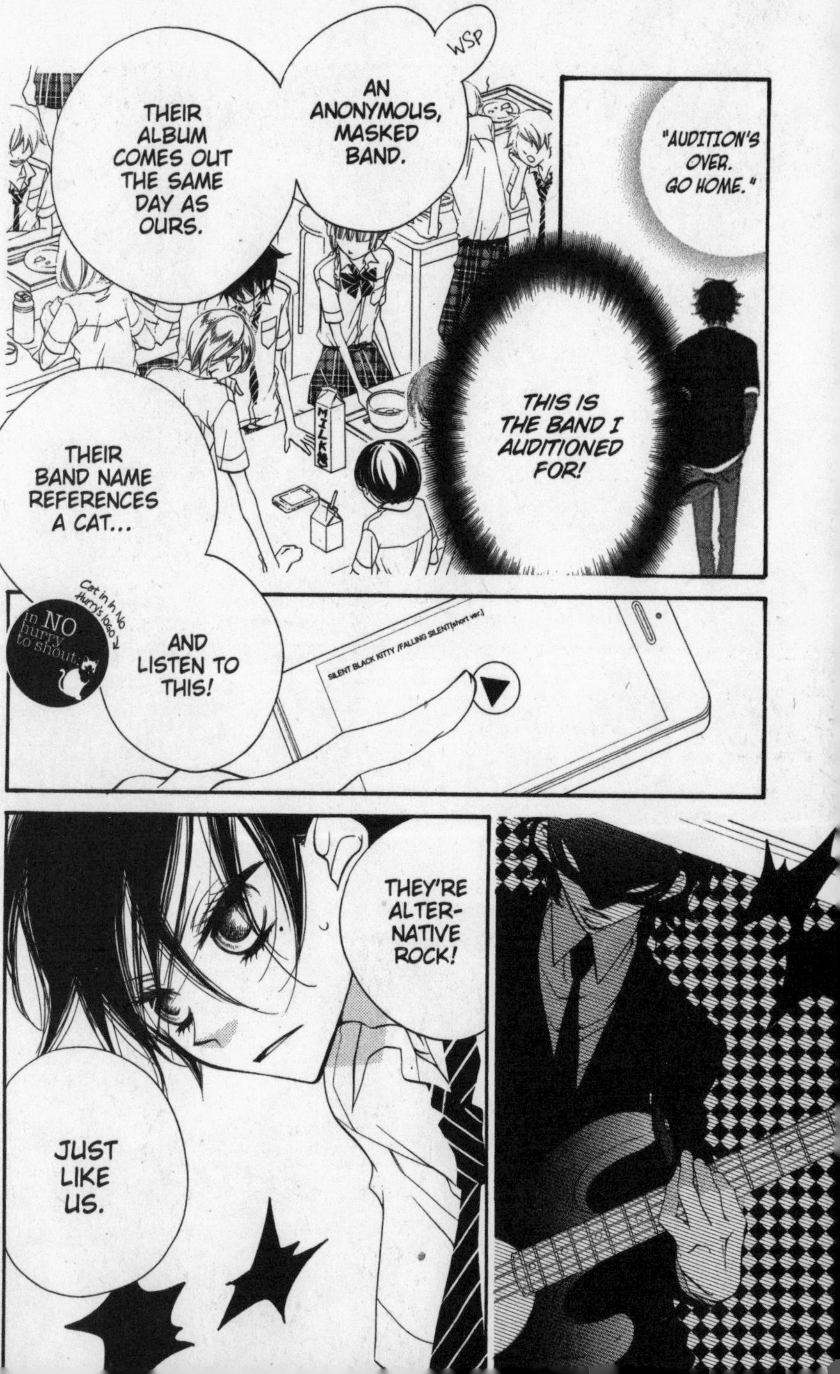
"AUDITION'S OVER. GO HOME."
THIS IS THE BAND I AUDITIONED FOR!
WSP
AN ANONYMOUS, MASKED BAND.
THEIR ALBUM COMES OUT THE SAME DAY AS OURS.
MILK
THEIR BAND NAME REFERENCES A CAT...
SILENT BLACK KITTY /FALLING SILENT[short ver.]
AND LISTEN TO THIS!
Cat in In No Hurry's logo
in NO hurry to shout;
THEY'RE ALTER-NATIVE ROCK!
JUST LIKE US.

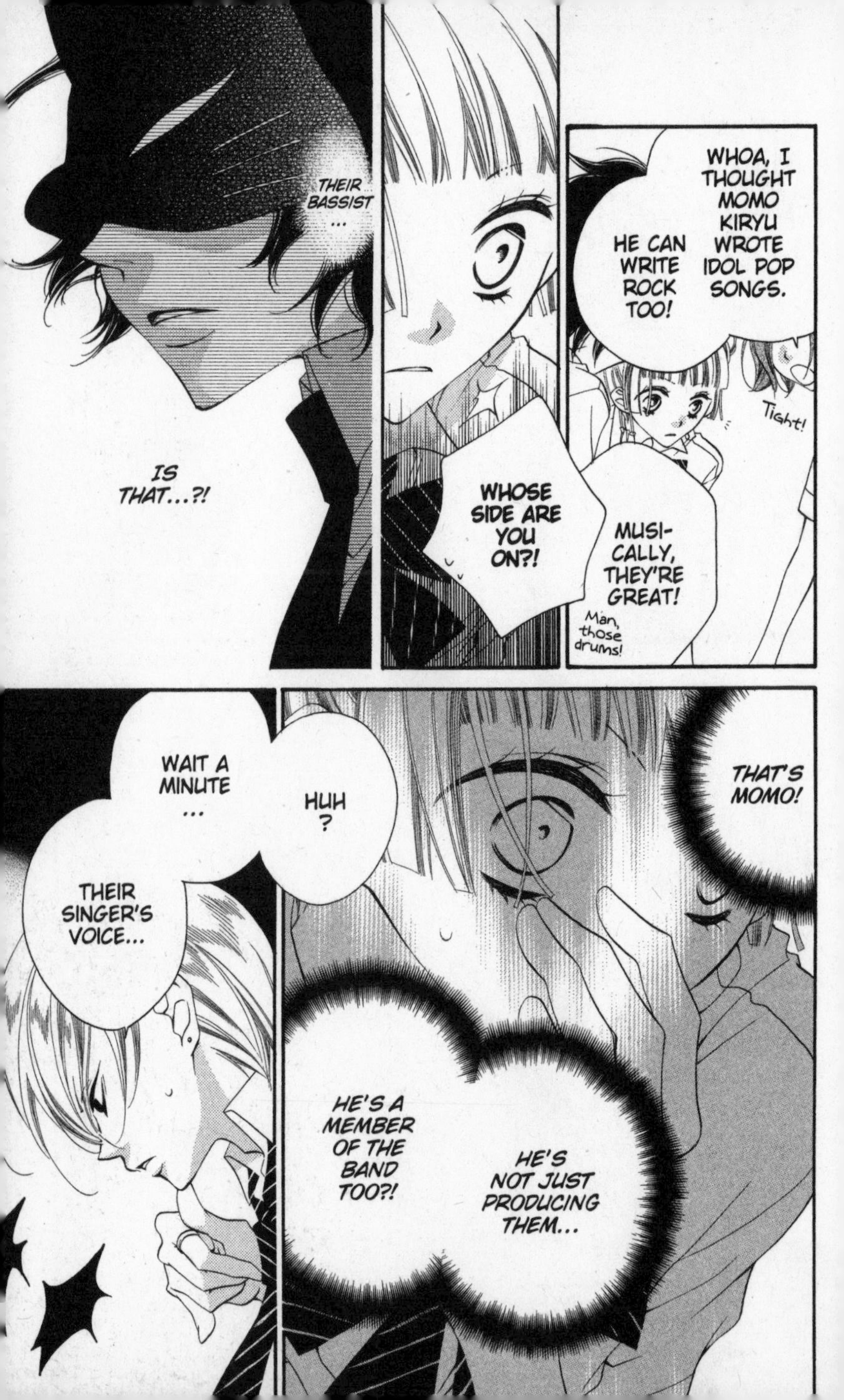
WHOA, I THOUGHT MOMO KIRYU WROTE IDOL POP SONGS.
HE CAN WRITE ROCK TOO!
Tight!
MUSI-CALLY, THEY'RE GREAT!
Man, those drums!
WHOSE SIDE ARE YOU ON?!
THEIR BASSIST ...
IS THAT...?!
THAT'S MOMO!
HUH ?
HE'S NOT JUST PRODUCING THEM...
HE'S A MEMBER OF THE BAND TOO?!
WAIT A MINUTE ...
THEIR SINGER'S VOICE...

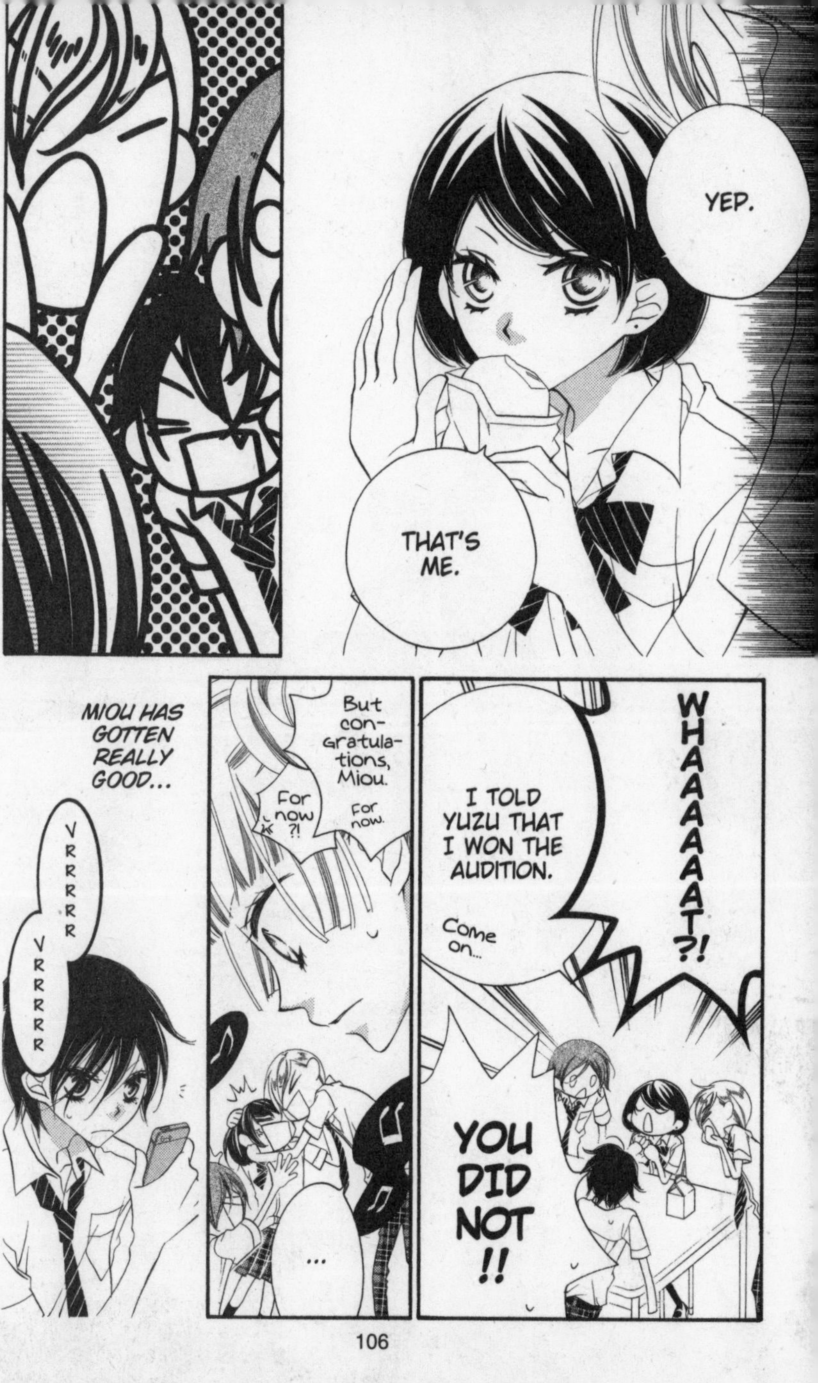
YEP.
THAT'S ME.
WHAAAAAAAT?!
I TOLD YUZU THAT I WON THE AUDITION.
Come on...
YOU DID NOT!!
But congratulations, Miou.
For now.
For now?!
...
MIOU HAS GOTTEN REALLY GOOD...
VRRRRR VRRRRR

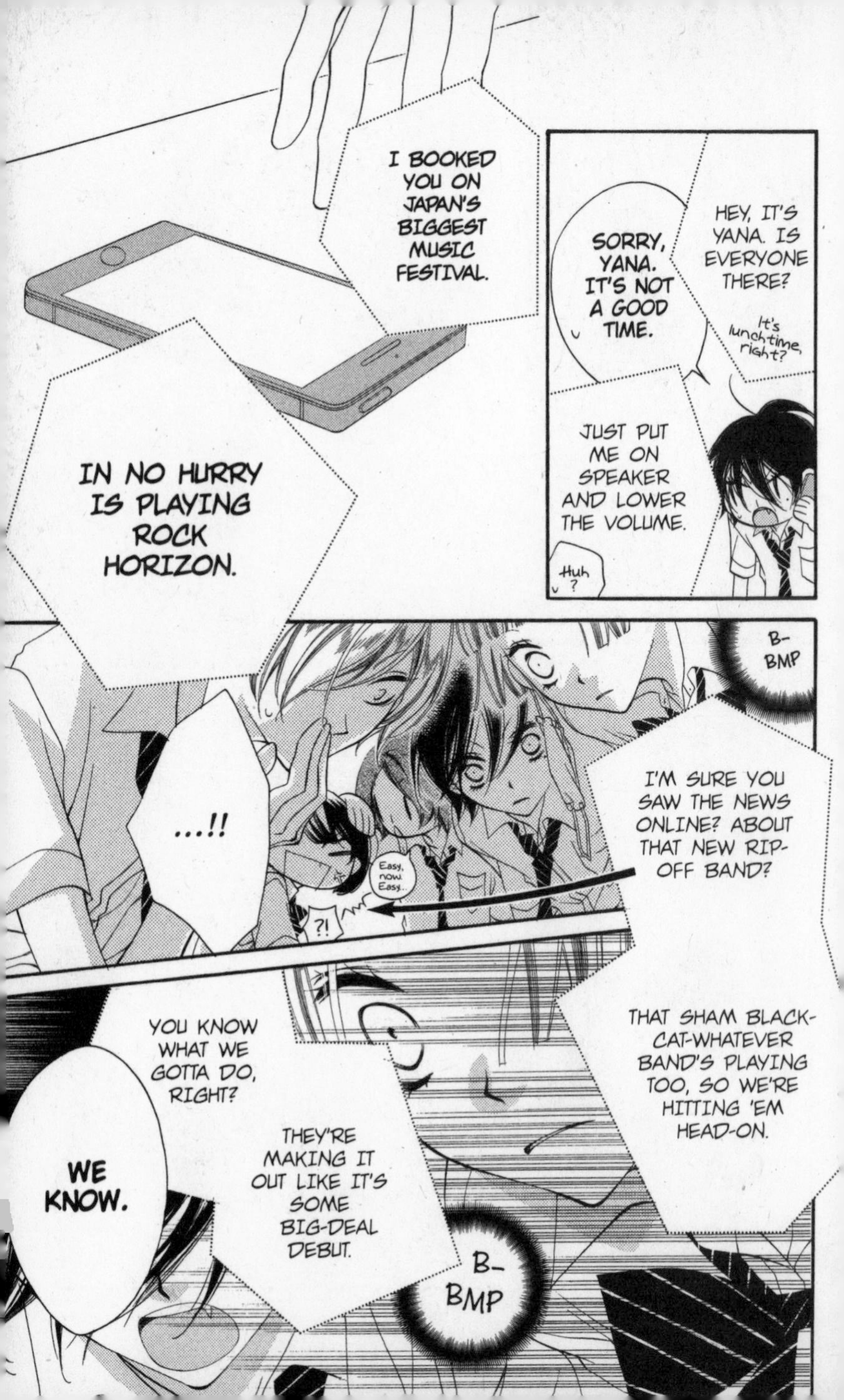
HEY, IT'S YANA. IS EVERYONE THERE?
It's lunchtime, right?
SORRY, YANA. IT'S NOT A GOOD TIME.
JUST PUT ME ON SPEAKER AND LOWER THE VOLUME.
Huh?
I BOOKED YOU ON JAPAN'S BIGGEST MUSIC FESTIVAL.
IN NO HURRY IS PLAYING ROCK HORIZON.
B-BMP
I'M SURE YOU SAW THE NEWS ONLINE? ABOUT THAT NEW RIP-OFF BAND?
Easy, now. Easy..
?!
...!!
THAT SHAM BLACK-CAT-WHATEVER BAND'S PLAYING TOO, SO WE'RE HITTING 'EM HEAD-ON.
YOU KNOW WHAT WE GOTTA DO, RIGHT?
THEY'RE MAKING IT OUT LIKE IT'S SOME BIG-DEAL DEBUT.
B-BMP
WE KNOW.

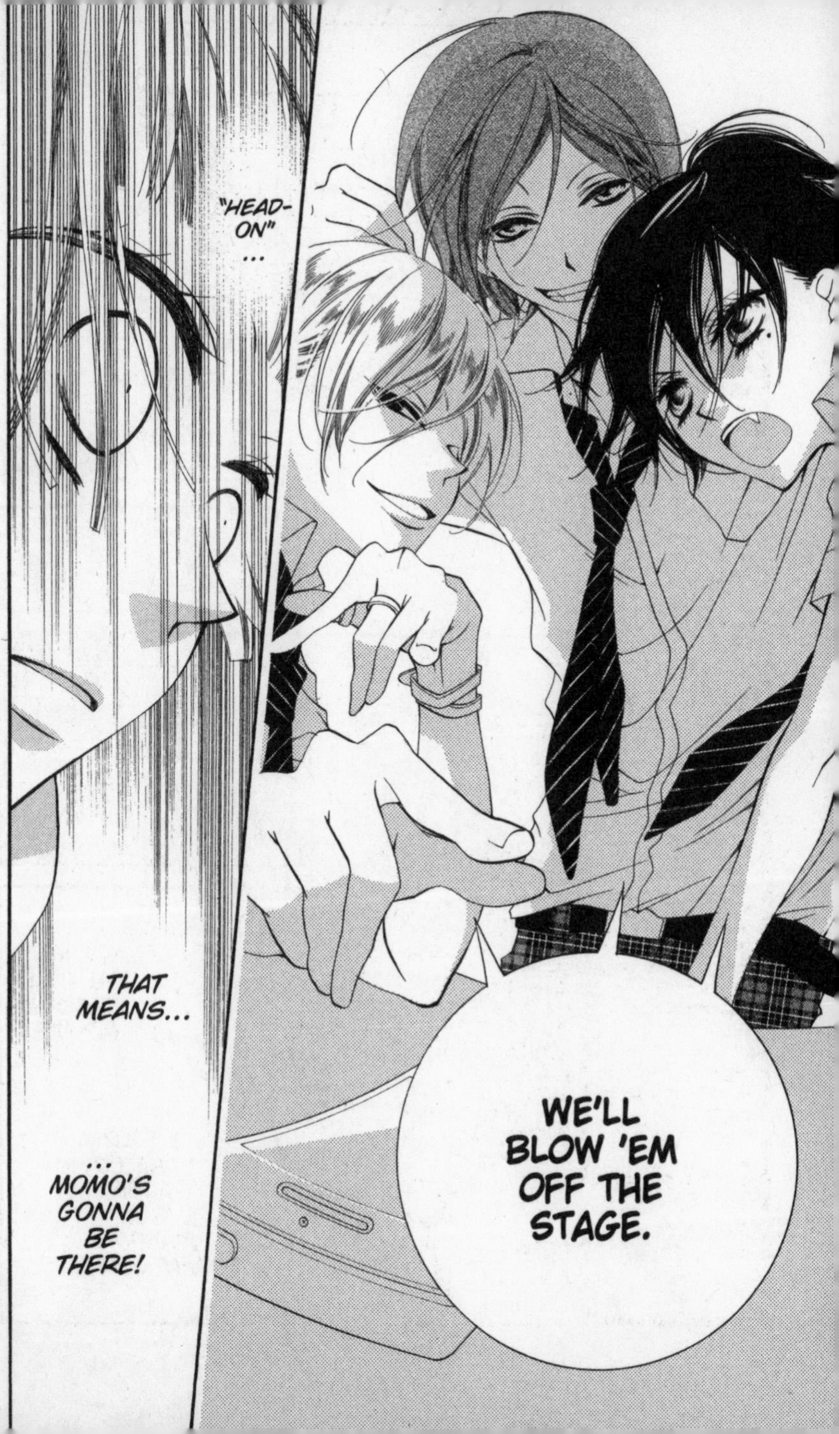
WE'LL BLOW 'EM OFF THE STAGE.
"HEAD-ON" ...
THAT MEANS...
... MOMO'S GONNA BE THERE!

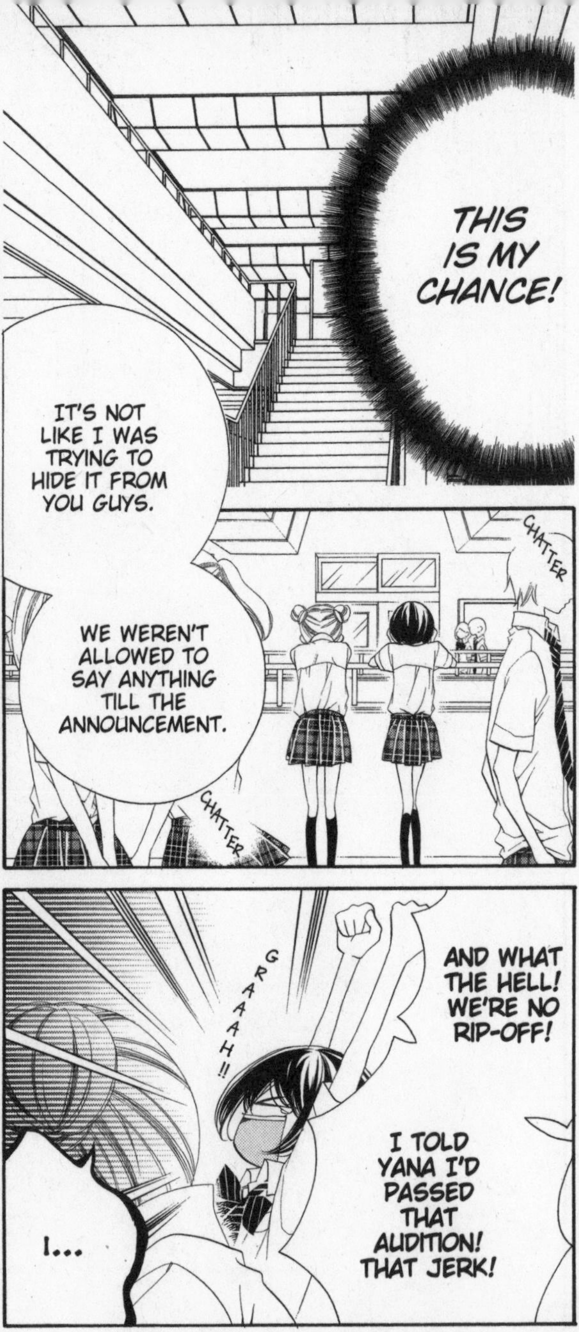
THIS IS MY CHANCE!
IT'S NOT LIKE I WAS TRYING TO HIDE IT FROM YOU GUYS.
CHATTER
WE WEREN'T ALLOWED TO SAY ANYTHING TILL THE ANNOUNCEMENT.
CHATTER
AND WHAT THE HELL! WE'RE NO RIP-OFF!
GRAAAAH!!
I TOLD YANA I'D PASSED THAT AUDITION! THAT JERK!
I...

4

I joined a gym last year, and at first I was going regularly, full of vim and vigor. But since then I've been so busy with work I've barely had a chance to leave the house, and I just realized I haven't gone in half a year!

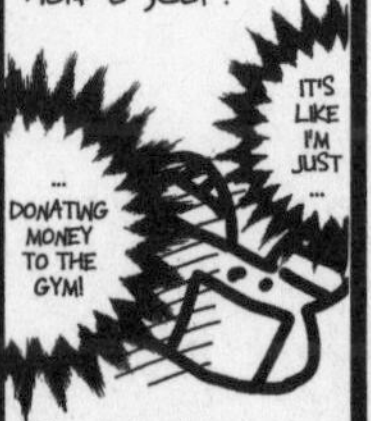
IT'S LIKE I'M JUST...
...DONATING MONEY TO THE GYM!

So I decided to cancel my membership, but then I started thinking, "With summer coming, where else will I be able to exercise?" And so...to this day, I'm still donating money to the gym. What should I do?

Signed,
A self-employed person in Yokohama

[NAMED WITHHELD BY REQUEST]

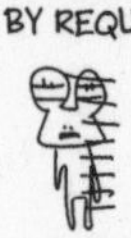

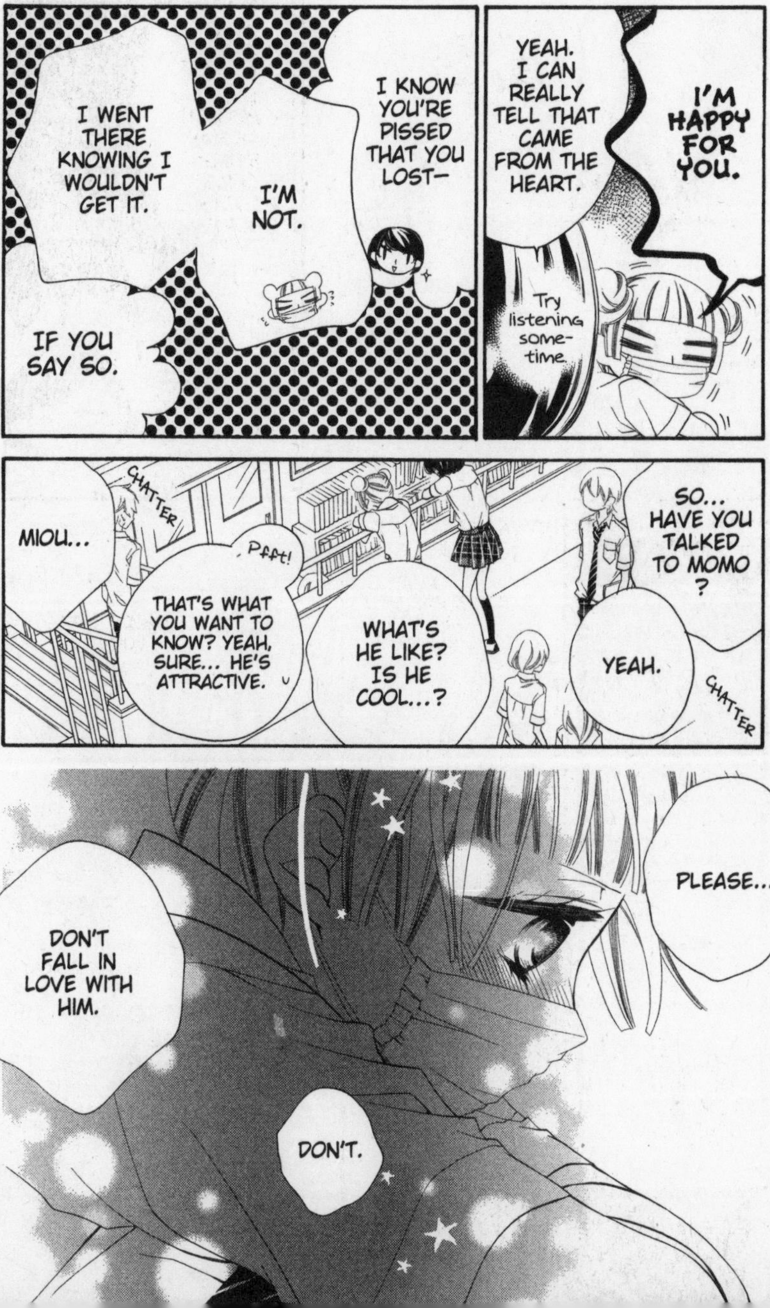
I'M HAPPY FOR YOU.
YEAH. I CAN REALLY TELL THAT CAME FROM THE HEART.
Try listening some-time.
I KNOW YOU'RE PISSED THAT YOU LOST—
I'M NOT.
I WENT THERE KNOWING I WOULDN'T GET IT.
IF YOU SAY SO.
SO... HAVE YOU TALKED TO MOMO?
YEAH.
CHATTER
WHAT'S HE LIKE? IS HE COOL...?
Pfft!
THAT'S WHAT YOU WANT TO KNOW? YEAH, SURE... HE'S ATTRACTIVE.
CHATTER
MIOU...
PLEASE...
DON'T FALL IN LOVE WITH HIM.
DON'T.

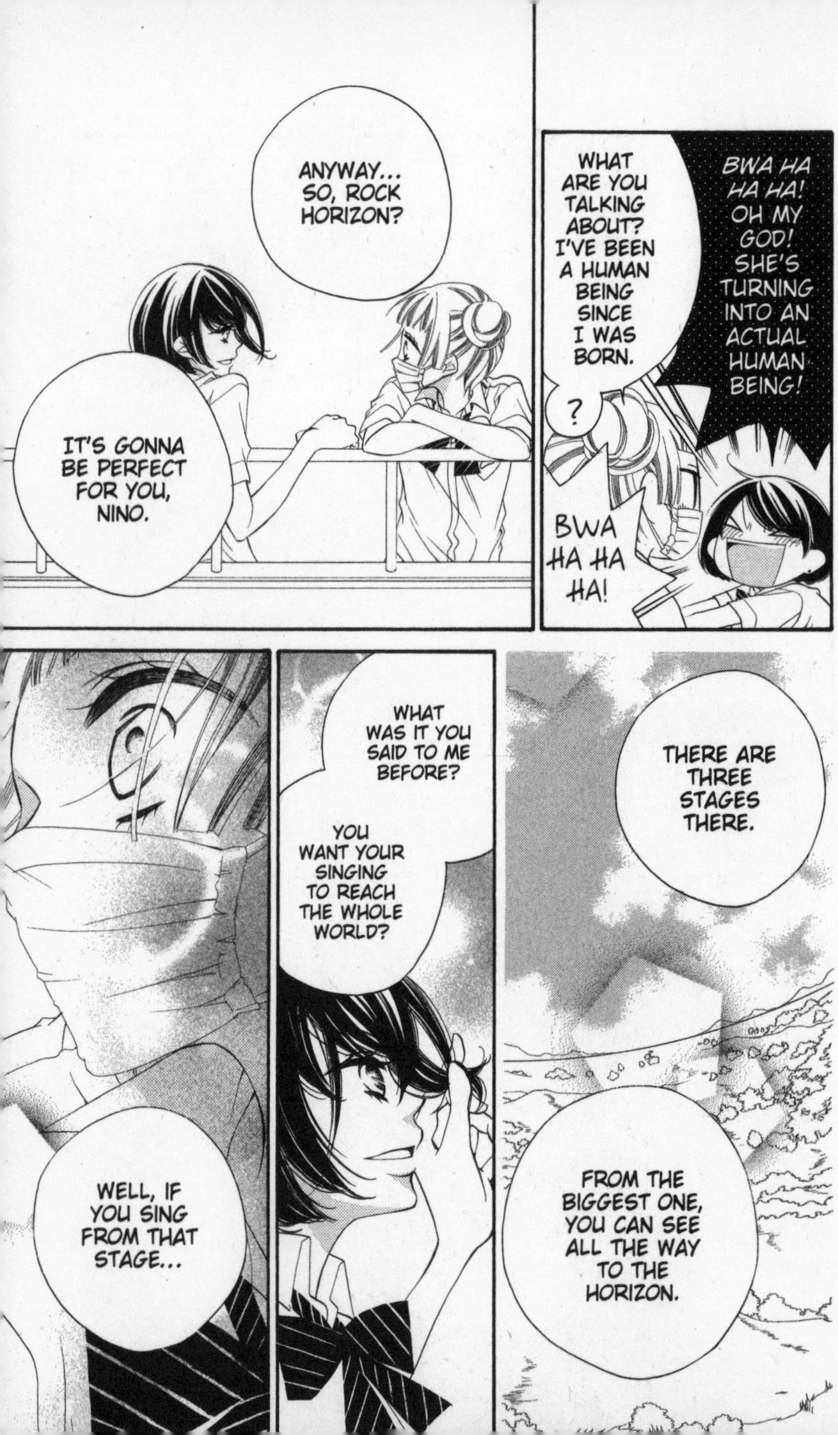
BWA HA HA HA! OH MY GOD! SHE'S TURNING INTO AN ACTUAL HUMAN BEING!
WHAT ARE YOU TALKING ABOUT? I'VE BEEN A HUMAN BEING SINCE I WAS BORN.
?
BWA HA HA HA!
ANYWAY... SO, ROCK HORIZON?
IT'S GONNA BE PERFECT FOR YOU, NINO.
THERE ARE THREE STAGES THERE.
FROM THE BIGGEST ONE, YOU CAN SEE ALL THE WAY TO THE HORIZON.
WHAT WAS IT YOU SAID TO ME BEFORE?
YOU WANT YOUR SINGING TO REACH THE WHOLE WORLD?
WELL, IF YOU SING FROM THAT STAGE...

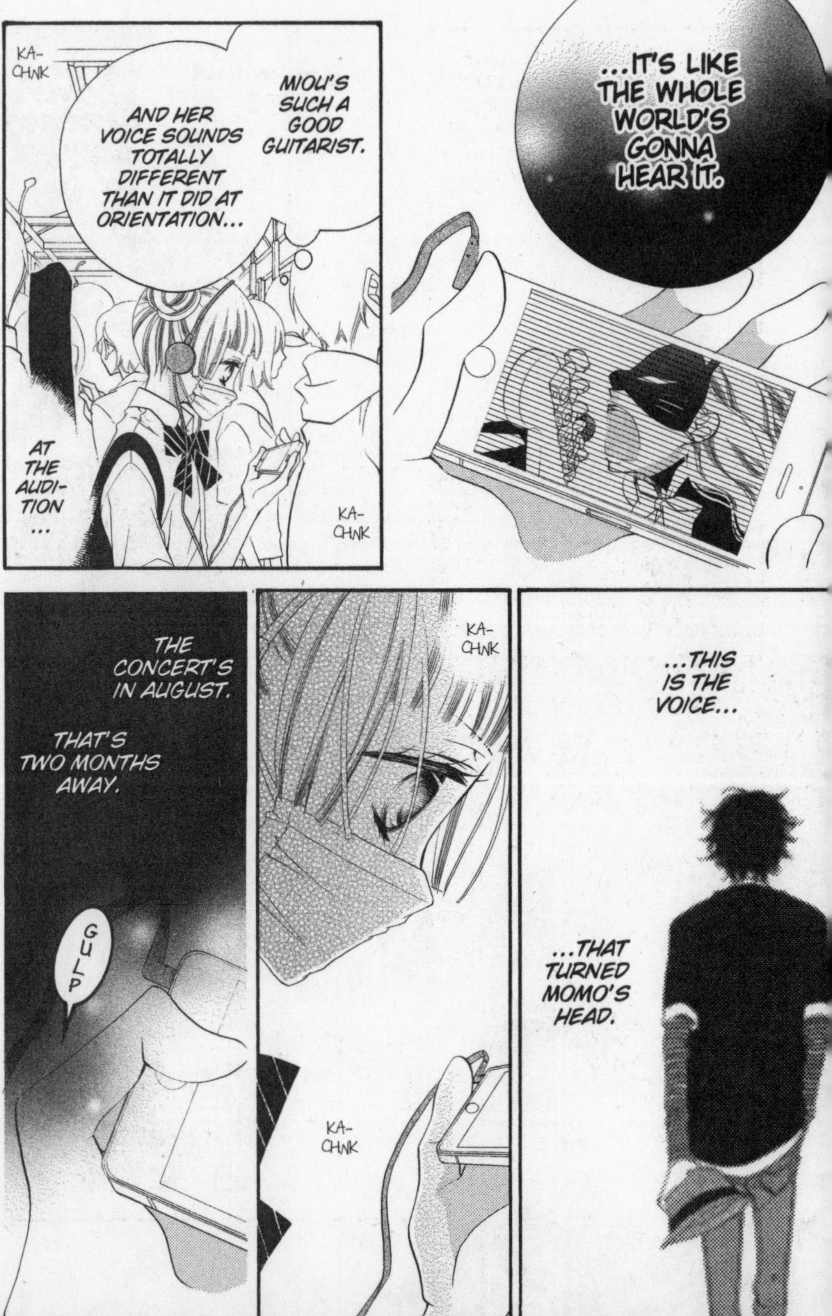
...IT'S LIKE THE WHOLE WORLD'S GONNA HEAR IT.
KA-CHNK
MIOU'S SUCH A GOOD GUITARIST.
AND HER VOICE SOUNDS TOTALLY DIFFERENT THAN IT DID AT ORIENTATION...
KA-CHNK
AT THE AUDITION...
...THIS IS THE VOICE...
...THAT TURNED MOMO'S HEAD.
KA-CHNK
KA-CHNK
THE CONCERT'S IN AUGUST.
THAT'S TWO MONTHS AWAY.
GULP

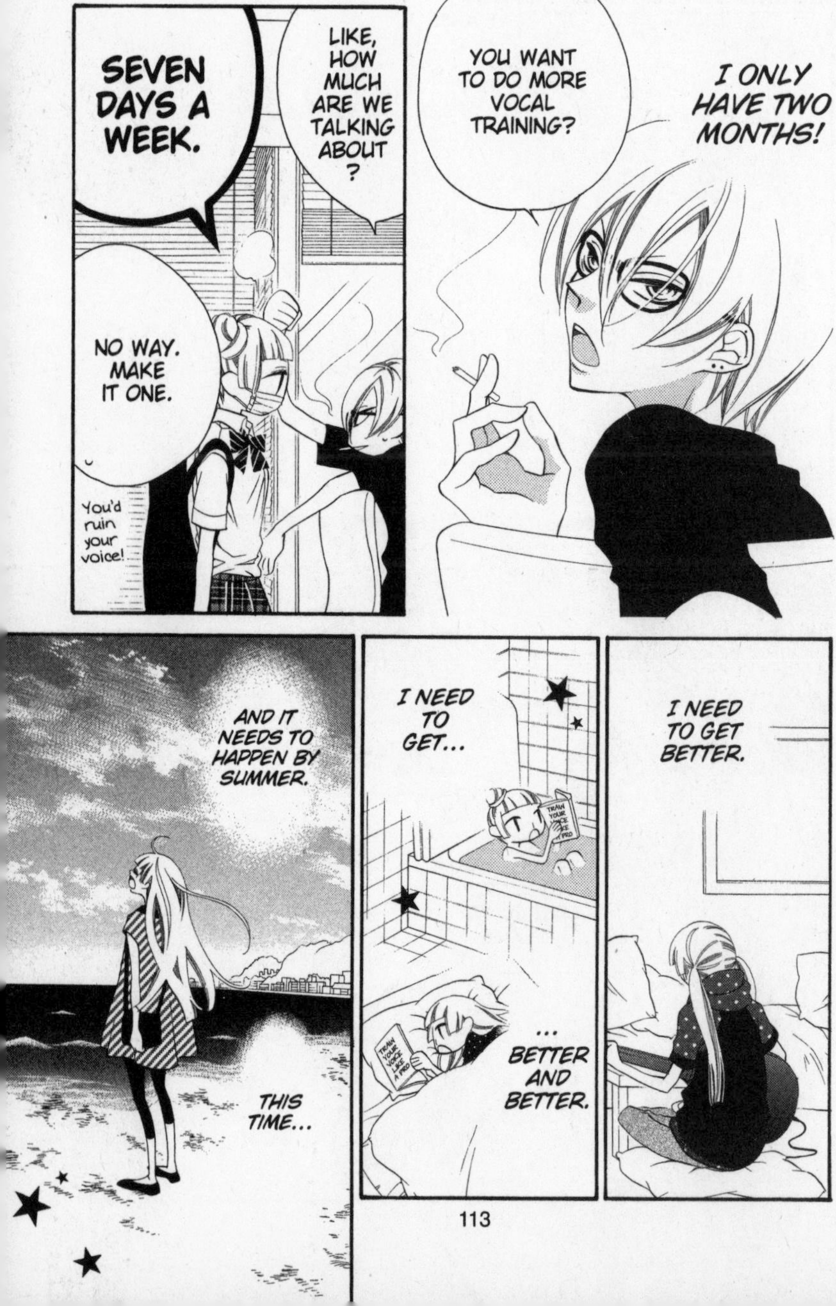
I ONLY HAVE TWO MONTHS!
YOU WANT TO DO MORE VOCAL TRAINING?
LIKE, HOW MUCH ARE WE TALKING ABOUT?
SEVEN DAYS A WEEK.
NO WAY. MAKE IT ONE.
You'd ruin your voice!
I NEED TO GET BETTER.
I NEED TO GET...
TRAIN YOUR VOICE LIKE A PRO
...BETTER AND BETTER.
AND IT NEEDS TO HAPPEN BY SUMMER.
THIS TIME...

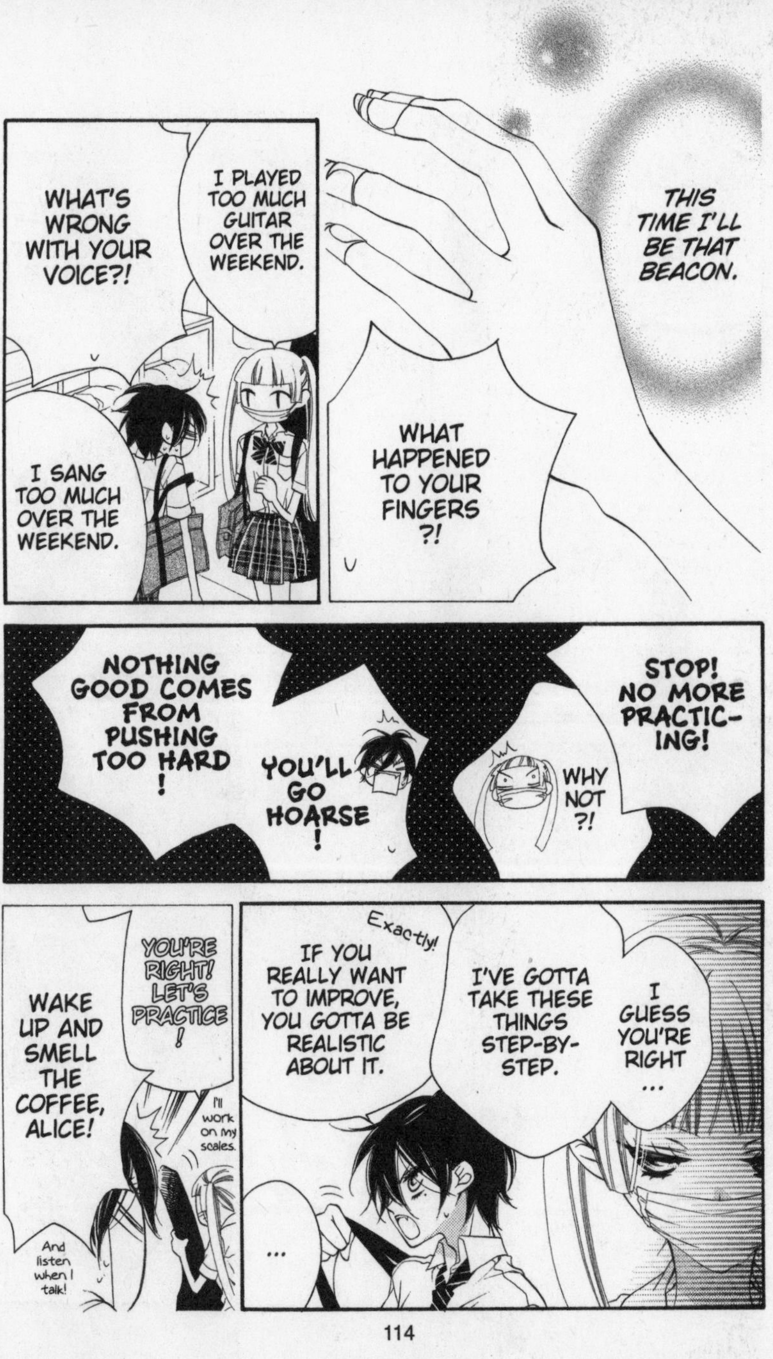
THIS TIME I'LL BE THAT BEACON.
WHAT HAPPENED TO YOUR FINGERS?!
I PLAYED TOO MUCH GUITAR OVER THE WEEKEND.
WHAT'S WRONG WITH YOUR VOICE?!
I SANG TOO MUCH OVER THE WEEKEND.
STOP! NO MORE PRACTICING!
WHY NOT?!
YOU'LL GO HOARSE!
NOTHING GOOD COMES FROM PUSHING TOO HARD!
I GUESS YOU'RE RIGHT...
I'VE GOTTA TAKE THESE THINGS STEP-BY-STEP.
Exactly!
IF YOU REALLY WANT TO IMPROVE, YOU GOTTA BE REALISTIC ABOUT IT.
...
YOU'RE RIGHT! LET'S PRACTICE!
WAKE UP AND SMELL THE COFFEE, ALICE!
I'll work on my scales.
And listen when I talk!

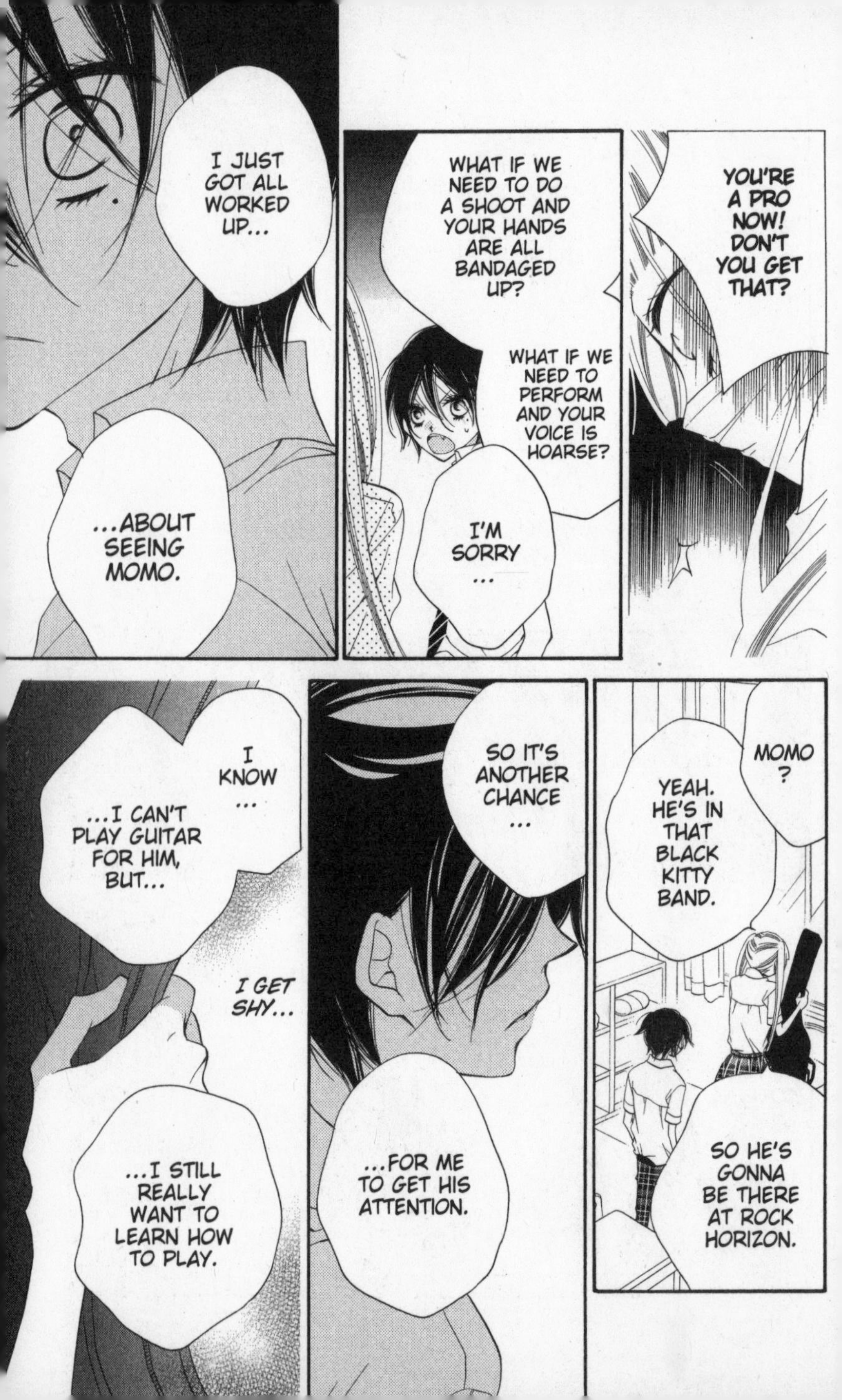
YOU'RE A PRO NOW! DON'T YOU GET THAT?
WHAT IF WE NEED TO DO A SHOOT AND YOUR HANDS ARE ALL BANDAGED UP?
WHAT IF WE NEED TO PERFORM AND YOUR VOICE IS HOARSE?
I'M SORRY...
I JUST GOT ALL WORKED UP...
...ABOUT SEEING MOMO.
MOMO?
YEAH. HE'S IN THAT BLACK KITTY BAND.
SO HE'S GONNA BE THERE AT ROCK HORIZON.
SO IT'S ANOTHER CHANCE...
...FOR ME TO GET HIS ATTENTION.
I KNOW...
...I CAN'T PLAY GUITAR FOR HIM, BUT...
I GET SHY...
...I STILL REALLY WANT TO LEARN HOW TO PLAY.

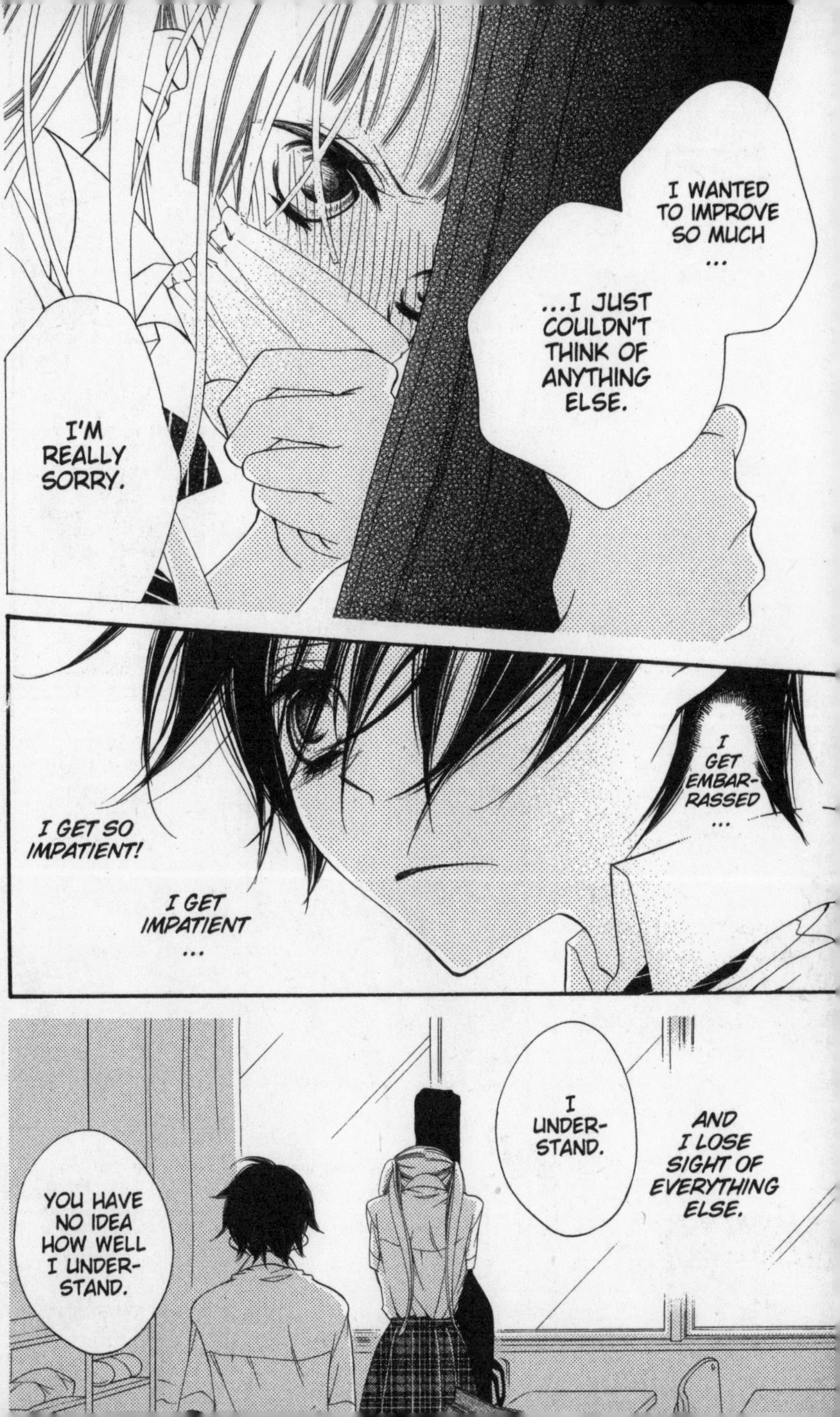
I WANTED TO IMPROVE SO MUCH ...
...I JUST COULDN'T THINK OF ANYTHING ELSE.
I'M REALLY SORRY.
I GET EMBAR-RASSED ...
I GET IMPATIENT ...
I GET SO IMPATIENT!
AND I LOSE SIGHT OF EVERYTHING ELSE.
I UNDER-STAND.
YOU HAVE NO IDEA HOW WELL I UNDER-STAND.

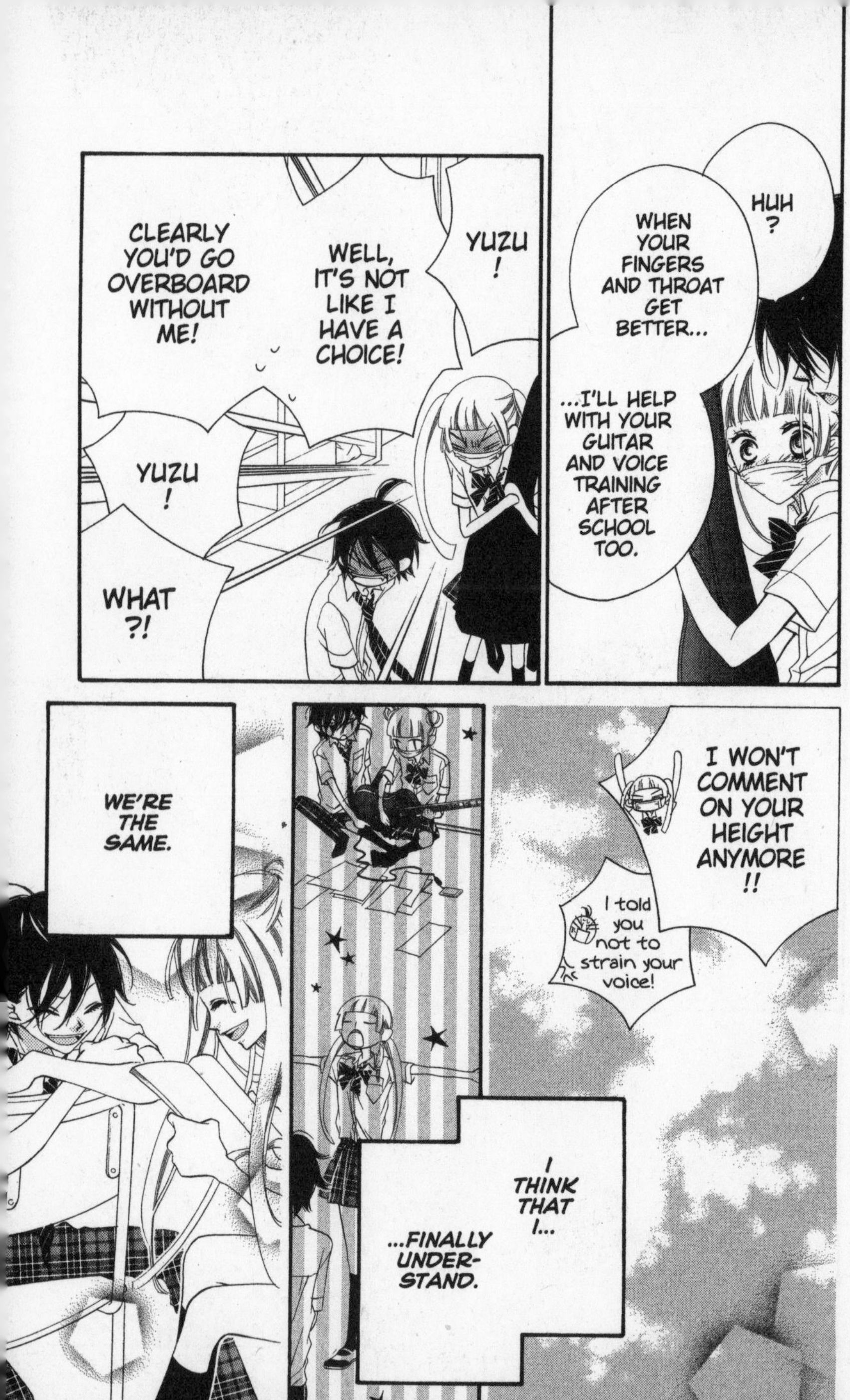
HUH?
WHEN YOUR FINGERS AND THROAT GET BETTER...
...I'LL HELP WITH YOUR GUITAR AND VOICE TRAINING AFTER SCHOOL TOO.
YUZU!
WELL, IT'S NOT LIKE I HAVE A CHOICE!
CLEARLY YOU'D GO OVERBOARD WITHOUT ME!
YUZU!
WHAT?!
I WON'T COMMENT ON YOUR HEIGHT ANYMORE!!
I told you not to strain your voice!
I THINK THAT I...
...FINALLY UNDER-STAND.
WE'RE THE SAME.

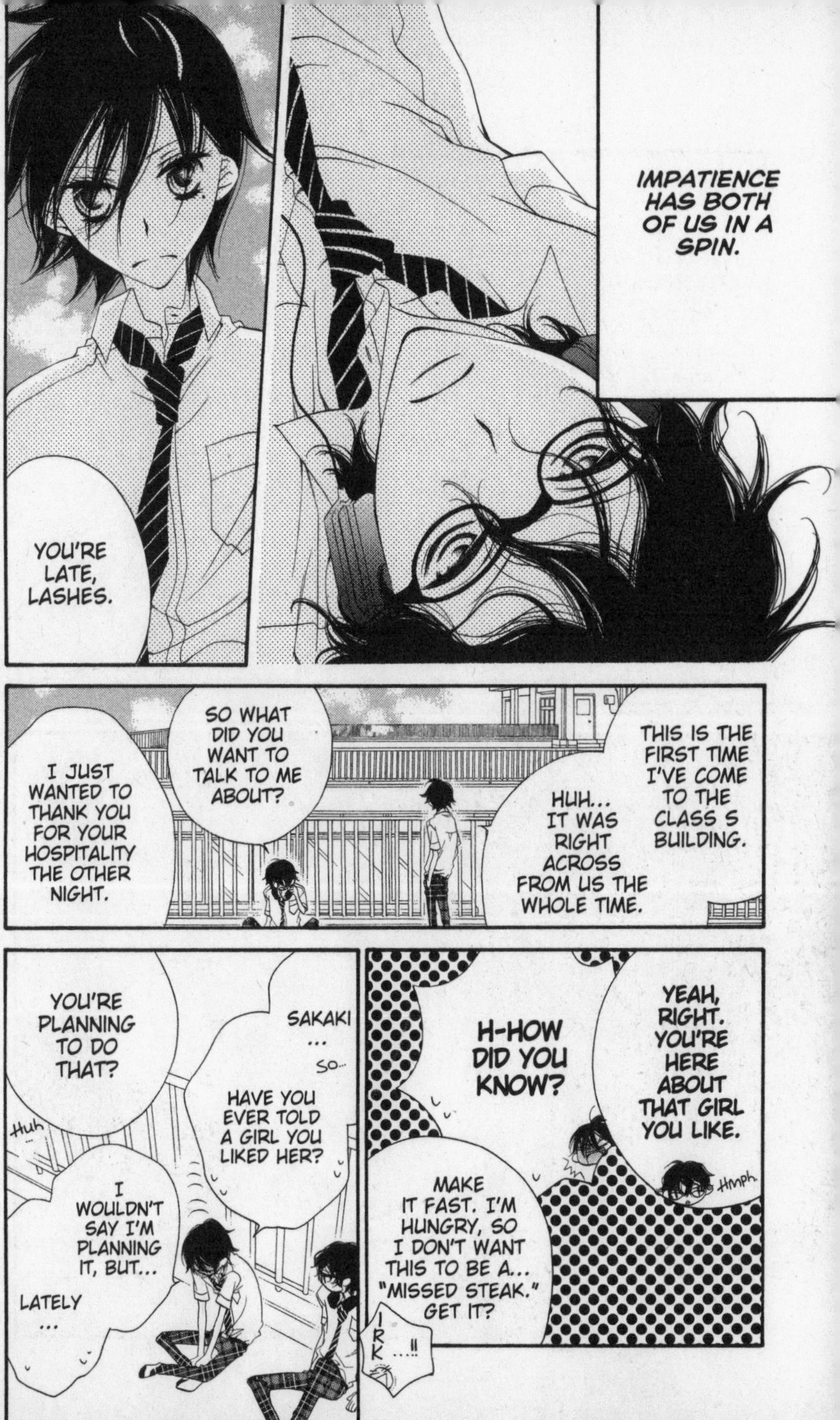

IMPATIENCE HAS BOTH OF US IN A SPIN.
YOU'RE LATE, LASHES.
THIS IS THE FIRST TIME I'VE COME TO THE CLASS S BUILDING.
HUH... IT WAS RIGHT ACROSS FROM US THE WHOLE TIME.
SO WHAT DID YOU WANT TO TALK TO ME ABOUT?
I JUST WANTED TO THANK YOU FOR YOUR HOSPITALITY THE OTHER NIGHT.
YEAH, RIGHT. YOU'RE HERE ABOUT THAT GIRL YOU LIKE.
Hmph.
H-HOW DID YOU KNOW?
MAKE IT FAST. I'M HUNGRY, SO I DON'T WANT THIS TO BE A... "MISSED STEAK." GET IT?
IRK ....!!
SAKAKI...
So...
HAVE YOU EVER TOLD A GIRL YOU LIKED HER?
YOU'RE PLANNING TO DO THAT?
Huh...
I WOULDN'T SAY I'M PLANNING IT, BUT...
LATELY...

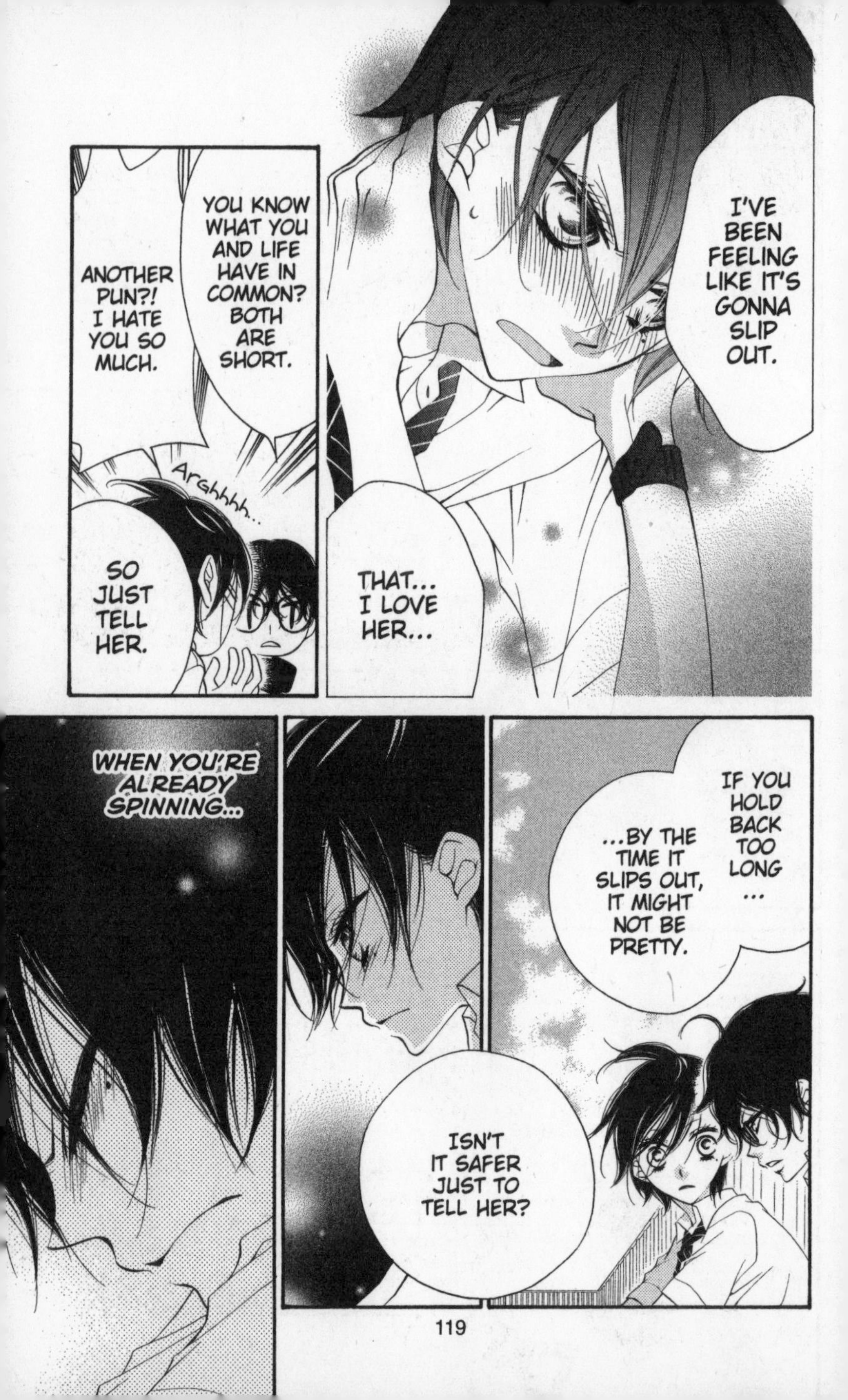
I'VE BEEN FEELING LIKE IT'S GONNA SLIP OUT.
THAT... I LOVE HER...
YOU KNOW WHAT YOU AND LIFE HAVE IN COMMON? BOTH ARE SHORT.
ANOTHER PUN?! I HATE YOU SO MUCH.
Arghhhh...
SO JUST TELL HER.
IF YOU HOLD BACK TOO LONG...
...BY THE TIME IT SLIPS OUT, IT MIGHT NOT BE PRETTY.
ISN'T IT SAFER JUST TO TELL HER?
WHEN YOU'RE ALREADY SPINNING...

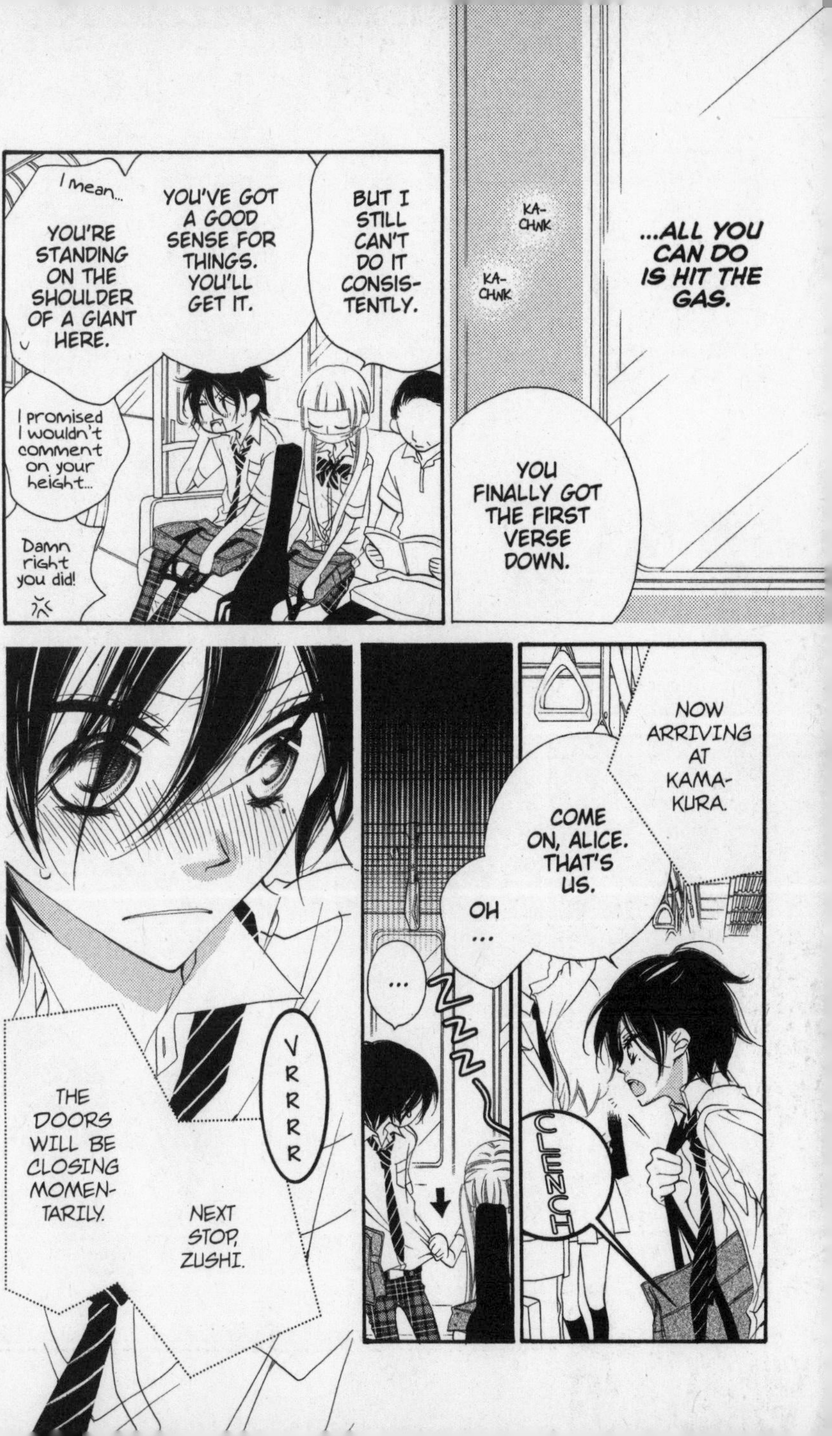
...ALL YOU CAN DO IS HIT THE GAS.
KA-CHNK
KA-CHNK
YOU FINALLY GOT THE FIRST VERSE DOWN.
BUT I STILL CAN'T DO IT CONSISTENTLY.
YOU'VE GOT A GOOD SENSE FOR THINGS. YOU'LL GET IT.
I mean... YOU'RE STANDING ON THE SHOULDER OF A GIANT HERE.
I promised I wouldn't comment on your height...
Damn right you did!
NOW ARRIVING AT KAMAKURA.
COME ON, ALICE. THAT'S US.
OH...
CLENCH
ZZZ
...
VRRRR
THE DOORS WILL BE CLOSING MOMENTARILY.
NEXT STOP, ZUSHI.

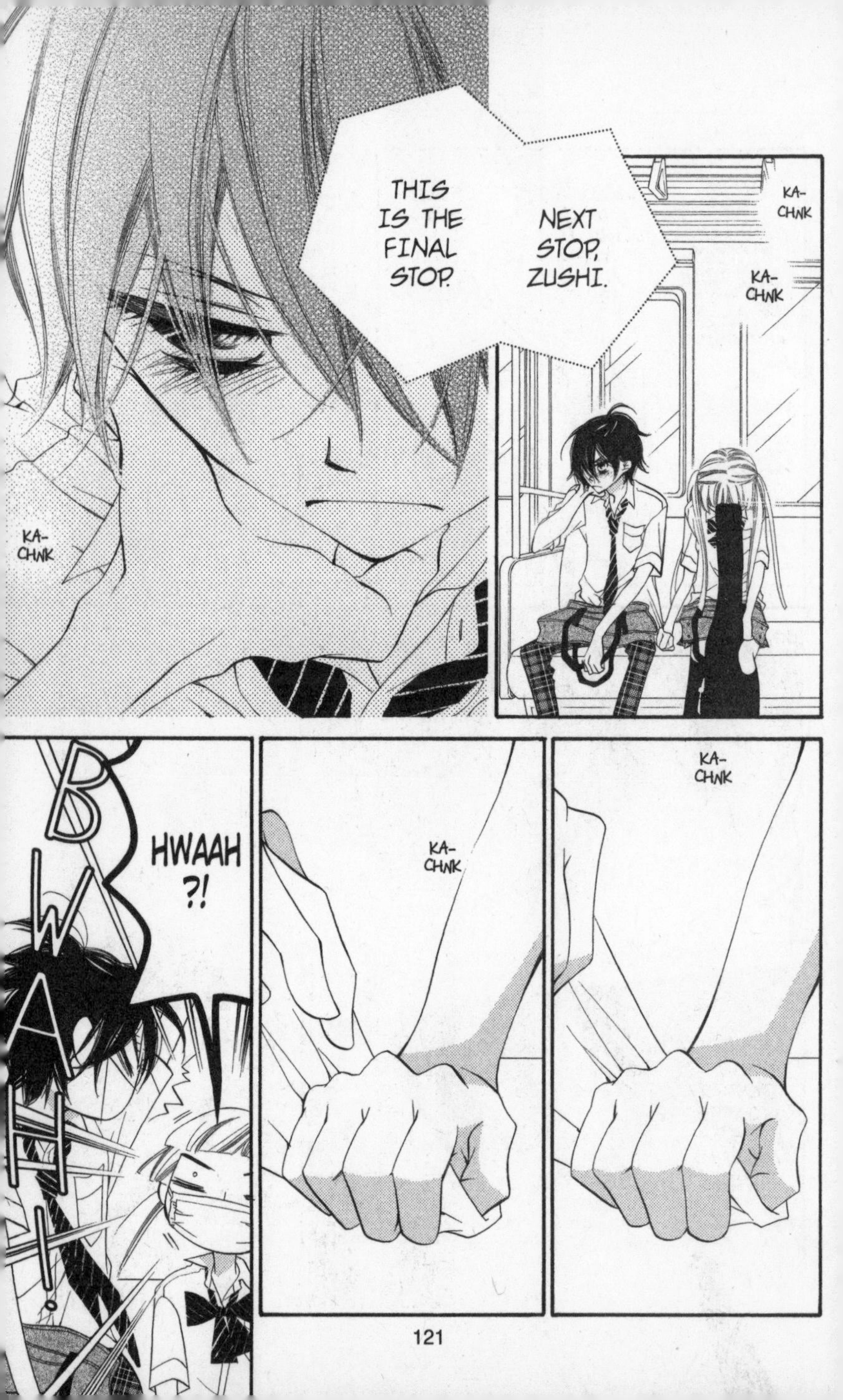
KA-CHNK
KA-CHNK
NEXT STOP, ZUSHI.
THIS IS THE FINAL STOP.
KA-CHNK
KA-CHNK
KA-CHNK
BWAAH
HWAAH ?!

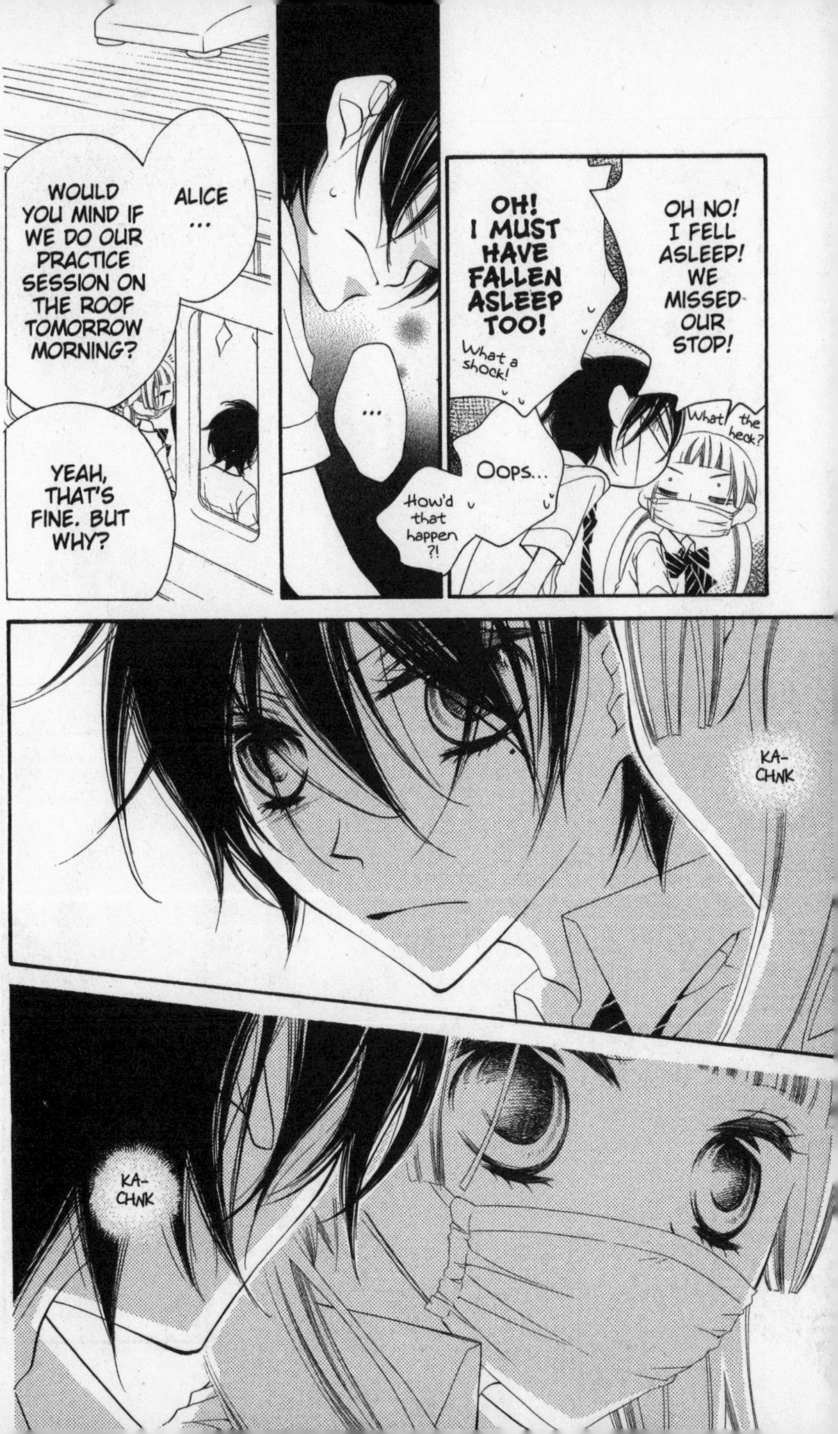
OH NO! I FELL ASLEEP! WE MISSED OUR STOP!
OH! I MUST HAVE FALLEN ASLEEP TOO!
What the heck?
What a shock!
Oops...
How'd that happen?!
...
ALICE ...
WOULD YOU MIND IF WE DO OUR PRACTICE SESSION ON THE ROOF TOMORROW MORNING?
YEAH, THAT'S FINE. BUT WHY?
KA-CHNK
KA-CHNK

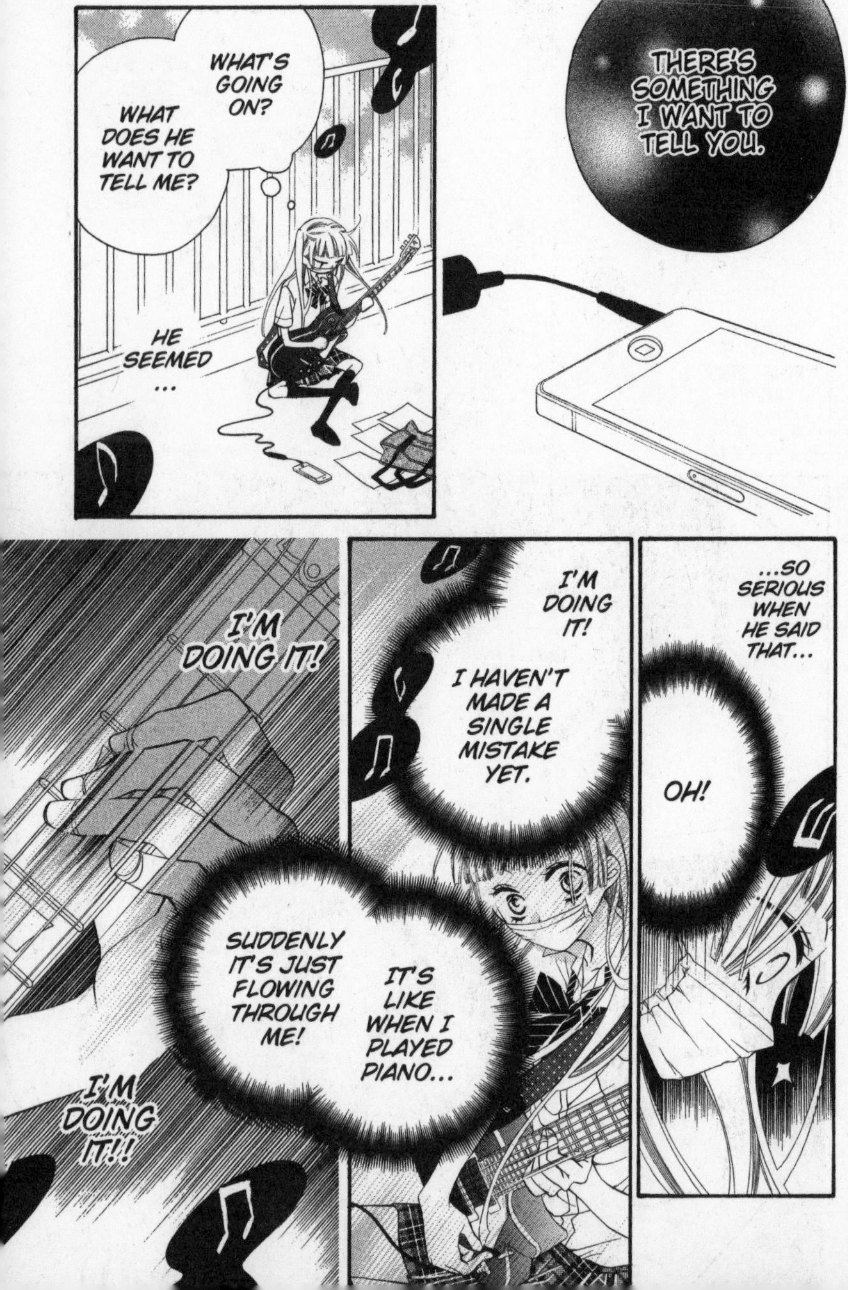
THERE'S SOMETHING I WANT TO TELL YOU.
WHAT'S GOING ON?
WHAT DOES HE WANT TO TELL ME?
HE SEEMED ...
...SO SERIOUS WHEN HE SAID THAT...
OH!
I'M DOING IT!
I HAVEN'T MADE A SINGLE MISTAKE YET.
IT'S LIKE WHEN I PLAYED PIANO...
SUDDENLY IT'S JUST FLOWING THROUGH ME!
I'M DOING IT!
I'M DOING IT!!

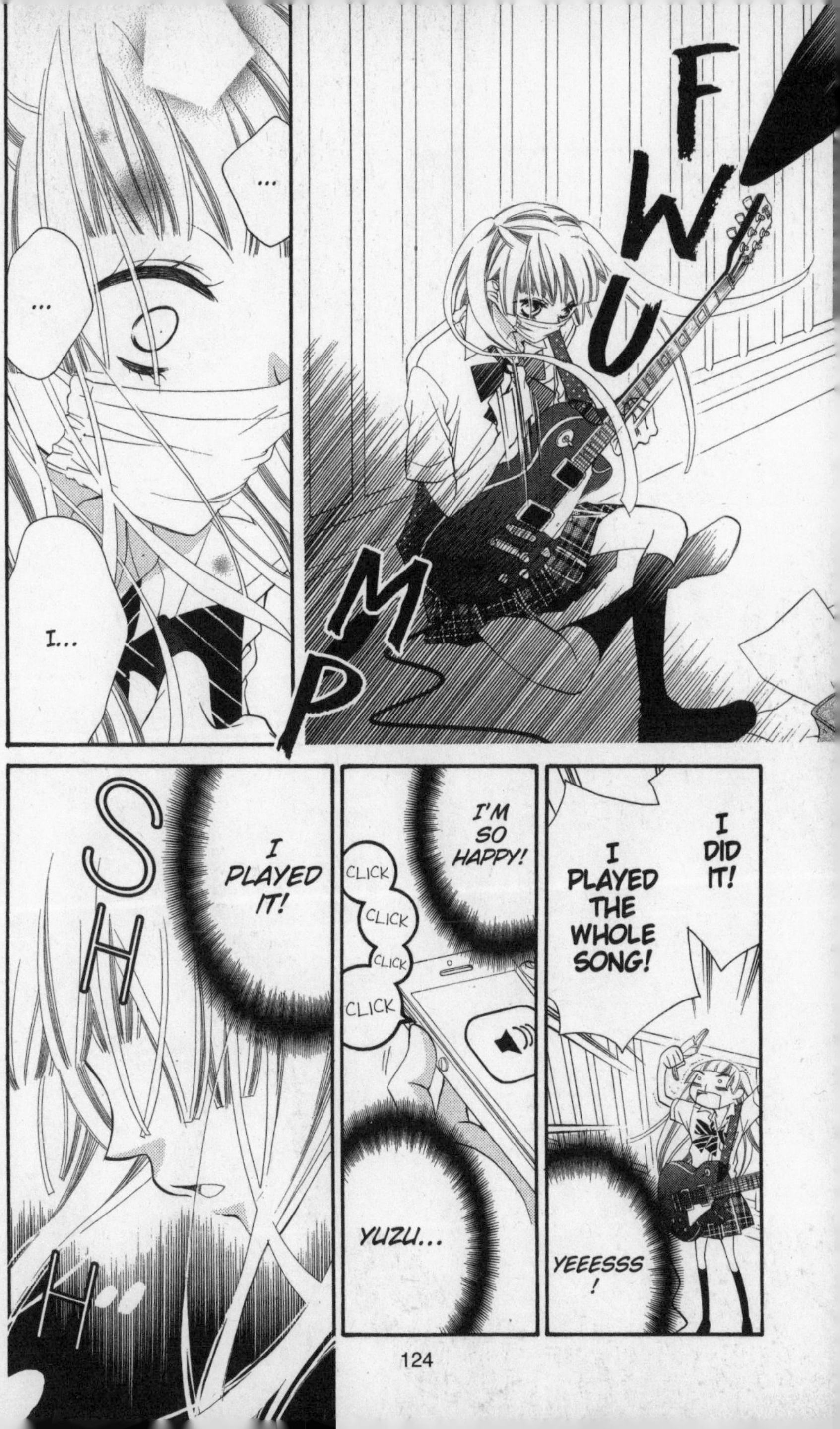
FWUMP
...
...
I...
I DID IT!
I PLAYED THE WHOLE SONG!
YEEESSS!
I'M SO HAPPY!
CLICK
CLICK
CLICK
CLICK
YUZU...
I PLAYED IT!
SHH...

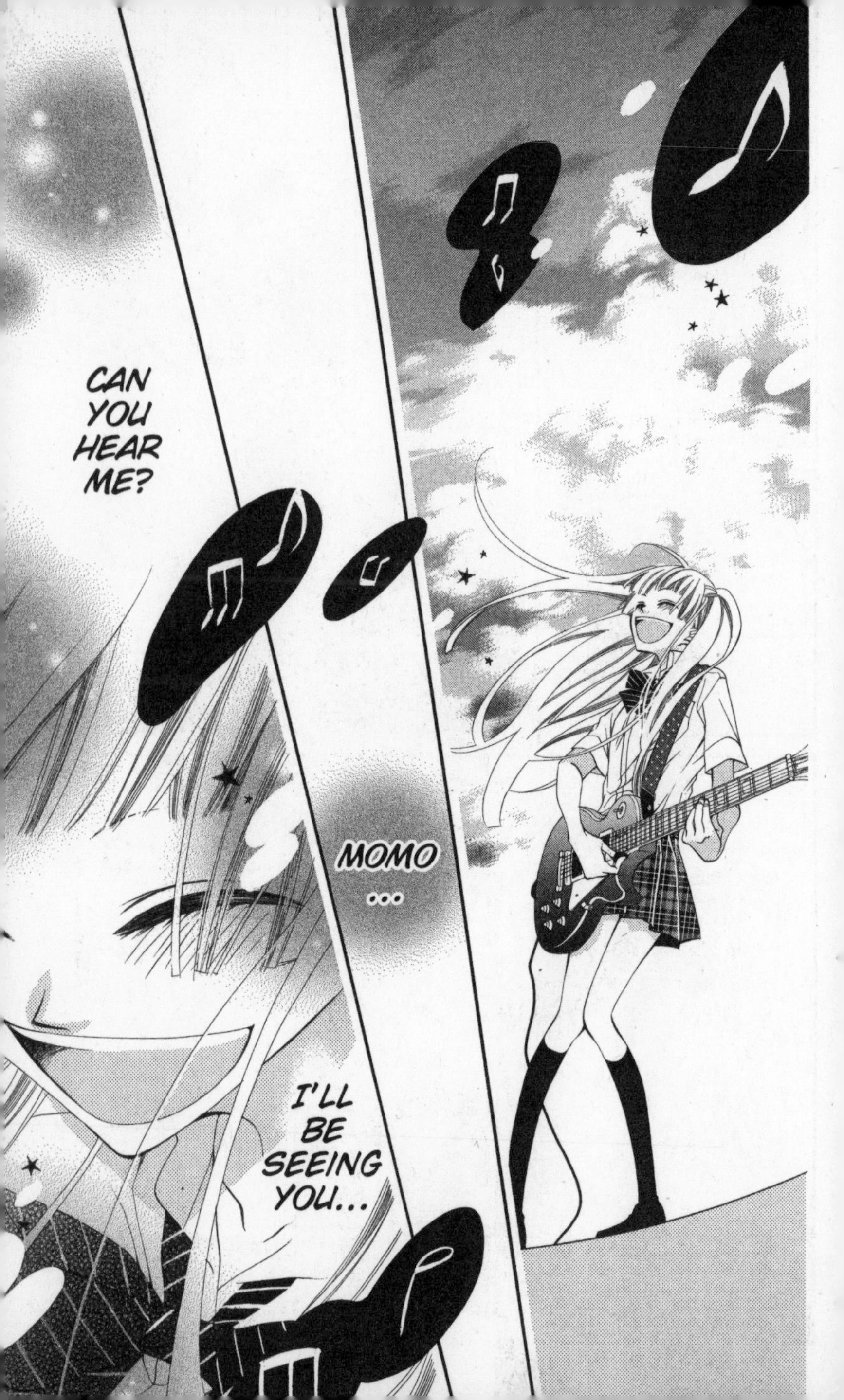
MOMO...
I'LL BE SEEING YOU...
CAN YOU HEAR ME?

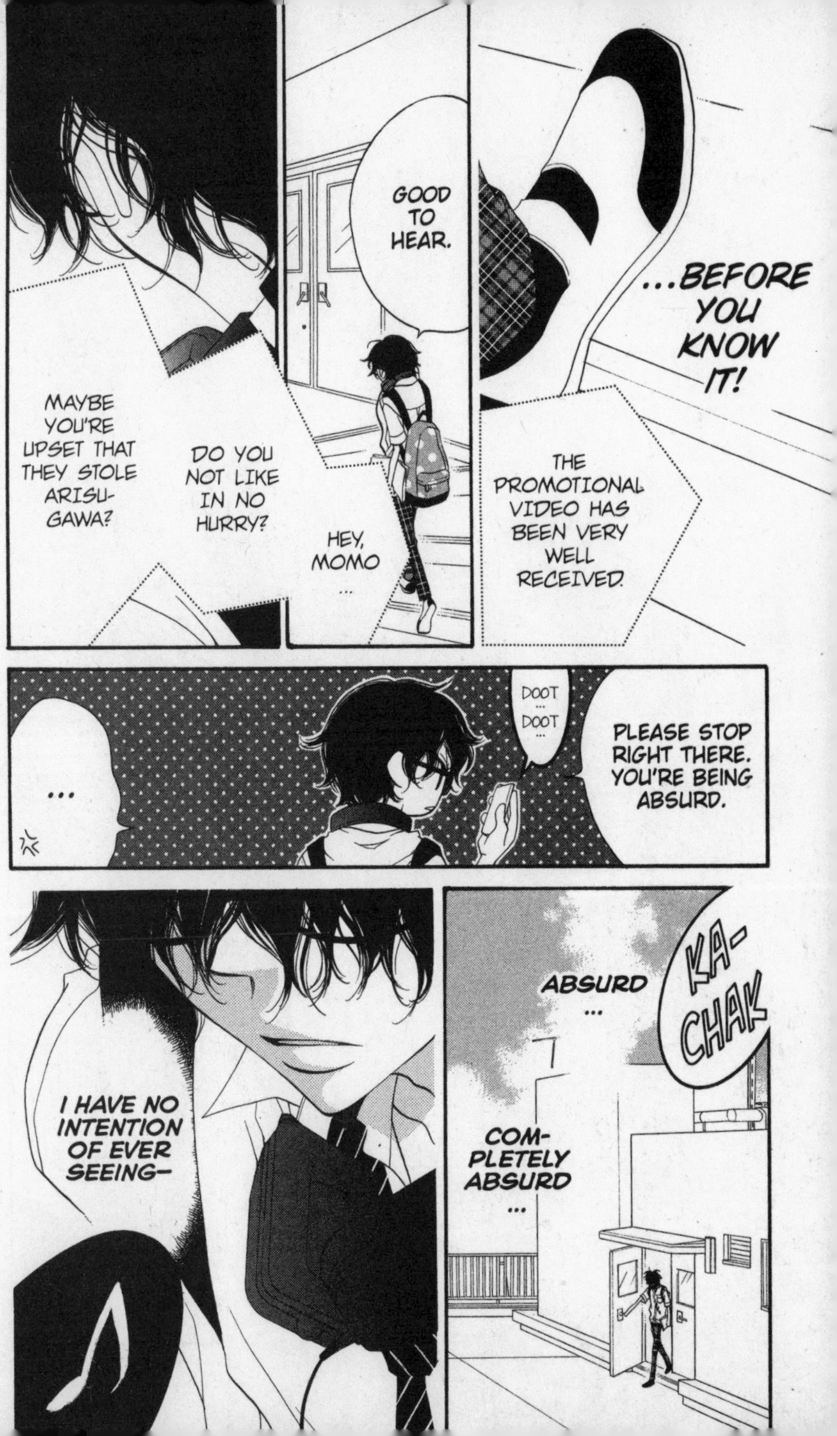
...BEFORE YOU KNOW IT!
THE PROMOTIONAL VIDEO HAS BEEN VERY WELL RECEIVED.
GOOD TO HEAR.
HEY, MOMO ...
DO YOU NOT LIKE IN NO HURRY?
MAYBE YOU'RE UPSET THAT THEY STOLE ARISU-GAWA?
PLEASE STOP RIGHT THERE. YOU'RE BEING ABSURD.
DOOT ... DOOT ...
...
KA-CHAK
ABSURD ...
COM-PLETELY ABSURD ...
I HAVE NO INTENTION OF EVER SEEING—

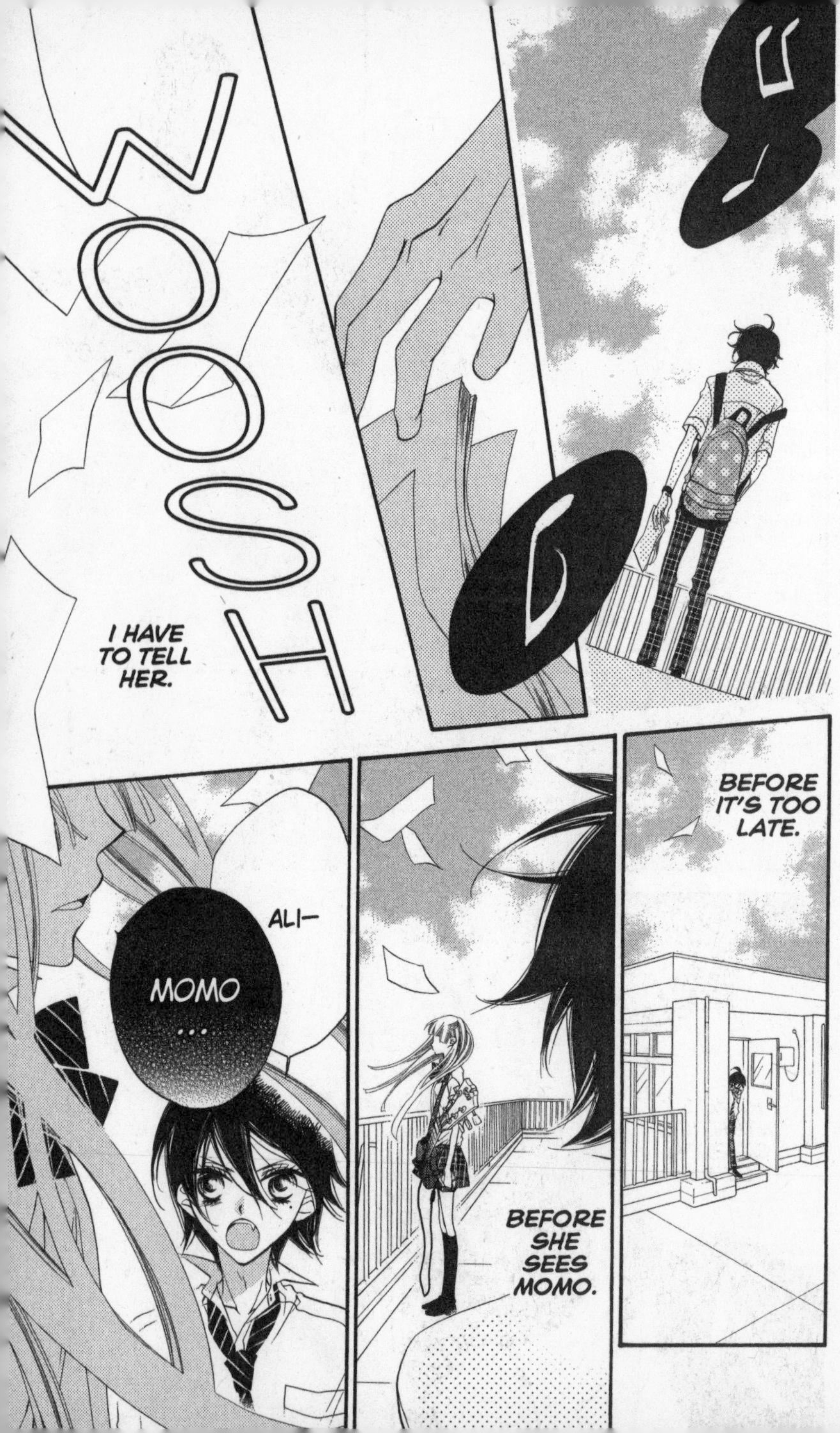
WOOSH
I HAVE TO TELL HER.
BEFORE IT'S TOO LATE.
BEFORE SHE SEES MOMO.
ALI—
MOMO ...

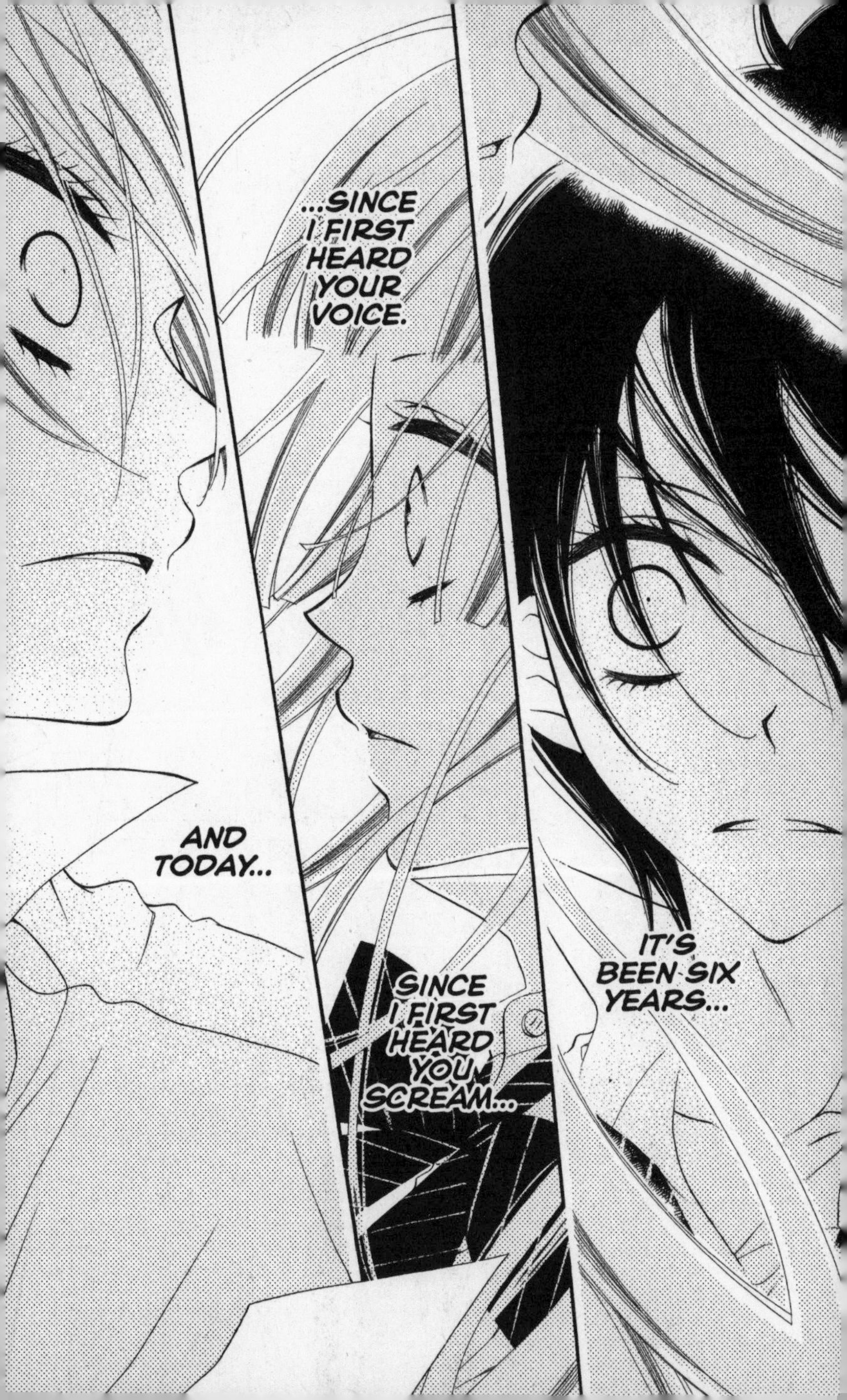
IT'S BEEN SIX YEARS...
SINCE I FIRST HEARD YOU SCREAM...
AND TODAY...
...SINCE I FIRST HEARD YOUR VOICE.

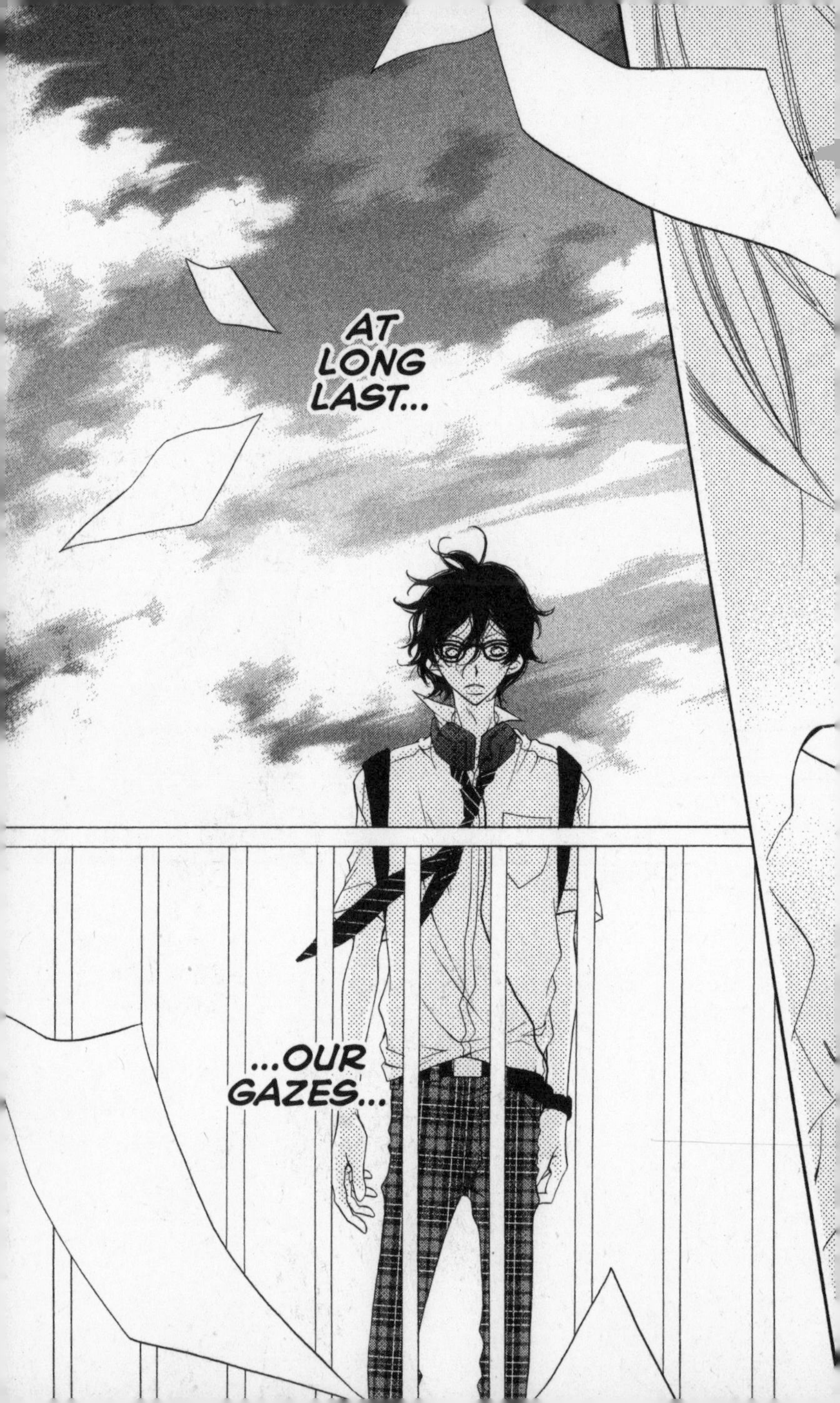
AT LONG LAST...
...OUR GAZES...

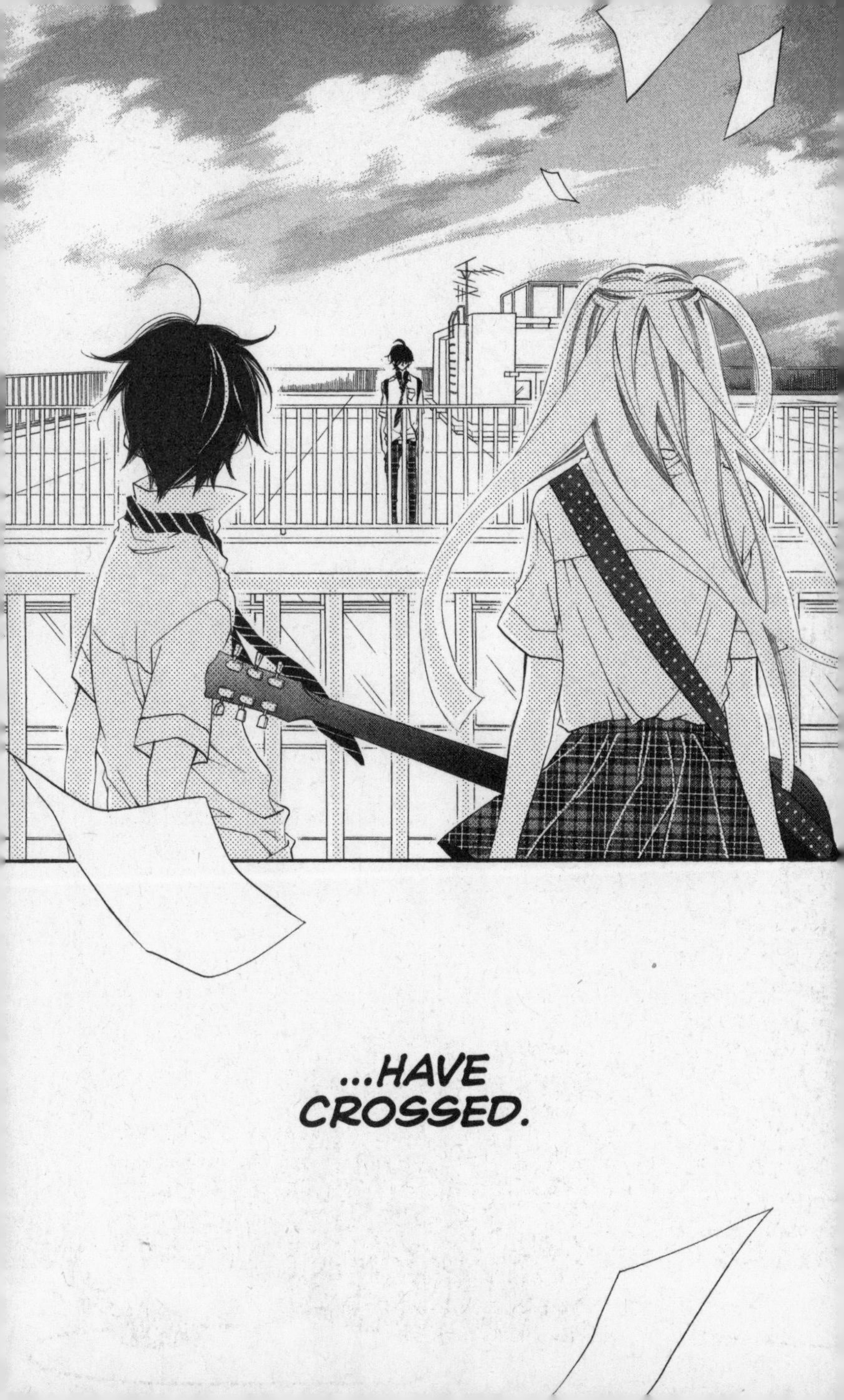
...HAVE
CROSSED.

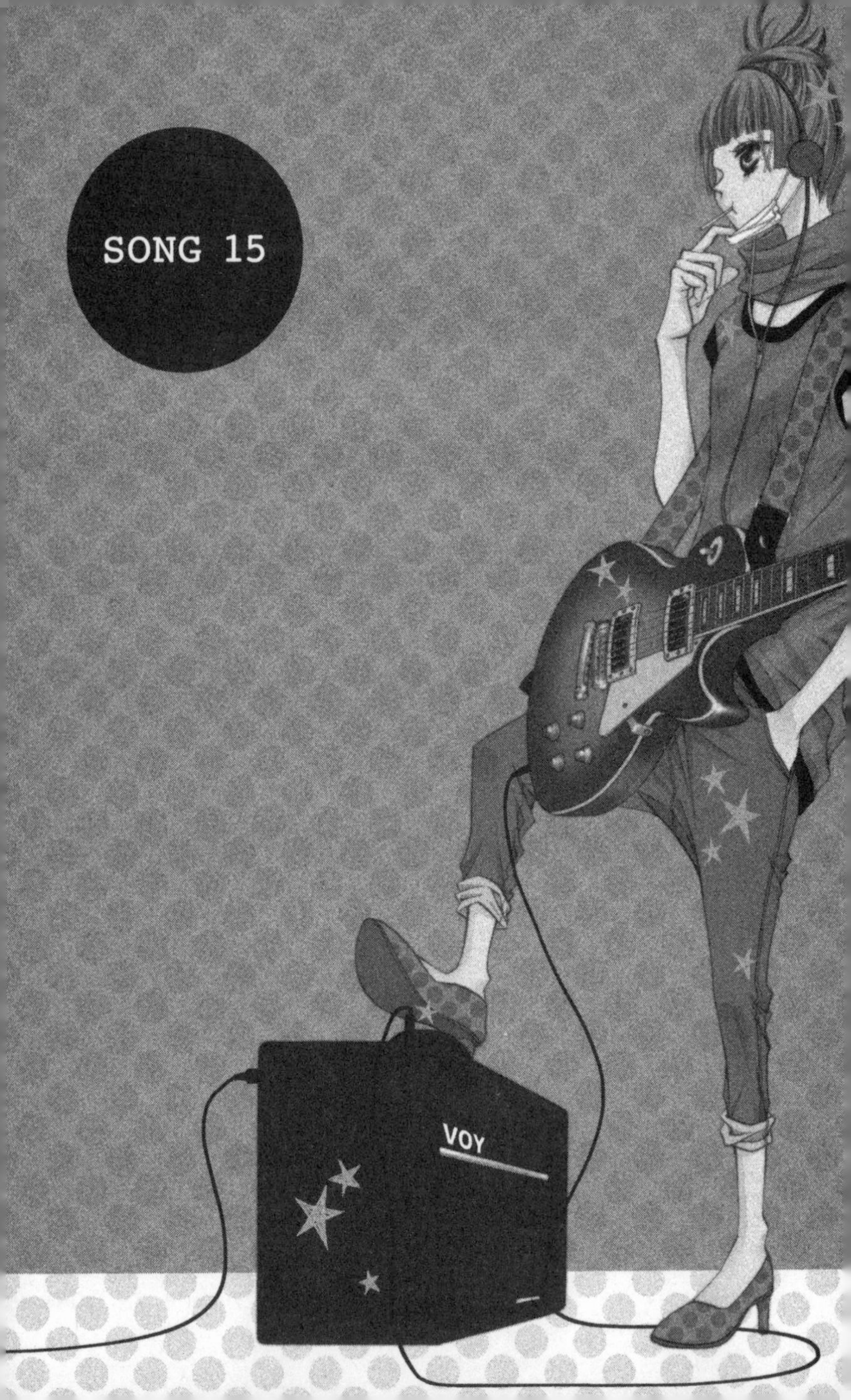
SONG 15
VOY

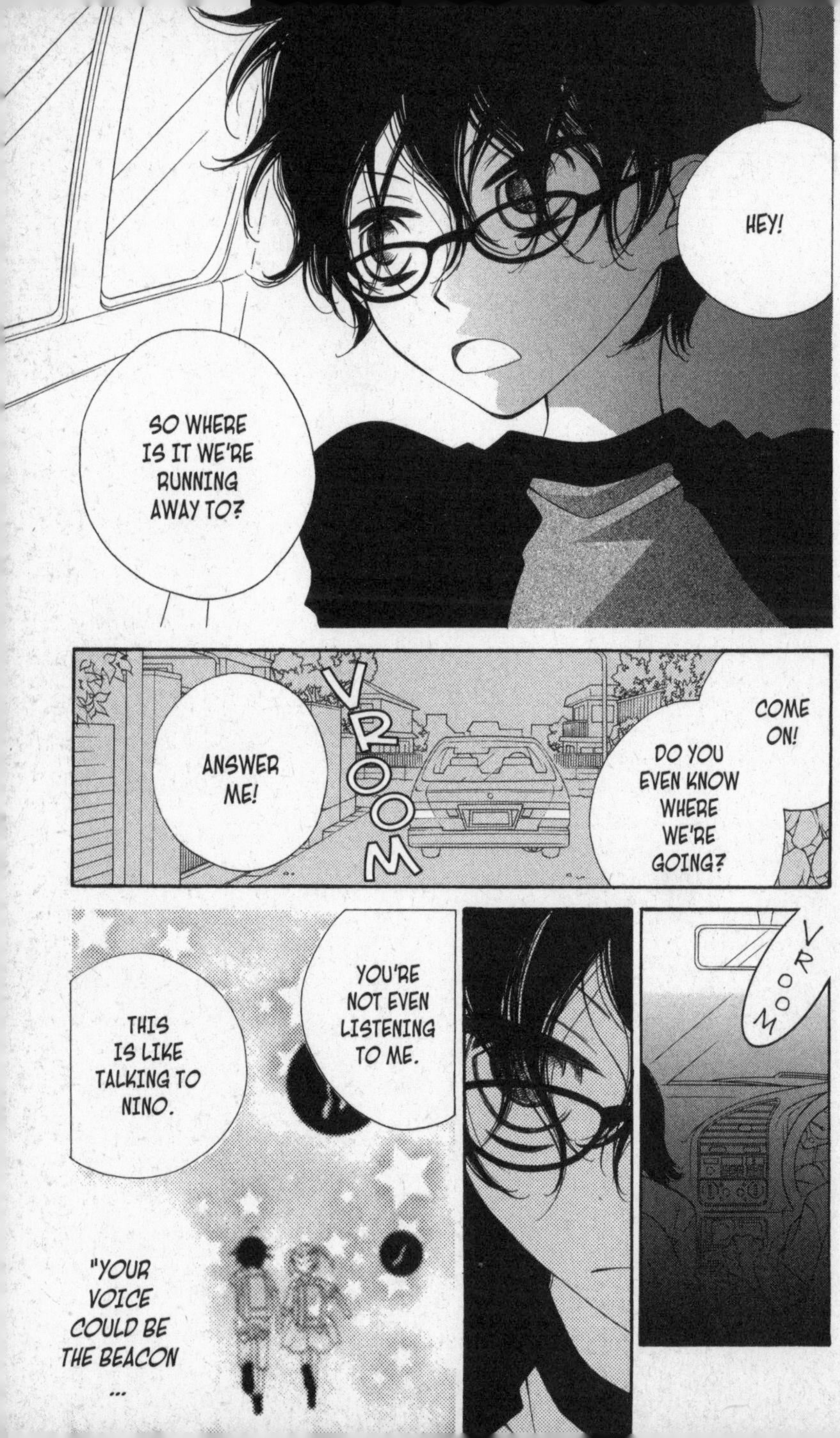
HEY!
SO WHERE IS IT WE'RE RUNNING AWAY TO?
COME ON!
DO YOU EVEN KNOW WHERE WE'RE GOING?
VROOM
ANSWER ME!
VROOM
YOU'RE NOT EVEN LISTENING TO ME.
THIS IS LIKE TALKING TO NINO.
"YOUR VOICE COULD BE THE BEACON ...

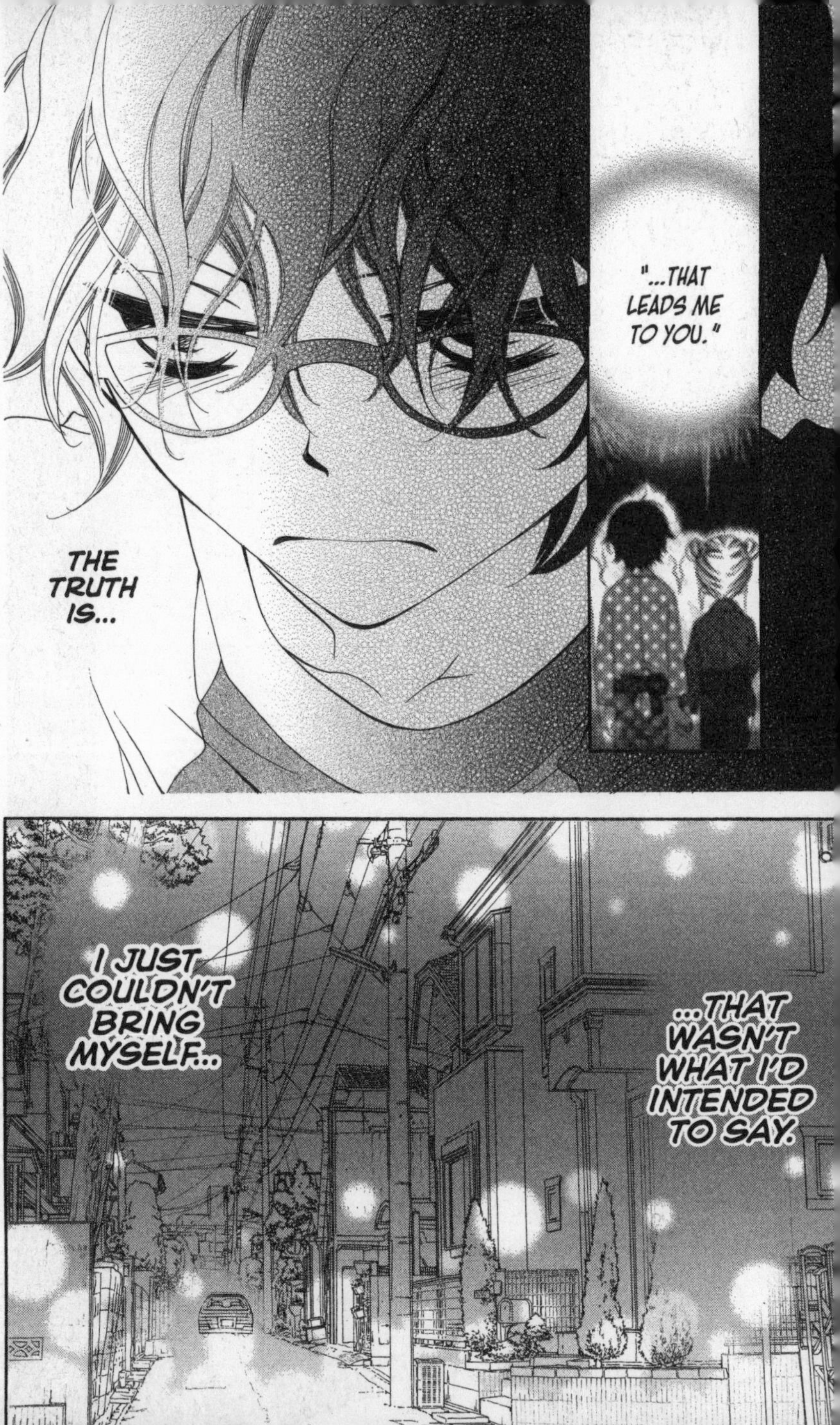
"...THAT LEADS ME TO YOU."
THE TRUTH IS...
...THAT WASN'T WHAT I'D INTENDED TO SAY.
I JUST COULDN'T BRING MYSELF...

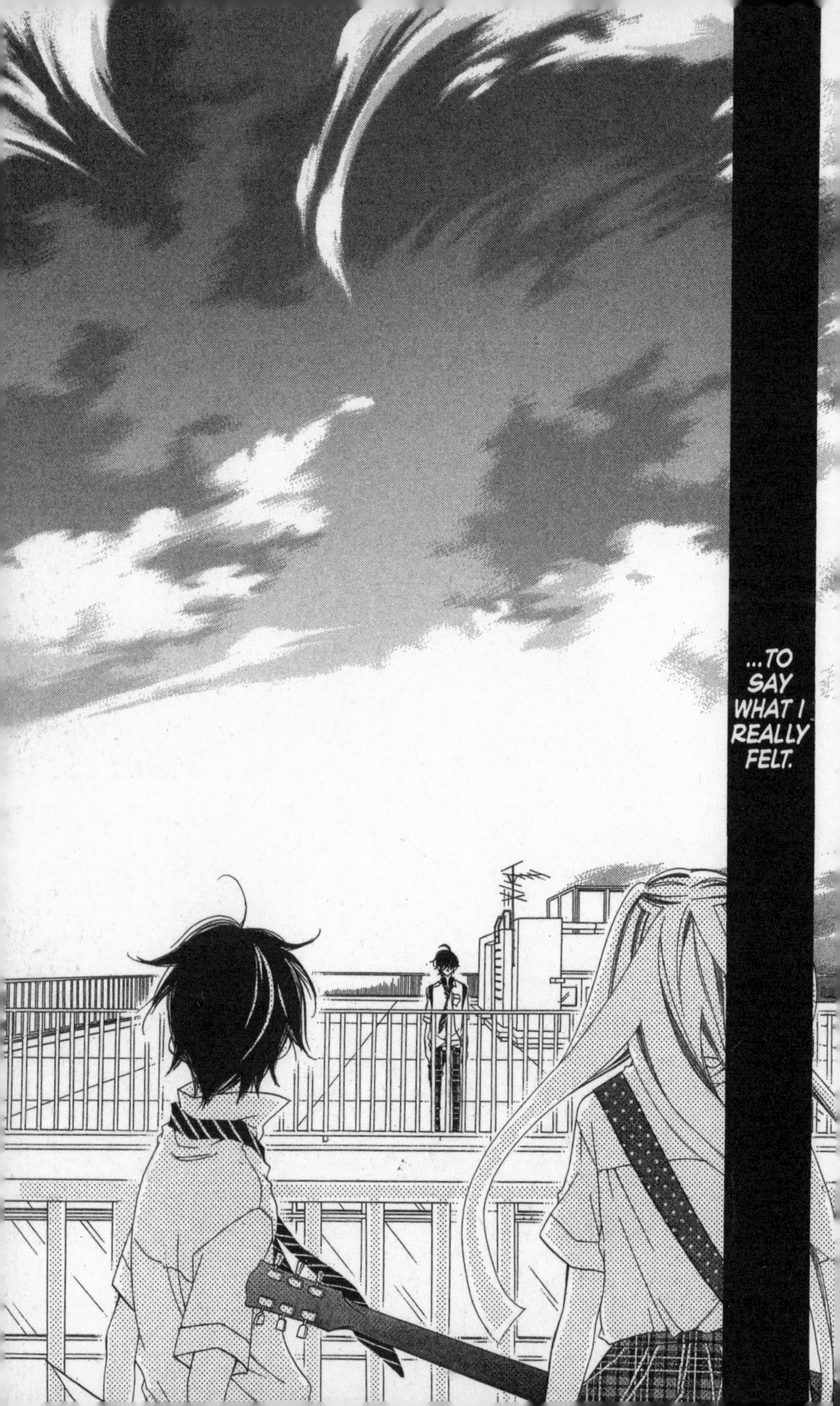
...TO SAY WHAT I REALLY FELT.

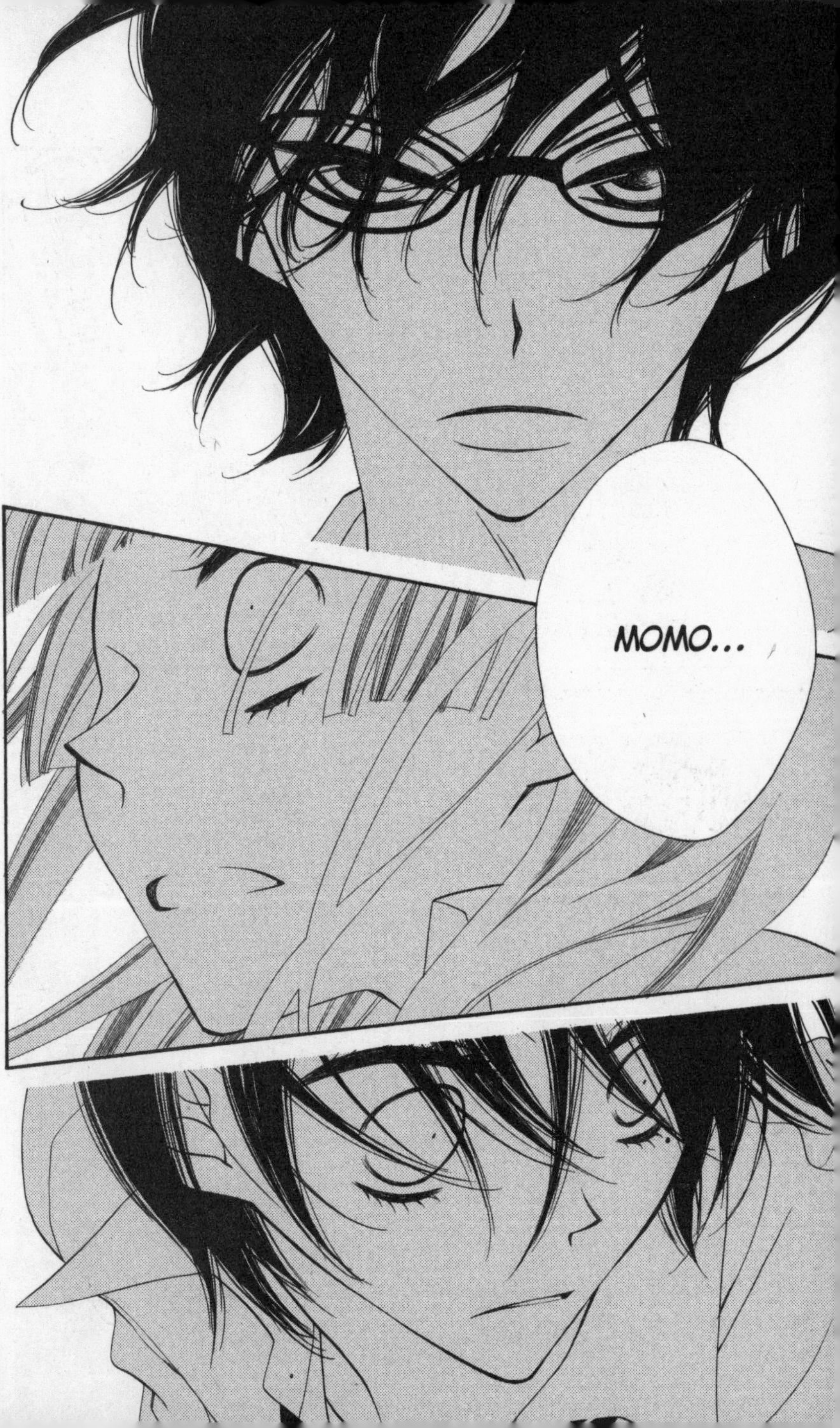
MOMO...

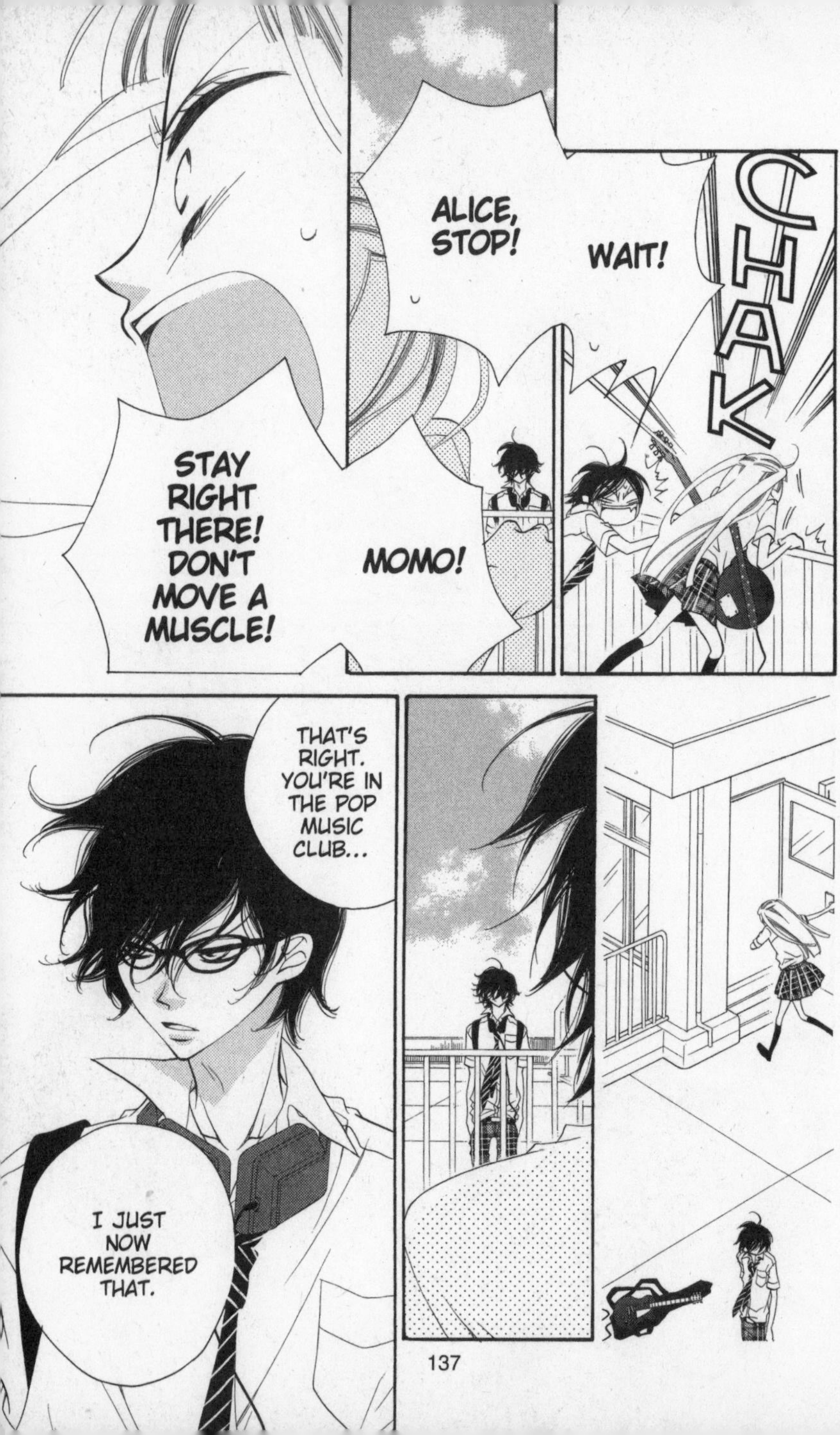
CHAK
WAIT!
ALICE, STOP!
MOMO!
STAY RIGHT THERE! DON'T MOVE A MUSCLE!
THAT'S RIGHT. YOU'RE IN THE POP MUSIC CLUB...
I JUST NOW REMEMBERED THAT.

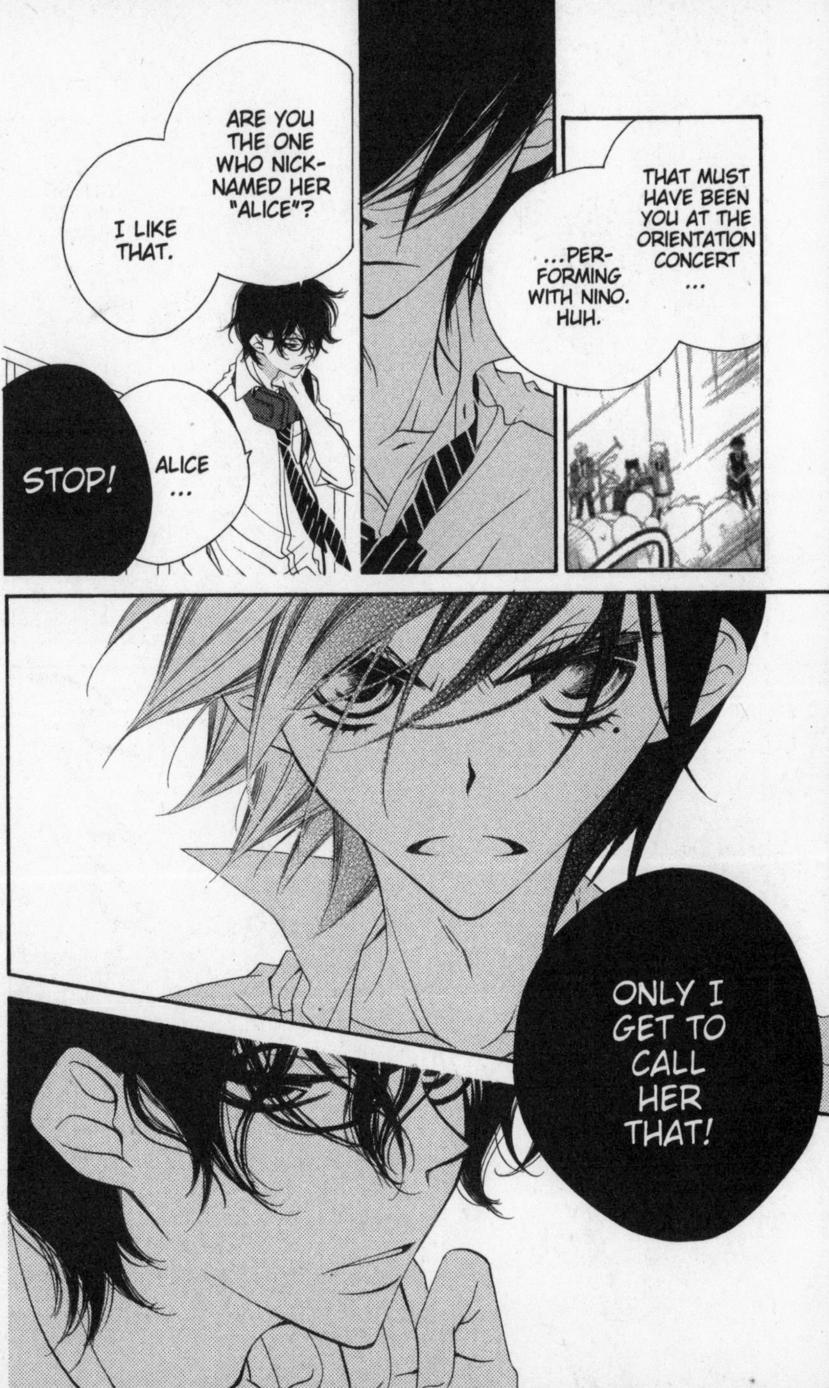
THAT MUST HAVE BEEN YOU AT THE ORIENTATION CONCERT ...
...PER-FORMING WITH NINO. HUH.
ARE YOU THE ONE WHO NICK-NAMED HER "ALICE"?
I LIKE THAT.
ALICE ...
STOP!
ONLY I GET TO CALL HER THAT!

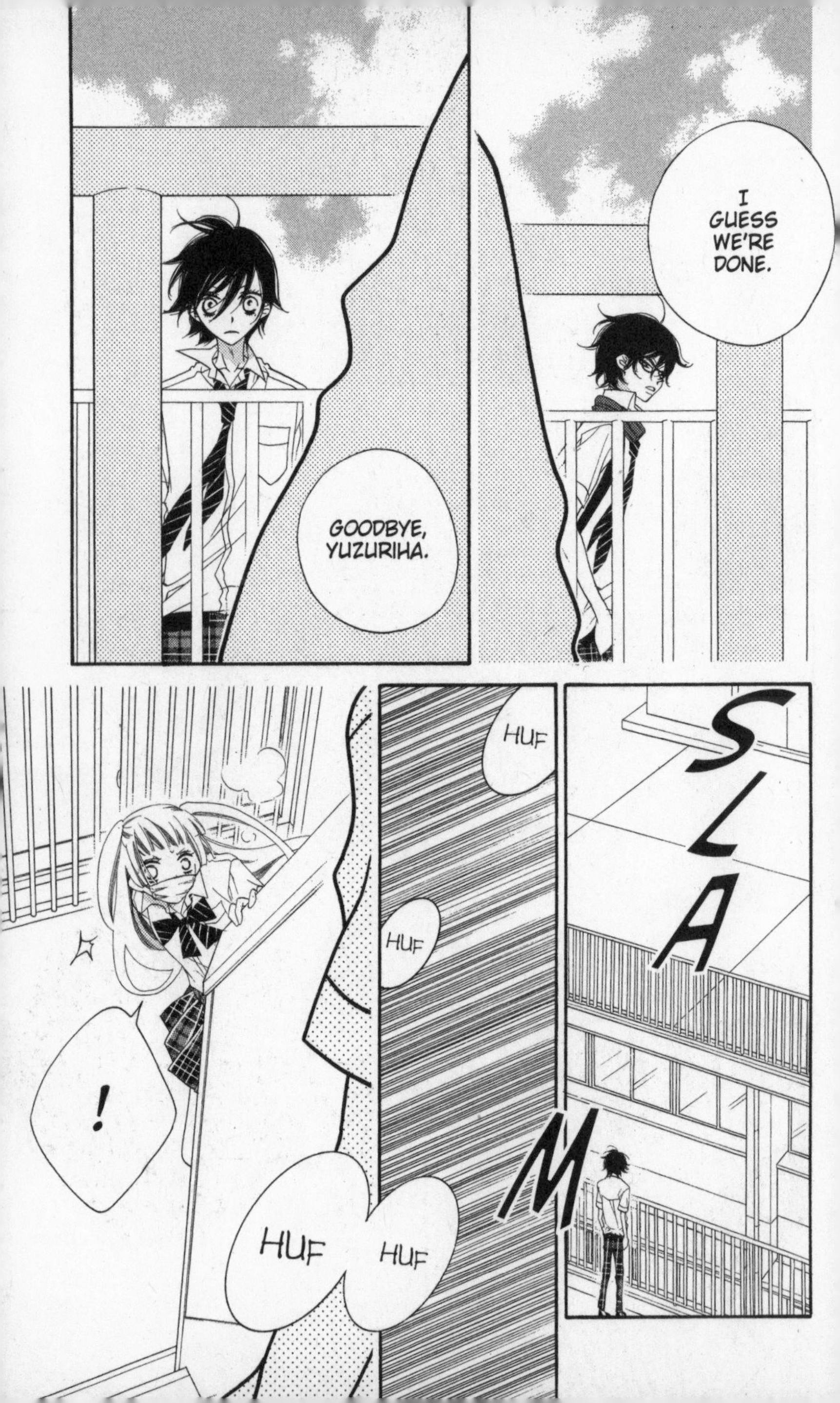

I GUESS WE'RE DONE.
GOODBYE, YUZURIHA.
SLAM
HUF
HUF
!
HUF
HUF

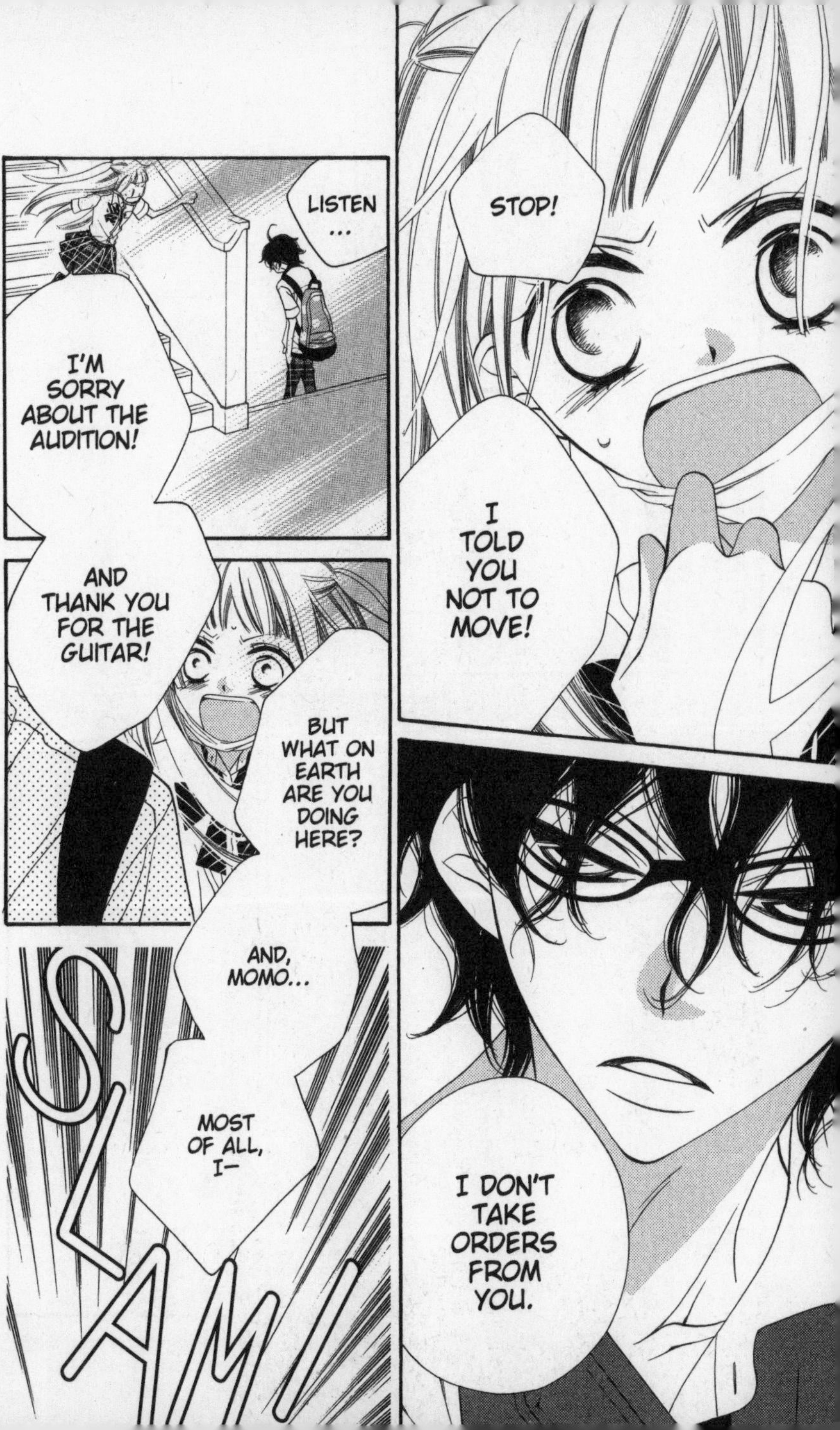
STOP!
I TOLD YOU NOT TO MOVE!
I DON'T TAKE ORDERS FROM YOU.
LISTEN...
I'M SORRY ABOUT THE AUDITION!
AND THANK YOU FOR THE GUITAR!
BUT WHAT ON EARTH ARE YOU DOING HERE?
AND, MOMO...
MOST OF ALL, I—
SLAM!

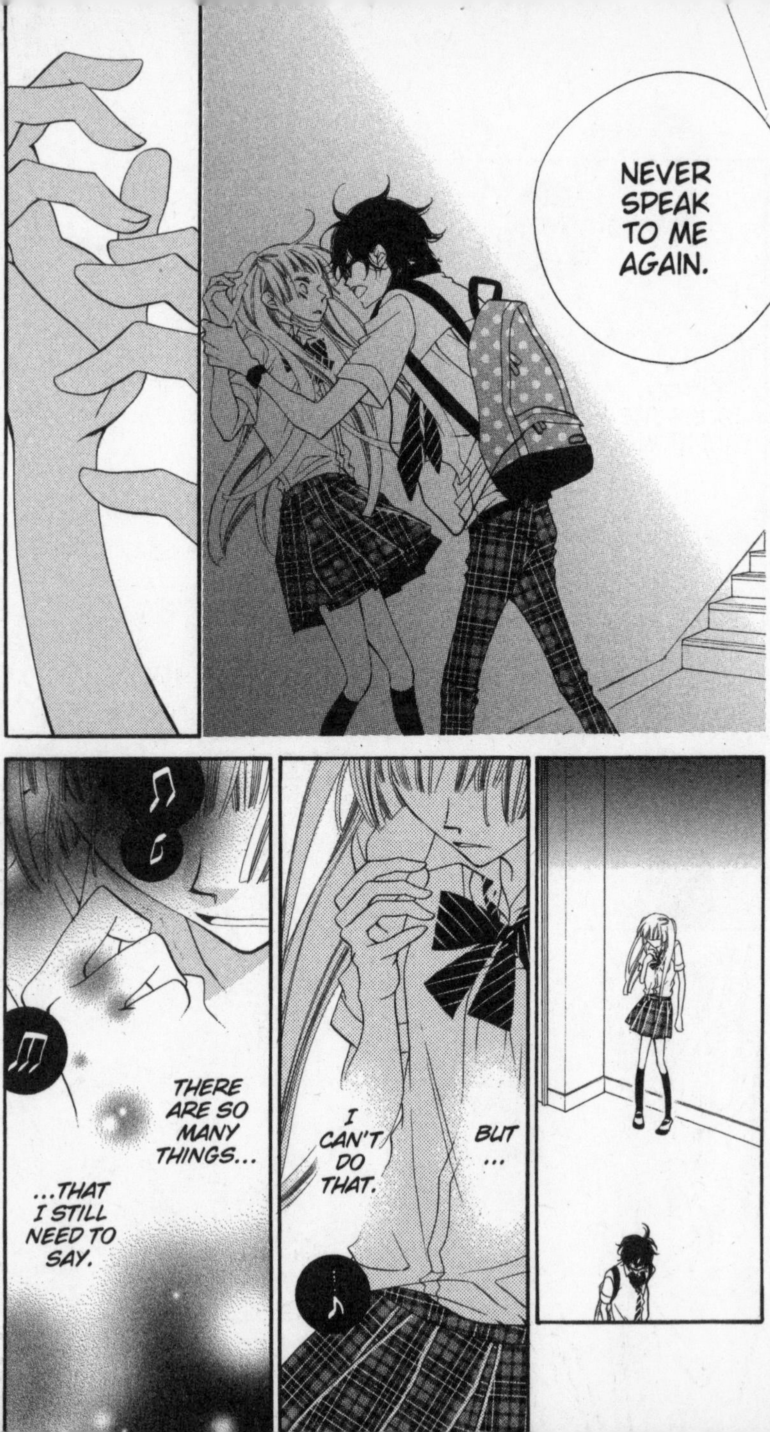
NEVER SPEAK TO ME AGAIN.
BUT ...
I CAN'T DO THAT.
THERE ARE SO MANY THINGS...
...THAT I STILL NEED TO SAY.

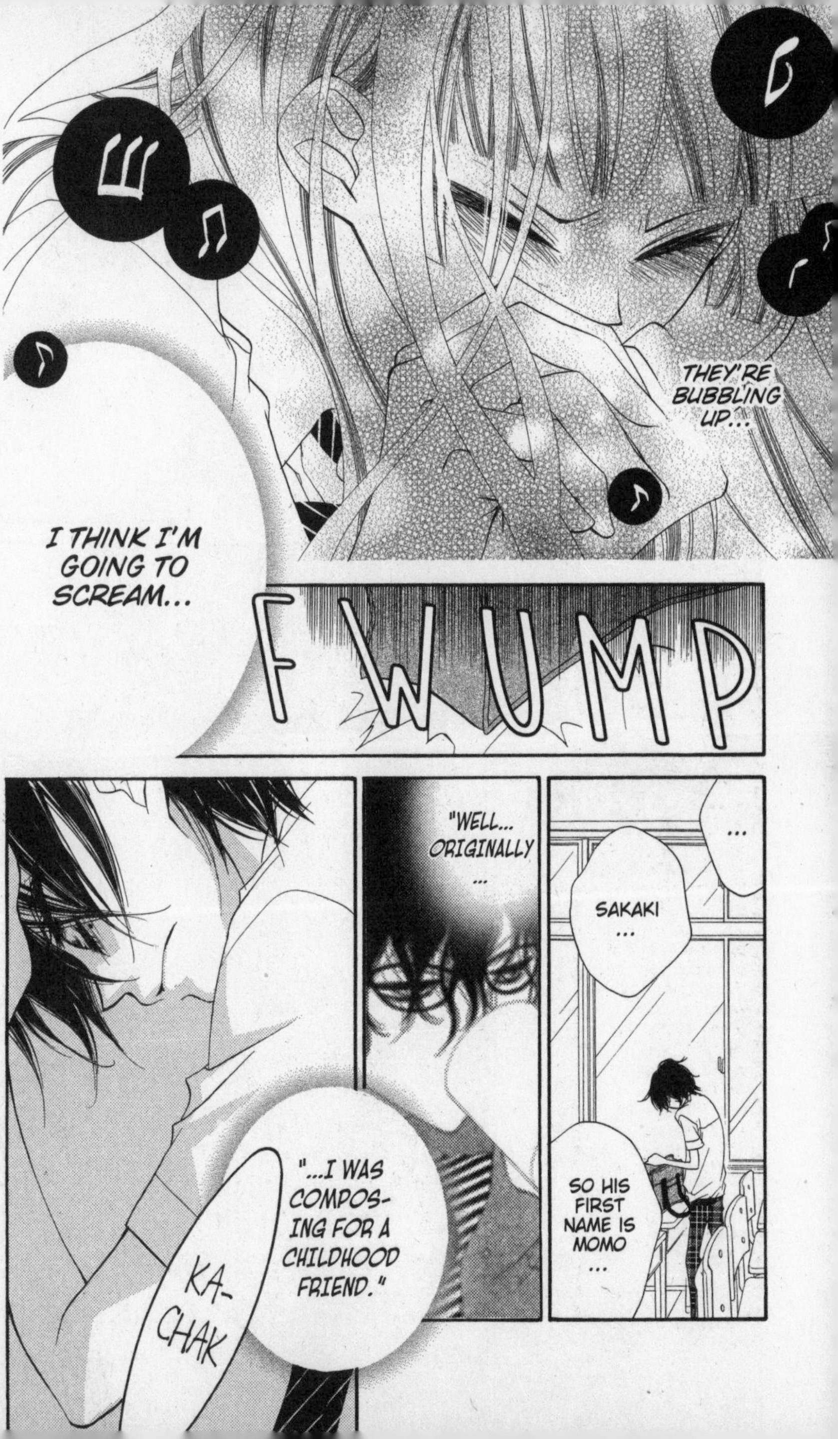
THEY'RE BUBBLING UP...
I THINK I'M GOING TO SCREAM...
FWUMP
...
SAKAKI ...
SO HIS FIRST NAME IS MOMO ...
"WELL... ORIGINALLY ...
"...I WAS COMPOS-ING FOR A CHILDHOOD FRIEND."
KA-CHAK

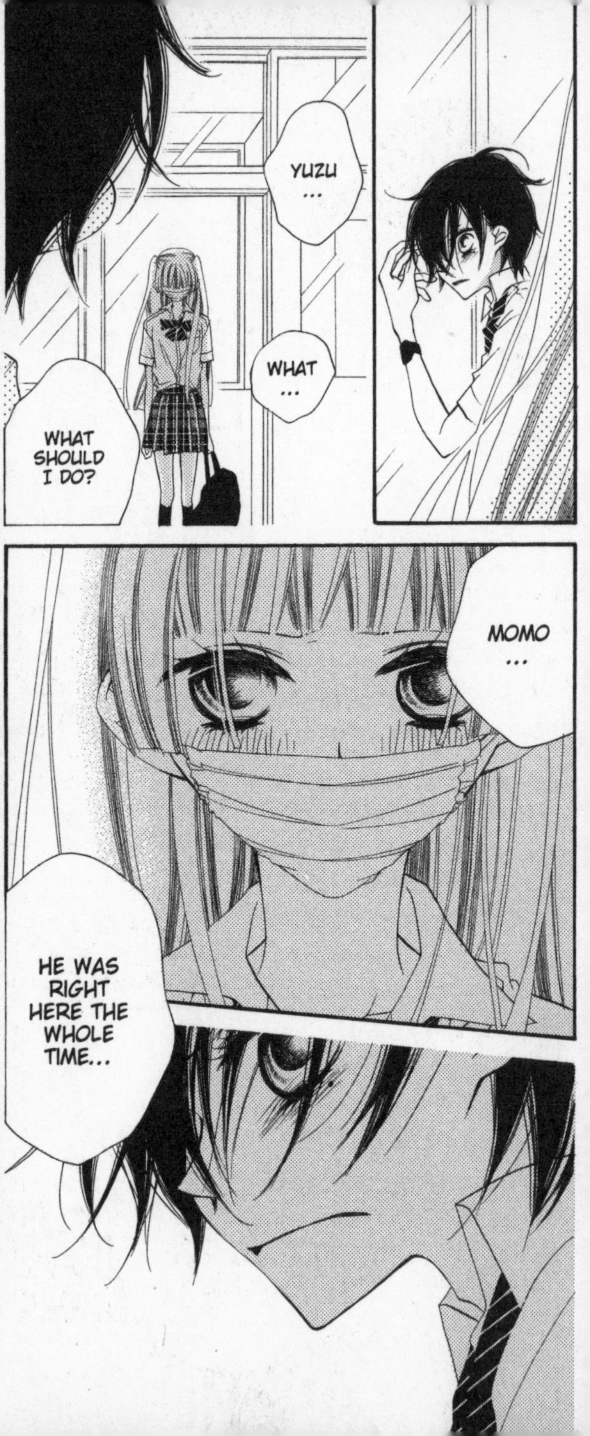
YUZU ...
WHAT ...
WHAT SHOULD I DO?
MOMO ...
HE WAS RIGHT HERE THE WHOLE TIME...

5

Okay, back to the gym talk! I tried, but I just can't fit a gym that opens at 10:30 into my lifestyle. So I've started taking walks instead!

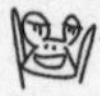
TA-DAH!

I know what you're all thinking—"Why didn't you just do that to begin with?!"

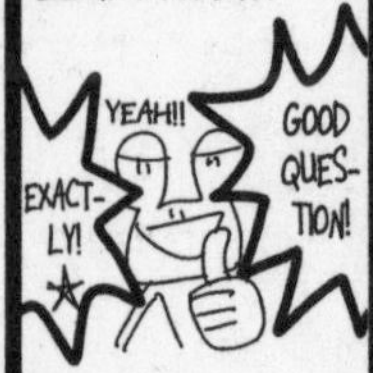
YEAH!!
GOOD QUESTION!
EXACTLY!

Anyway, I've been listening to my beloved Tokyo FM and J-Wave as I explore the streets of Yokohama. I can't believe how many shops and restaurants I'm discovering in my own neighborhood that I never knew existed! Walking is great!

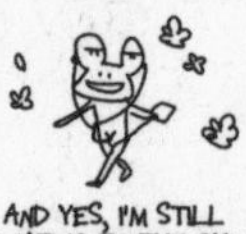

AND YES, I'M STILL DONATING TO THE GYM.

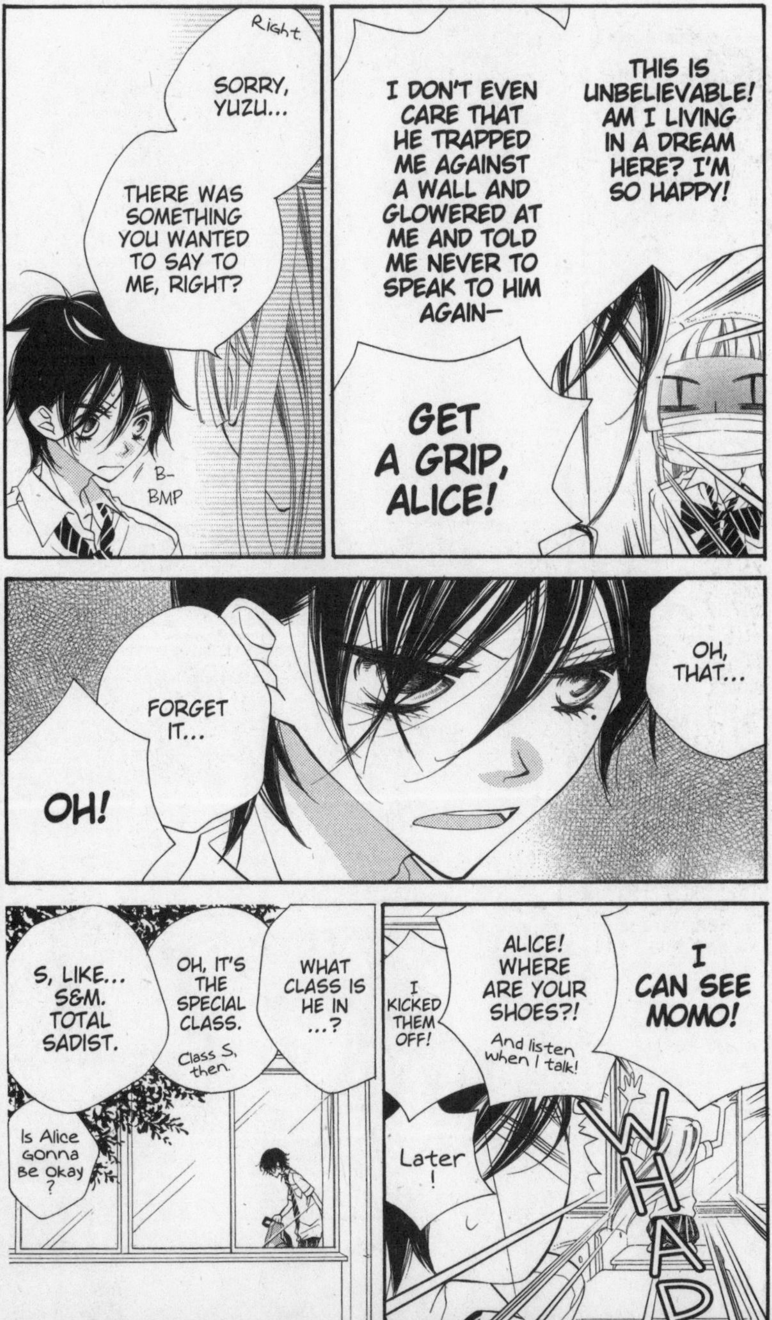
THIS IS UNBELIEVABLE! AM I LIVING IN A DREAM HERE? I'M SO HAPPY!
I DON'T EVEN CARE THAT HE TRAPPED ME AGAINST A WALL AND GLOWERED AT ME AND TOLD ME NEVER TO SPEAK TO HIM AGAIN—
GET A GRIP, ALICE!
Right.
SORRY, YUZU...
THERE WAS SOMETHING YOU WANTED TO SAY TO ME, RIGHT?
B-BMP
OH, THAT...
FORGET IT...
OH!
I CAN SEE MOMO!
ALICE! WHERE ARE YOUR SHOES?!
And listen when I talk!
I KICKED THEM OFF!
Later!
WHAP
WHAT CLASS IS HE IN ...?
OH, IT'S THE SPECIAL CLASS.
Class S, then.
S, LIKE... S&M. TOTAL SADIST.
Is Alice gonna be okay?

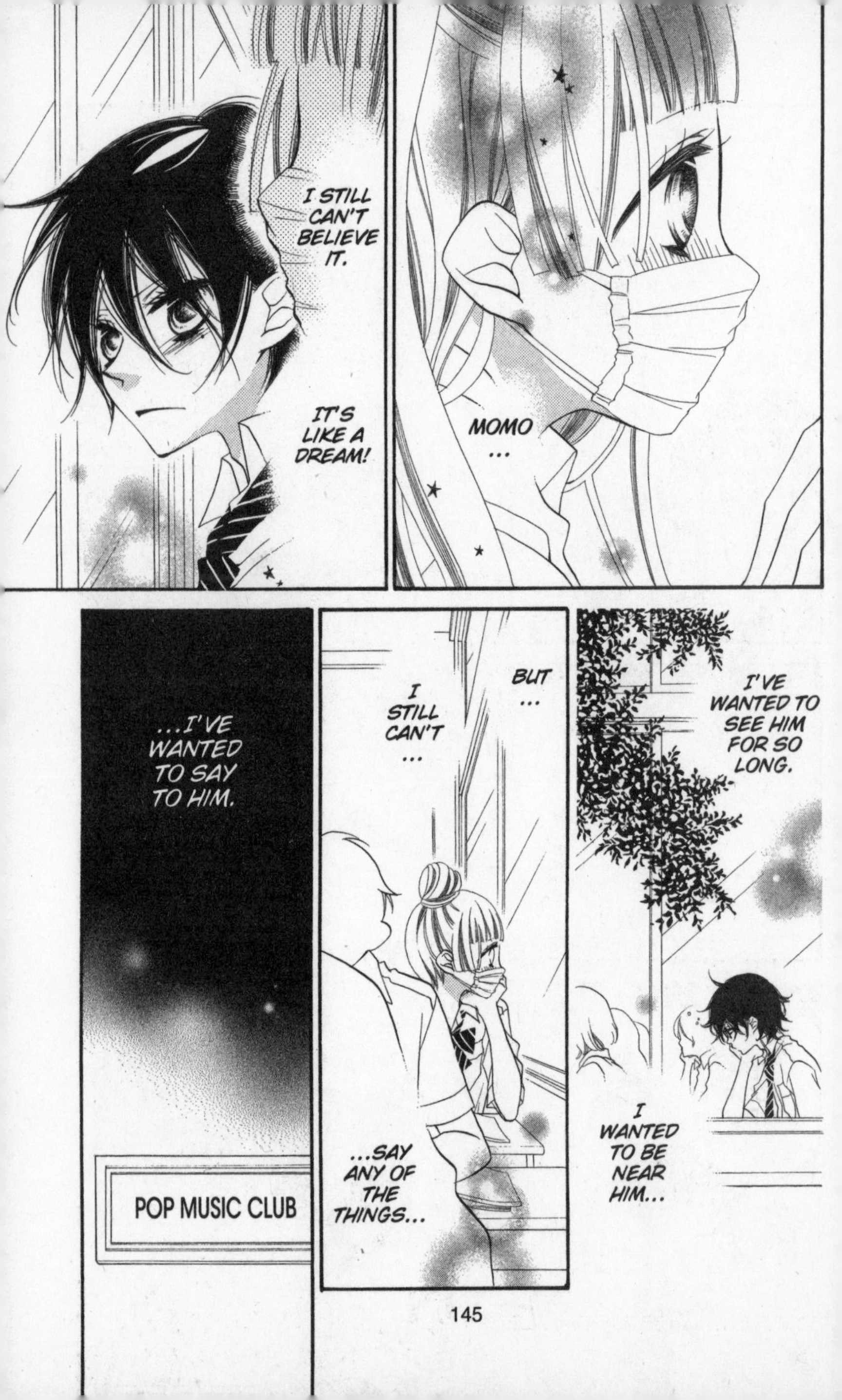
MOMO ...
I STILL CAN'T BELIEVE IT.
IT'S LIKE A DREAM!
I'VE WANTED TO SEE HIM FOR SO LONG.
I WANTED TO BE NEAR HIM...
BUT ...
I STILL CAN'T ...
...SAY ANY OF THE THINGS...
...I'VE WANTED TO SAY TO HIM.
POP MUSIC CLUB

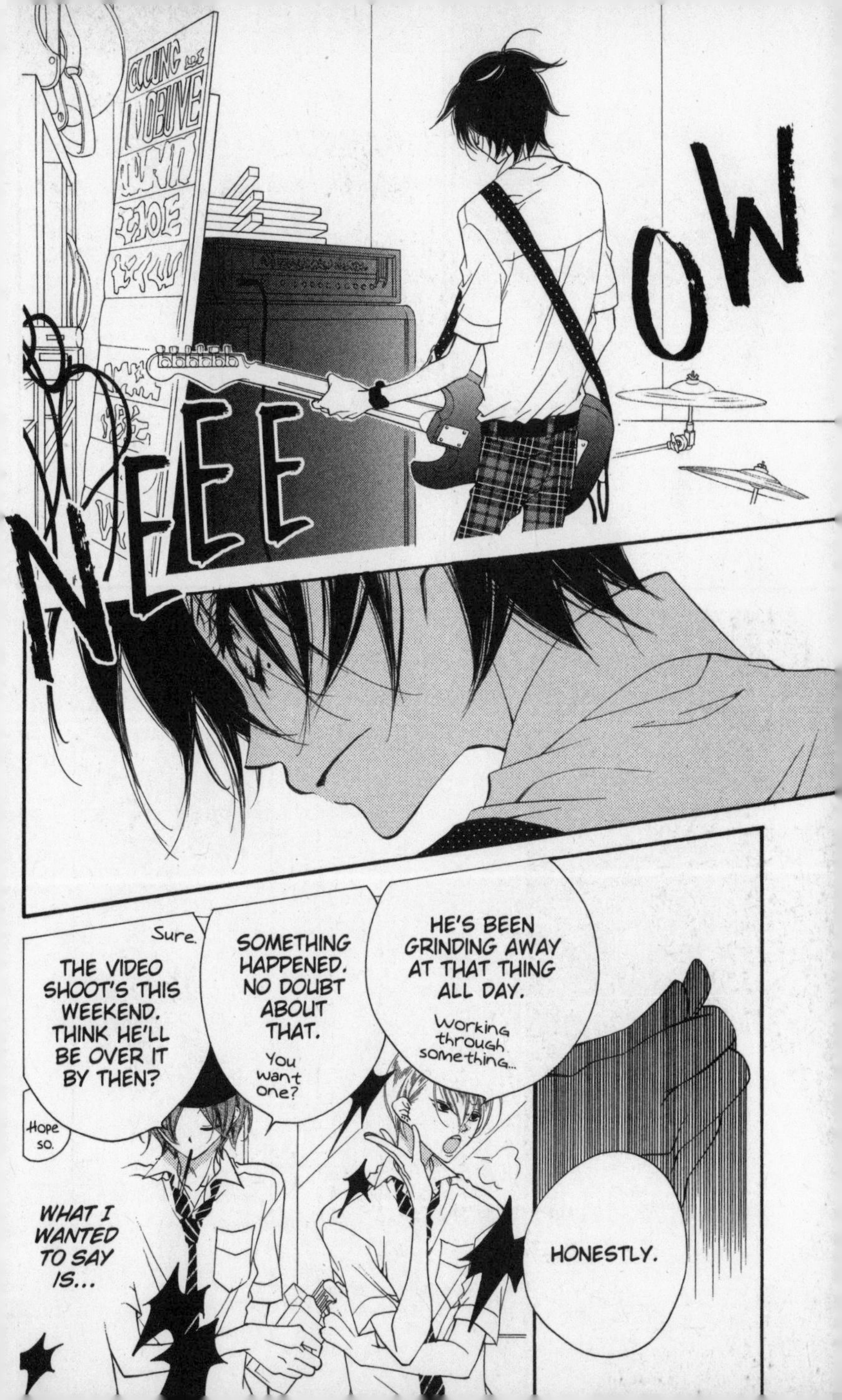
NEEEOW
HE'S BEEN GRINDING AWAY AT THAT THING ALL DAY.
Working through something...
SOMETHING HAPPENED. NO DOUBT ABOUT THAT.
You want one?
Sure.
THE VIDEO SHOOT'S THIS WEEKEND. THINK HE'LL BE OVER IT BY THEN?
Hope so.
HONESTLY.
WHAT I WANTED TO SAY IS...

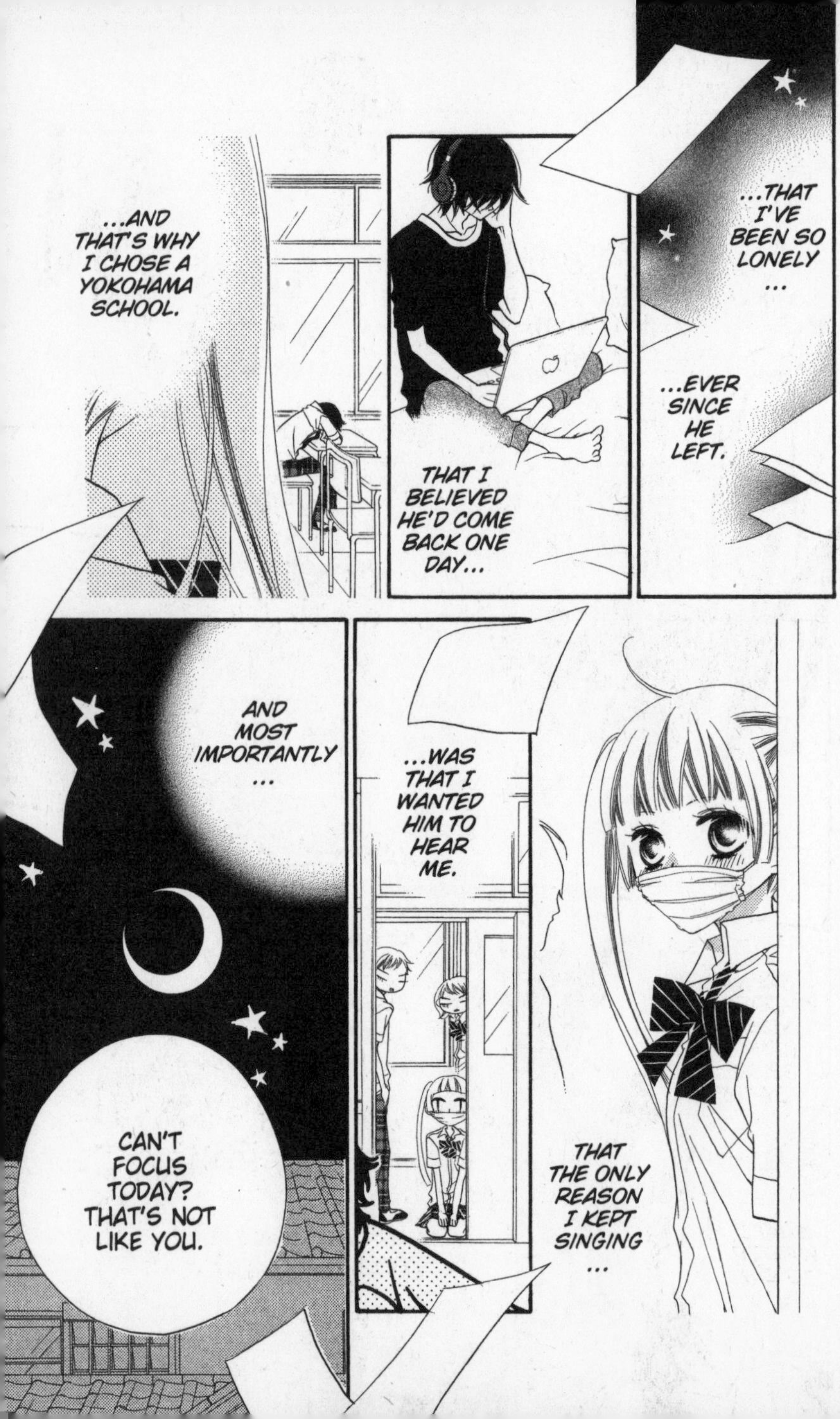
...THAT I'VE BEEN SO LONELY ...
...EVER SINCE HE LEFT.
THAT I BELIEVED HE'D COME BACK ONE DAY...
...AND THAT'S WHY I CHOSE A YOKOHAMA SCHOOL.
THAT THE ONLY REASON I KEPT SINGING ...
...WAS THAT I WANTED HIM TO HEAR ME.
AND MOST IMPORTANTLY ...
CAN'T FOCUS TODAY? THAT'S NOT LIKE YOU.

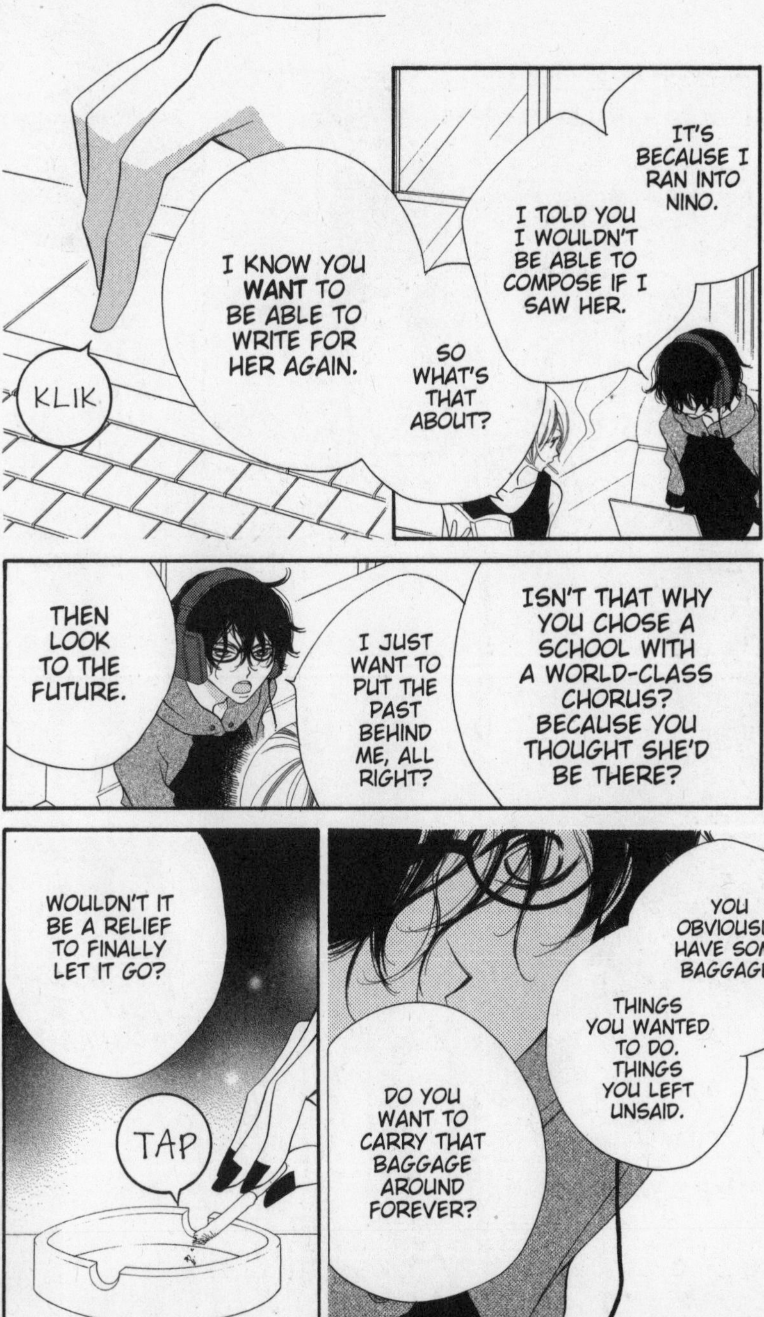
IT'S BECAUSE I RAN INTO NINO.
I TOLD YOU I WOULDN'T BE ABLE TO COMPOSE IF I SAW HER.
I KNOW YOU WANT TO BE ABLE TO WRITE FOR HER AGAIN.
SO WHAT'S THAT ABOUT?
KLIK
ISN'T THAT WHY YOU CHOSE A SCHOOL WITH A WORLD-CLASS CHORUS? BECAUSE YOU THOUGHT SHE'D BE THERE?
I JUST WANT TO PUT THE PAST BEHIND ME, ALL RIGHT?
THEN LOOK TO THE FUTURE.
YOU OBVIOUSLY HAVE SOME BAGGAGE.
THINGS YOU WANTED TO DO. THINGS YOU LEFT UNSAID.
DO YOU WANT TO CARRY THAT BAGGAGE AROUND FOREVER?
WOULDN'T IT BE A RELIEF TO FINALLY LET IT GO?
TAP

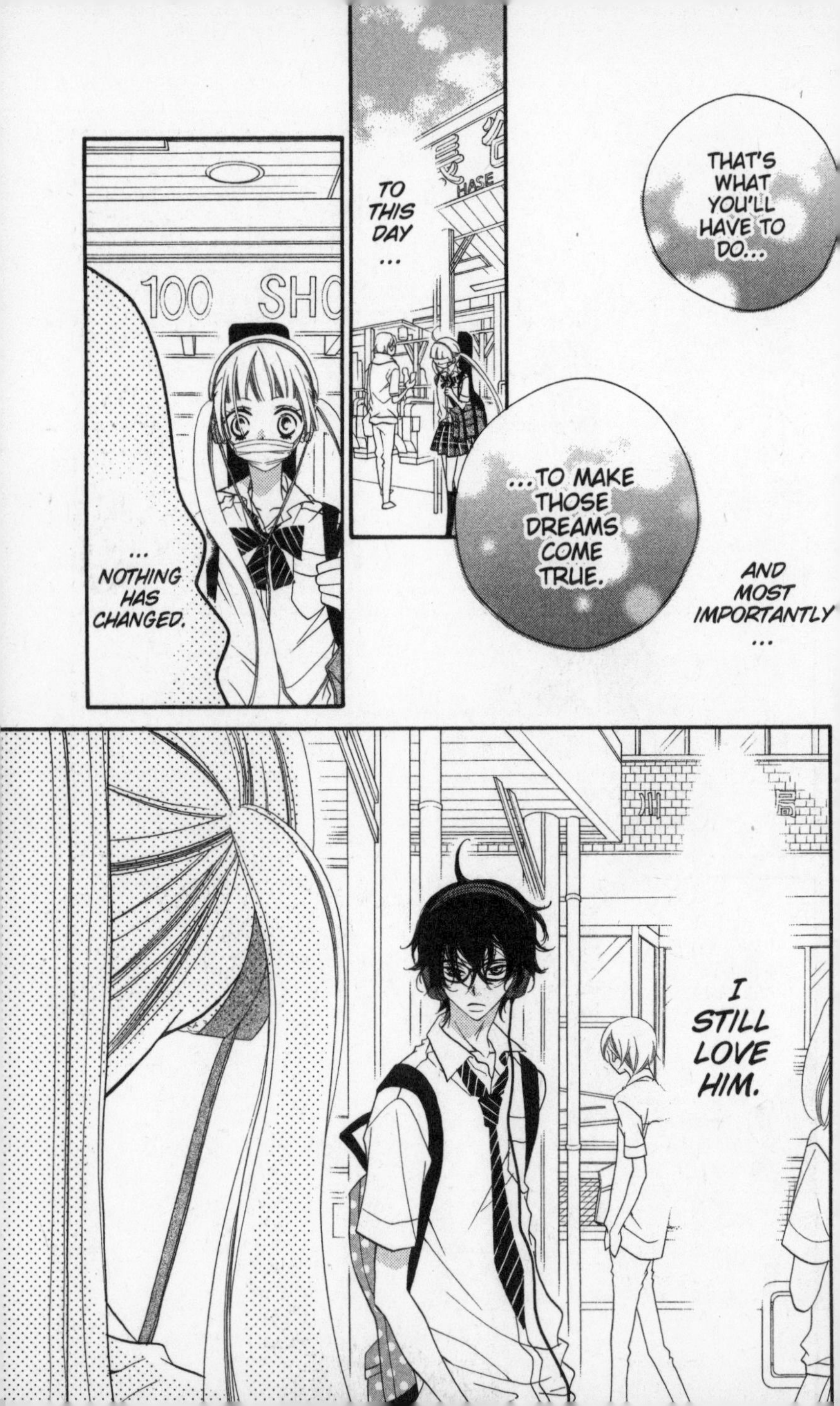
THAT'S WHAT YOU'LL HAVE TO DO...
...TO MAKE THOSE DREAMS COME TRUE.
TO THIS DAY ...
HASE
100 SHO
... NOTHING HAS CHANGED.
AND MOST IMPORTANTLY ...
I STILL LOVE HIM.

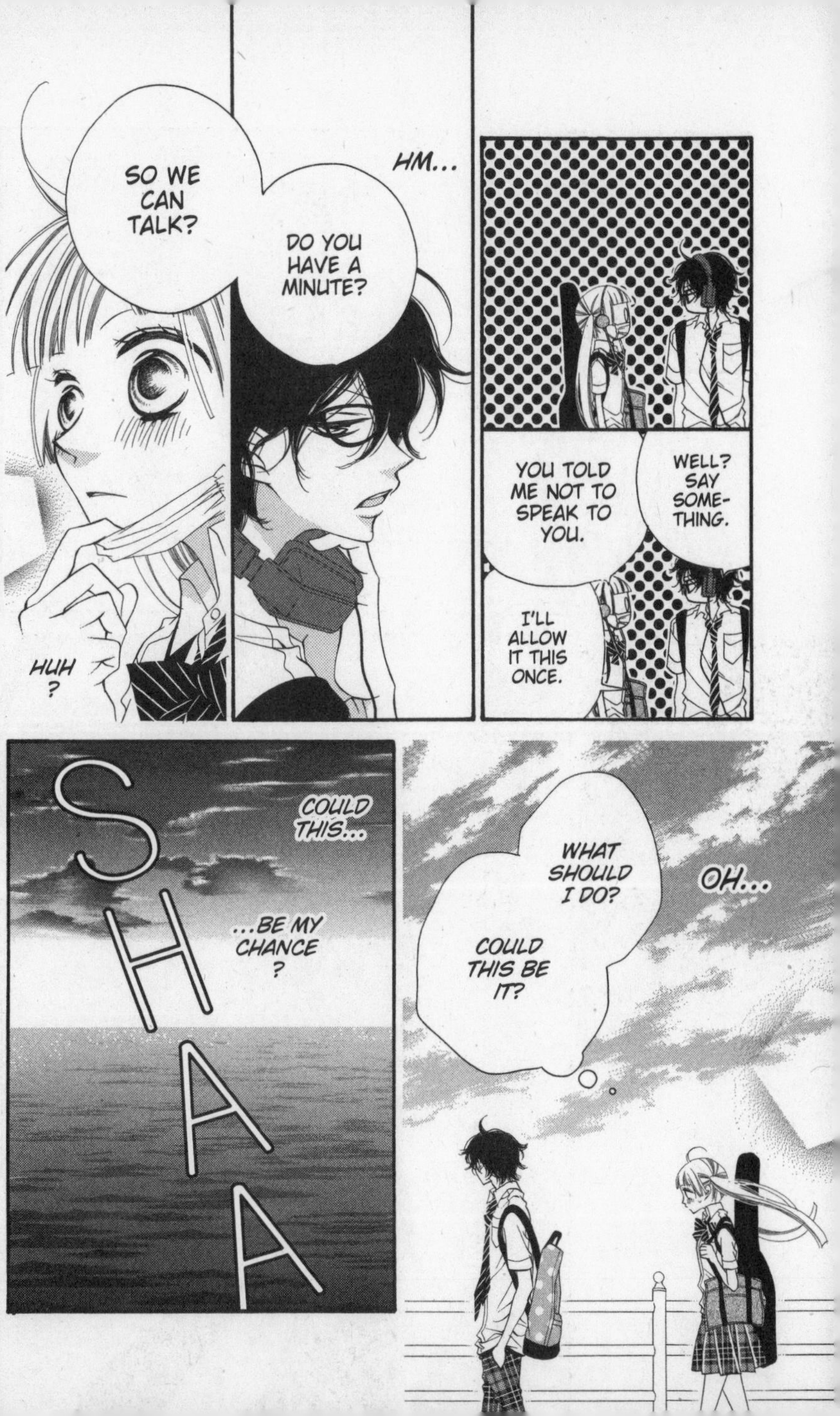
WELL? SAY SOME-THING.
YOU TOLD ME NOT TO SPEAK TO YOU.
I'LL ALLOW IT THIS ONCE.
HM...
DO YOU HAVE A MINUTE?
SO WE CAN TALK?
HUH?
OH...
WHAT SHOULD I DO?
COULD THIS BE IT?
SHAA
COULD THIS...
...BE MY CHANCE?

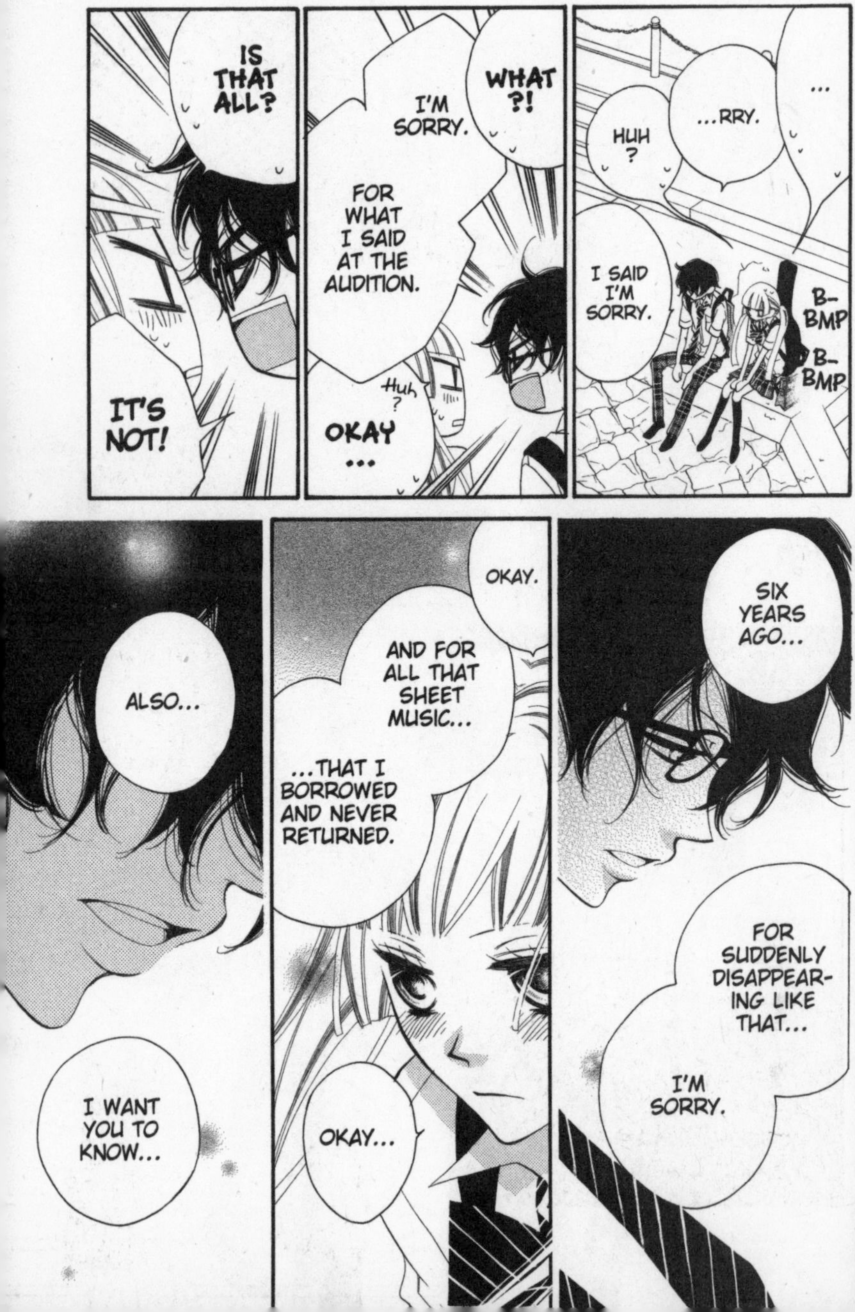
...
...RRY.
HUH?
I SAID I'M SORRY.
B-BMP
B-BMP
WHAT?!
I'M SORRY.
FOR WHAT I SAID AT THE AUDITION.
Huh?
OKAY...
IS THAT ALL?
IT'S NOT!
SIX YEARS AGO...
FOR SUDDENLY DISAPPEARING LIKE THAT...
I'M SORRY.
OKAY.
AND FOR ALL THAT SHEET MUSIC...
...THAT I BORROWED AND NEVER RETURNED.
OKAY...
ALSO...
I WANT YOU TO KNOW...

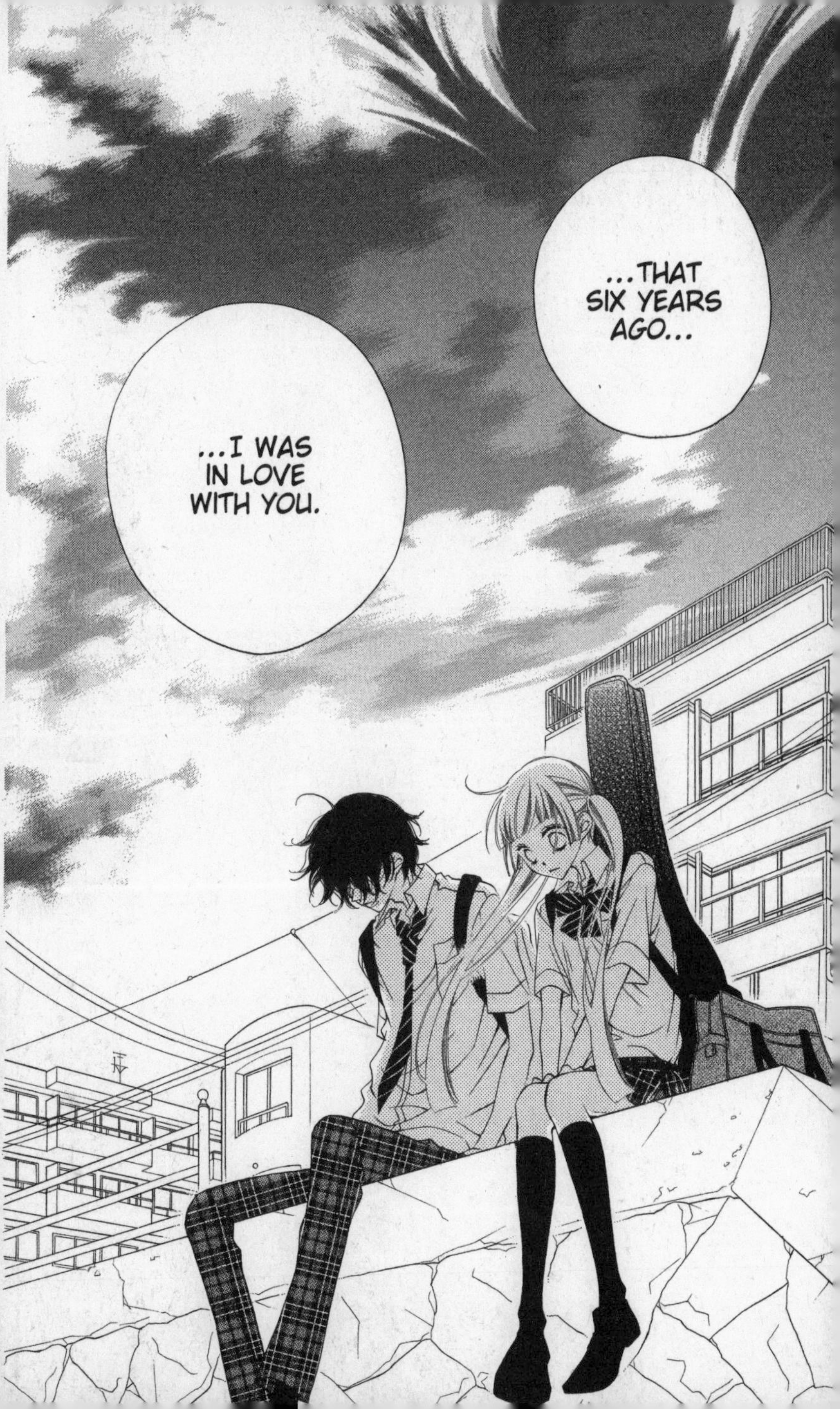
...THAT SIX YEARS AGO...
...I WAS IN LOVE WITH YOU.

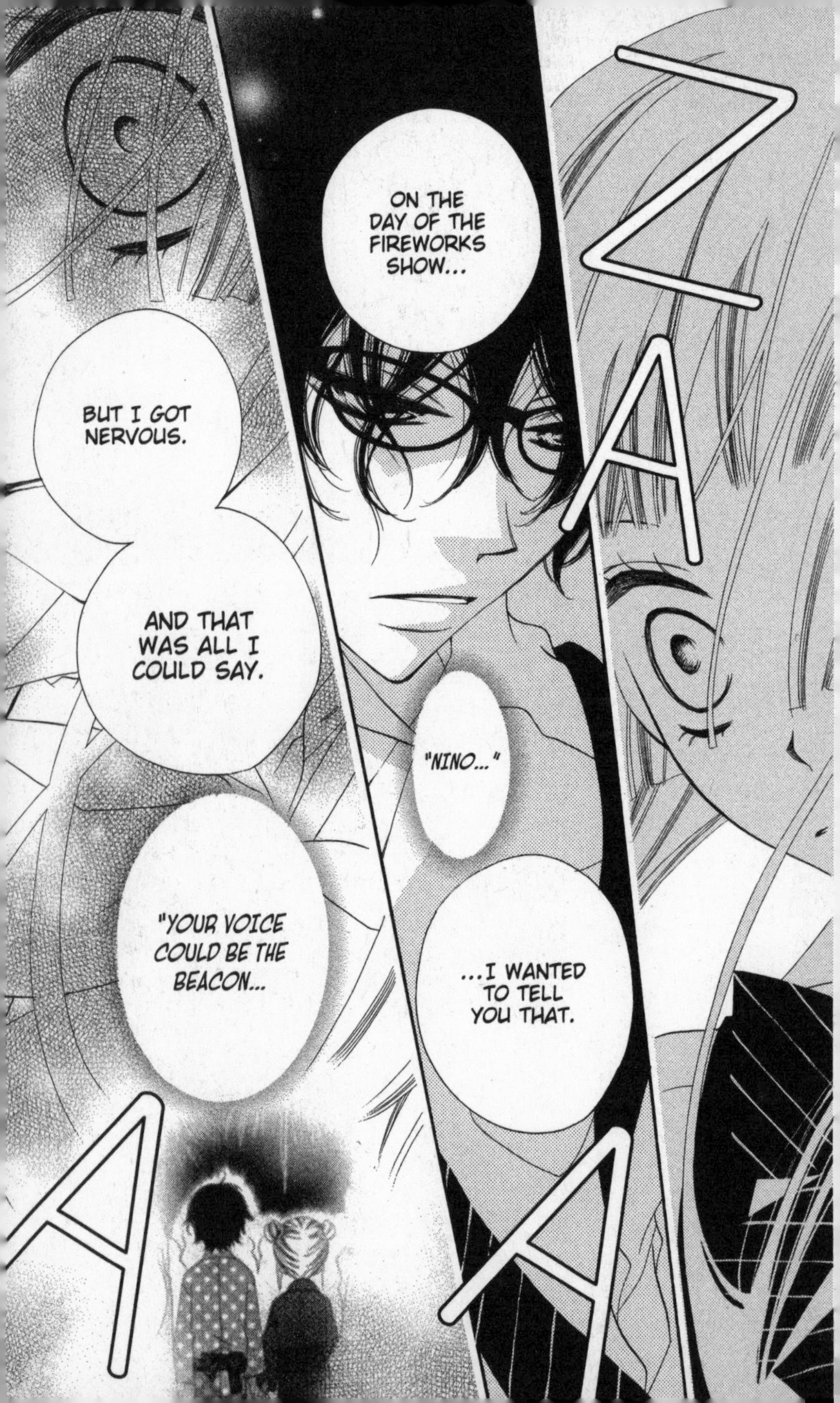
ZAAA
ON THE DAY OF THE FIREWORKS SHOW...
"NINO..."
...I WANTED TO TELL YOU THAT.
BUT I GOT NERVOUS.
AND THAT WAS ALL I COULD SAY.
"YOUR VOICE COULD BE THE BEACON...

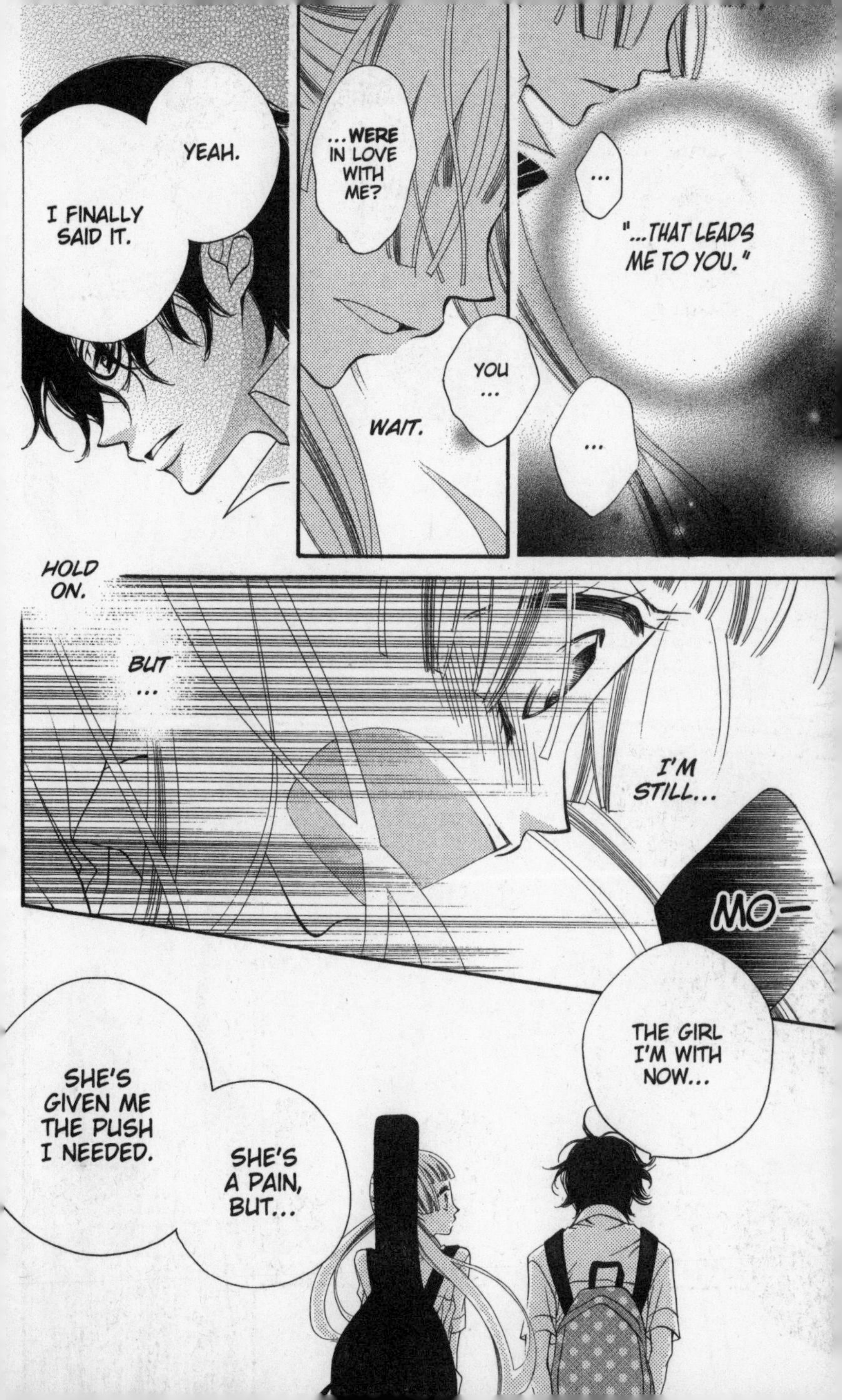
...
"...THAT LEADS ME TO YOU."
...
YOU ...
...WERE IN LOVE WITH ME?
WAIT.
YEAH.
I FINALLY SAID IT.
I'M STILL...
MO—
BUT ...
HOLD ON.
THE GIRL I'M WITH NOW...
SHE'S A PAIN, BUT...
SHE'S GIVEN ME THE PUSH I NEEDED.

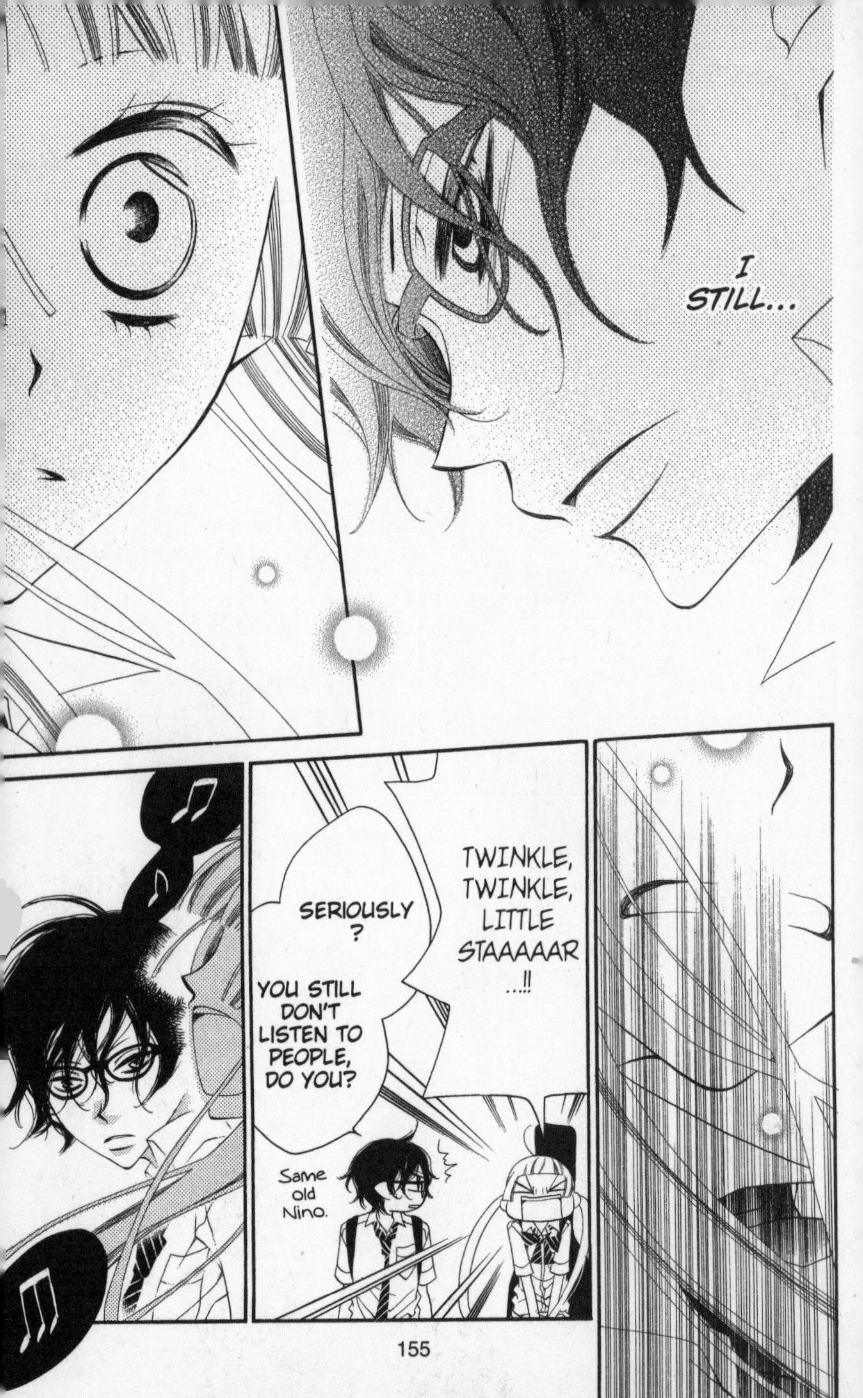

I STILL...
TWINKLE, TWINKLE, LITTLE STAAAAAR ...!!
SERIOUSLY?
YOU STILL DON'T LISTEN TO PEOPLE, DO YOU?
Same old Nino.

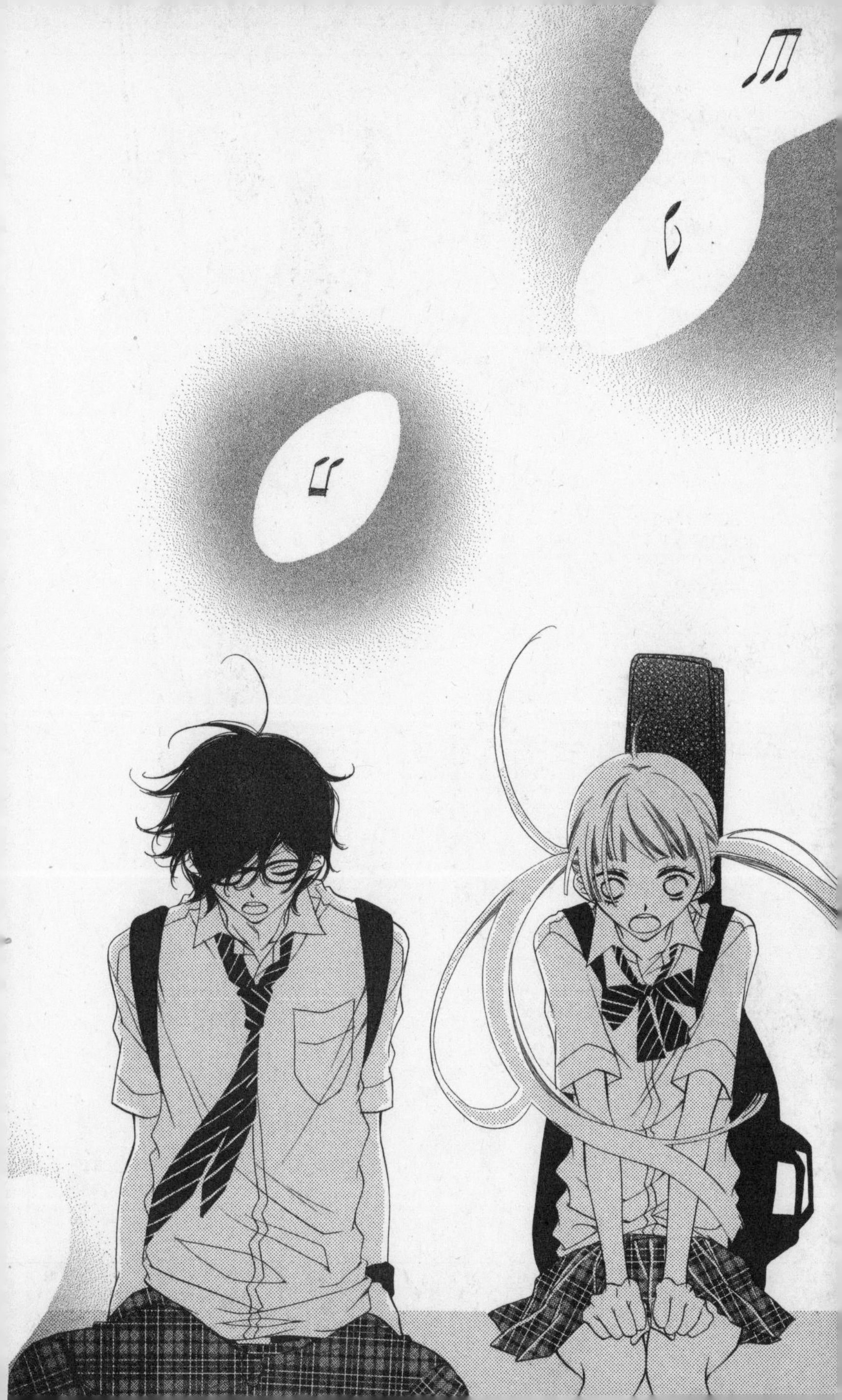

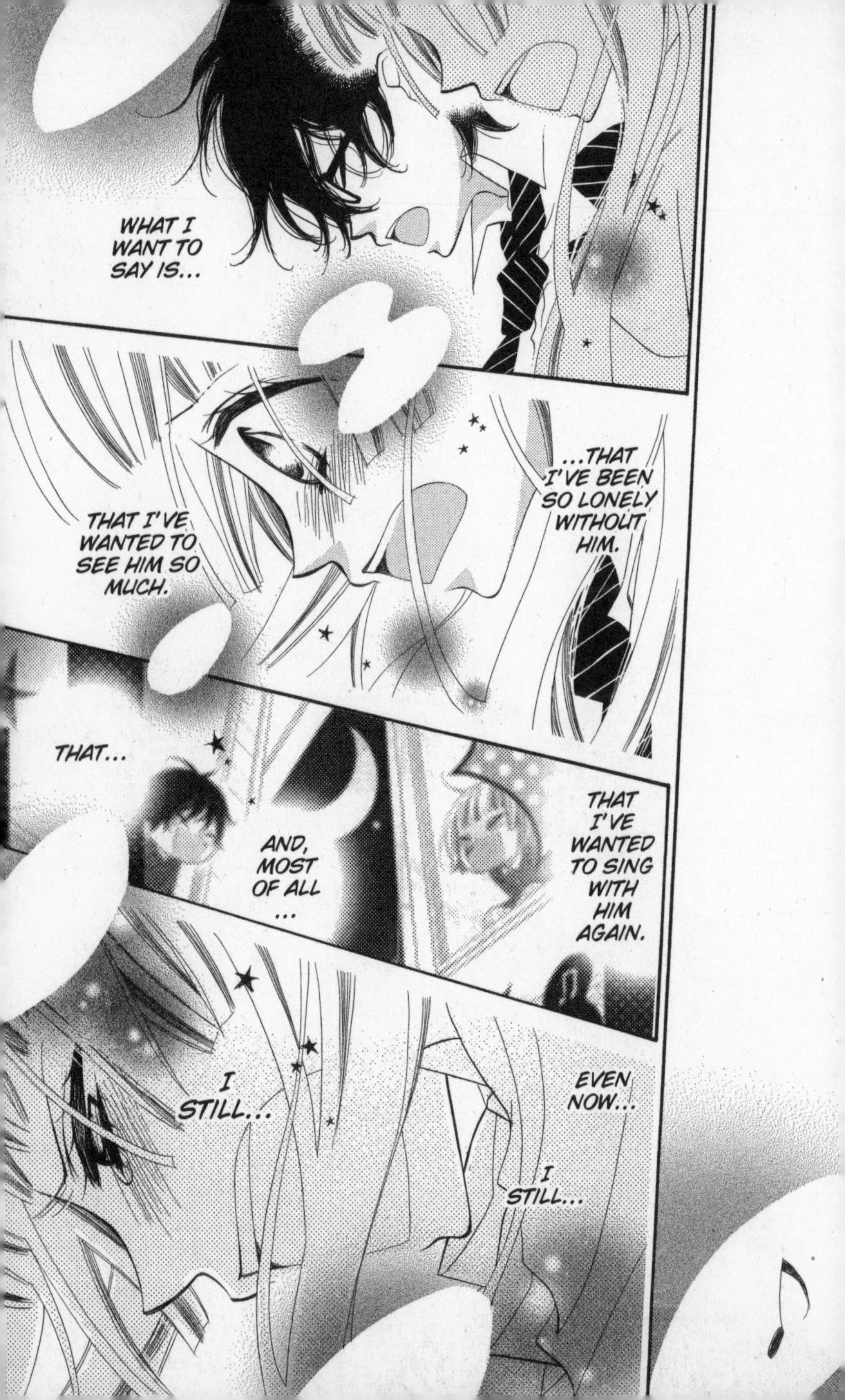
WHAT I WANT TO SAY IS...
...THAT I'VE BEEN SO LONELY WITHOUT HIM.
THAT I'VE WANTED TO SEE HIM SO MUCH.
THAT I'VE WANTED TO SING WITH HIM AGAIN.
AND, MOST OF ALL...
THAT...
EVEN NOW...
I STILL...
I STILL...

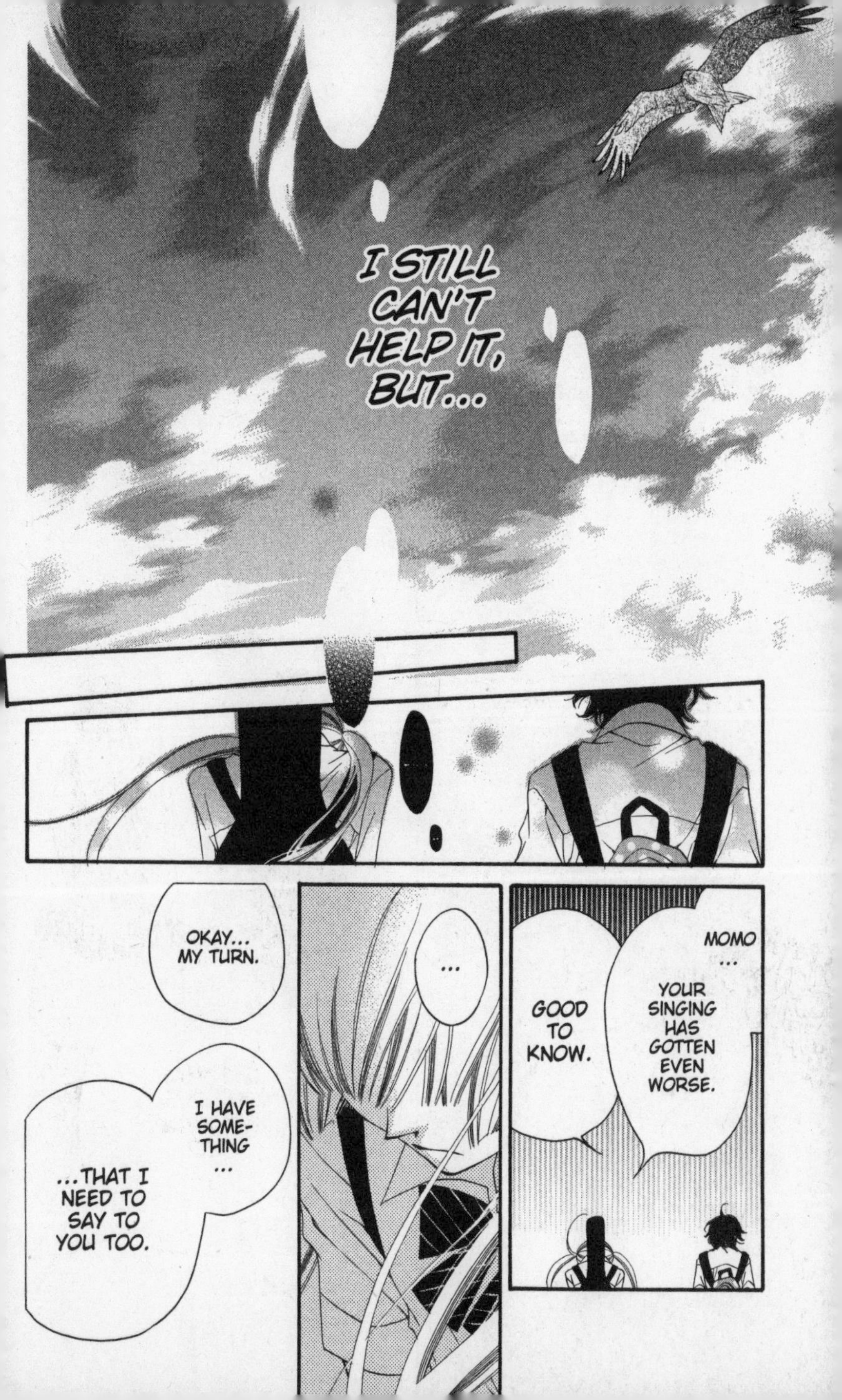
I STILL CAN'T HELP IT, BUT...
MOMO ... YOUR SINGING HAS GOTTEN EVEN WORSE.
GOOD TO KNOW.
...
OKAY... MY TURN.
I HAVE SOME-THING ...
...THAT I NEED TO SAY TO YOU TOO.

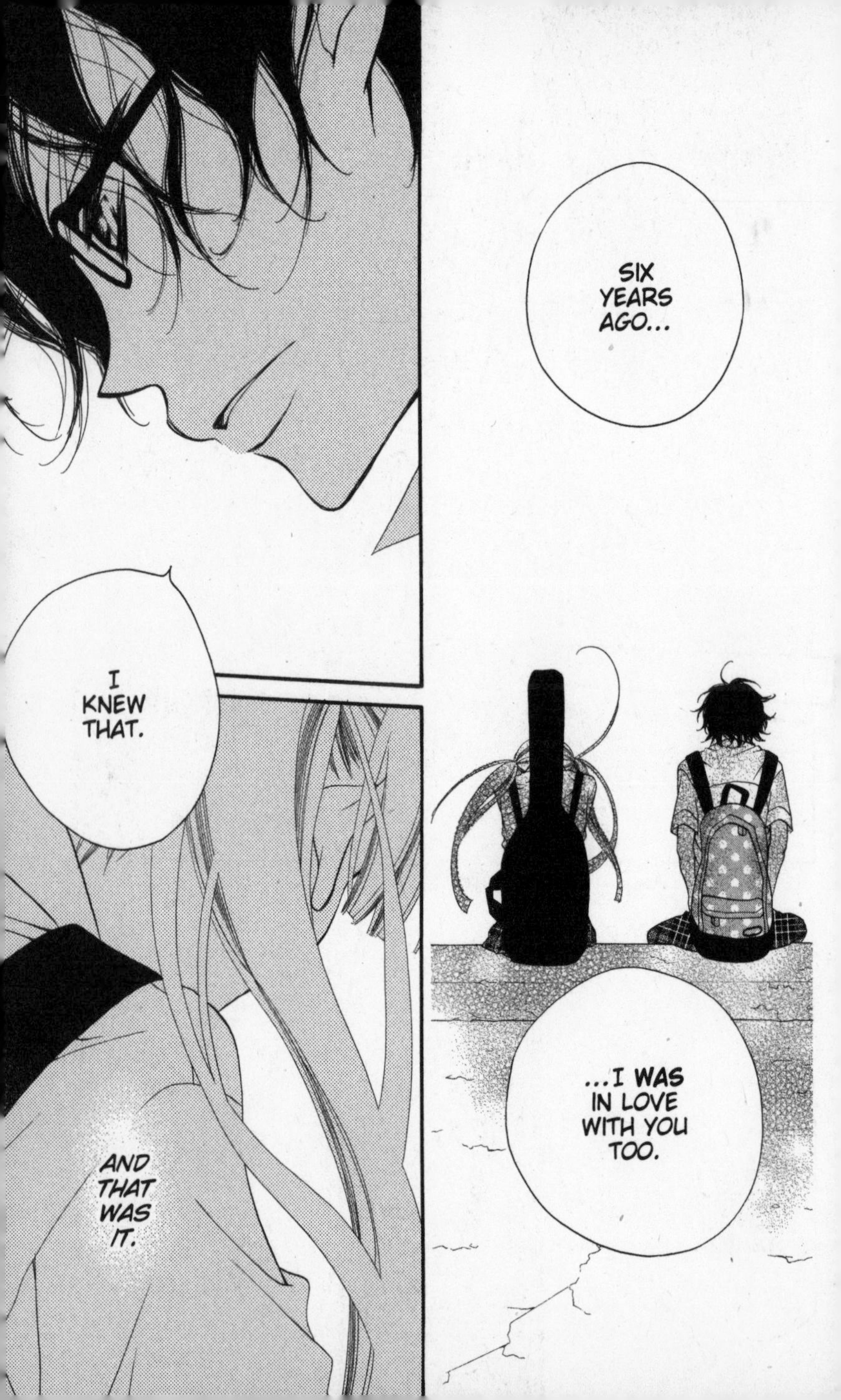
SIX YEARS AGO...
...I WAS IN LOVE WITH YOU TOO.
I KNEW THAT.
AND THAT WAS IT.

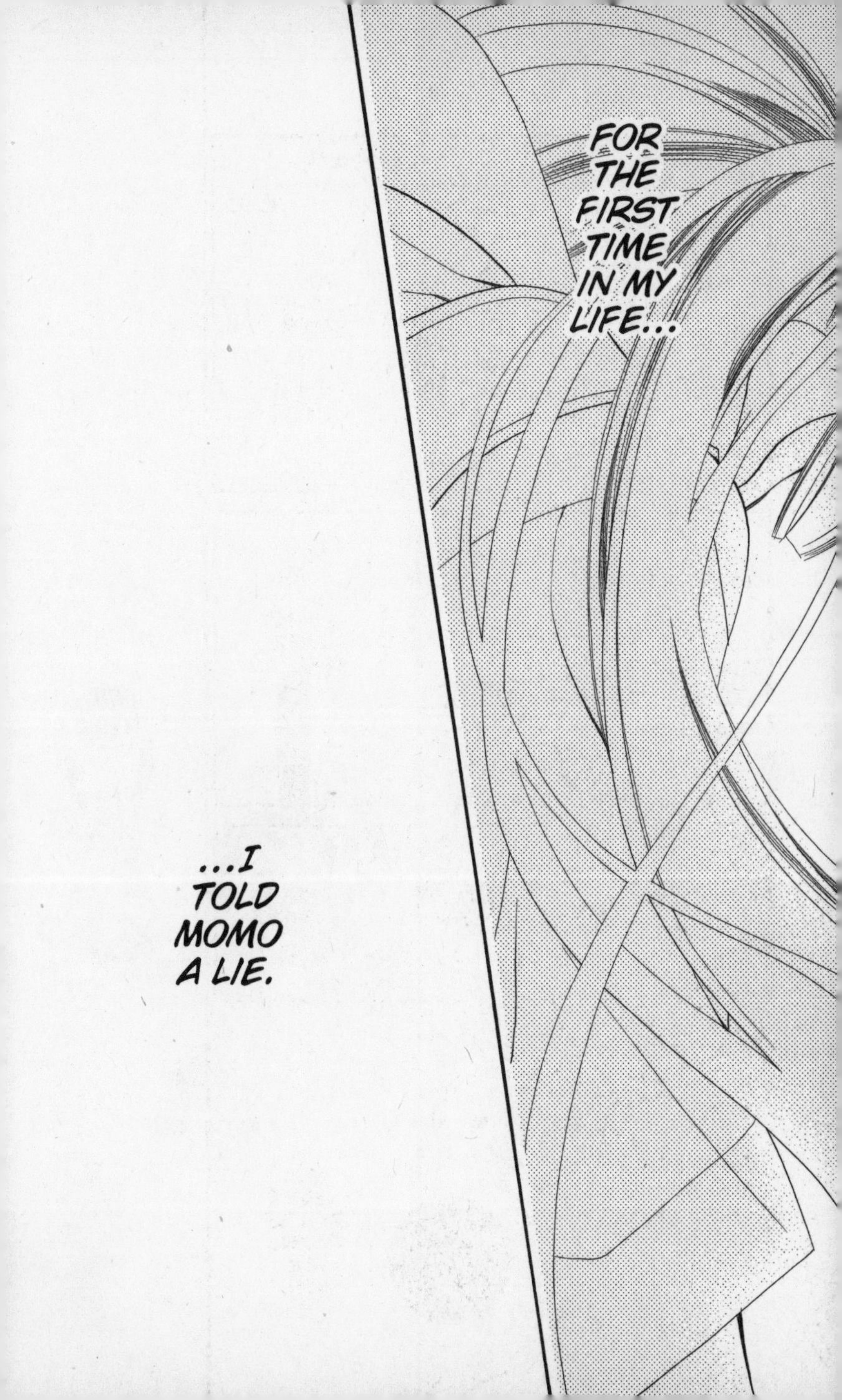
FOR THE FIRST TIME IN MY LIFE...
...I TOLD MOMO A LIE.

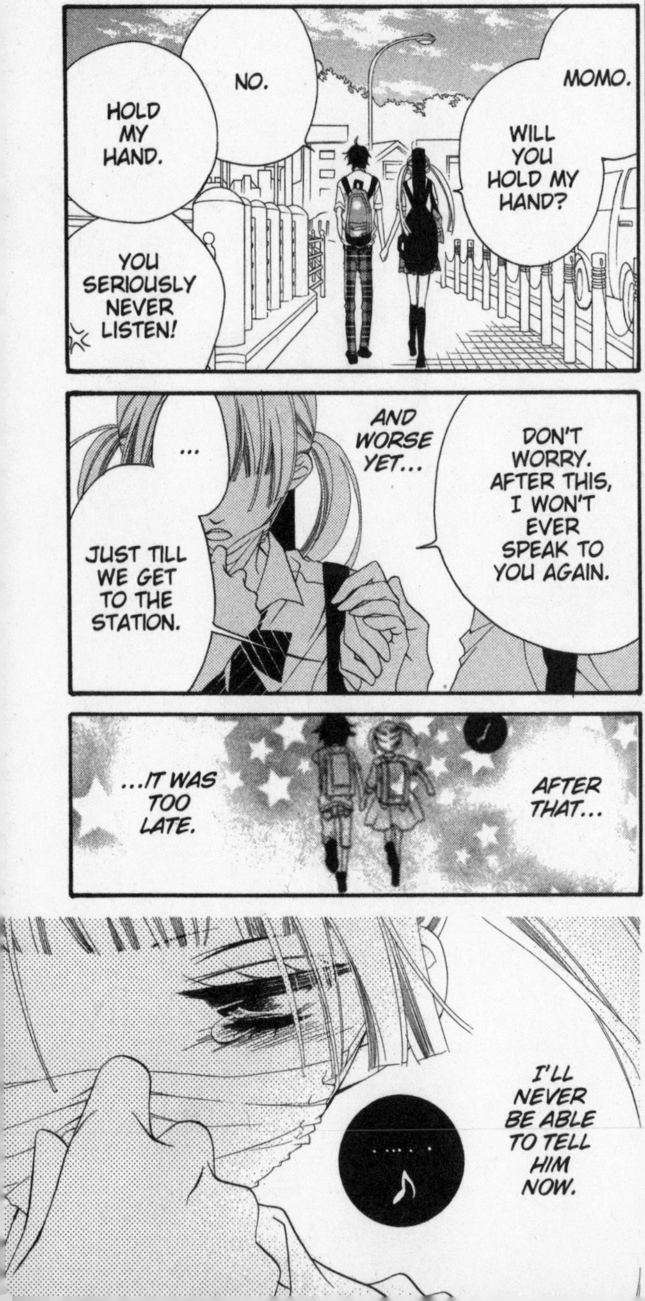
MOMO.
WILL YOU HOLD MY HAND?
NO.
HOLD MY HAND.
YOU SERIOUSLY NEVER LISTEN!
DON'T WORRY. AFTER THIS, I WON'T EVER SPEAK TO YOU AGAIN.
AND WORSE YET...
...
JUST TILL WE GET TO THE STATION.
AFTER THAT...
...IT WAS TOO LATE.
I'LL NEVER BE ABLE TO TELL HIM NOW.

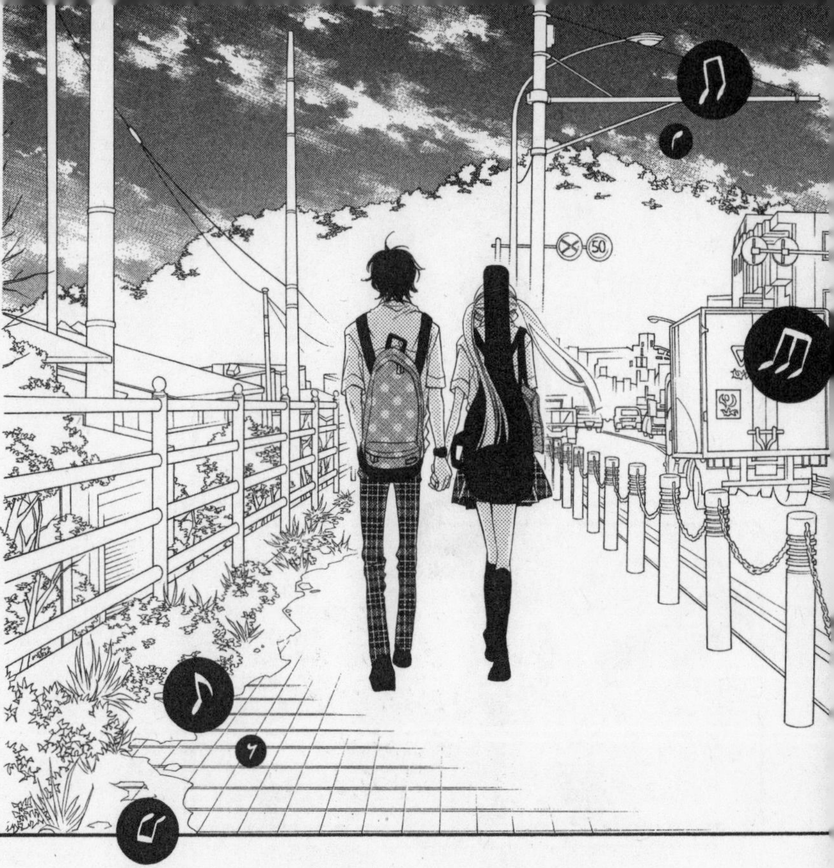
50

I JUST
HAVE TO
KEEP
HIDING
IT.

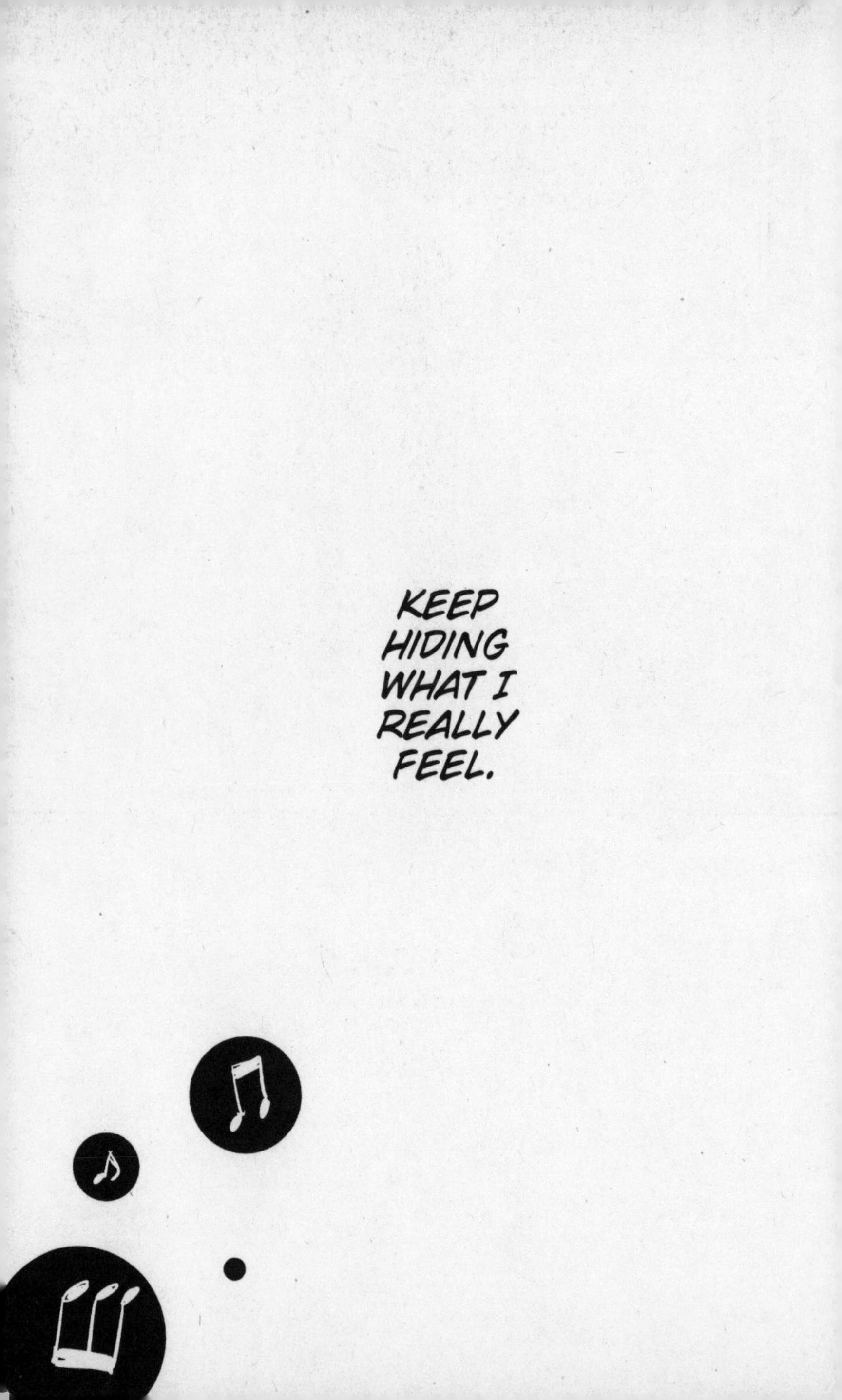
KEEP HIDING WHAT I REALLY FEEL.

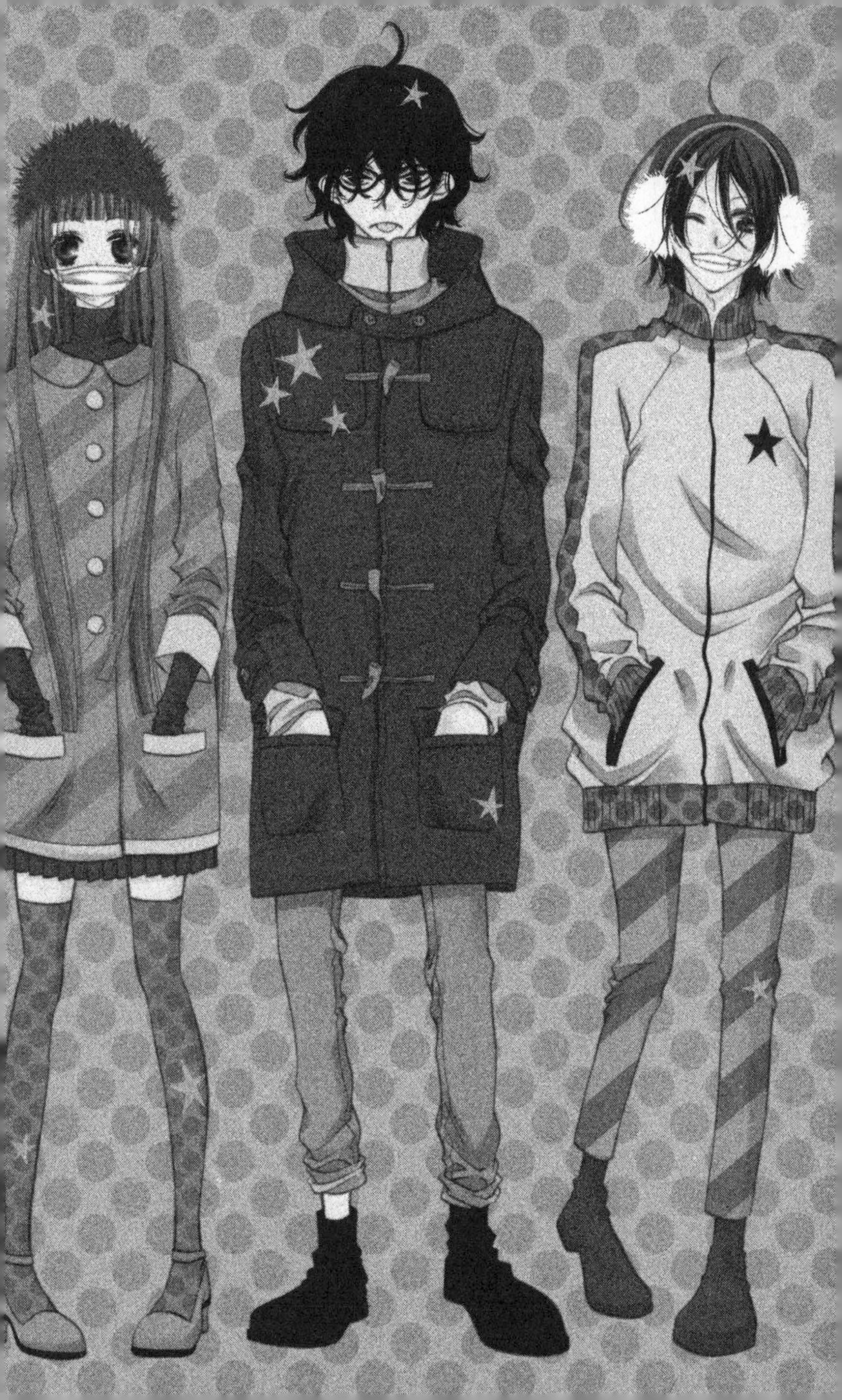

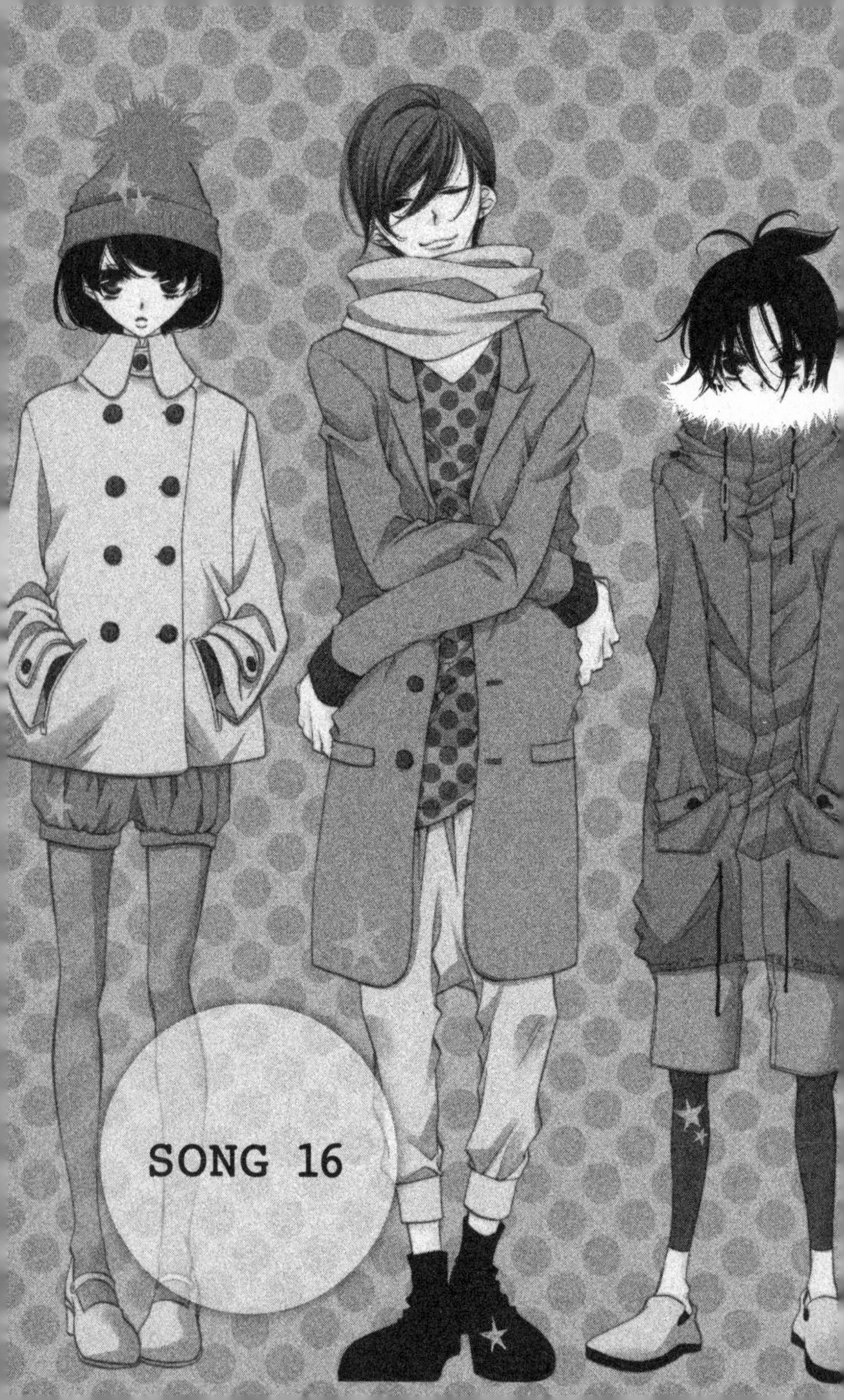
SONG 16

THE HEART-POUNDING EPIC SAGA OF YUZU AND HIS MILK EPISODE 5

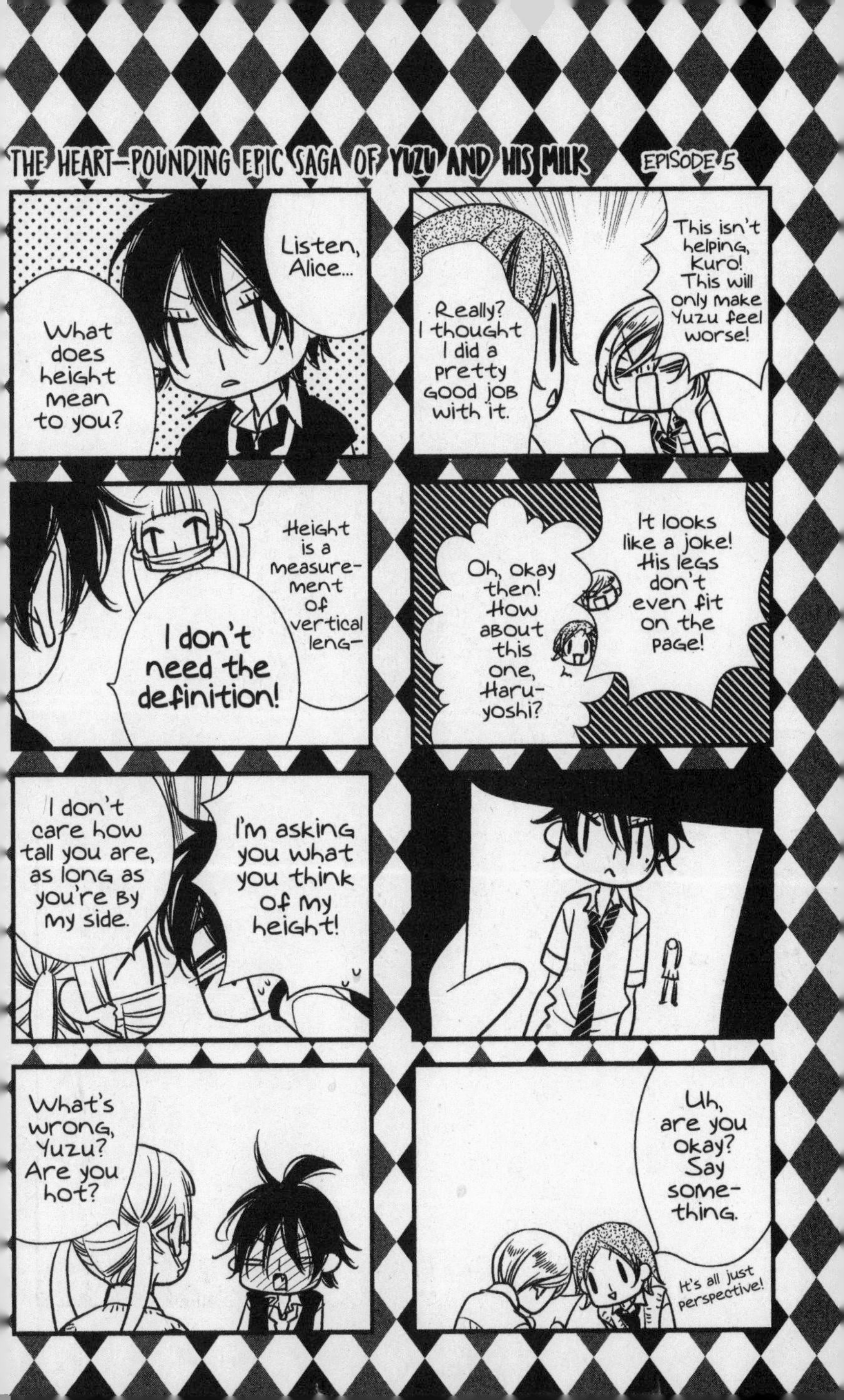
This isn't helping, Kuro! This will only make Yuzu feel worse!
Really? I thought I did a pretty good job with it.
It looks like a joke! His legs don't even fit on the page!
Oh, okay then! How about this one, Haruyoshi?
Uh, are you okay? Say some-thing.
It's all just perspective!
Listen, Alice...
What does height mean to you?
Height is a measure-ment of vertical leng-
I don't need the definition!
I'm asking you what you think of my height!
I don't care how tall you are, as long as you're by my side.
What's wrong, Yuzu? Are you hot?

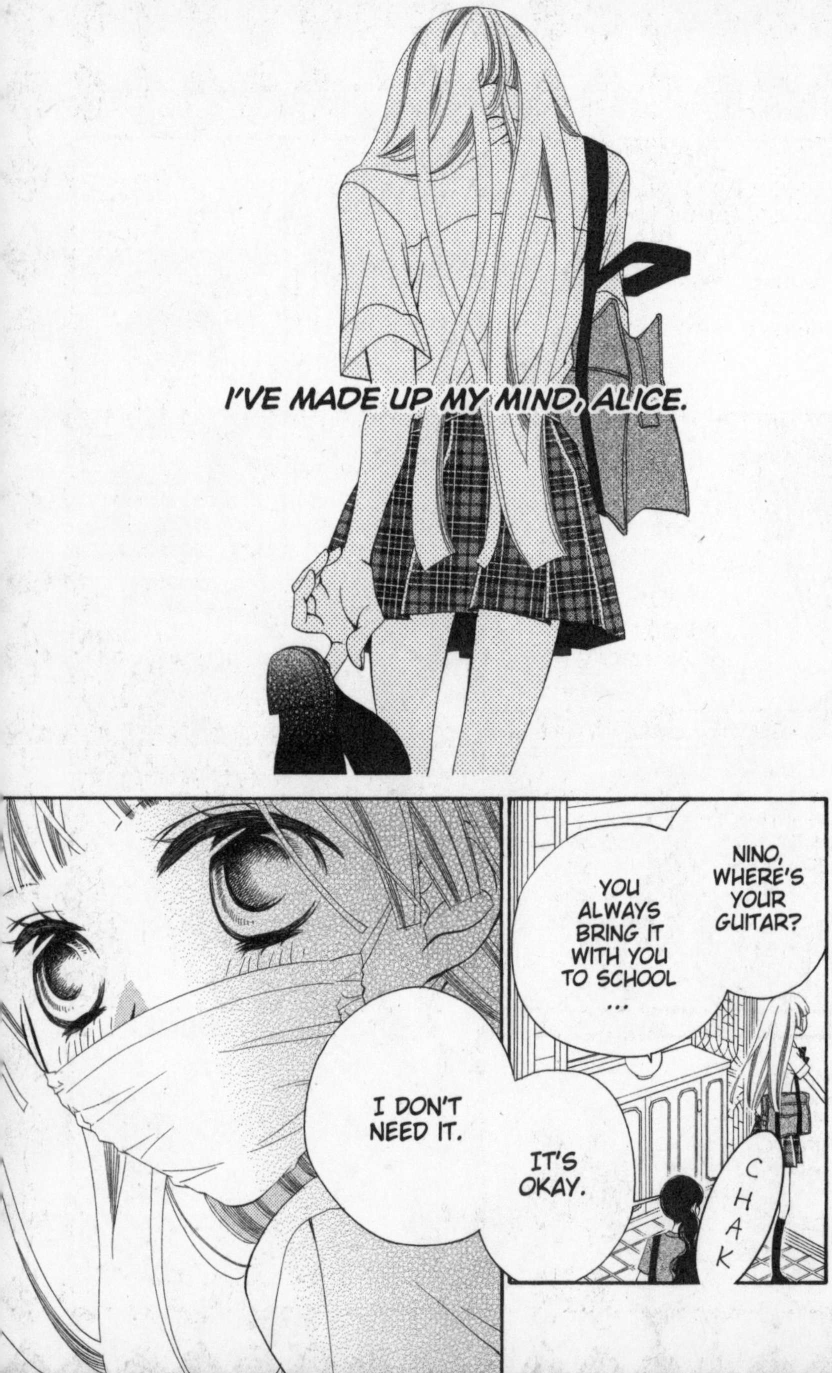
I'VE MADE UP MY MIND, ALICE.
NINO, WHERE'S YOUR GUITAR?
YOU ALWAYS BRING IT WITH YOU TO SCHOOL ...
CHAK
I DON'T NEED IT.
IT'S OKAY.

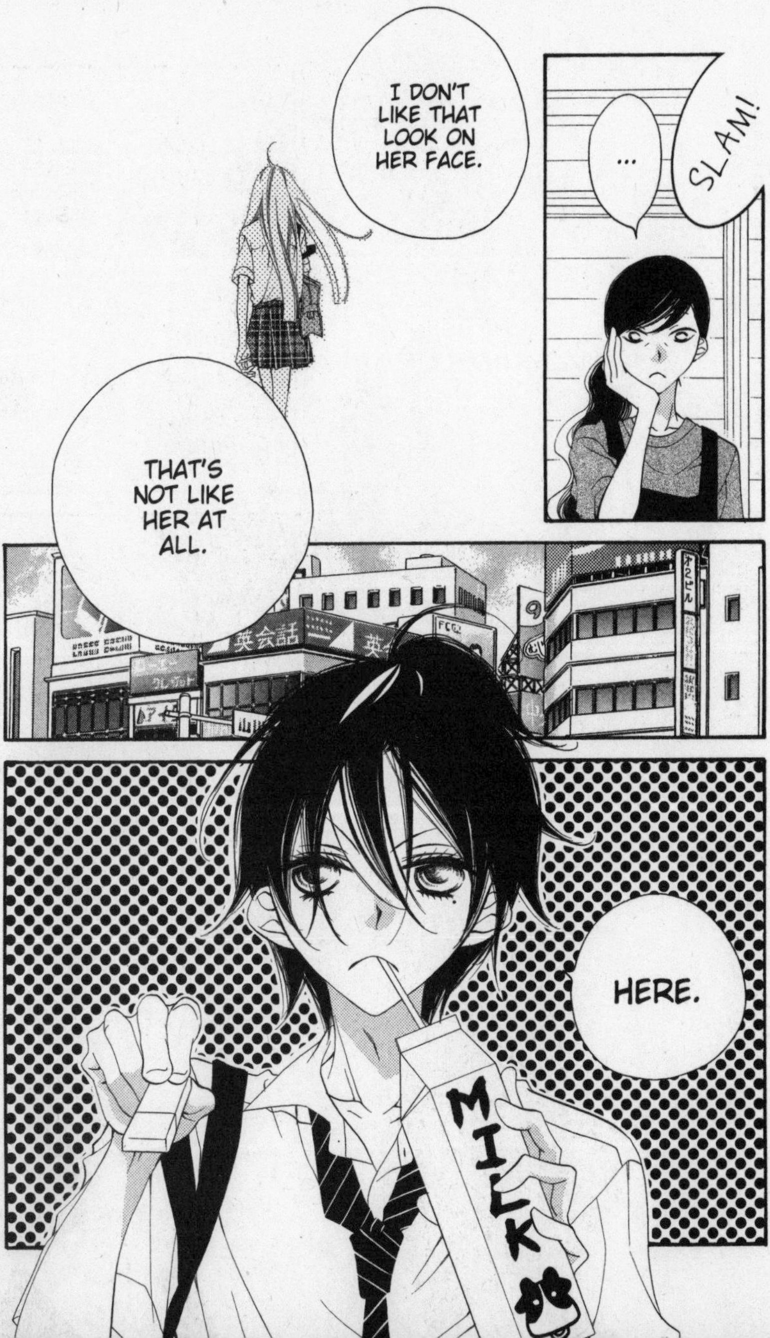
SLAM!
...
I DON'T LIKE THAT LOOK ON HER FACE.
THAT'S NOT LIKE HER AT ALL.
英会話
HERE.
MILK

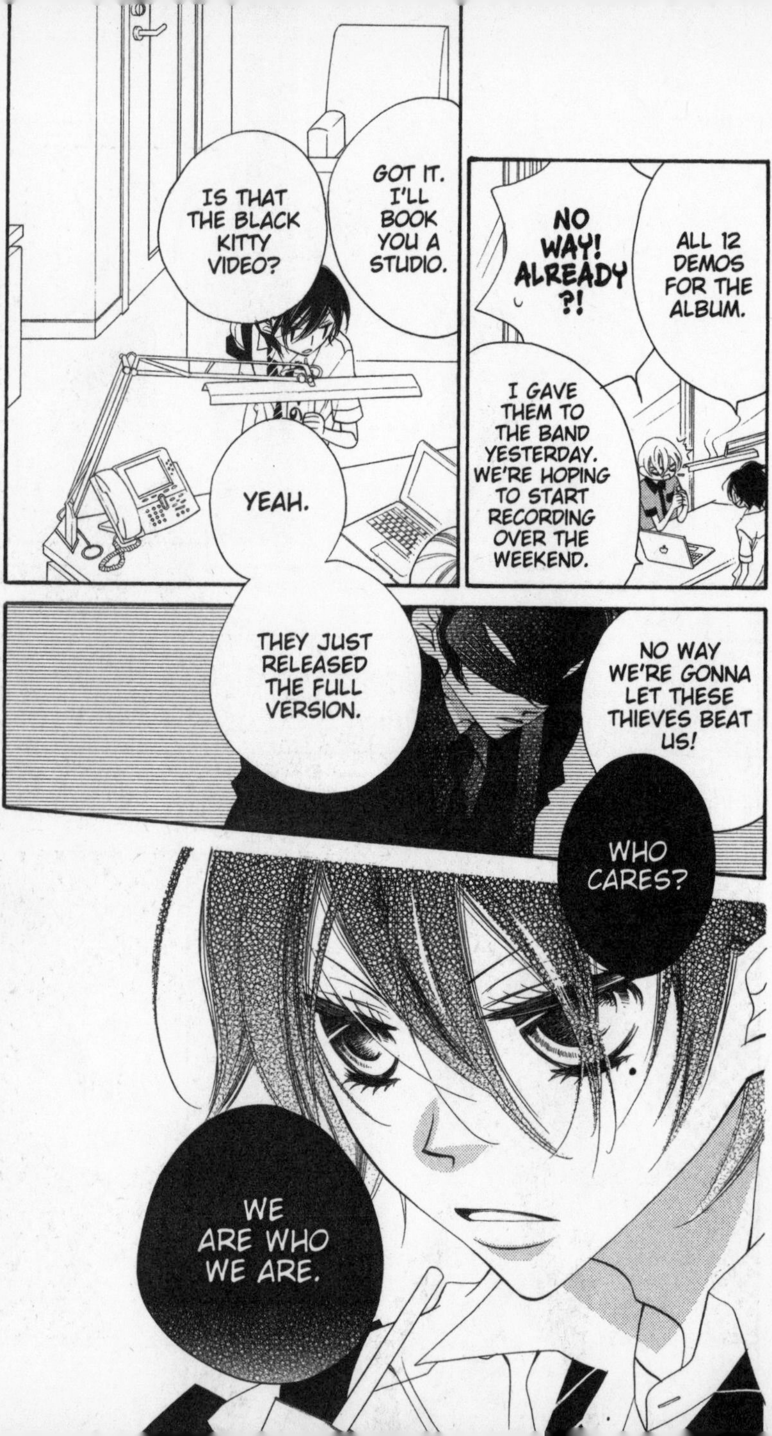
ALL 12 DEMOS FOR THE ALBUM.
NO WAY! ALREADY?!
I GAVE THEM TO THE BAND YESTERDAY. WE'RE HOPING TO START RECORDING OVER THE WEEKEND.
GOT IT. I'LL BOOK YOU A STUDIO.
IS THAT THE BLACK KITTY VIDEO?
YEAH.
THEY JUST RELEASED THE FULL VERSION.
NO WAY WE'RE GONNA LET THESE THIEVES BEAT US!
WHO CARES?
WE ARE WHO WE ARE.

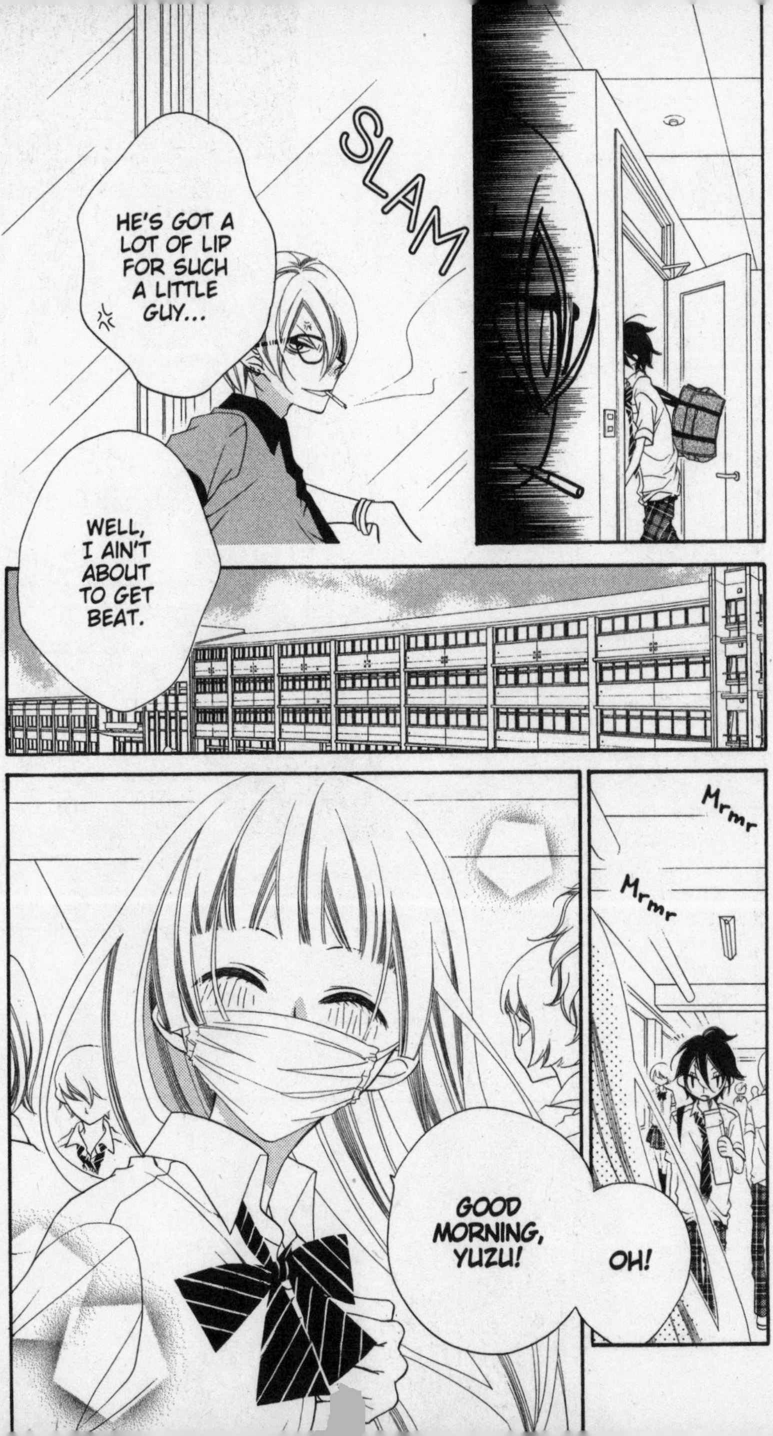
SLAM
HE'S GOT A LOT OF LIP FOR SUCH A LITTLE GUY...
WELL, I AIN'T ABOUT TO GET BEAT.
Mrmr
Mrmr
OH!
GOOD MORNING, YUZU!

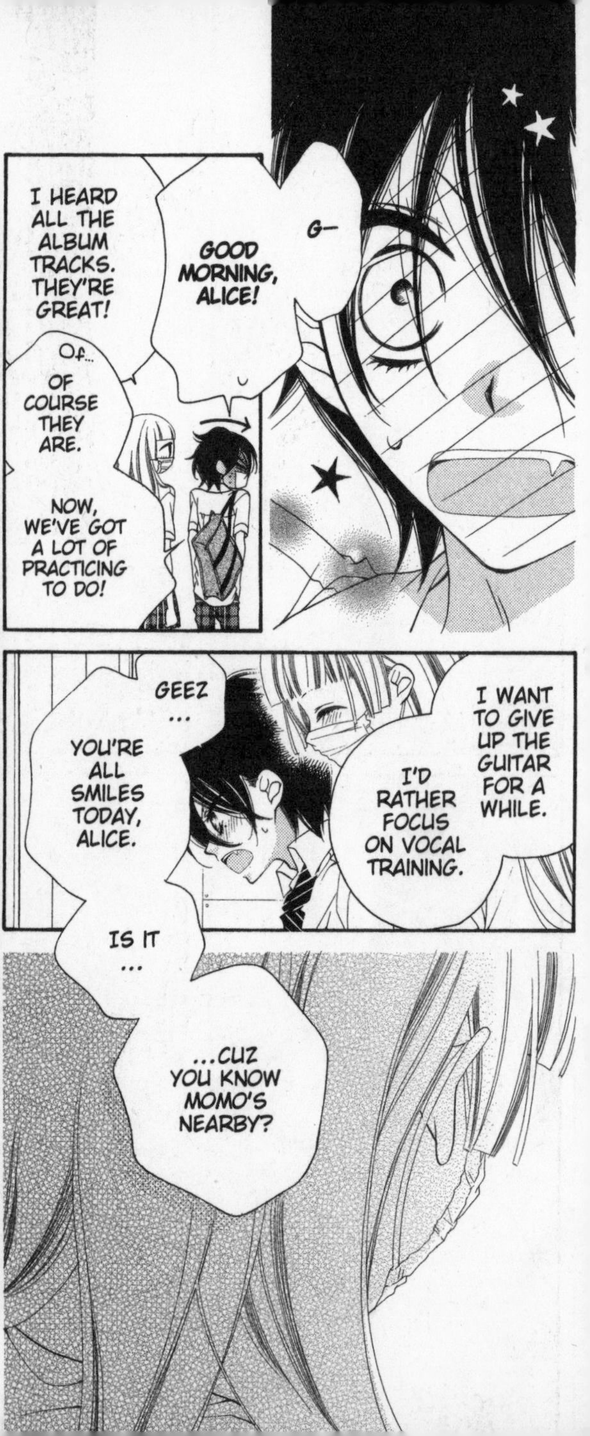
G—
GOOD MORNING, ALICE!
I HEARD ALL THE ALBUM TRACKS. THEY'RE GREAT!
Of...
OF COURSE THEY ARE.
NOW, WE'VE GOT A LOT OF PRACTICING TO DO!
I WANT TO GIVE UP THE GUITAR FOR A WHILE.
I'D RATHER FOCUS ON VOCAL TRAINING.
GEEZ...
YOU'RE ALL SMILES TODAY, ALICE.
IS IT...
...CUZ YOU KNOW MOMO'S NEARBY?

6

This is my last column?! Already?! What did you all think of Anonymous Noise 3? I'm sure everyone's wondering, "What the hell is Yuzu doing?" But I sure hope to see you all back for volume 4! Thank you so much for reading this far!

Ryoko Fukuyama
6/20/2014

[SPECIAL THANKS]
IZUMI HIOU
MINI KOMATSU
TAKAYUKI NAGASHIMA
KENJU NORO
KENJI KATAGAI
RINAKO TANAKA
AI SHIBATA
SAORI TAO
MY FAMILY
MY FRIENDS
AND YOU!!

Ryoko Fukuyama
c/o Anonymous Noise Editor
VIZ Media
P.O. Box 77010
San Francisco, CA 94107

http://ryoco.net/
@ryocoryocoryoco
http://facebook.com/ryocoryocoryoco

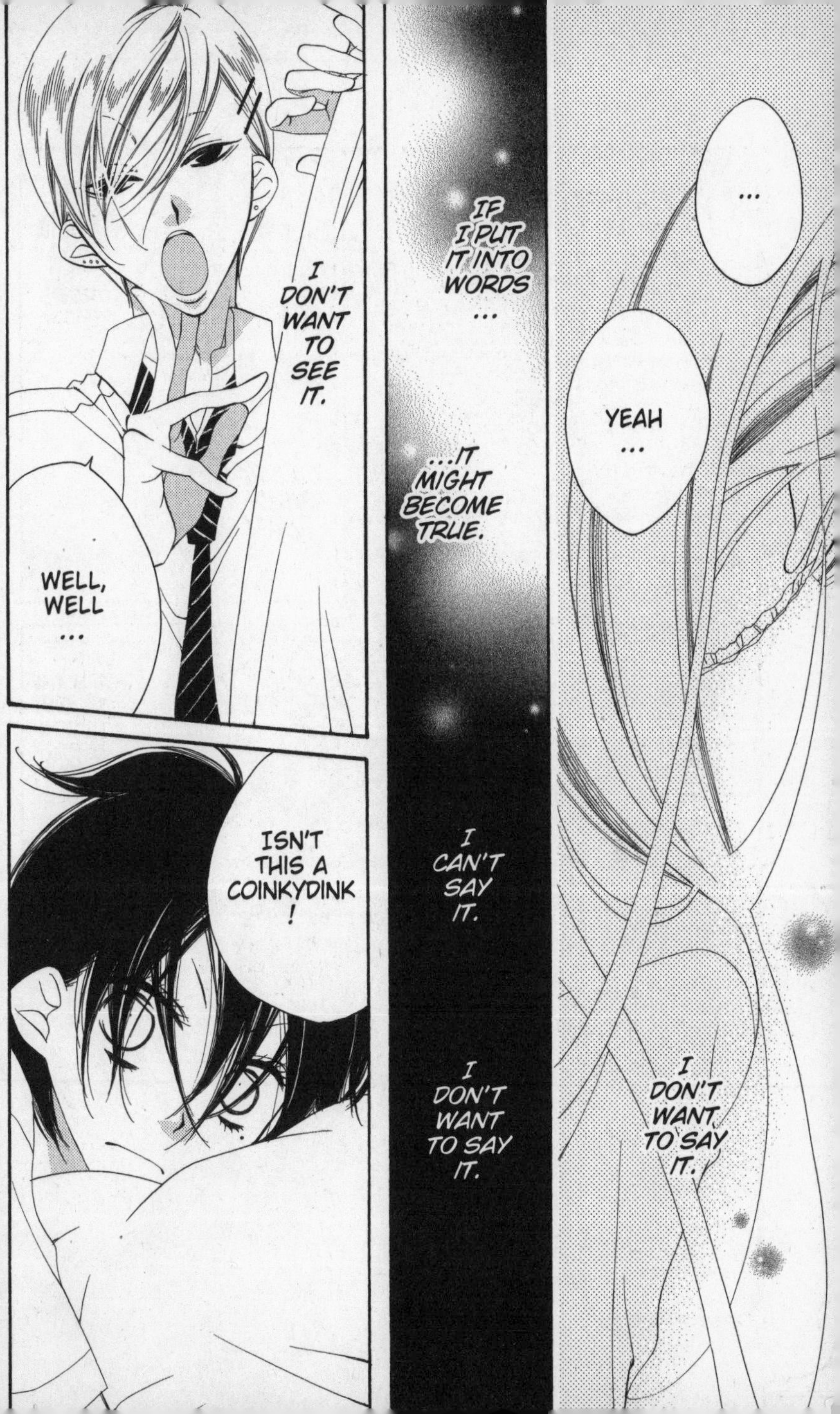
...
YEAH ...
I DON'T WANT TO SAY IT.
IF I PUT IT INTO WORDS ...
...IT MIGHT BECOME TRUE.
I CAN'T SAY IT.
I DON'T WANT TO SAY IT.
I DON'T WANT TO SEE IT.
WELL, WELL ...
ISN'T THIS A COINKYDINK!

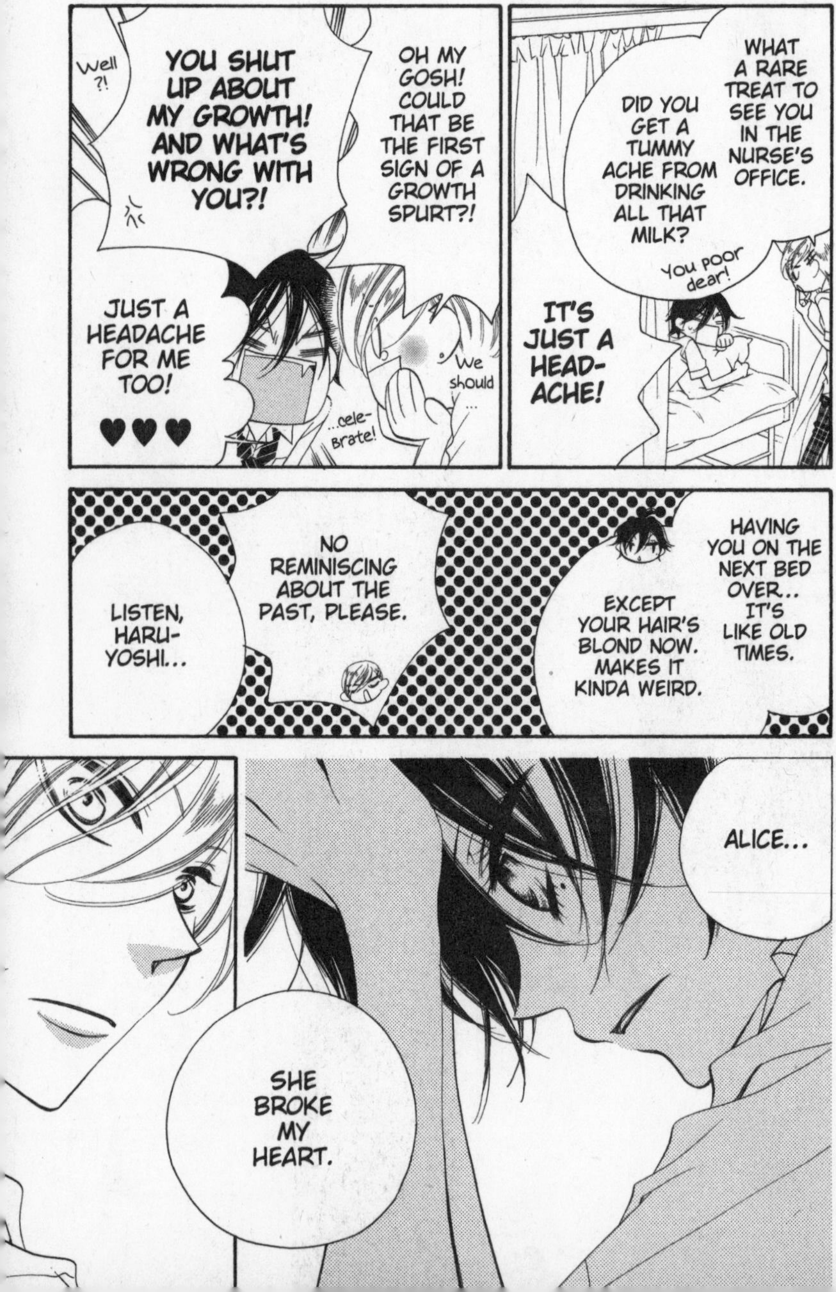
WHAT A RARE TREAT TO SEE YOU IN THE NURSE'S OFFICE.
DID YOU GET A TUMMY ACHE FROM DRINKING ALL THAT MILK?
You poor dear!
IT'S JUST A HEAD-ACHE!
OH MY GOSH! COULD THAT BE THE FIRST SIGN OF A GROWTH SPURT?!
YOU SHUT UP ABOUT MY GROWTH! AND WHAT'S WRONG WITH YOU?!
Well ?!
We should ...
...cele-brate!
JUST A HEADACHE FOR ME TOO! ♥♥♥
HAVING YOU ON THE NEXT BED OVER... IT'S LIKE OLD TIMES.
EXCEPT YOUR HAIR'S BLOND NOW. MAKES IT KINDA WEIRD.
NO REMINISCING ABOUT THE PAST, PLEASE.
LISTEN, HARU-YOSHI...
ALICE...
SHE BROKE MY HEART.

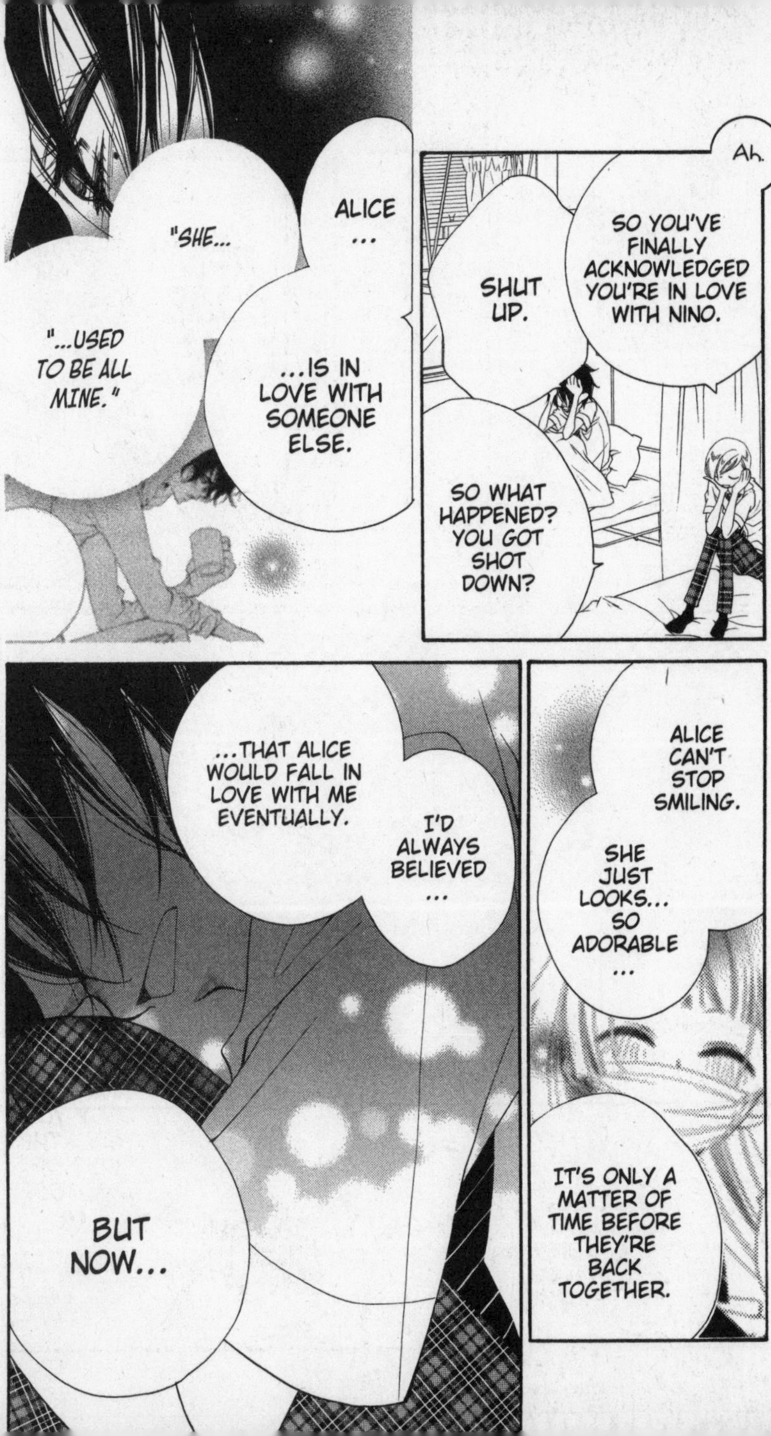
Ah.
SO YOU'VE FINALLY ACKNOWLEDGED YOU'RE IN LOVE WITH NINO.
SHUT UP.
SO WHAT HAPPENED? YOU GOT SHOT DOWN?
ALICE ...
"SHE...
...IS IN LOVE WITH SOMEONE ELSE.
"...USED TO BE ALL MINE."
ALICE CAN'T STOP SMILING.
SHE JUST LOOKS... SO ADORABLE ...
IT'S ONLY A MATTER OF TIME BEFORE THEY'RE BACK TOGETHER.
I'D ALWAYS BELIEVED ...
...THAT ALICE WOULD FALL IN LOVE WITH ME EVENTUALLY.
BUT NOW...

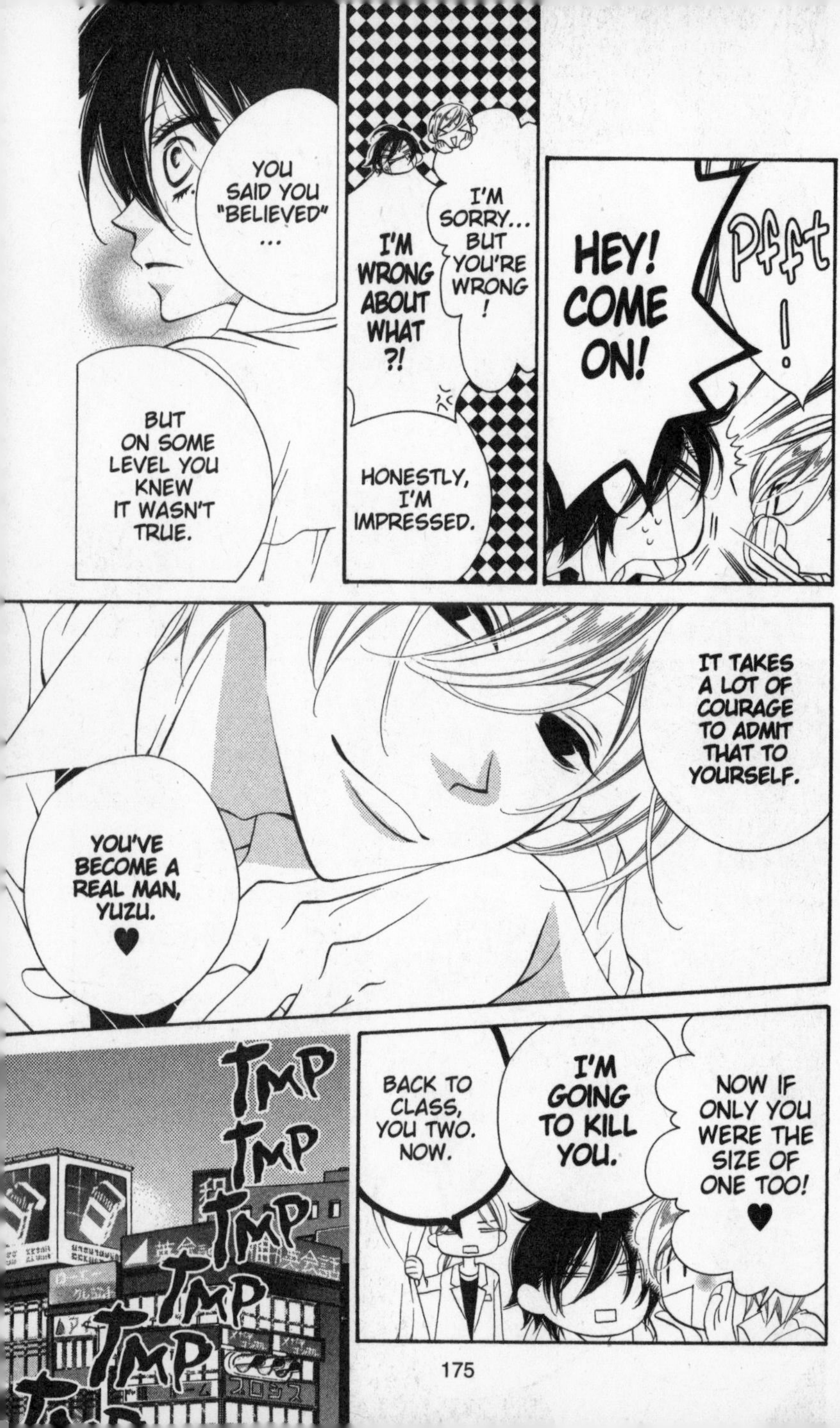
Pfft!
HEY! COME ON!
I'M SORRY... BUT YOU'RE WRONG!
I'M WRONG ABOUT WHAT?!
HONESTLY, I'M IMPRESSED.
YOU SAID YOU "BELIEVED"...
BUT ON SOME LEVEL YOU KNEW IT WASN'T TRUE.
IT TAKES A LOT OF COURAGE TO ADMIT THAT TO YOURSELF.
YOU'VE BECOME A REAL MAN, YUZU. ♥
NOW IF ONLY YOU WERE THE SIZE OF ONE TOO! ♥
I'M GOING TO KILL YOU.
BACK TO CLASS, YOU TWO. NOW.
TMP TMP TMP TMP TMP

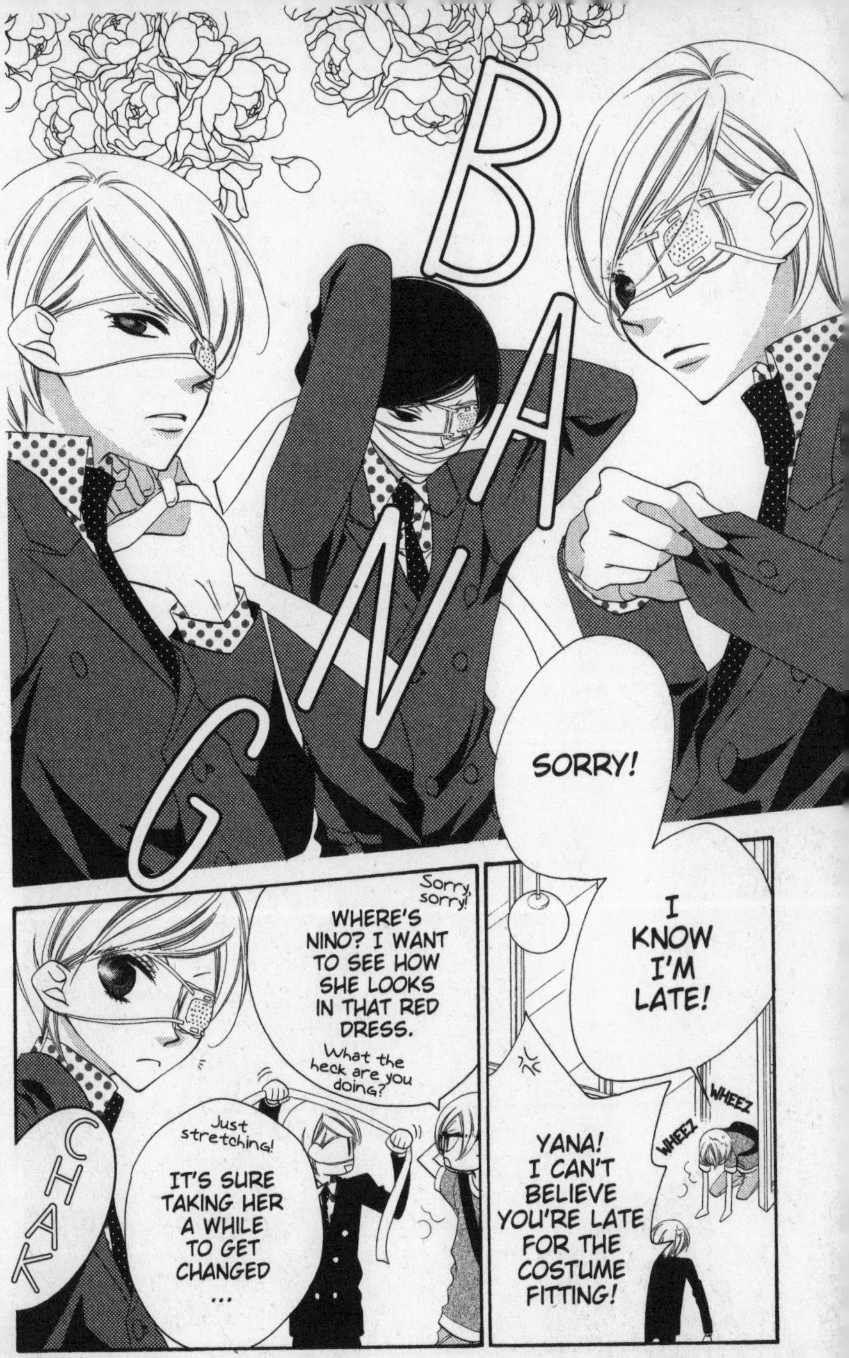
BANG
SORRY!
I KNOW I'M LATE!
YANA! I CAN'T BELIEVE YOU'RE LATE FOR THE COSTUME FITTING!
WHEEZ
WHEEZ
Sorry, sorry!
WHERE'S NINO? I WANT TO SEE HOW SHE LOOKS IN THAT RED DRESS.
What the heck are you doing?
Just stretching!
IT'S SURE TAKING HER A WHILE TO GET CHANGED ...
CHAK

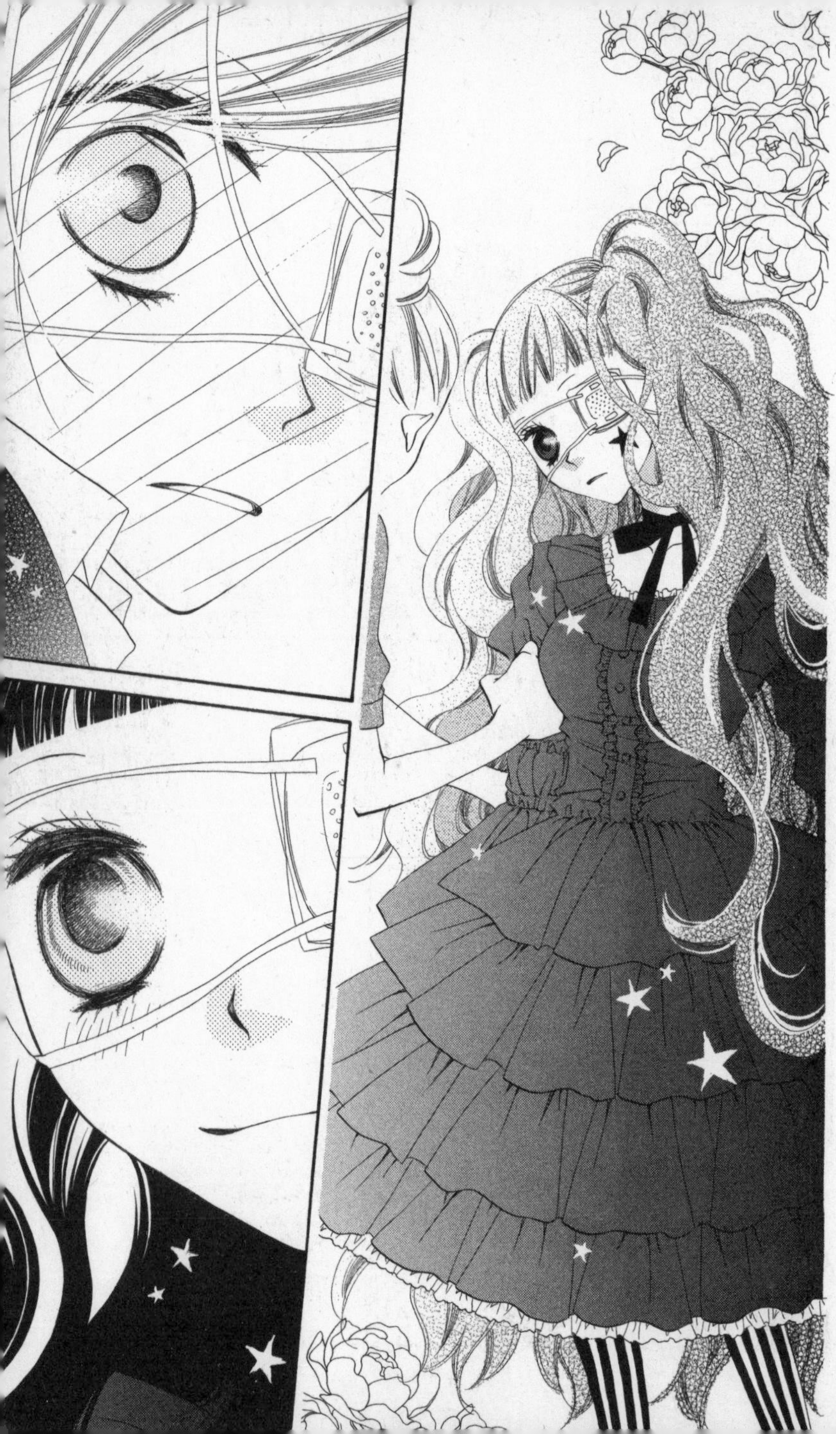

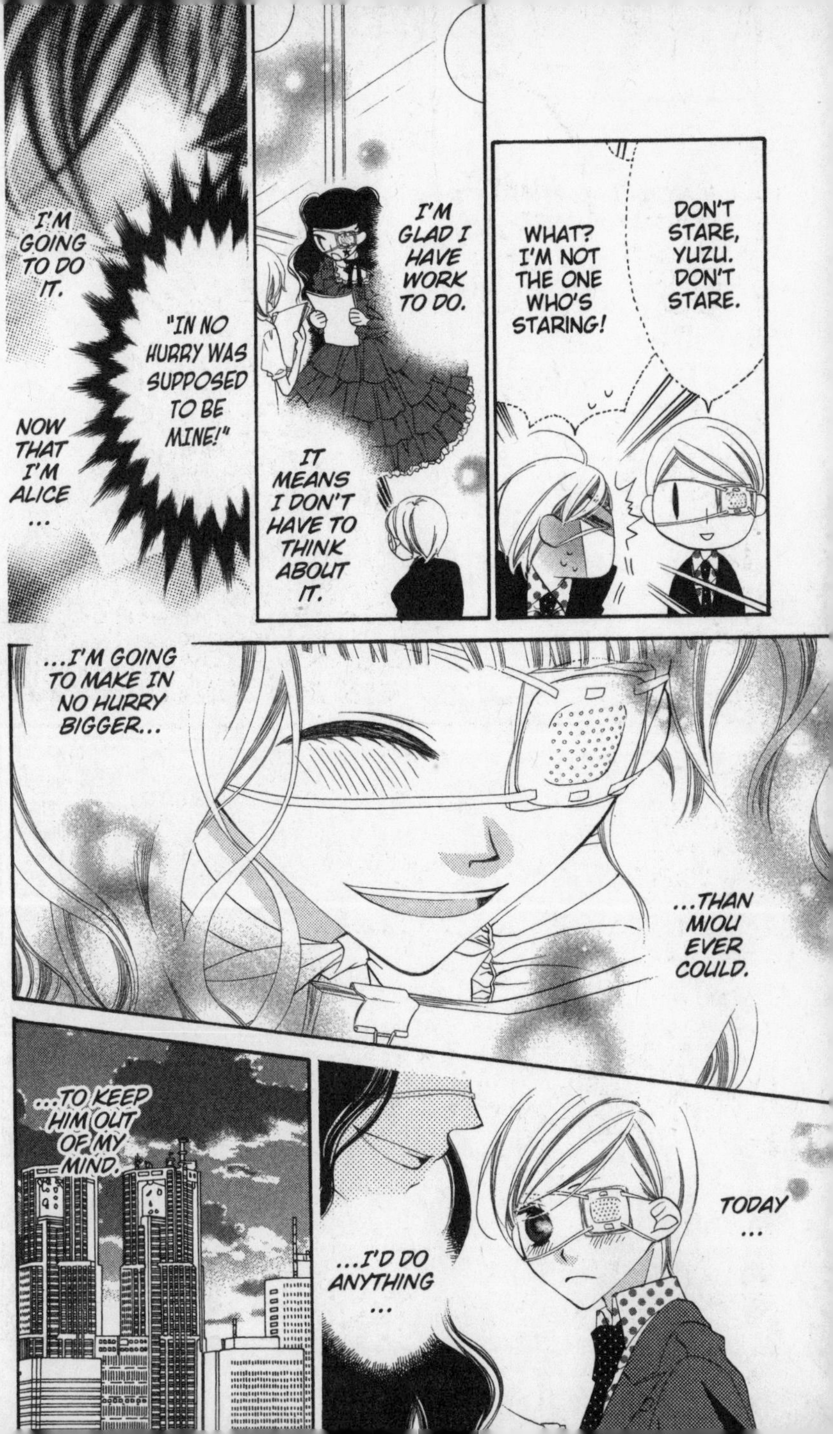
DON'T STARE, YUZU. DON'T STARE.
WHAT? I'M NOT THE ONE WHO'S STARING!
I'M GLAD I HAVE WORK TO DO.
IT MEANS I DON'T HAVE TO THINK ABOUT IT.
"IN NO HURRY WAS SUPPOSED TO BE MINE!"
NOW THAT I'M ALICE ...
I'M GOING TO DO IT.
...I'M GOING TO MAKE IN NO HURRY BIGGER...
...THAN MIOU EVER COULD.
TODAY ...
...I'D DO ANYTHING ...
...TO KEEP HIM OUT OF MY MIND.

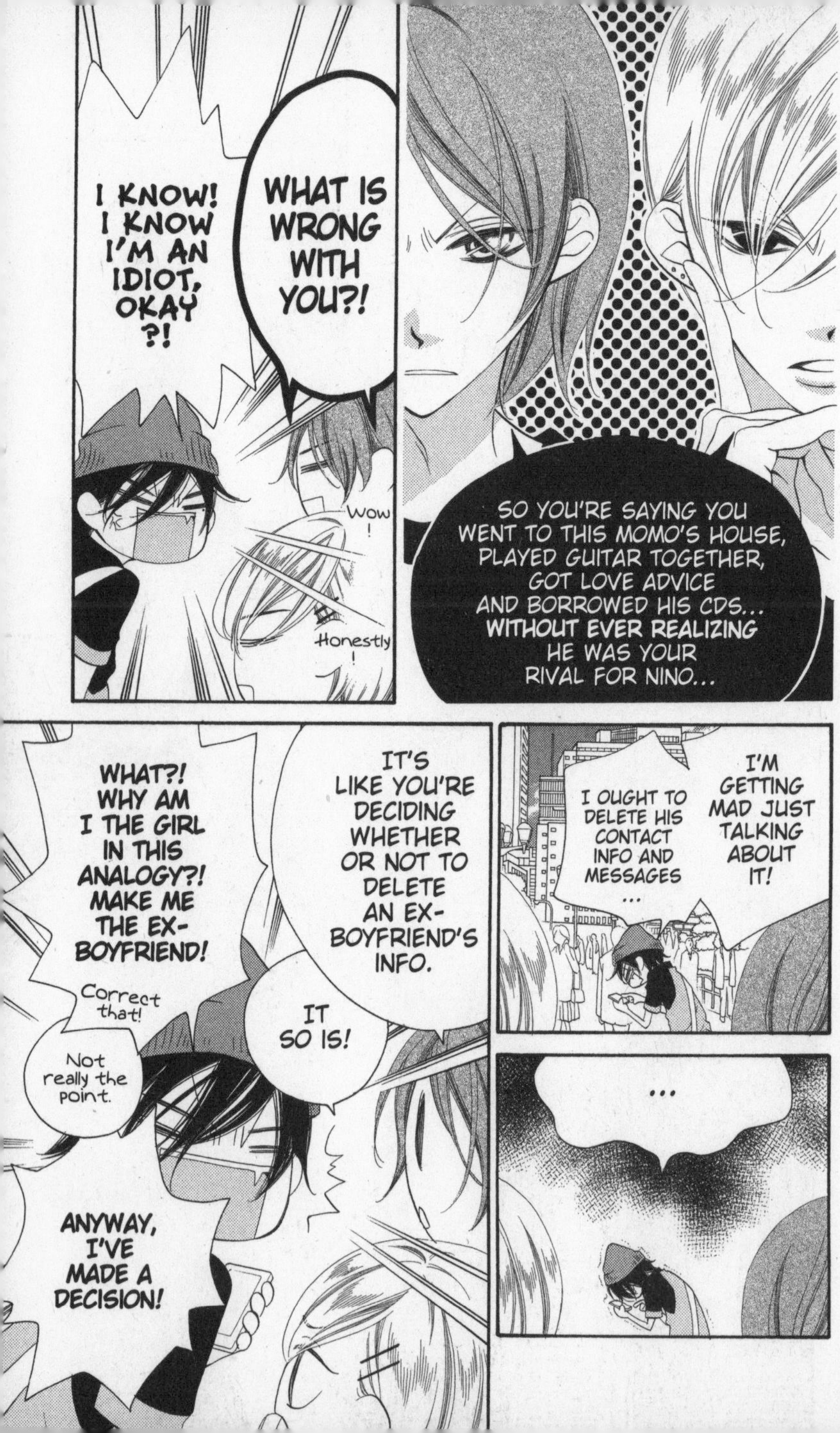
SO YOU'RE SAYING YOU WENT TO THIS MOMO'S HOUSE, PLAYED GUITAR TOGETHER, GOT LOVE ADVICE AND BORROWED HIS CDS... WITHOUT EVER REALIZING HE WAS YOUR RIVAL FOR NINO...
WHAT IS WRONG WITH YOU?!
I KNOW! I KNOW I'M AN IDIOT, OKAY ?!
Wow !
Honestly !
I'M GETTING MAD JUST TALKING ABOUT IT!
I OUGHT TO DELETE HIS CONTACT INFO AND MESSAGES ...
...
IT'S LIKE YOU'RE DECIDING WHETHER OR NOT TO DELETE AN EX-BOYFRIEND'S INFO.
WHAT?! WHY AM I THE GIRL IN THIS ANALOGY?! MAKE ME THE EX-BOYFRIEND!
IT SO IS!
Correct that!
Not really the point.
ANYWAY, I'VE MADE A DECISION!

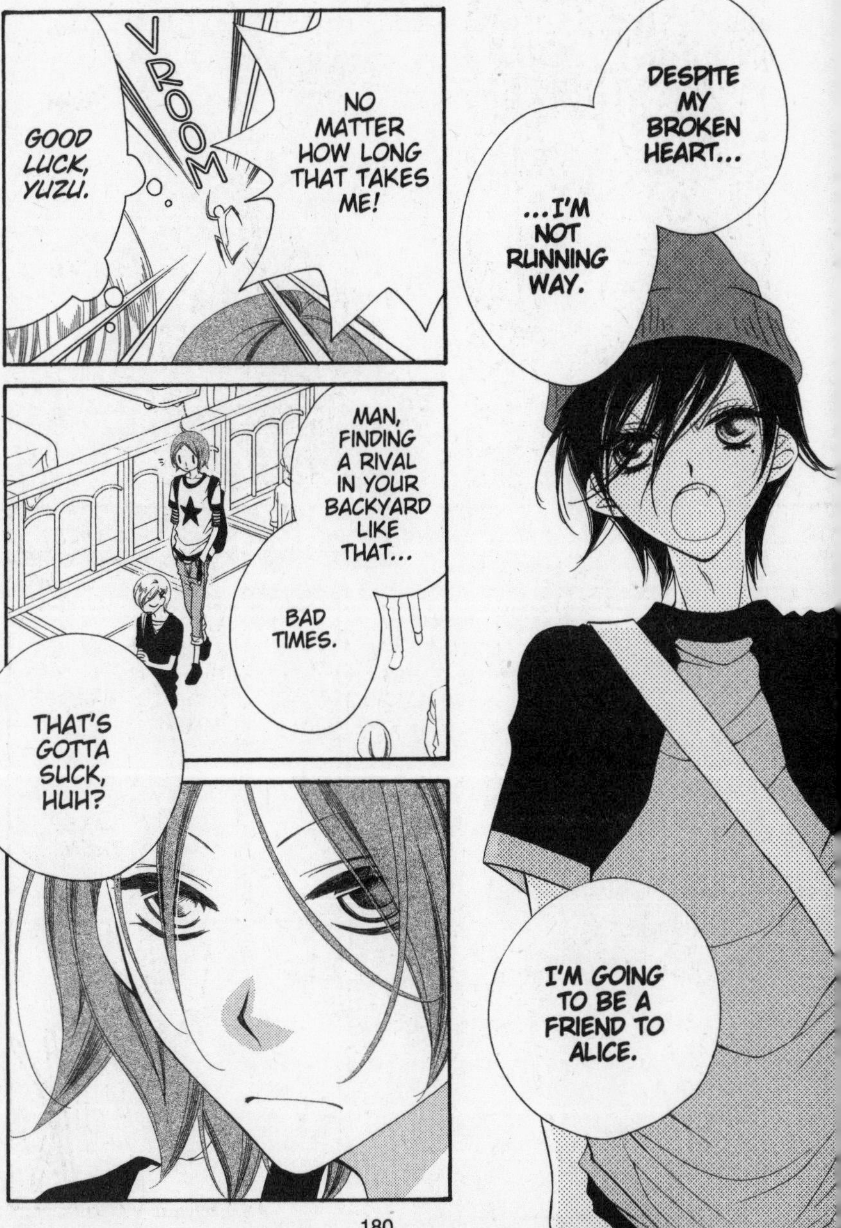
DESPITE MY BROKEN HEART...
...I'M NOT RUNNING WAY.
I'M GOING TO BE A FRIEND TO ALICE.
NO MATTER HOW LONG THAT TAKES ME!
VROOM
GOOD LUCK, YUZU.
MAN, FINDING A RIVAL IN YOUR BACKYARD LIKE THAT...
BAD TIMES.
THAT'S GOTTA SUCK, HUH?

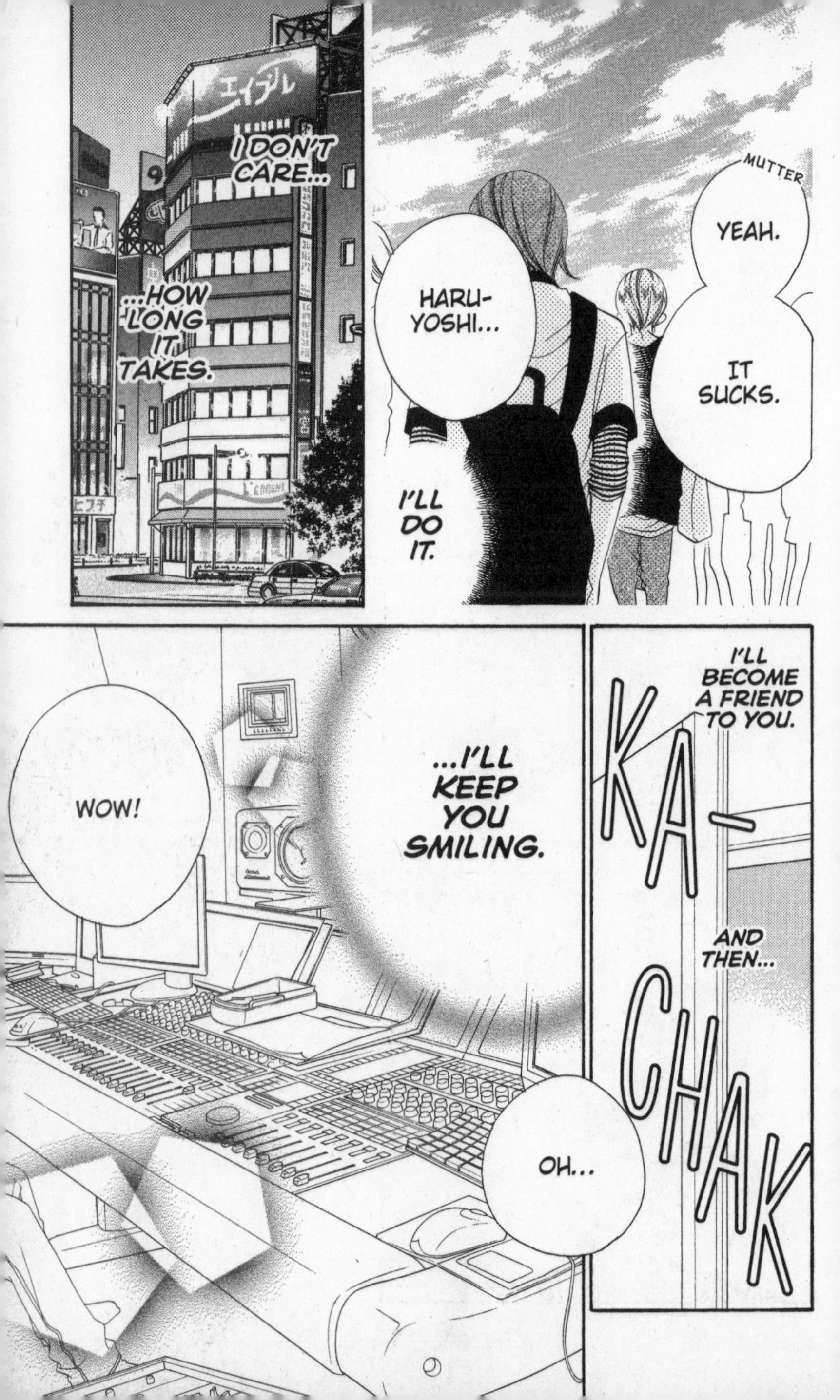
MUTTER
YEAH.
IT SUCKS.
HARU-YOSHI...
I'LL DO IT.
エイプル
I DON'T CARE...
...HOW LONG IT TAKES.
I'LL BECOME A FRIEND TO YOU.
KA-CHAK
AND THEN...
...I'LL KEEP YOU SMILING.
WOW!
OH...

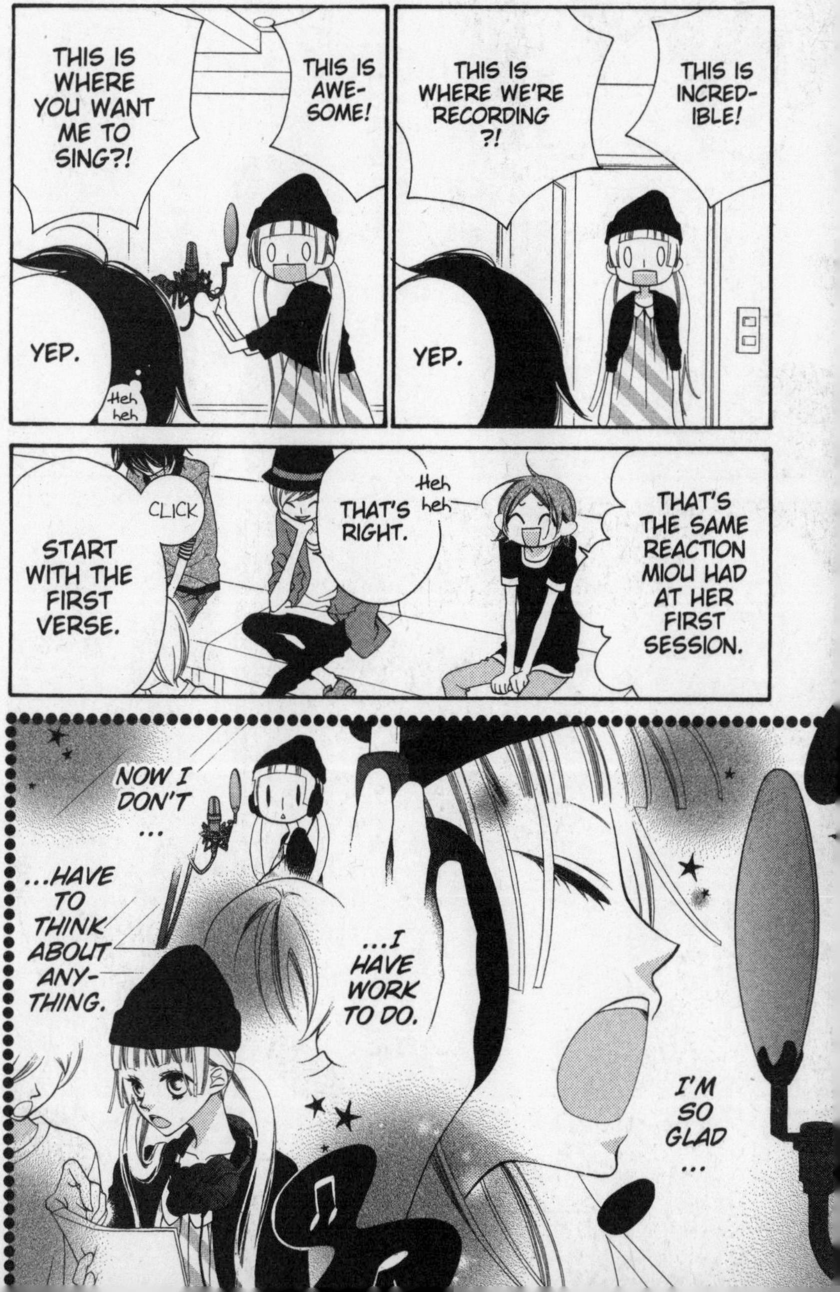
THIS IS INCRED-IBLE!
THIS IS WHERE WE'RE RECORDING ?!
YEP.
THIS IS AWE-SOME!
THIS IS WHERE YOU WANT ME TO SING?!
YEP.
Heh heh
THAT'S THE SAME REACTION MIOU HAD AT HER FIRST SESSION.
Heh heh
THAT'S RIGHT.
CLICK
START WITH THE FIRST VERSE.
I'M SO GLAD ...
...I HAVE WORK TO DO.
NOW I DON'T ...
...HAVE TO THINK ABOUT ANY-THING.

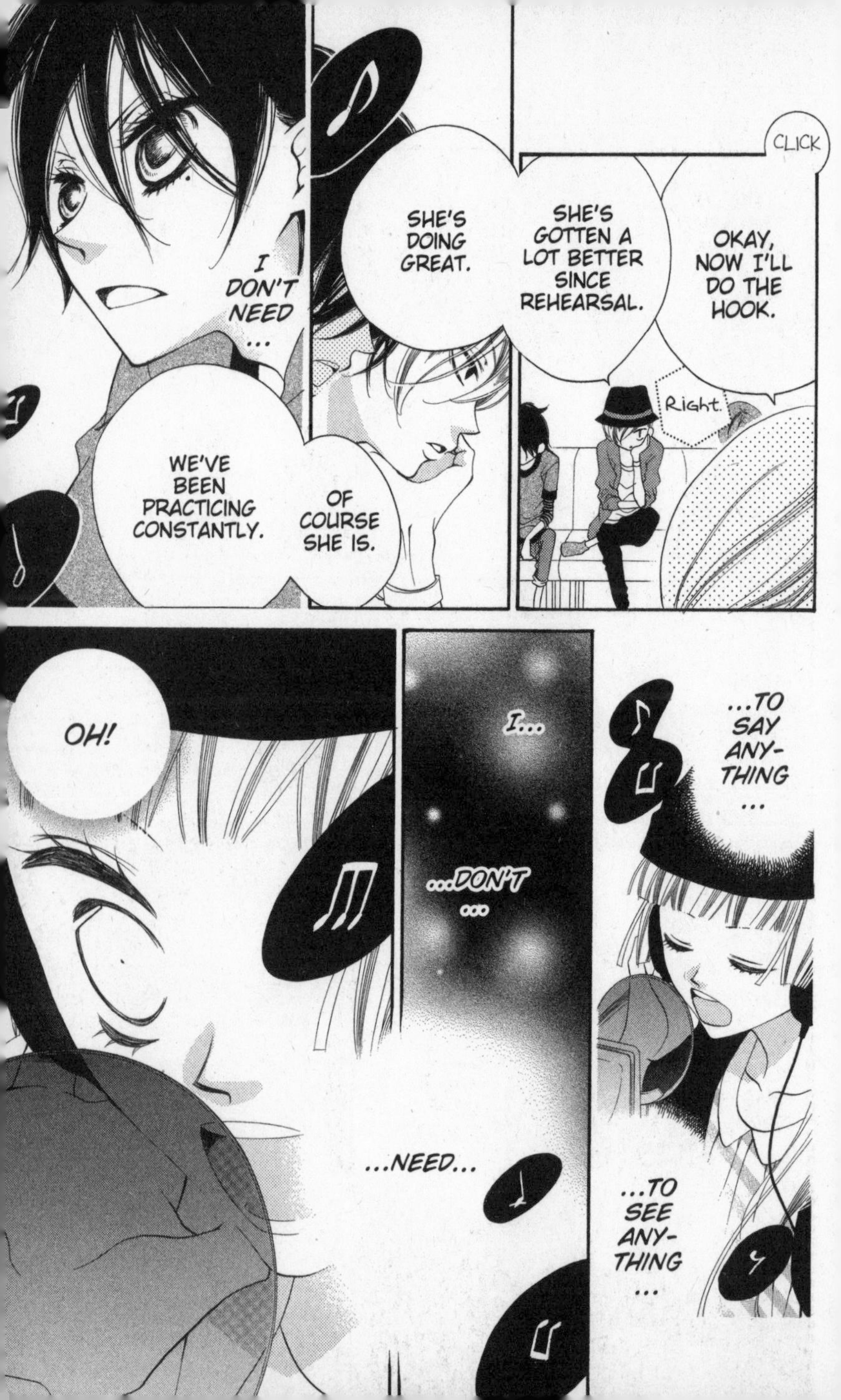
CLICK
OKAY, NOW I'LL DO THE HOOK.
SHE'S GOTTEN A LOT BETTER SINCE REHEARSAL.
Right.
SHE'S DOING GREAT.
OF COURSE SHE IS.
WE'VE BEEN PRACTICING CONSTANTLY.
I DON'T NEED...
...TO SAY ANY-THING...
...TO SEE ANY-THING...
I...
...DON'T...
...NEED...
OH!

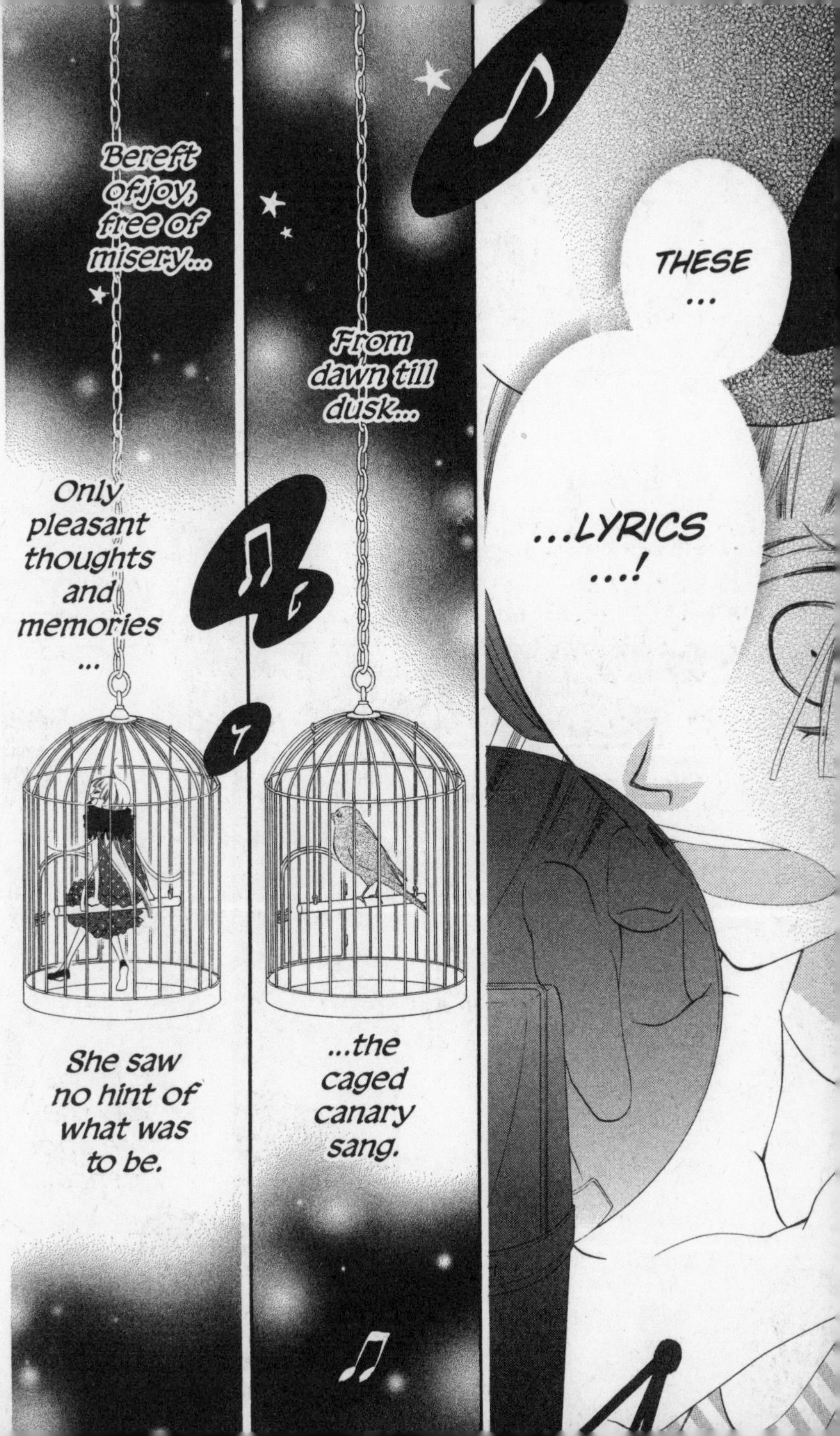
THESE ...
...LYRICS ...!
From dawn till dusk...
...the caged canary sang.
Bereft of joy, free of misery...
Only pleasant thoughts and memories ...
She saw no hint of what was to be.

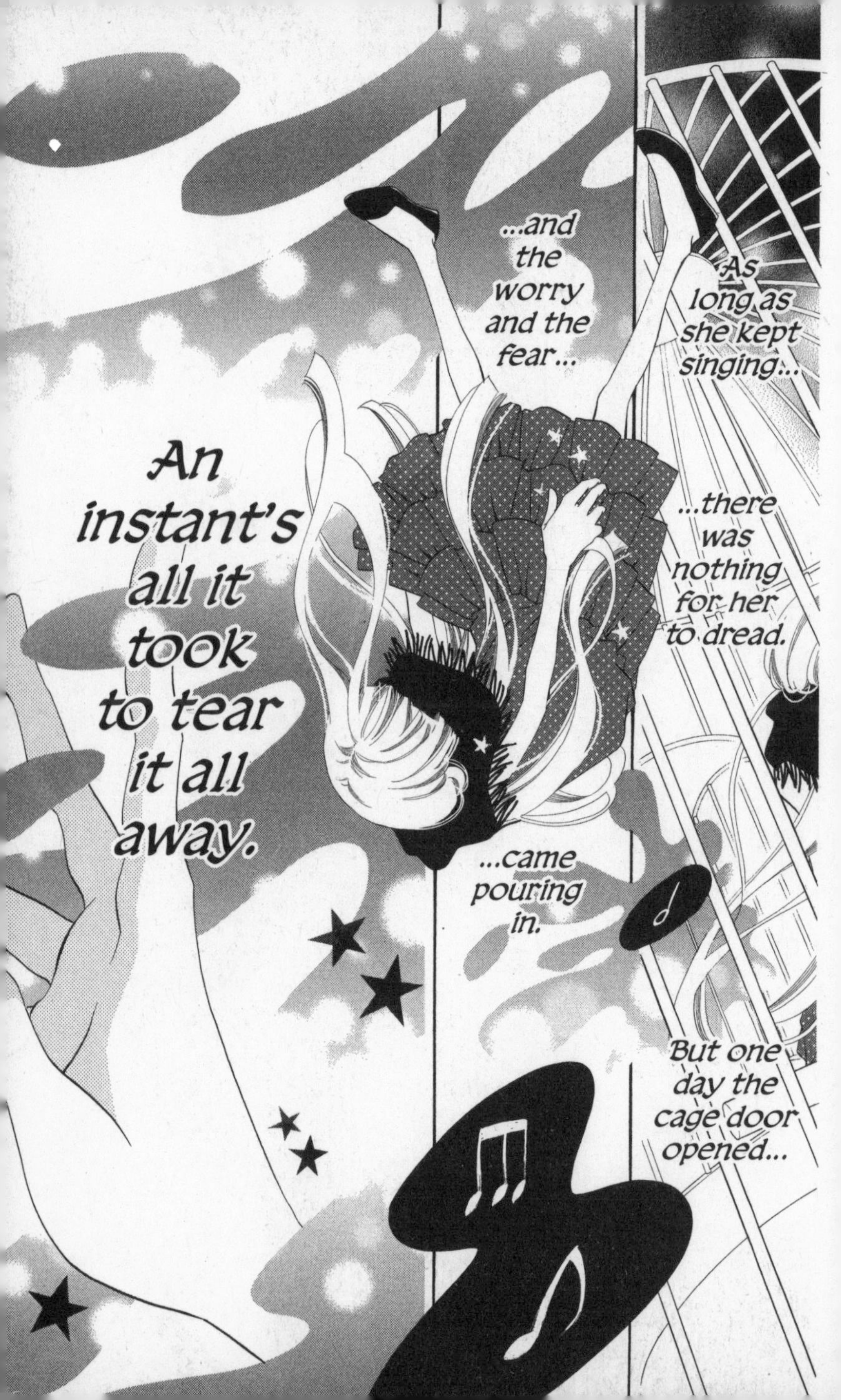
As long as she kept singing...
...there was nothing for her to dread.
But one day the cage door opened...
...and the worry and the fear...
...came pouring in.
An instant's all it took to tear it all away.

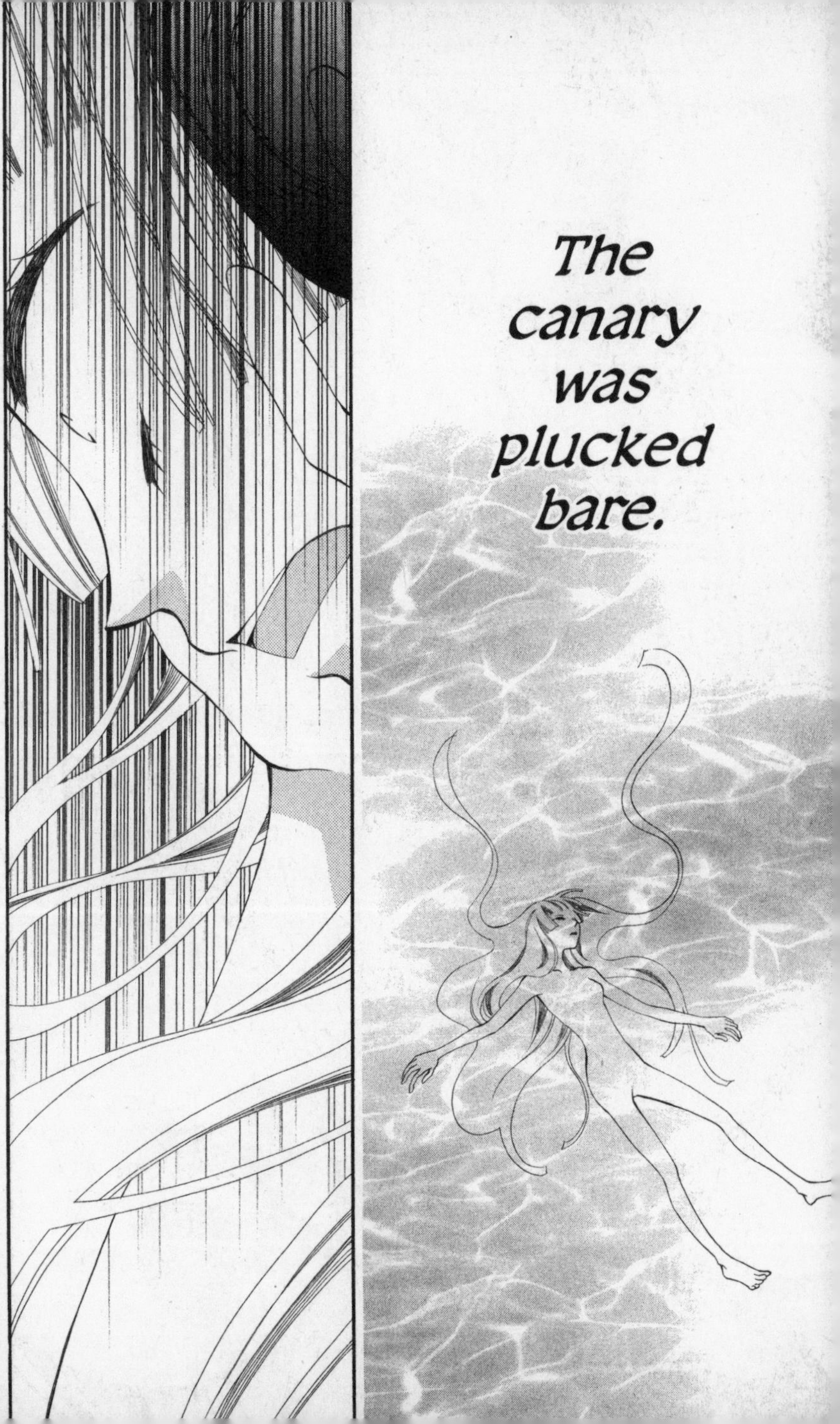
The canary was plucked bare.

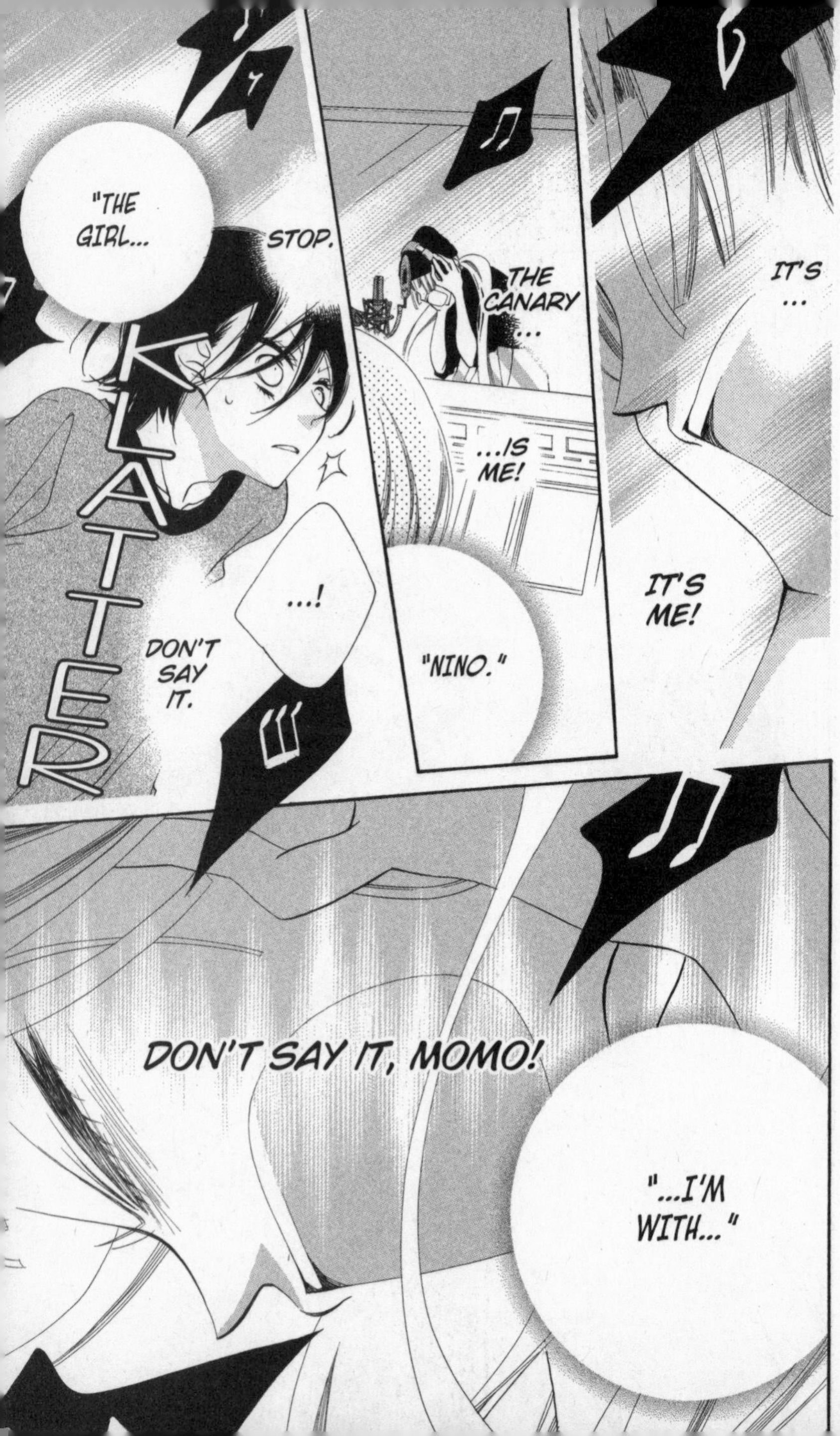

IT'S ...
IT'S ME!
THE CANARY ...
...IS ME!
"NINO."
"THE GIRL...
STOP.
...!
DON'T SAY IT.
KLATTER
DON'T SAY IT, MOMO!
"...I'M WITH..."

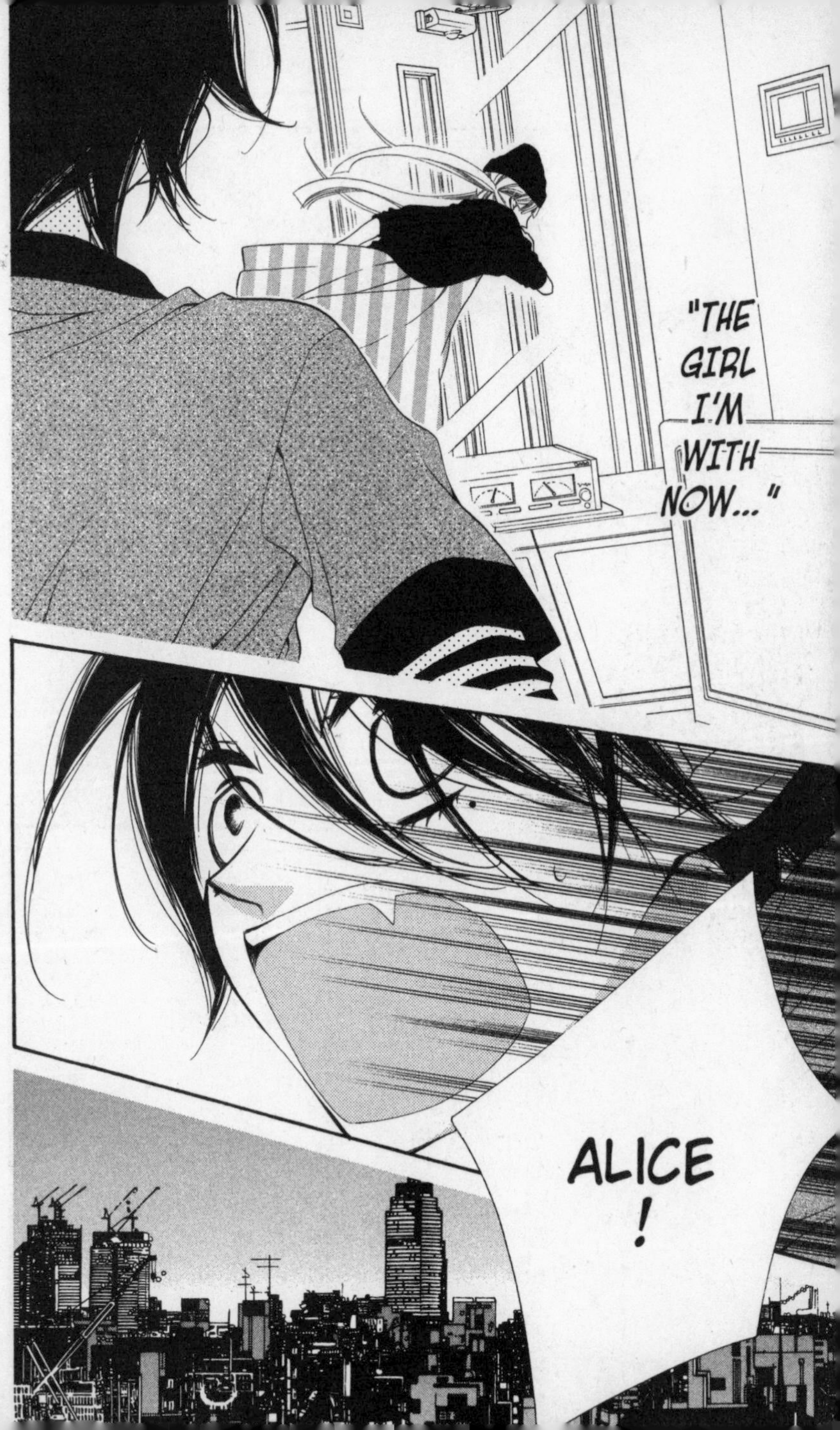
"THE GIRL I'M WITH NOW..."
ALICE!

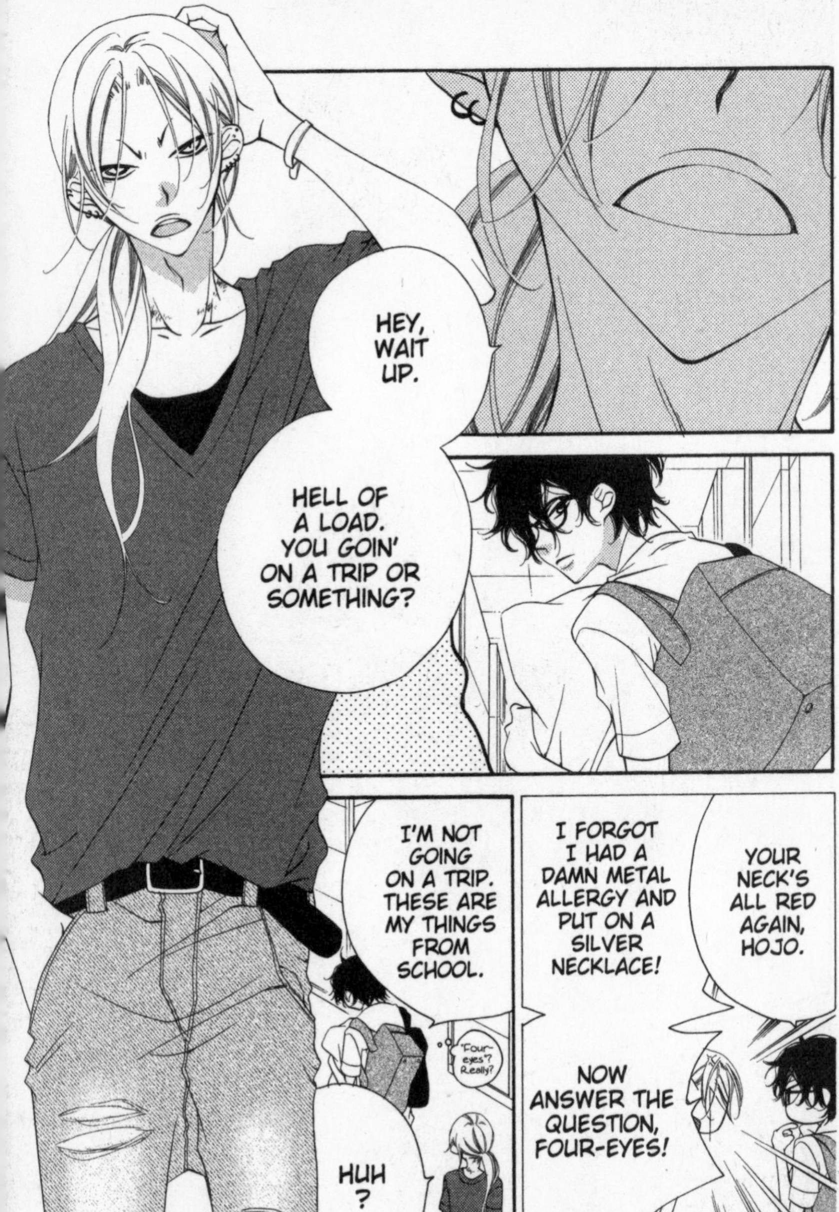

HEY, WAIT UP.
HELL OF A LOAD. YOU GOIN' ON A TRIP OR SOMETHING?
YOUR NECK'S ALL RED AGAIN, HOJO.
I FORGOT I HAD A DAMN METAL ALLERGY AND PUT ON A SILVER NECKLACE!
NOW ANSWER THE QUESTION, FOUR-EYES!
I'M NOT GOING ON A TRIP. THESE ARE MY THINGS FROM SCHOOL.
"Four-eyes"? Really?
HUH?

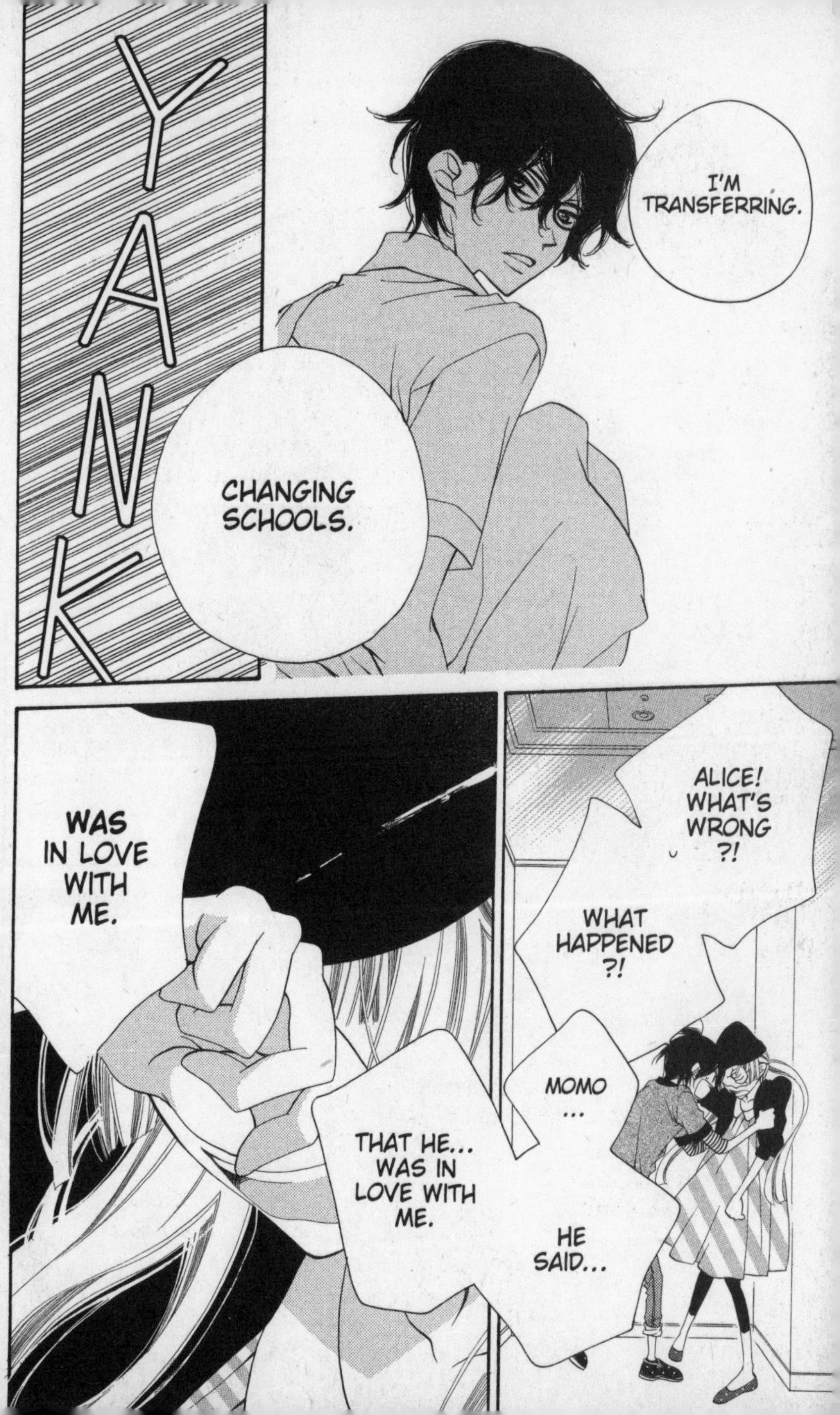
I'M TRANSFERRING.
CHANGING SCHOOLS.
YANK
ALICE! WHAT'S WRONG ?!
WHAT HAPPENED ?!
MOMO ...
HE SAID...
THAT HE... WAS IN LOVE WITH ME.
WAS IN LOVE WITH ME.

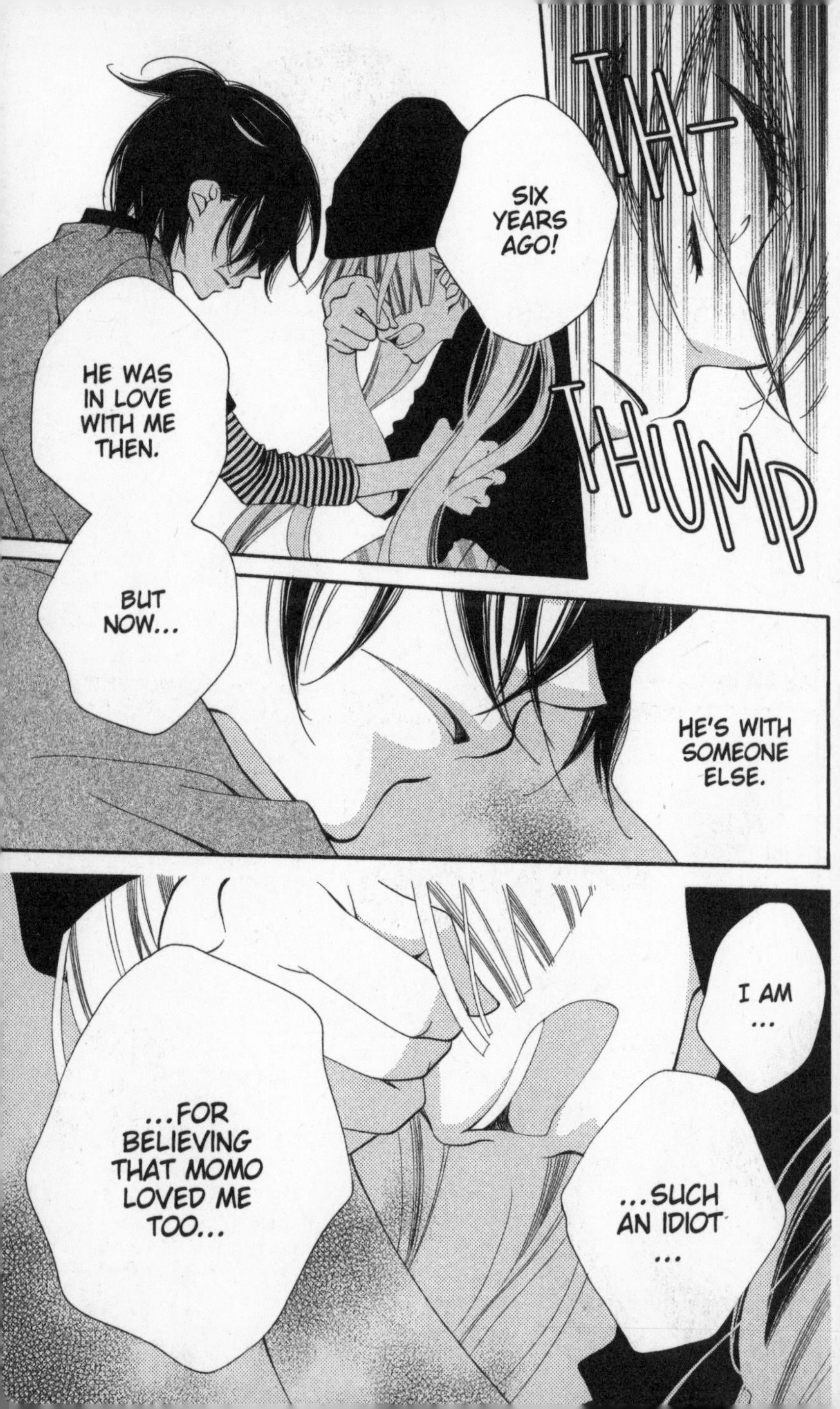
TH-THUMP
SIX YEARS AGO!
HE WAS IN LOVE WITH ME THEN.
BUT NOW...
HE'S WITH SOMEONE ELSE.
I AM...
...SUCH AN IDIOT...
...FOR BELIEVING THAT MOMO LOVED ME TOO...

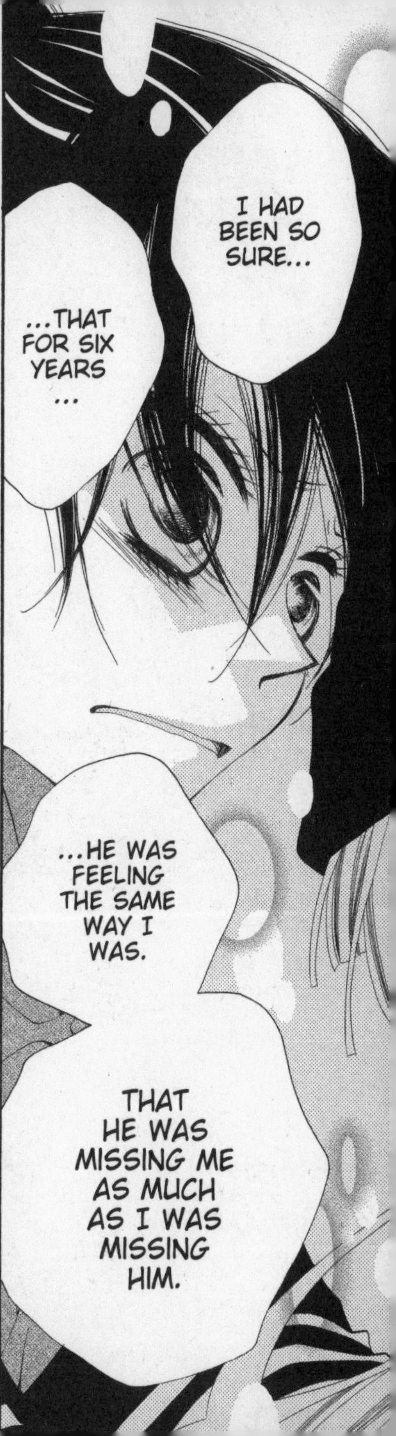
I HAD BEEN SO SURE...
...THAT FOR SIX YEARS ...
...HE WAS FEELING THE SAME WAY I WAS.
THAT HE WAS MISSING ME AS MUCH AS I WAS MISSING HIM.

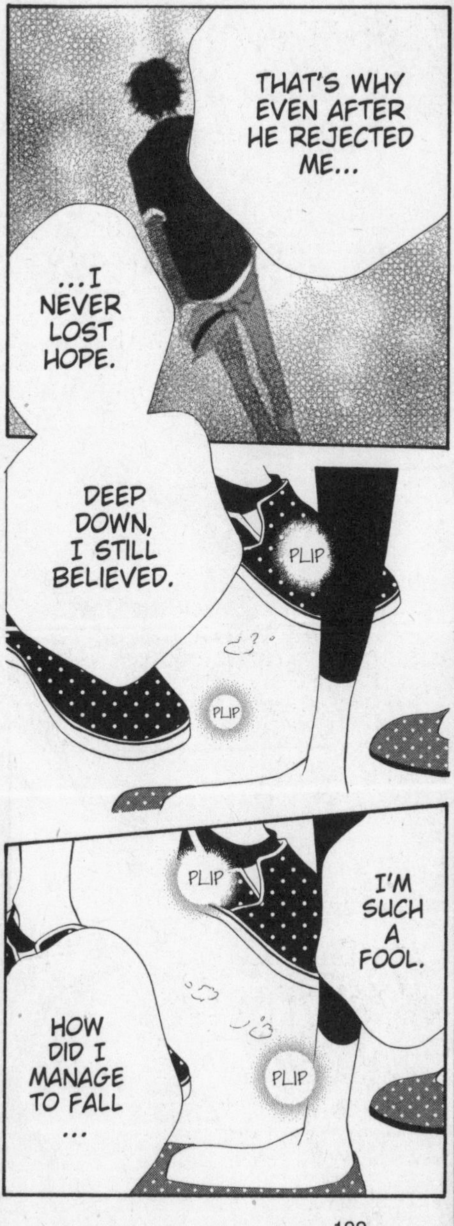
THAT'S WHY EVEN AFTER HE REJECTED ME...
...I NEVER LOST HOPE.
DEEP DOWN, I STILL BELIEVED.
PLIP
PLIP
PLIP
I'M SUCH A FOOL.
HOW DID I MANAGE TO FALL ...
PLIP

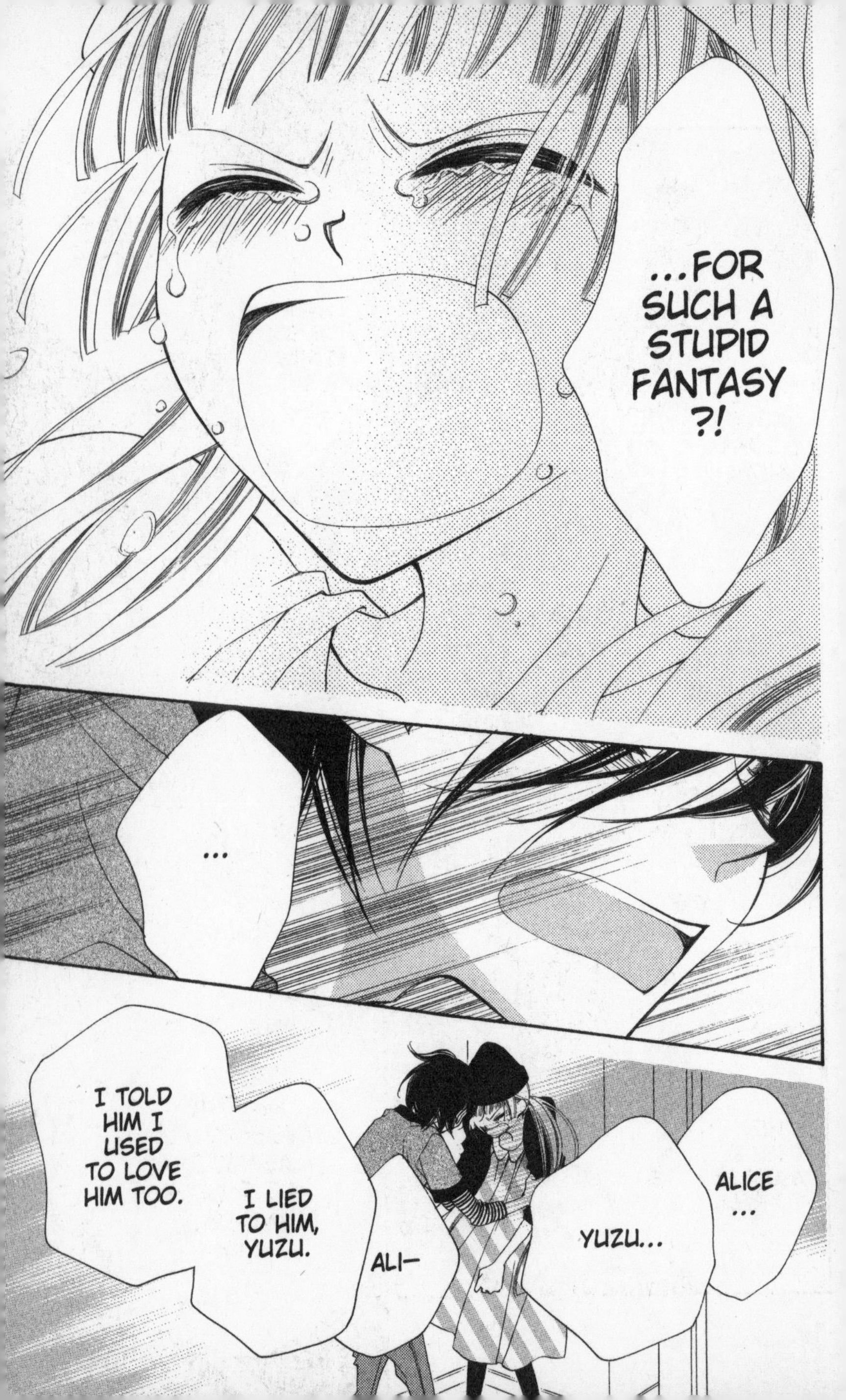
...FOR SUCH A STUPID FANTASY?!
...
ALICE...
YUZU...
ALI—
I LIED TO HIM, YUZU.
I TOLD HIM I USED TO LOVE HIM TOO.

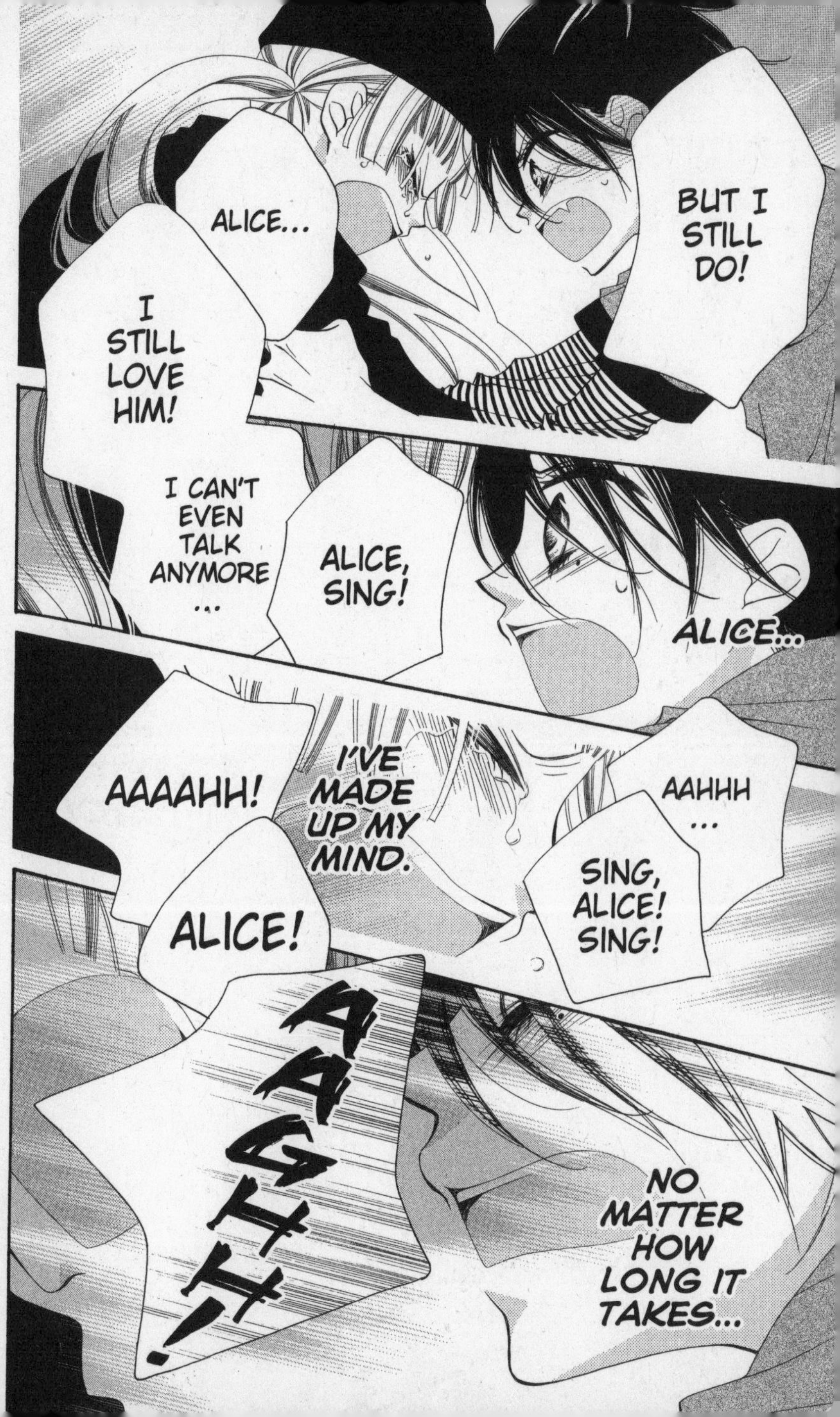
BUT I STILL DO!
ALICE...
I STILL LOVE HIM!
ALICE...
ALICE, SING!
I CAN'T EVEN TALK ANYMORE...
AAHHH...
I'VE MADE UP MY MIND.
AAAAHH!
SING, ALICE! SING!
ALICE!
NO MATTER HOW LONG IT TAKES...
AAGHH!

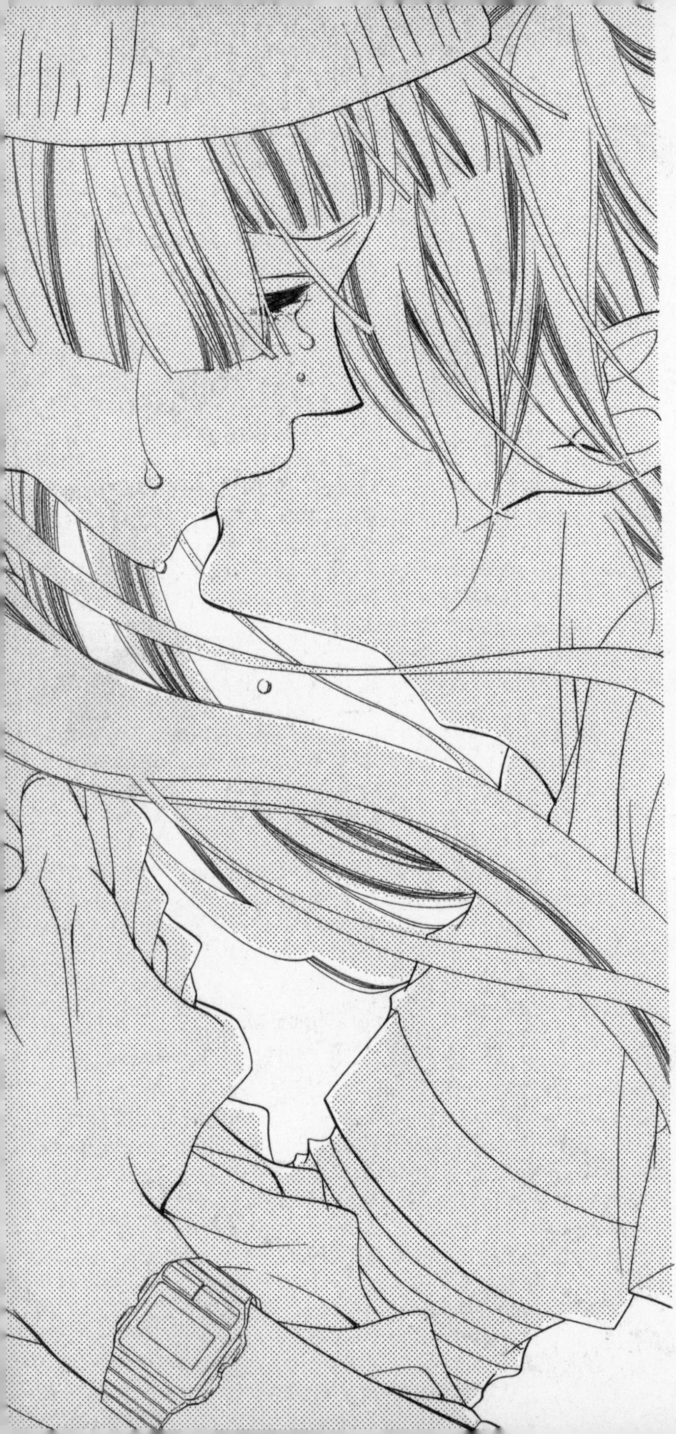

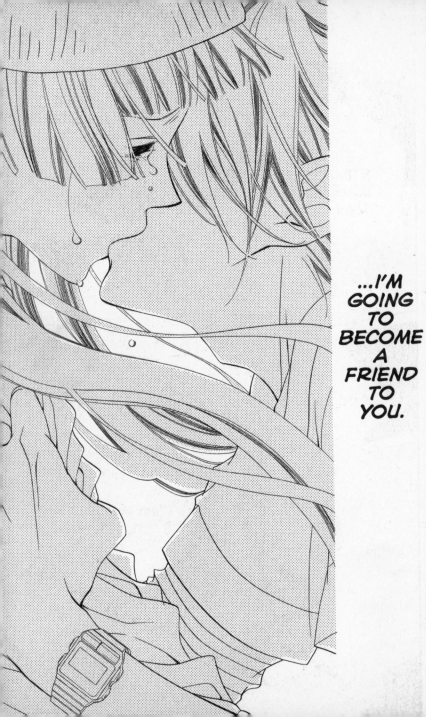

...I'M GOING TO BECOME A FRIEND TO YOU.

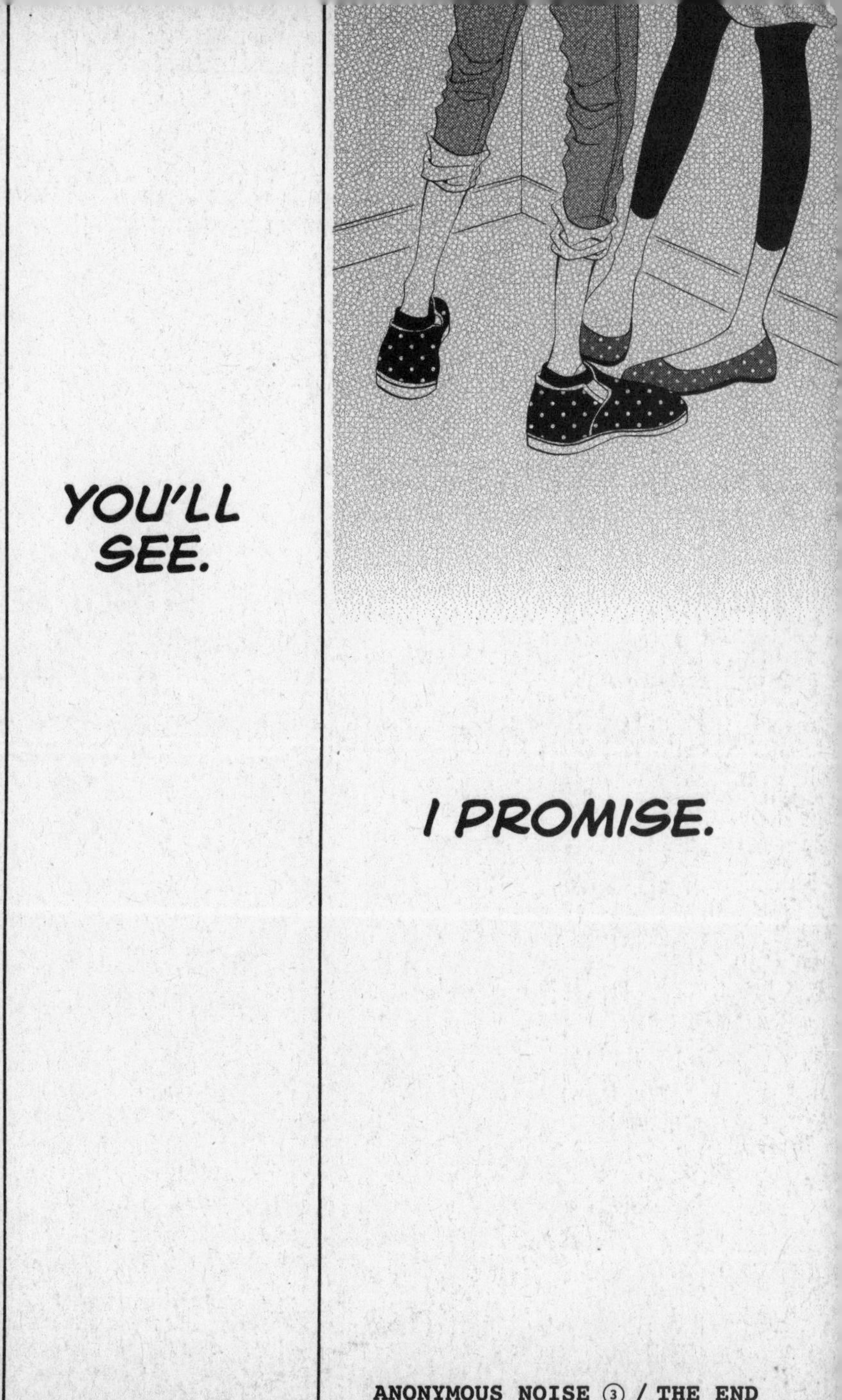
I PROMISE.
YOU'LL SEE.

ANONYMOUS NOISE ③ / THE END

TO BE CONTINUED IN ANONYMOUS NOISE 4

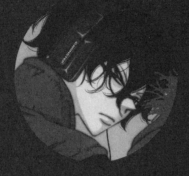

To celebrate the one-year
anniversary of my serialization in
Hana to Yume, I visited Yuigahama
Beach for the first time in a year.
It really is a special place—I always
feel wonderful being there.
I'd love to visit again!

- Ryoko Fukuyama

Born on January 5 in Wakayama Prefecture in
Japan, Ryoko Fukuyama debuted as a manga
artist after winning the Hakusensha Athena
Shinjin Taisho Prize from Hakusensha's *Hana
to Yume* magazine. She is also the author
of *Nosatsu Junkie*. *Anonymous Noise* was
adapted into an anime in 2017.

ANONYMOUS NOISE
Vol. 3
Shojo Beat Edition

STORY AND ART BY
RYOKO FUKUYAMA

English Translation & Adaptation/Casey Loe
Touch-Up Art & Lettering/Joanna Estep
Design/Yukiko Whitley
Editor/Amy Yu

Fukumenkei Noise by Ryoko Fukuyama
© Ryoko Fukuyama 2014
All rights reserved.
First published in Japan in 2014 by HAKUSENSHA, Inc., Tokyo.
English language translation rights arranged with HAKUSENSHA, Inc., Tokyo.

Printed in Canada

Published by VIZ Media, LLC
P.O. Box 77010
San Francisco, CA 94107

10 9 8 7 6 5 4 3 2 1
First printing, July 2017

www.viz.com   www.shojobeat.com

Surprise!

You may be reading the wrong way!

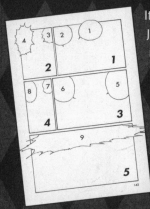

It's true: In keeping with the original Japanese comic format, this book reads from right to left—so action, sound effects and word balloons are completely reversed. This preserves the orientation of the original artwork—plus, it's fun! Check out the diagram shown here to get the hang of things, and then turn to the other side of the book to get started!

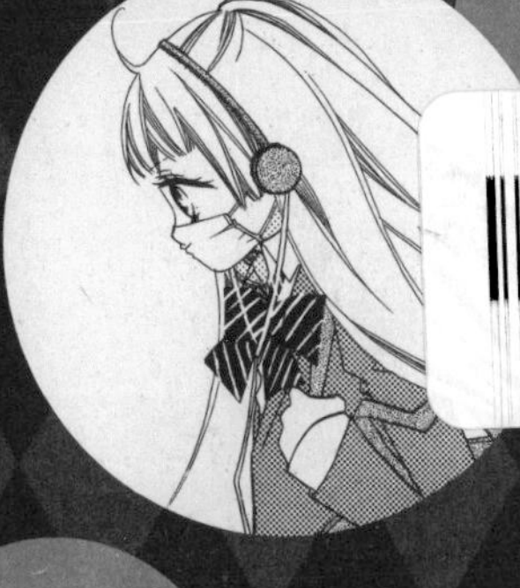